Under the editorship of
Ernest Q. Campbell
Vanderbilt University

AN INTRODUCTION
TO THE SOCIOLOGY
OF LEARNING

Sarane Spence ͏Boocock

University of Southern California

LC
189
B58

Houghton Mifflin Company / Boston

New York / Atlanta / Geneva, Illinois / Dallas / Palo Alto

Library of Congress Catalog Card Number: 78–160671

ISBN: 0–395–12565–0

To the Johns Hopkins University
Department of Social Relations,
where this all began

Editor's Introduction

The sociology of education badly needs definition, structure, and purpose. This book is a major contribution toward meeting these needs. I regard it as the best general work in the area since Waller's *The Sociology of Teaching* which appeared some forty years ago. Further, it is timely. Today's sociologists are pressured as never before to make their work relevant to social policy. Yet, I shudder to think how few sociologists have crisp minds, are able to ask the right questions, appreciate and apply defensible criteria of proof, and put it all together to draw useful implications for educational practice. Sarane Boocock demonstrates in this book that she is one sociologist who has that ability.

For Dr. Boocock, the real problem is not the coherence of a body of knowledge called the sociology of education, but the public schools themselves: how to improve them and how to realize their promise for all Americans. Her book is addressed to the important questions of our time. It is a provocative inquiry into the effects of school facilities, classmates, teachers, and students upon how much children learn in schools. The author believes passionately that our schools are not doing the educational job that must be done. She seeks empirical data, typically quantitative, and she speaks not of correlation but of causal systems. Each chapter has its own virtues, but I should like to mention especially Chapter 5 on "Sex Differences"; Chapter 6 on "Individual Abilities," which is the best sociological perspective on this subject I have seen; Chapter 13, which introduces a much needed comparative perspective into the question of America's educational accomplishments; and Chapter 14, which attempts a brief look at the prospects for substantial innovation.

Dr. Boocock writes with great respect for the reader. At first glance, the intensity of her style may not reassure all readers: there are no pictures, no breezy asides, no long illustrations and case studies, no study guides and discussion questions. There is simply a big and important question to be considered—what can we, together, learn from sociology about why so many children learn less than they should in school, and about how they might learn more? Dr. Boocock moves immediately into that question on the first page of her book and she continues to ask it (and answer it) through the last page. She pays all of us the large compliment of assuming that we share her sense of crisis and that we are ready to explore the evidence. I think she is right to proceed that way. Her work has substance and provocativeness for the graduate student in sociology. Also it is readable and useful for the undergraduate preparing for a teaching career in the public schools. Moreover, it will be shared widely with other social scientists, with school administrators and educators, and with political decision makers. This is as it should be; if we sociologists can talk only to each other, how can we ever expect to have an effect on decisions made in public life?

I have admired Dr. Boocock's ability for synthesis and extension ever since reading her article," The Sociology of Learning," in the Winter 1966 issue of *Sociology of Learning*. I am pleased indeed that I could play a part in extending her work into its present form. Few texts offer us so large a learning experience, or stretch and provoke us so fully, as this one.

Ernest Q. Campbell
Vanderbilt University

Preface

This book was born almost seven years ago when I began to explore simulation and gaming, at that time a new technique to most sociologists. In the course of trying to formulate a theoretical rationale for instructional gaming as well as to develop some game models, I turned to the literature of educational sociology for some kind of overview of the social factors related to learning.

I did not find what I was looking for. There were descriptions of the school and the classroom as social environments, and a multitude of studies on the relationship of one or more social indicators to indicators of academic success, but no discussion pulled all the bits and pieces of evidence together in a comprehensive way. Waller's *The Sociology of Teaching,* published in 1932, remained the most comprehensive treatment of the subject.

Consequently, I decided to write my own synthesis. The resulting forty-five-page review and bibliography was published in 1966 in *Sociology of Learning.* As readers began to request reprints and send me further references and data from their own research, I was persuaded by Ernest Campbell, among others, to expand my work to book length.

I gained additional impetus from the growing evidence of the ghastly conditions and gross inequalities prevailing in many of our schools, highlighted by the urban riots and school desegregation struggles of the mid-1960's and documented in both scholarly and popular accounts. Benjamin Bloom has estimated that only about one-third of our students have a successful learning experience, although he judges that an overhaul of our learning system would enable over ninety per cent to learn what is currently taught. Few other institutions would tolerate such a low success rate, and surely our society cannot afford to have so many children not "making it" at school.

Journalistic complaints that sociologists "aren't doing anything" to help solve our most pressing social problems also goaded me to write this book. Notable among these was Joseph Alsop's 1969 blast at the "final bankruptcy" of the social sciences. In Alsop's view social scientists are to be blamed for everything from the rising use of heroin in New York City's schools to the "cruelly false hopes that were raised by the Supreme Court's decision desegregating the schools."

The purpose of this book then is to describe and place in context some of the best research and the most important findings in the sociology of learning. It should be viewed as a progress report rather than a final report. So much of the relevant work is recent or in progress that the thoroughness and the perspective possible in a more established field will be missing. I hope this will be compensated for by the reader's sense of participation in the rapid development of a timely new field. I hope also to show that our educational problems are more complex than Mr. Alsop would lead one to believe, and that "soft" sociologists do have something to contribute to their understanding and solution.

I fear that my treatment of the American educational system may be perceived by some readers as disrespectful. While this is not my attitude, I do feel that many of the structural features of our schools and school systems are at the crux of learning problems. Further, I believe that we must change such structures quite radically. Surely sacred cows are an indulgence when children need sustenance. While I make no claim for emotional detachment in the matter of education, I hope that my biases and sense of urgency are balanced by the quality of my scholarship.

My intellectual debts are great. James Coleman, author of *The Adolescent Society* and *Equality of Educational Opportunity,* gave me the original encouragement I needed. Indeed, he has been a constant source of ideas and "feedback." To those who feel that too much attention has been given to Coleman's studies, I can only reply that in my opinion they are not only landmarks by any standards but also more stimulative of creative thinking and empirical research than any others in the sociology of learning. Edward McDill, another Johns Hopkins sociologist, gave generously of intellectual and personal help. As first director of the Center for the Study of Social Organization of Schools, at Johns Hopkins, he also gave funds for clerical expenses incurred. (The University of Southern California Research and Publication Fund provided additional funds.) Professor McDill's 1967–1968 interdisciplinary seminar on educational research—whose influential participants included Julian Stanley, Peter Rossi, and James McPartland—scrutinized relentlessly and rewardingly several of the studies included here.

Colleague-friends with whom I carried on extensive discussions about education problems in general and this book in particular deserve special thanks. They are Michael Inbar and Erling Schild, now both at Hebrew University in Jerusalem; Clarice Stoll, now at California State College at Sonoma; and Jerry Zaltman, now at Northwestern University.

In his Foreword to *The New Industrial State,* John Kenneth Galbraith states, "At least until late middle age, all American authors of serious purpose are required to thank their families for their forbearance and thus, more than incidentally, show that they have a wholesome family life." I am not sure that any special forbearance was required of my husband Brett and my son Paul in connection with my writing. Indeed, I half suspect that they viewed my activity as minimizing interference with their own. I thank them for other qualities. As a veteran teacher and educational administrator, my husband served as a sensitive sounding board for my ideas and as an invaluable source of information on what "really happens" in schools. My son's cheerful presence not only eased the strains of writing but also acted as a constant reminder of one of this book's central themes: children are so eager to master their world that they even may manage to overcome the obstacles of formal education.

Sarane Spence Boocock
University of Southern California

Contents

PART ONE

Introduction

The Field Chapter 1

. . . if there was ever a time and a country in which the sociological point of view was indicated, in a particularly urgent fashion, for pedagogues, it is certainly our country and our time. . . . It is not because sociology can give us ready-made procedures which we need only use. Are there, in any case, any of this sort? But it can do more and it can do better. It can give us what we need most urgently; I mean to say a body of guiding ideas that may be the core of our practice and that sustain it, that give a meaning to our action, and that attach us to it; which is the necessary condition for this action to be fruitful.
Emile Durkheim

How well are children learning in our schools? Every year in the United States, and in most other countries, more resources are devoted to formal education and more people spend more time in school. Can we assume that there is an increase in total learning—that is, that we are getting our money's worth? What should we do about those who fail to learn?

The mass media, as well as professional education journals and conferences, debate these questions, or variations of them, and, in the process, often generate more heat than light. Part of the problem is that before the question of whether students are learning "enough" can be approached, a host of other questions must be answered. For example, what are students supposed to be learning? How is the amount or the quality of learning to be measured? Are we talking about all students, or schools, or just certain types?

This book explores a relatively new field or subfield of sociology. Its subject is the learning environment, which includes the social characteristics of schools and their surroundings, and the student's relationships with other individuals and groups, inside and outside of school, that effect his

3

academic success. We want to explain what—and under what conditions—social factors have an impact upon school performance.

The sociology of learning is to be distinguished from the psychology of learning, which focuses upon the internal mechanisms by which the individual responds to and assimilates stimuli of various kinds. Although the ultimate advantages of interdisciplinary linkages are obvious—we shall, in fact, use findings from psychological research as the frameworks or "givens" in our discussion—so far, sociology lags far behind psychology in the learning field. This book's premise is that sociology has a contribution to make which is independent of this psychological "learning theory" dominant in the field.

Although the study of education and educational institutions began with modern sociology (Bidwell, 1967), surprisingly little sociological attention has been directed toward the central function of schools, learning itself. The relationship between sociology and education has been, at best, uncomfortable (see, for instance, Hansen, 1967). Until the mid-1950's, the research literature on the sociology of education was small and tended to avoid the more controversial educational issues. For example, a number of studies described the structure and functioning of the school as a social system, in particular the degree to which schools share the characteristics of bureaucratic organizations generally. Many studies described the social background of teachers. Only during the past decade or so, when research in educational sociology began to grow at a much faster rate, did sociologists attack directly the problems of how and under what conditions children learn, or fail to learn.

Learning in Schools

Let us clarify further what we are trying to explain. Our title is *An Introduction to the Sociology of Learning*. Strictly speaking, learning consists of a cognitive change leading to a measurable increase in knowledge or skills. A student who can perform some academic task which he could not perform at all or as well at some earlier point in time is assumed to have learned something. With many academic tasks, however, adequate performance requires more than purely intellectual skills. Our *dependent variable*—that is, the dimension we shall be trying, in this book, to explain and understand—thus encompasses the whole set of factors which designate how well a student is succeeding in the role of student, or how well he is "making it" in the school system.

We should note three components of learning, as it is conceived in this book. First is *change*. Something happens to a person in a learning experience, so that he is in some sense not the same person afterwards.

A second component is some kind of *interaction between the learner and an instructor,* whether this be a teacher, another student, or some nonhuman teaching device. (As noted above, academic success also is dependent upon *recognition* by others in the educational system of one's adequacy of performance.) The point here is that school learning occurs in a social setting, and success may depend more upon social skills than upon strictly academic-intellectual ones, especially in the early years. This is the view held by Talcott Parsons, who in an analysis of the school class as a social system (1959) breaks down school achievement into "cognitive" and "moral" components. A "good" student fuses the two, although the weight given to one or the other varies during the course of a school career. At the elementary level, says Parsons, the high achievers:

> are both the "bright" pupils, who catch on easily to their more strictly intellectual tasks, and the more "responsible" pupils, who "behave well" and on whom the teacher can "count" in her difficult problems of managing the class. . . . In many such cases, it can be presumed that the primary challenge to the pupil is not to his intellectual, but to his "moral" capacities (Parsons, 1959: 304).

Jerome Bruner also suggests that mastery of certain social skills is a prerequisite to active "engagement" in the formal instructional process, partly because it shapes the school's perception and treatment of children. Thus children coming from groups alienated from the larger society—for instance, from low-income, rural migrants to large cities—are least likely to benefit from and to be successful at school (Bruner, 1966: 199ff).

A third component of learning is *substance*. Individuals do not just "learn"—they learn, or fail to learn, *something*. What is learned can be classified into two general categories: information; and things a person can *do*, such as reading or working with tools. A possible additional category is the general capacity to think clearly and to take action based upon a fresh and reasoned analysis of a problem,[1] although this category may be viewed as the synthesis of the other two—as the ability to apply skills to information and vice versa.

Finally, it should be underscored that this book is about learning in schools.[2] Although obviously learning occurs in other institutions, the skills and attitudes children acquire outside of school will be included in the discussion only when they help to explain differences in school performance. This limitation is imposed not only to provide a structure for the book, but because the discussion of formal educational functions increasingly is becoming synonymous with the discussion of schools. In small, simply organized societies, education can be carried out largely within the family, but in complex, industrially developed (or developing) societies, families rarely can communicate the specialized knowledge and skills required for many adult roles. The assignment of more and more educative functions to the schools, which is to some degree in opposition to the rights and interests of the family, has been described by Durkheim (1956) and by Eisenstadt (1956).[3] Contemporary critics see the school as "distilling from other institutions their normal educative functions and transferring them to the school: e.g., vocational training, auto safety and driver training, rehabilita-tion of the disadvantaged, early childhood training, homemaking" (Newman and Oliver, 1967: 75).

The influence of the school also is extending into the period of people's lives *after* they leave the formal education system. Because "the creden-tials awarded by the school are taken seriously by institutions and publics outside the school," a person's opportunities, including access to the jobs, income and other accoutrements of the "good life," increasingly are deter-mined by his educational attainment. "What is important here is not that school-awarded credentials are relevant or irrelevant, but simply that *they are taken seriously* as screening devices for access to social roles and to subsequent education" (Green, 1969: 244–245).

The kinds of things that can be learned at schools are sometimes con-fused with the goals or functions of schools, about which there is as much debate and as little agreement as about whether children are learning "enough." While most educational sociologists would agree with Durkheim that education is "above all the means by which a society perpetually recreates the conditions of its very existence" (Durkheim, 1959: 123), there is less consensus on just what it is that should be preserved and recreated. Some observers feel that confusion over goals is at the heart of our educa-tional problems; that because our society is not sure of its own basic values, it "cannot be clear about the goals it wishes education to serve" (Keppel, 1966). Others feel that it is not that we lack clear goals but that we have so many of them. We expect our schools to do so much that our expecta-tions are often unrealistic and conflicting. The literature on American edu-cation is filled with typologies and debates about goals. The following list seems to comprise those that appear most often:

cognitive goals—the school should produce individuals equipped with em-pirical knowledge and technological mastery;

moral or value goals—the schools should produce good citizens equipped with the proper values for participation in a democracy;

socialization goals—the school should produce well-adjusted individuals skilled in interpersonal relations;

social mobility goals—the schools should constitute an avenue to social betterment of the individual. (The compensatory side of this goal assigns to the schools the task of overcoming the disadvantages of poverty, ethnic background, and weak family structure.)

As we shall see in a later chapter, the particular combination of social idealism and material considerations that appear simultaneously in many of our educational discourses is not a universal phenomenon; other cultures have different educational goals and subsequently different types of educa-tional systems. Even within our own society, there is disagreement between those who think schools should focus upon a single function (e.g., the "Rick-over syndrome," which would have the school concentrate on the first goal on the above list, dismissing the others as frills) and those who worry about the lack of balance between the various areas. As one such critic complains, "Marks in school subjects are virtually useless as predictors of creativity, inventiveness, leadership, good citizenship, personal and social maturity, family happiness, and honest workmanship" (Goodlad, 1966: 49). The typical response to such criticism is that even if present school success is not a good predictor of future moral character, it *is* a good predictor of future school success which is in turn a good predictor of future social position. Finally, there are those, among whom Kenneth Boulding (1966) is the leading spokesman, who say that the major function of schools today is to prepare students for the surprises of the future. Since the world of tomorrow will be one of ever-accelerating change, both technological and social, accompanied by an explosion of knowledge, formal education must develop in the young the habit of continual learning as well as the capacity for "social invention" to correct the discontinuities that result from rapid change.

From the foregoing arguments, we see that the conception of learning to be used in this book is a fairly broad one, and that our dependent variable may be termed more accurately academic or school success than learning. In the following chapters, we shall include studies about attitudes, decisions, and behaviors which are not direct measures of cognitive learning per se but which signify that a certain level of knowledge or skill has been or is likely to be reached. One such measure is the decision to go to college. Our conception focuses upon cognitive development as it occurs within the formal education system, while recognizing the close relationship between cognitive and other forms of development, and using the latter when they help to explain intellectual achievement.

The View of the Child

The goals a society sets for its educational system and what and how children are taught in school depend not only upon what is perceived as valuable and necessary for the smooth functioning of society but also upon society's view of what children are like. Although we tend to take for granted the way children are treated in our own society, it is important to remember that what we see—the aspects of children's behavior to which we are sensitive—is filtered through a cultural lens. As the following passages from Philippe Aries' classic study, *Centuries of Childhood,* make clear, our view of children has not always been the prevailing one, even in Western culture:

> Olivier Le Fevre d'Ormesson was born in 1525 of a father who was a clerk in the record office of the High Court, and a mother who was the daughter of an attorney in the Audit Office. He had two brothers and three sisters, who all died except for his brother Nicolas. He lost his father when he was five. At the age of eight, Olivier went to Navarre College. . . . How-

ever, the le Fevre family was not rich, and the widow could not afford to keep her two children at school. . . . Thus Olivier stayed at school only from the age of eight or nine to the age of eleven. At eleven "he was lodged with an attorney in the Audit Office to learn to write (that is to say to 'write to perfection,' to write deeds, the equivalent of typing today) and to earn his living" (Aries, 1962: 191–192).

In the sixteenth and seventeenth centuries, childhood could be very brief, with the young person early absorbed into the adult world to study or hold a job on the same basis as any adults. (Adolescence, to which behavioral scientists and educators now attach so much importance, was not even a recognized period in the life cycle until the late eighteenth century.) Formal schooling was available to only a small segment of the population and often was limited to three or four years, even for a person entering a profession. Some, like Olivier Le Fevre, "did not amass the necessary knowledge to ply a trade before entering it, but . . . acquired the necessary knowledge through everyday practice, from living and working with adults who were already fully trained" (Aries, 1962: 192). Moreover, because the function of the school was to communicate the knowledge and skills necessary to the operation of certain institutions—originally the music and literature connected with the ceremonies of the church; later the writing, arithmetic, and manual skills used in commercial activities—"for a long time the school remained indifferent to the separation and distinction of the ages, because it did not regard the education of children as its essential aim. . . . Thus it welcomed equally and indifferently children, youths, adults, the precocious and the backward, at the foot of the magisterial rostrum" (Aries, 1962: 330). Another boy described by Aries entered a Jesuit college at the age of nine and had worked his way through several years of the classical philosophy curriculum before being pulled out by his father, a military man, to take command of a company in the father's regiment. He was the same age, thirteen, as several of his brother officers at the siege of La Motte in 1634 (Aries, 1962: 202).

While these brief excerpts do not do justice to the richness of Aries' study, two conclusions are clear:

1. The very notion of childhood is a relatively recent conceptualization and one which is constantly adapting to the changing structure and needs of a particular society;

2. The image of the child held by a society affects the kinds of educational system it provides for him.

Although there is no single unified view held by all segments of our population, and the debate over the proper translation of views into actual educational practice is endless, two themes have been emerging in recent years. Both are illustrated by work in learning psychology and thus exemplify how developments in one discipline can provide a framework for development in another.

Among the individuals whose influence upon the field of child development has been especially strong in recent years is the Swiss-born psychologist Jean Piaget.[4] In Piaget's conceptualization of mental development, the child passes through an ordered sequence of phases. Each phase has its own distinct view of the world, modes of thinking and so on; at the same time, each has roots in and entails repetitions of the previous phases, although on a higher level of organization and differentiation. There is a continuity of development over the entire series, a continuous trend from simplicity to ever greater complexity, from focus upon the physical world to the societal and finally to the ideational, from emphasis upon activity and doing to emphasis upon thought about what is being done and finally to abstract conceptualization.

Although there is within each individual the possibility of full development at each phase, in fact children achieve at different levels within each stage and many fail to realize their full potential. The implication for educators is that it is crucial both to understand a child's developmental stage and to provide him with learning tasks that will enable him to reach his capacity. This does *not* mean pushing children to achieve academic tasks faster or younger—such efforts would, on the contrary, go directly against Piaget's theory—but rather structuring and enriching the learning environment to provide the fullest development congruent with each cognitive phase.

Piaget's image of the child is not a new one. (Piaget himself was born in 1896 and published his first studies on children's conceptual development in the 1920's.) But it has been more or less ignored until the past decade, when national and international events, including the post Sputnik agitation for higher academic standards in American schools, and the civil rights movement's identification of the intellectual consequences of poverty and racial prejudice, have shifted our education focus away from social skills and adjustment and back to a focus upon intellectual development and achievement. In this country, Piaget's ideas have been studied by those involved in the education of young children, in particular in connection with Head Start and other programs to reduce the intellectual waste among lower-income groups in our population. His influence has been even more extensive in Europe. The last chapter of this book includes a description of an English primary classroom which incorporates many ideas from Piaget's developmental theories, in particular the degree to which young children are encouraged to learn through self-directed activity and to shape a mental scheme of the world through direct, repeated experience using all of these senses.

During the past two decades, learning psychologists working with animals discovered that their subjects often would continue to explore mazes and try to master other learning tasks even when such behavior would not be predicted on the basis of their bodily condition (hunger, thirst, need for rest, and so on) or the stimulus-reward structure of the environment. The traditional view of learning motivation—that learning occurs because a response produced by a stimulus is followed by the reduction in a primary drive—would not explain the experimental finding that:

> monkeys will learn to solve a three-device mechanical puzzle apparatus for no other reward than the activity itself. Other experiments with monkeys show an orderly increase in the number of correct responses in the learning of a six-device mechanical puzzle over a twelve-day period, though no reduction of hunger, thirst, pain or sexual gratification has followed manipulation of the puzzle. . . . Butler has shown that monkeys will learn which of two differently colored windows to press when they are put into an opaque box, and the only reward following their response is the chance to look out of the window for a 30-second period. . . . Montgomery ran animals in a Y maze in which one arm of the letter Y led to a large maze that they could explore and the other arm was a blind alley. The animals learned to enter the arm leading to the opportunity to explore, which here functioned to reinforce their instrumental response at the choice point.
>
> These recent studies of manipulation, exploration, and curiosity highlight the limitations of the drive-reduction theory of reinforcement. The activity of manipulating a puzzle and the activity of exposing the visual receptors to sufficiently complex and novel stimulation are, apparently, as capable of reinforcing antecedent actions as are the activities of eating when hungry and drinking when thirsty (Atkinson, 1966: 185–186).

That children, like rats and monkeys, have a natural curiosity and desire for knowledge and skill is the current conclusion of most learning psychologists. The term used to explain this phenomenon is *competence motivation,* defined as behavior which is "directed, selective, and persistent," and which continues "not because it serves primary drives, which indeed it cannot serve until it is almost perfected, but because it satisfies an intrinsic need to deal with the environment" (White, 1959: 318). Moreover, mastery of a skill or subject has a positive effect upon the child's interest in it. He begins to *like* the subjects in which he achieves some competence and to want to learn more about them. On the negative side, a child who continually fails to master something begins to lose interest in it. Thus competence can be a cause of interest as well as a result of it.

The significance of this view of the child is obvious and it has been incorporated into much of the recent criticism of American schools. The unifying theme of a recent collection of articles entitled *Revolution in the Schools* is that:

> Children of all levels and kinds of ability and from all kinds of backgrounds can learn more, learn it earlier, and learn it better. . . . Furthermore, children can do this without any "pushing," propelled by their own curiosity and innate desire to discover and know and understand (Gross and Murphy, 1964: 138).

As we shall see in later chapters of the book, however, the slowness with which new research about and attitudes toward children are being translated into restructuring of the learning system is a clear example of culture lag. Indeed, one of the remarkable features of the formal educational system is the efficiency with which it squelches the potentially powerful competence motivation of many children rather than using it to promote learning.

The Learning System

Perhaps the best way to gain an overview of the field of sociology of learning is to describe the territory which will be covered. Exhibit 1–1 is a map of the social components of learning system, which can be used to organize the myriad of theoretical formulations and research findings discussed in the main body of this book.

Since the school system is set up for the purpose of effecting a particular kind of change (learning) in a particular class of individuals (students), we shall enter this complex system at the level of the individual student, in the left center of Exhibit 1–1. In understanding the student role, it is important to remember that the child does not enter school untouched by the past and the outside world. Each child brings to school a number of characteristics which differentiate that child from other children, which determine in part the nature of the school experience, and which may have effects upon the school system itself. These characteristics include the individual's abilities and interests, his values and his attitudes toward school and learning, and the knowledge and skills he possesses already.

It is not really possible, moreover, to understand what is happening at the individual level without taking into account how the individual is affected by factors and processes occurring at other levels of the learning system. As Exhibit 1–1 indicates, personal characteristics of an individual student are themselves affected by outside factors—by the structure, status, and values of his family, by his neighborhood, and by other layers of his environment. In sum, when he arrives at school, the student has already been shaped by his background and environment, so that he possesses a set of qualities, experiences, and expectations through which the influence of the school experience must filter. Part Two of this book will focus upon the student role, identifying the characteristics of the individual which are importantly related to success in this role and showing how they are interrelated with factors in both the in-school and in the out-of-school environment.

The individual level meshes with the group or system level of the learning system when the individual enters the school. Within the school, he interacts with other individuals—among them teachers. The first chapter in Part Three will include speculations and findings on the type of teacher performance and teacher-student relationship that seem most productive of learning.

Exhibit 1-1
The Learning System

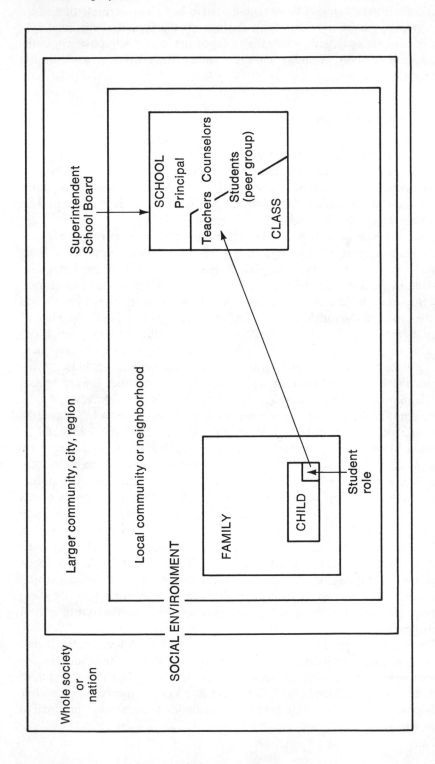

In addition to teachers, the student interacts with other adults in the school system—counselors, the principal, and various administrators. Note that the behavior of teachers and other school personnel, like that of students, is affected by characteristics and experiences which they bring to school with them. Finally there is the student's peer group, the majority segment of the school population, which as we shall see (Chapter 11) has a strong influence upon his attitudes toward school and learning and his actual school performance.

These interactions occur within the school. The structure and dynamics of the school as a social system and as a learning environment comprise the content of Part Three. Chapters 7 and 8 deal with the classroom, the subdivision of the school in which teaching is normally conducted. Chapters 9 and 10 deal with the sociological characteristics of schools in general and the factors which distinguish one school from another in ways which affect student learning.

Part Four deals with the school's environment as a part of the learning system. As Exhibit 1–1 indicates, the school system, like the individual student, is surrounded by a series of environmental levels, from the immediate neighborhood to the community, city or region, to the larger society or nation. At each level, the values and resources of the system affect the school's goals, resources, autonomy and so on—and so the school is in a very real sense a sociocultural product. Chapter 12 in Part Four will analyze the role of the superintendent and his professional staff, the school board, and the other groups that together constitute the school's external social environment, with particular reference to the way in which the interaction of these groups may affect academic productivity. Chapter 13 will be devoted to some crosscultural comparisons of learning expectations and achievement.

It is hoped that Exhibit 1–1 will serve as a frame of reference for Parts Two, Three, and Four. Although individual chapters must of necessity be treated as separate units, it is important to keep in mind that the components of the learning system are closely related. Also, although each chapter will pursue a different branch of the sociology of learning, each is organized around the same set of general questions:

1. What do sociologists know about learning? What kinds of social factors are related most strongly to learning at a particular level of the learning system?

2. What are the implications of (1)? Given what we know, what components of the learning system can be manipulated to increase learning efficiency?

3. What *don't* sociologists know about learning at a particular level, or what additional knowledge would be most valuable?

The interdependence of the topics discussed in different parts of the book will be underscored further by the handling of certain issues which are generally treated as separate topics—the effects of socioeconomic status generally and the problem of socioeconomic disadvantage in particular. Our current knowledge about the "disadvantaged" student indicates that he is disadvantaged at more than one level. He comes to school with characteristics and aspirations which are at variance with the goals, expectations, and procedures of the school system; his relationships with school personnel are poisoned by ineffective communication patterns, low expectations, and hostility (on both sides of the relationship); and the neighborhood in which he lives typically lacks the resources to support a strong school and the expertise to obtain a fair share of the resources available to education in the community or city as a whole. Obviously effective change must consist of a *set* of solutions which attack several levels simultaneously or in some meaningful sequence. In fact, however, not only have most proposed solutions to the problems of disadvantaged students been partial, but few have identified clearly the part of the learning system they are supposed to change or strengthen. Since this is a sociological study, and since the failure of sociologists to make a real contribution to learning theory is at least in part a failure to locate the issues in their proper social context, we shall, at the risk of repetitiousness, organize the discussion systematically in terms of social structure and levels. It is hoped that the recurrence of certain issues and themes throughout the book will lead toward a deeper understanding of learning problems and away from simplistic conclusions and solutions.

In the final part, we shall attempt to pull together the answers to the three kinds of questions raised above—by analyzing the directions in which our educational system seems to be moving, and examining the extent to which some recent educational innovations are congruent with a sociology of learning.

Before plunging into the discussion of substantive findings, we shall take a detour which can be considered part of the introduction to the field. Anyone who has explored the education literature in any depth is aware that the quality of research on learning is very uneven. Chapter 2 will try to put into perspective the kinds of research strategies available to educational sociologists and the kinds of data that are already available. We shall begin with descriptions of a few "landmark" studies in the field, selected to illustrate the range of design possibilities, then move on to a more systematic discussion of research alternatives. The purpose of Chapter 2 is to help the reader who has not had extensive research experience to understand the structure and functioning of the learning system. That is, we shall not attempt to teach the reader how to *do* the educational research, but simply how to read and weigh the findings reported in the succeeding chapters of the book. Readers who have had previous courses or experience in research methodology can skim over Chapter 2, or go directly to Chapter 3.

Notes

1. "Education ought to provide society with people who are capable of doing new things, rather than repeating what other generations have done, and with people who can analyze and verify so that they do not readily accept available trends of thought" (Glaser, 1968: 740).

2. It is also, in the main, about late elementary and secondary school learning. Although a few studies concerned with the beginning and postcompulsory school years will be included in the following chapters, these years—with their special characteristics and problems—will not be treated directly.

3. "Economic and professional specialization in modern societies is based on an accumulation of technical knowledge, the transmission of which lies beyond the powers of any family, and also necessitates a period of learning and preparation, the length of which is usually directly related to the extent of specialization. This also holds true of many aspects of ideological, philosophical and religious knowledge, the acquisition of which constitutes a necessary prerequisite for the performance of many roles and for the attainment of full membership and status within the total society. The transmission of this knowledge is effected in special, institutionalized, educational organizations—the schools. While various types of professional and educational schools exist in many societies, it is only in modern societies (and perhaps to some extent in certain sectors of the societies of classical antiquity) that they have gradually become an almost universal institutional device for the transmission of knowledge necessary for the attainment of full social status. Their first distinct characteristic is that, unlike the so-called initiation schools of the primitives, they organize the life of children for a long period of time, usually for several years. The second basic characteristic is their very strong technical-preparatory emphasis" (Eisenstadt, 1956: 163).

4. Piaget's scholarly output on the development in the child of causality, quantity, numbers and measurement, chance, morality, and other aspects of thinking, is too voluminous to be fully documented here. A recent estimate was 25 books and over 160 articles. Among the basic references are Piaget, 1948; 1951; and 1952.

The Design of
Educational Research

One of the great unsolved problems of American education, or of education anywhere in the world is that of providing a continuous flow of dependable information on how well the schools are meeting the developmental needs of children and in what respects they are failing to do so.　　H. S. Dyer

There is another reason why I cannot get excited about the failure to disseminate research findings in education: many of the so-called findings are not worth disseminating.　　A. W. Halpern

Most of us are so familiar with schools that we forget how puzzling a school must appear to someone entering it for the first time. Moments of calm, with the corridors deserted and only the faintest sounds coming from behind rows of closed doors, alternate with intervals of pure chaos, with bells ringing, lockers clanging, books dropping, voices raised to a deafening pitch, and adults and children moving at high speed in all directions. Even persons familiar with the general sequence of activity in schools run the risk of being pushed and shouted at if they make the mistake of being in the halls "between classes" without knowing the traffic pattern of that particular school.

If a stranger decided, despite physical risk, to persevere in his efforts to understand the workings of schools, he would begin to notice certain patterns. In many of the rooms, he would observe a group of children or adolescents, probably between twenty and forty in number, seated in identical chairs or desks—reading or writing quietly or listening with varying degrees of attention to an adult who stands or sits before them. This adult is clearly in a position of leadership, although his control of the situation, as well as the extent to which all the young people are engaged in the same activity, varies from one room to another.

In addition to these rooms, there are others where the activities and personnel are quite different. There is usually a large room or rooms where women are answering telephones, typing and filing, and talking to a stream of adults and children who pass in and out. Often there are additional rooms with titles—"Principal," "Assistant Principal," "Guidance Counselor"—on the door. Entrance to these rooms is on a formal basis, usually by permission of someone who acts as a kind of gatekeeper. Some schools have rooms fitted out with special equipment for teaching special skills, including science laboratories, studios for music and art, and shops for woodworking and other manual activities. Finally, there may be one or more rooms large enough for all or most of the school population to assemble simultaneously, for large-group communication, eating, or sports.

At various points in the school day, subgroups of the population may be outside the building, engaged in sports or informal socialization. This is, however, nearly always on property immediately surrounding the school building and clearly separated from the outside world. Leaving the school area is frowned upon, if not altogether forbidden.

To which of these persons and activities should the observer turn his attention? How should he gather and organize information? This is the dilemma of the educational researcher who wants to explain how children learn and what structural arrangements facilitate or impede the learning of children with given sets of characteristics. To have been a student oneself and thus an "insider" to the very system one is studying is both an advantage and a hazard to the researcher. On the one hand, past experience may sensitize the researcher to certain things—upon entering a new school, he often notices things that are atypical or "feels" that the students are more or less friendly or interested; that the classes or certain classes are more or less stimulating, anxiety producing, or rigid; that the adult personnel are more or less competent; or that the general atmosphere is more or less attractive than in other schools. On the other hand, familiarity may cause the researcher to overlook or take for granted things that a stranger would find noteworthy. While we tend, for example, to assume that the formal classroom structure and the modes of interaction between teacher and students are the only or the best ways to educate the young, an outsider (and indeed some of the educational critics and innovators within our own society) may find these patterns of interest in themselves, and not entirely congruent with the goal of efficient communication of information and skills.

A research design is in a sense always a compromise. A "full" study of even a single classroom would require recording everything that went on during a given period of time (probably on a film or video tape, since no single researcher could see and record everything and no two researchers would see the scene in exactly the same way), plus questioning the members of the group and examining any available information on them to fill in attitudes and past behavior which would not show up in observation alone.

To collect data in this depth would be an ambitious project in a single class, and to extend it to a whole school, or several schools, would be for all practical purposes impossible. Thus the researcher makes a choice out of all the things that could be studied and the methods of gathering and analyzing data. In order to gain some notion of the range of research alternatives, let us begin by considering briefly, from among the studies that will be discussed in the following chapters, a few that represent very different approaches.

In a classroom study directed by Flanders, which is excerpted and discussed in Chapter 7, the question raised was what teaching "style" produced the greatest increase in student learning in two academic subjects. Rather than trying to record "everything" that went on in the classes studied, the observers were trained in advance to use a rather elaborate coding scheme which categorized each unit of interaction. The coding scheme was based upon a well developed theory of interaction patterns in small groups, and Flanders made some predictions about the results he would get before the data were analyzed.

Another classroom study, also discussed in Chapter 7, is Rosenthal's analysis of the effects of teacher expectations upon pupil performance. Here the researcher manipulated the classroom situation, by assigning some of the children to a special treatment which was not accorded to their classmates. Rosenthal's study illustrates the application of a particular kind of research design, the classical experiment, to the classroom situation. To the extent that a design meets the rigorous requirements of the experiment (including random assignment to the experimental treatment, a matched group of subjects for purposes of comparison, and measurement of all subjects before and after the experimental treatment), the researcher is justified in drawing certain kinds of conclusions that he could not draw in nonexperimental research.

A very different kind of study is the widely publicized and controversial *Equality of Educational Opportunity* survey, designed by James Coleman, Ernest Campbell, and a research team of sociologists, statisticians, and educational research specialists, under the auspices of the U.S. Office of Education and in fulfillment of one of the mandates of the Civil Rights Act of 1964. In this gigantic survey of approximately five per cent of the schools in the United States, all students at five grade levels were given a battery of ability and achievement tests; further information about them, their schools, and their communities was obtained from principals and teachers. The tests and questionnaires were produced and distributed by a national testing agency but usually were administered by the regular teaching staff in each school. The mountains of data returned were processed and analyzed by computer. At every stage of this ambitious undertaking, the research activity involved a variety of research specialists and the most meticulous attention to the technical details of administration and data handling. In keeping with the size and scope of this project, the empirical findings cover a wide range of topics, and they will be introduced in several different chapters in this book.

A final contrast is provided by the Strodtbeck study discussed in Chapter 3, which is based upon a small sample of high school boys purposely selected to contain equal numbers of boys designated as over- and underachievers. In this study, the researchers went into the homes of their subjects, taking recording equipment with them, and interviewed boys and parents at some length, both individually and as a family group.

These four studies illustrate only some of the design possibilities available. They also sensitize us to the need for caution in making comparisons between studies. Given that the way a study is designed and executed affects its outcomes and the confidence we can place in them, it is important to understand some of the basic dimensions of research design. Although the following discussion does not constitute a comprehensive presentation, it points to the alternatives that seem to have special relevance for sociological learning research. (For a more thorough treatment of the alternatives of research design, see Riley, 1963; or Selltiz *et al.,* 1959.)

The Sample

At the start, the researcher must decide whom or what he will study—the research unit (individual students, schools, communities, or so forth) he will use and the selection of cases he will study out of the total population. The samples in the four studies described above range from 48 boys in Strodtbeck's study to some 900,000 children from schools all over the United States in the *Educational Opportunity* survey.

The latter study, one of the largest and most rigorously designed of those to be studied in this book, is based upon what is called a stratified, two-stage probability sample. Stratification involves choosing a similar or equal number of cases from each of a designated set of categories. Since the major objective of the *Educational Opportunity* survey was to compare the opportunities and performances of majority and minority group students, roughly half the respondents were white and the other half nonwhite. The total sample was also distributed so that there were over 75,000 subjects at each of grades 1, 3, 6, 9, and 12. Since the geographical area and total population studied were so immense, the sampling was done in stages, the first to select the set of counties and metropolitan areas from which, in the second stage, the actual schools would be drawn. Within each of the strata designated, the individual cases were chosen randomly. A probability or random sample, in which every case in a population or population stratum has an equal likelihood of being included in the final sample, is the only kind that allows the researcher to make estimates about the total population and to compute the degree of confidence to be placed in his estimates.

As in all national surveys, there were difficulties in obtaining the truly representative sample specified in the original research design. For example, certain schools selected refused to participate in the study. Some of the data collected were unusable because of incompleteness, or coding and other kinds of processing errors. One important segment of the potential school population—school dropouts, for whom the issue of equality of educational opportunity is particularly relevant—is not discussed in the report.[1] These and other problems are discussed in the report and estimates of the amount of bias introduced are calculated. It seems safe to conclude that the author's findings and their interpretation of them represent an unusually accurate picture of the American schools.[2]

The stratified, two-stage, probability sample was appropriate for this particular study, but it is neither practical nor desirable for many kinds of research. Rosenthal, who wanted to study closely the effect of a particular aspect of teacher behavior and to manipulate the classroom situation, limited his sample to the children in the first six grades in a single school. He made no claims for the representativeness of his sample, but deliberately chose a school with a high turnover rate and a high proportion of students from a racial minority group, two variables related to low academic performance.

Yet another approach was that of Flanders. Here the population sampled was all *classes* in grade 7 social studies and grade 8 mathematics in one large metropolitan area. Class averages on questionnaire responses concerning the kinds of social patterns existing in the classes were calculated, and the eight highest and eight lowest classes were selected for the study. The important criterion in evaluating a study sample is the extent to which it fits the basic objectives of the study. While samples vary, and can be judged, in many ways, some of the more important variables are the *size* of the sample and whether or not it is *representative* of some designated larger population. (In the *Educational Opportunity* survey, the objective was "to provide estimates for a large number of school, pupil, and teacher characteristics for the Nation as a whole." Thus it was necessary to have a probability or random sample, and one large enough to assure sufficient cases in all the strata to be compared.) Another important variable is the sampling *unit,* which in educational research can be the classroom (in the Flanders study) or the school as a whole (as in the Coleman *et al.* survey) as well as the individual student.

Data-Gathering Techniques

A second important decision is what kind of data to gather from the sample one has chosen. The four studies we have used as examples illustrate considerable variety in data-gathering techniques. Again the reader is referred to a text on research methodology for a full discussion, and we shall simply outline the major alternatives.

1. *Observation.* This may range from simply putting a researcher into a class or other school situation to record all he can about what is going on to the highly structured form of observation developed by Flanders, in which pretrained observers classified selected aspects of teacher-student interaction according to an elaborate coding scheme.

2. *Interviewing or questioning.* The Strodtbeck study relied mainly on this technique, including individual interviews with boys and their parents and a special kind ot group interviewing in which the family members were asked to resolve differences of opinion which had been revealed in the individual interviews. The group interviews were recorded, and by listening to the tapes, the researchers were able to give each family member a "power" score based upon his amount of participation and the number of final decisions in accordance with his original opinion.

3. *Written tests and questionnaires.* With this technique, subjects produce their own data, which means that the researcher does not have to be present throughout the period of data gathering and that comparable data can be collected from a large number of subjects in a short time. The tests and questionnaires for the *Educational Opportunity* survey were mailed out to the thousands of schools in the sample and were administered in large assemblies or in a number of classrooms simultaneously. Coleman and his associates were thus able to collect a vast amount of information about the 900,000 students within a period of a few months.

This is the only practical method of gathering new data on a large sample. At the same time, it has certain limitations. Since it depends upon written communication, it is not an appropriate technique for use with young children or with older students who have severe learning problems. And when the researcher is not present during the administration, he cannot be sure that all respondents took the questionnaire under the same conditions and interpreted the questions in the same way. The researcher can overcome these weaknesses to some degree by careful pretesting of the data collection instruments.

4. *Available data.* In addition to generating new data by observing or interviewing members of the school system or by obtaining written information from them, the researcher who can gain access to the great amount of data that schools and other educational organizations gather themselves can often save time and expense and get information he would be unable to obtain any other way. Most schools keep detailed records about individual students (grades, test scores, health, behavior and other problems, and family information) and about the school as a whole (class size, special classes and services, teacher and curriculum characteristics, and expenditures). The sample for the Strodtbeck study was based upon inspection of school records. Coleman and his colleagues used a variety of available data resources, including U.S. Census population surveys, the Office of Education National Inventory of School Facilities and Personnel, and school inventories from state departments of education. They also collected statistics on the physical facilities of schools and the academic and extracurricular programs from superintendents' and other administrative offices in each school district.

Many studies combine two or more of these basic data-gathering techniques. For example, Flanders and his staff also gave achievement tests to the students in the classrooms they observed. The Coleman and Strodtbeck studies illustrate the many studies which use available data as background for or in conjunction with the gathering of new data. The important thing in evaluating a study is whether or not the researchers have gathered data which have direct bearing upon the questions they are asking, and whether the technique used is the most efficient means of getting relevant information.

The Time Factor

According to the conceptualization of learning developed in Chapter 1, learning is a dynamic phenomenon. That is, learning by definition assumes *change over time*—the student who learns knows something he did not know at some previous time. Given this inherent characteristic of our dependent variable, the ideal research design would consider a set of students, classes, or schools at more than one point in time.

Two decisions about the time factor which must be made for any study are the *length of time* encompassed in the study and whether it is *longitudinal,* a more or less continuous study of the same sample over some length of time, as opposed to a pair or series of cross-sectional views. To borrow imagery from photography, the longitudinal study is analogous to a film for which the camera follows the same subject or subjects for a given interval of time. The cross-sectional study is analogous to a film for which the camera takes a series of snapshots taken from the same position—with whatever happens to be in the camera's range being recorded and the same subjects not necessarily appearing in all the shots.

In real life, it is rarely practical to study any group of students, classes, or schools continuously for long periods of time, and a study generally is classified as longitudinal if measurements are taken of all subjects at fairly regular intervals over a fairly long period. None of our four sample studies can be said to be truly longitudinal, although the students in Flanders' sample were given attitude and achievement tests before, during, and at the end of the two-week teaching units, and Rosenthal's subjects were tested at the beginning and end of a school year. In this book, we will come across few true developmental studies—in the sense of their being both longitudinal and long-term. The preponderance of what one analyst has termed "snapshot" studies (which "look at particular aspects of the school learning process for a relatively brief moment") is particularly disadvantageous when one is trying to make long-term decisions, such as whether the introduction of a particular subject or method of teaching in the earlier grades will have a substantial impact upon learning in high school (Carroll, 1965: 249–252).

In the *Educational Opportunity* survey, Coleman, Campbell, *et al.* attempt to draw conclusions about differential patterns of academic development among different racial-ethnic groups from data that are cross-sectional rather than longitudinal. During the 1965–1966 school year, the test batteries were administered to a sample of children at five different grade levels. The research staff began their analysis with the results of the twelfth graders, which they then compared with results from the other grade levels. From these comparisons the authors concluded that the gap which existed between white and minority group children when they entered school increases as they progress through the grade levels. What must be understood is that this conclusion was reached not by following a group of children through their school career but *by comparing different groups of children at different age and grade levels.*

Given the scope of the survey and the limited time available (a requirement of the Civil Rights Act of 1964 was that the report be submitted in the summer of 1966), a longitudinal study was clearly impossible. The study was thus designed to approximate the longitudinal model as closely as possible, by "matching" the older and younger respondents as follows:

> For each secondary school selected in the sample, the lower grade schools which feed their students into the secondary school were identified by the local school administrators, together with the per cent of the feeder school students who would ordinarily attend the sampled high school. Each feeder school sending 90 per cent or more of its student to a sampled secondary school was selected with certainty, and other feeder schools were selected with probability equal to the per cent of students who go on to the sampled secondary school (Coleman, Campbell, *et al.,* 1966: 554).

The researchers felt that, although they were not able to trace the educational growth of individual students over time, comparisons controlling for age and grade level could, "with appropriate caution, give some indication of relative growth rates among each of the ethnic and regional groups examined" (Coleman, Campbell, *et al.,* 1966: 219).

The Setting: Field vs. Laboratory Studies

Carroll's complaint about "snapshot" studies in the laboratory points to another dimension upon which educational research can vary. In three of our four sample studies, the work was conducted in the school. (In the Strodtbeck study, the researchers collected initial data in schools, but did their interviewing in the homes of a selected group of subjects.) Since the dependent variable we are trying to understand is scholastic achievement, the school is the "natural" setting in which to conduct research—it constitutes the "field" for studying formal education.

The major advantage of the field setting is that it allows one to observe the social system operating more or less normally (keeping in mind that simply entering a social system for research purposes usually has some effect upon that system). Its disadvantage, when the field is as complex and busy as that of most schools, is that the researcher cannot take in everything, and that he has little control over subjects and activities. He can rarely ask a teacher to repeat a class or lesson, separate some students for special study, or make major changes in the content of a course or the teaching method used. Even in the Rosenthal study, in which the researcher intervened in the learning process to identify certain children as academic "bloomers," there was very little interference in the regular classroom procedures.

When one wishes to study a specific portion or aspect of the learning system, with certain other aspects controlled, a more appropriate setting is a laboratory. In educational research, this may be a specially constructed research facility with recording equipment, one-way glass for observation, and other technological devices, or it may be simply the researcher's office or an unused room in the school. The point is that the subjects are removed from their regular setting.

The first part of the Flanders study was a laboratory experiment "designed to study relationships between controlled teacher influence and its effect on dependent behavior among students. The laboratory approach was essential to the control of the students' goal perceptions and the assessment of dependence" (Flanders, 1960: 22). This part of the study was conducted in a spare room of the school, with students selected so that each of the thirteen groups had the same number of boys and girls and the same distribution of IQ scores. They were then assigned to one of four kinds of "treatment," based upon variation in the degree of teacher influence and the degree of clarity of presentation. By conducting his initial tests in this manner, Flanders was able to control certain characteristics of the student-subjects, the presentation of the learning tasks, and the subsequent behavior of the "teacher" (a trained member of the research staff in this part of the study). He was thus able to study the way in which these variables were related to each other without having to take into account the possible effects of a host of other things which could be operating in a normal classroom.

As is the case with the other decisions the researcher must make, his choice of setting determines the kinds of information he will obtain and how he can interpret them. Obviously, a full understanding of the learning process and the social factors which affect it requires studies from both field and laboratory settings. In this respect, the Flanders study is a very strong one, since the laboratory phase was followed by a field study with a larger sample.

Experimental Design

Any piece of educational research in which the researcher is trying to determine the effects of some social variables upon learning or to evaluate some change in the structure of the learning environment can be judged in terms of the extent to which it meets the assumptions and requirements of the controlled experiment. To compare an actual research design with a model of this sort indicates how much confidence can be placed in the results and may help the researcher locate sources of possible bias.

The classical experimental design is shown in Exhibit 2–1. The experimental group, which can consist of individuals or groups (classes), is subjected to a given situation or treatment with one or more control groups similar to it in all respects except the treatment factor. An important assumption of the ideal model is that subjects are assigned to the experimental or control group on a random basis. Thus if d is different from d' (see Exhibit 2–1), this difference is assumed to be the result of the experimental variable—or of chance variation, the probability of which can be estimated.

The experimental treatment normally is thought of as something new which the researcher introduces into the situation (for example, a new method of teaching or a particular way of grouping students). However, many research studies consist basically of a comparison between two or more groups which vary in one or more respects but where the variation was not controlled by the researcher—for example, comparison of the performance of a given type of student in different schools or programs of study, or with different kinds of teachers.

The classical experiment has been the subject of countless articles and papers, many of which suggest additions to the basic design to allow the researcher greater confidence in his results. Among the most thorough analyses of experimental design in educational research is a long paper by Campbell and Stanley (1963). Among the many additions or variations which they discuss, two are especially relevant. One elaboration is to test a pair of experimental and control groups only *after* the introduction of the experimental variable, to control for a possible effect of test 1. (When no "before" test is given, it is especially important that the requirement of random assignment to groups be met.)

A second extension of the classical design controls for the novelty effect —that is, separates the effects of the new program or equipment per se

Exhibit 2–1
Classical Experimental Design

	Before	Treatment	After	
Experimental Group	Test 1	Presence of sociological factor or new teaching method	Test 2	d = results of Test 2 minus results of Test 1
Control Group	Test 2	Absence of sociological factor or new teaching method	Test 2	d' = results of Test 2 minus results of Test 1

from the efforts of simply doing something new or receiving special attention.[3] An example of a study designed to control for the novelty effect is Miller's (1967) experiment on Omar Moore's "responsive environment," otherwise known as the ERE, or the "talking typewriter." One of the most widely touted innovations of the past decade, the ERE consists of an electric typewriter with keys that cannot jam, a window or screen in which letters, words, or sentences can be displayed, and a microphone-speaker, all of which are connected to a computer. The child works at the typewriter —at first simply exploring its possibilities at will—and the responsive environment provides continuous audio-visual "feedback," either repeating what the child has just typed or itself providing stimulus letters, words, and sentences (Pines, 1965).

Some early field studies with the ERE equipment reported astonishing results. Very young children and children with severe learning handicaps worked voluntarily for long periods of time and gained reading and writing skills far ahead of their peers. Miller's study controlled for the special attention typically given to the young subjects trying out the ERE, by allowing only the regular teacher or staff member administering the program to be in the experimental classroom. All reporters, visiting educators, equipment designers, and so on were excluded. The result: the children averaged less than five minutes per session on the typewriter, and few learned even the alphabet—let alone how to read. The moral is that a good experimental design builds in some control for the powerful effects of attention or novelty, either by carefully approximating in the study the normal classroom conditions or by adding one or more control groups in which an alternative treatment or novel factor is introduced, preferably by the same persons who introduced the experimental treatment.

Another kind of effect to be guarded against is the "experimenter effect," or the tendency of our research results to turn out the way we want them to. Rosenthal, the designer of the study on teacher effects described earlier in this chapter, also has written a full-length book on the experimenter effect (Rosenthal, 1966), which serves as background and companion piece to his own experimental work. In an example taken from psychology, experimenters who were told that they were working with genetically bright rats reported better performance in maze tasks than experimenters who believed they were working with dull or untrained animals—even though the animals actually had been assigned randomly to one or the other group. The experimenter effect, as Rosenthal conceptualizes it, combines the observer's tendency to "see" things consistently with his own expectations with a parallel tendency to influence his subjects so that they actually *behave* in the expected manner. The general strategy for avoiding this kind of bias is for the experimenter to remove himself as much as possible from the administrative process of the experiment, and to "blind" the data gatherers and analysts as to which are the experimental and control subjects.

There are, however, numerous difficulties in translating a model into an actual research design. Just to set up comparable experimental and control groups in an educational setting is more difficult in practice than in theory. In most schools, assignment by classes rather than individuals to the experimental or control treatment is the only practical procedure, and the researcher can consider himself lucky if he can match the groups on some aggregate level measures (say, mean IQ or achievement scores), assure that the matched classes are taught by the same teachers, and assign the classes to treatments randomly. (Whether matching is done on the individual or group level, the requirement of random assignment to experimental or control treatment is an important one, since the possibility of bias is so large otherwise. It is difficult, for example, to evaluate much of the early work on progressive education, because children who attended progressive schools usually differed from the general population of children in background, motivation, and abilities. It is likewise difficult to evaluate the results of teaching innovations which are tested with students who have volunteered or been selected by teachers to try them.)

Another dilemma is whether the researcher should, or can, control the behavior of the persons administering the experiment. "It is well known that almost any course works well in the classroom if it is taught by its inventors or by a few of their highly trained converts. . . . To get a valid test of feasibility, you must turn over the program to teachers who are a fair sample of the people who would be teaching if it were adopted on the scale for which it was intended" (Moise, 1964: 175). But can a teacher who has always run her classes along, say, authoritarian lines give a fair test to a teaching method involving much informal interaction among students and with no predetermined "correct" answers to problems—assuming such a teacher is willing to participate in such an experiment? How can the researcher be sure that two or more teachers supposedly using the same approach are in fact administering the experiment in the same way? In fact, how can the researcher be sure the experimental treatment is being administered in the intended manner unless he does it himself, or is at least present to observe? The dilemma is essentially the one described in connection with the field vs. laboratory setting—is the researcher more concerned with having the environment operate as "normally" as possible, or does he want to control factors which might complicate the particular process he wants to understand? To add to the dilemma, the more the researcher separates himself from the experimental situation (in order to avoid novelty and experimenter effects), the less he knows about what is really happening.

To summarize, while the complexity of the school makes it difficult, often impossible, to carry out educational research in accordance with all the requirements of the classical model, it can provide a standard against which to compare an actual research design. One way to evaluate the studies in the following chapters is to check the ways in which they adhere to and deviate from the controlled experiment model.

The Empirical Measurement of Learning

In Chapter 1, we discussed the concept of learning. Here, we shall elaborate upon our dependent variable by considering how the researcher translates the general concept into empirical measures.

Educational researchers disagree about the general approach to measuring learning. On one side are those who feel that all educational objectives should be defined in terms of observable human behavior. To this group, of whom Robert Gagné is the principal spokesman, statements of objectives such as—"The student should *acquire a developing awareness* of the magnitude of the solar system" or "The child should *become increasingly confident* in extemporaneous oral expression" are insufficient ("weasel worded" is the judgment made by Gagné) because they do not specify what the student must *do* to show his "developing awareness" or his "increasing confidence" (Gagné, 1965: 6).

Gagné's approach is to break down a given learning objective into a set of specific behaviors or performances which reflect achievement of that objective, each of which can be described by a set of "tasks," the smallest unit of performance which has a distinct or independent purpose. Thus the general objective of reading French should be defined in terms of the specific task of reading a French newspaper, the objective of understanding trigonometry should be defined in terms of being able to solve problems requiring the use of sine, cosine, tangent, and so on. Gagné does not, however claim that all learning tasks are of the same type or level, and he proposes a series of learning categories, going from simple *connections* (as when a young child learns to say "mama" when his mother gives the stimulus "mama") through *concepts* (learning to group classes of objects or events) to *general principles* (Gagné, 1965: 18–20).

Critics of the "behavioral objectives" approach to measuring and evaluating learning argue that much learning, particularly creative and scholarly work, does not proceed in a way that could be translated into a specific behavioral sequence, and, moreover, that analysis does not necessarily aid performance:

> A designer of "paint by numbers" kits might point out, as I believe information theorist Claude Shannon has, that any painting is essentially a collection of areas of discernibly different solid colors. It does not follow that painting by numbers is the best way to paint a Mona Lisa (Stake, 1968: 4–5).

The danger of defining learning only in terms of measurable behavior is that it can lead to a curriculum based upon factual information and readily measured skills.

The debate between Gagné and his critics is far from resolved, and there are, as in most educational debates, good points on both sides. Whichever side one favors, there is no doubt that greater clarity in defining and measuring learning outcomes should be a goal of all researchers. In Chapter 7, for example, we shall see that the disappointing results of many studies of teacher "effectiveness" are largely a consequence of lack of precision in defining what kinds of outcomes represent "good" student or teacher behavior, and that a general fault of much educational research is vague conceptualization.

The studies in this book use a wide range of empirical indicants of learning. In evaluating them we should consider how good a fit there is between the researcher's conceptualization of learning and the empirical indicants he chooses to measure it. While a first glimpse suggests endless variation in the measures used (which complicates the task of comparing the results of different studies), a closer examination shows that most studies use one or a combination of a few basic types of indicants.

Course grades are among the most common measures of learning. Given by the teacher of a course, they supposedly reflect how well a student has learned the subject matter. For this very reason, however, they are especially susceptible to personal biases. (Recent studies of college grading suggest that the consistently improving grade averages over a four-year college career reflect the expectations of the faculty regarding achievement at the various levels rather than a truly objective measure of actual performance.) Another weakness of grades as a measure of learning is their lack of comparability. As college admissions directors know, a B or a C from different schools, or even from different programs or teachers in the same school, does not always mean the same thing. However, whatever grades measure, they affect one's subsequent educational career and are a good predictor of subsequent educational achievement. Within a given system, they can be used as a means of ranking individual students, providing one keeps in mind the possible subjectivity of the graders.

Tests are another commonly used indicant of learning. *Standard tests,* as the name implies, were developed to provide more objective and comparable indicants of academic abilities and achievement. Standard tests are of two general types: achievement tests, which measure the accomplishments and information the student has acquired from his school and other learning experiences; and ability tests, which measure the student's aptitude for scholastic work. There has been much recent debate, however, about whether there is a clear boundary between the two kinds of tests and whether they are "fair" to certain kinds of children, in particular to the culturally deprived, whose backgrounds have not afforded them the kinds of experiences and skills called for by the tests. This problem will be discussed further in Chapter 6.

The fact that researchers have reservations about standard tests and teachers' own tests and grades is indicated by the many *tests and questionnaires designed by researchers* for their own studies. For example, the achievement tests used in the Flanders study were designed by the research staff. Self-designed tests have the advantage of getting directly at what the researcher wants to measure, and they are necessary in areas where standard tests are not available (for instance, in measuring learning from a new kind of teaching device or method. For discussion of the problems of evaluating the effects of educational innovations, see Part Five). Their weaknesses are their lack of comparability with results from other tests and the researcher's, as compared with the teacher's, possible biases.

Another way to overcome the biases of grades and tests is to provide students with some *new learning task,* distinct from their regular school work, and observe how quickly and well they master it. As we shall see in Part Two, this approach has been useful with children from disadvantaged or minority groups whose lack of familiarity with and confidence in formal classroom situations may have such a depressant effect upon their performance that it does not reflect their real capabilities.

While all of the above are methods of measuring *directly* students' information or skills, more indirect measures are also used. These include the highest education level reached (the assumption being that a student who reaches a relatively high level has learned more than one who leaves school at a lower level); or future educational plans or aspirations, even more removed from learning per se than education level achieved but strongly correlated with it. The major justification of such indicants is that they identify quite accurately those students who have mastered the behavior and attitudes needed to get the training which leads to the good jobs, high income, and the other accoutrements of success in our society.

Choice and measurement of *independent* variables, or factors which relate to or affect learning, present equally thorny problems. The researcher's task involves selecting from among the vast number of variable dimensions of classes, schools, and school systems, as well as students, those which have most direct bearing upon the questions he wants to answer and which can be measured with some degree of accuracy. (Even a study of the scope of the *Equality of Educational Opportunity* survey has been criticized for the omission of possibly important variables as well as for the modes of analysis and interpretation of the information that was collected.)

Finally, a word about the selection and handling of studies for this book. The ultimate goal of this book is the construction of credible models which will organize the sociology of learning. To this end we shall describe and try to place in context some of the best of past and ongoing empirical research, to synthesize the most important findings from a large number of studies from educational sociology and related fields. Our general strategy will be to look for consistent patterns in a multitude of studies which may themselves vary in type and quality.[4] Two chapters (7 and 11) are organized around "landmark" studies which represent levels of theoretical and methodological sophistication not now available in all areas of sociology of learning. However, some studies—among them, the Rosenthal study—will be given considerable attention because they test especially powerful ideas, even though on strictly methodological grounds they do not merit such attention.

In sum, we want to make clear that the studies presented in the following chapters are not perceived to be of equal weight. While we shall attempt to be candid and accurate in judging studies, our major concern is with what they add up to. By compiling a large number of empirical results, we hope not only to compensate to some degree for the deficiencies of individual studies, but also to move toward a dynamic, total model of the learning system.

Notes

1. However, a separate sample which included school dropouts was drawn and is being analyzed at Florida State University.

2. For the full sequence of steps by which this sample was chosen, see Coleman, Campbell, *et al.,* 1966: Appendix 9.2.

3. The novelty effect is often referred to in the research literature as the Hawthorne effect, after the industrial research project where it was "discovered." See, for example, Riley, 1963: Chapter 11.

4. For a discussion of this strategy of analysis and inference, see Campbell and Stanley, 1963: 36.

PART TWO

The Student

The schools must sort all the human material that comes to them, but they do not subject all children to the same sorting process. Other things being equal, the schools tend to bring children at least up to an intellectual level which will enable them to function in the same economic and social structure as their parents.   Willard Waller

Individuals are born into families. The family into which a child is born is one of the major determinants of his subsequent success in school. Two kinds of family effects are especially important. First, the family has certain characteristics including socioeconomic status, race, and religion, which are attributed to the child simply by virtue of his family membership. The second set of variables has to do with the way the family is structured and the attitudes and behavior of the members with respect to one another. These two types of variables are the subject of Chapters 3 and 4 respectively.

Socioeconomic status, race or ethnic group, and religion, the family attributes most strongly related to a child's school career, all affect academic success both directly and indirectly, through their interaction and through their effects on other variables related to achievement. Race differs from the other two attributes in its visibility (usually an individual's race can be identified on sight)[1] and its permanence (a person cannot move up or down within or out of his race as he can move within or out of his social class or religion). On the other hand, the conceptual distinction between ethnic group and religion is not always clear-cut. To be Jewish, for example, is a religious characteristic, but the identification of many Jewish persons is with an ethnic group or nation (Israel) rather than with a religion.

Socioeconomic Status

The family characteristic that is the most powerful predictor of school performance is socioeconomic status (SES): the higher the SES of the student's family, the higher his academic achievement. This relationship has been documented in countless studies and seems to hold no matter what measure of status is used (occupation of principal breadwinner, family income, parents' education, or some combination of these). It holds with a variety of achievement-aspiration variables, including grades, achievement test scores, retentions at grade level, course failures, truancy, suspensions from school, dropout rates, college plans, and total amount of formal schooling. It also predicts academic honors and awards, elective school offices, extent of participation in extracurricular activities, and other indicators of "success" in the informal structure of the student society. It holds, moreover, even when the powerful variables of ability and past achievement are controlled.[2]

Reexamination of these studies shows that the relationship may be more complicated than the previous paragraph implies. First, SES is related to other characteristics of the family which are independently related to achievement. One such characteristic is family size. Lower-SES children often start school with a verbal disadvantage simply because they are more likely to be born into large families where the opportunities for verbal communication with adults are limited, quite apart from the verbal facility or lack of it that parents may have (also class-related). And since mothers and older siblings in lower-SES families are more likely to be working and to spend less time at home, conversational opportunities are still further restricted. The social class-verbal skill relationship was consistently supported in a series of studies reviewed by Bernstein (1961), who concluded that middle-class children are exposed to a richer, more varied, and more grammatically correct verbal communication, which gives them a head start in school. Moreover, family size itself is related to other family characteristics which are also related to SES and to achievement. The following summation of the interactive relationship of SES with the factors of family size, birth order, and mother's age, each of which is also related to achievement motivation,[3] will, if nothing else, convince the reader of the complexity of the subject:

> It is not very helpful in predicting an individual's achievement motivation to know his position in the birth order—indeed this information can be misleading rather than useful—unless the social class and size of his family of orientation are also known. In small middle class families, for example, the effect of original position seems to be relatively unimportant; the oldest and youngest child in a two-child, middle class family have almost identical motivation scores, but as the size of the family increases, the scores for the oldest child in the middle class family become higher than those for the youngest child. However, in the lower class the reverse is true: the youngest child has a higher achievement motivation-score on the average than the

oldest child—a position that is maintained even when the size of the family increases. Similarly, the effect of mother's age upon the child's achievement motivation varies with the size of her family and social class. Thus the hypothesis that the sons of young mothers would have higher achievement motivation than the sons of old mothers proved to be correct, but only when the family is small. As the size of the family increases, particularly in the lower class, the scores of sons of young mothers drop rapidly and are surpassed by the scores of sons of middle-aged and old mothers (Rosen, 1961: 585).

In addition to the complex interactive relationship of SES and other background variables, SES is related to a number of attitudinal variables which may serve as intervening or explanatory variables in the SES-school performance relationship. Communication by middle-class parents of a certain set of values and of an outlook on life that incorporates educational and occupational success in turn produces higher actual achievement when the child gets to school. For example, in a reanalysis of a number of public opinion surveys done in the early 1950's, Hyman found that higher status respondents were more likely to perceive college education as essential to advancement, and to plan it for their own children, while among lower-SES respondents there was ". . . reduced striving for success . . . an awareness of the lack of opportunity, and a lack of valuation of education, normally the major avenue to achievement of high status" (Hyman, 1953: 438). In a study of high school sophomore boys, Rosen (1956) found the middle-class groups higher on individual "need achievement" (measured by TAT type tests), on cultural value orientations having to do with the implementation of achievement motivation (measured by questions on modes of coping with various physical and social environments—for example, "All I want out of life is a secure, not too difficult, job.") and on orientation toward the time dimension (the value of planning for the future). In fact, Rosen has characterized the typical middle-class family value system and child rearing patterns as an "achievement syndrome," with all efforts bent toward success in school and later life.

During the past two decades, Melvin Kohn and his associates at the National Institute of Mental Health have been conducting studies on the relationships between social class and parents' values for their children (Kohn, 1969a; Kohn and Schooler, 1968) and their behavior with respect to them, particularly their methods of discipline (Kohn, 1959b; Kohn, 1963). Kohn's studies are characterized by carefully designed samples. One consisted of 200 middle-class and 200 working-class white families with fifth-grade children. It was drawn by a two-step procedure. A selection of Washington, D.C., census tracts was made—based upon tract distributions of such status characteristics as occupation, income, and rent or value of home. Then families within these tracts were selected at random from lists of fifth graders compiled from public and parochial school records. In the early 1960's, Kohn compared this sample with a parallel one in Turin, Italy (Pearlin and Kohn, 1966), the findings of which will be discussed in the chapter on crosscultural differences in academic achievement. The other major sample used in Kohn's studies was of 3,100 men, chosen to represent all American men in civilian occupations, and interviewed by the National Opinion Research Center in 1964.

Respondents in this latter sample were asked to designate on a list of thirteen personal qualities: (1) which three they considered most important for their child; (2) which *one* of these three was the most important of all; (3) which three were the *least* important; and (4) which one of these three was least important of all. On each of the thirteen items, a mean rating was obtained for each of the five social class subgroups, based upon a combination of responses to all four of the above questions. The items for which there is a statistically significant linear relationship between social class and mean rating—that is, the value of the correlation coefficient *r* is significant at the .05 level—and which the *lower*-SES parents perceive as more important than the higher-SES parents are:

good manners,

neat and clean,

obeys his parents well,

good student.

Those for which the linear relationship is reversed—which are more highly valued by the *higher*-SES parents—are:

self control,

responsible,

considerate of others,

interested in how and why things happen.

In other words, the middle-SES families, by comparison with their lower-SES counterparts, place greater emphasis upon *self*-direction. They want their children to be responsible and to control their own behavior, and this includes exploration of the world around them (finding out "how and why things happen" as opposed to simply being a "good student"). By contrast, the items which are relatively more important to the lower-SES parents are those which reflect conformity or obedience to external rules or authority (obeying parents and teachers) and having the *external* appearance or qualities that make a child acceptable to adults (good manners and cleanliness, in addition to obedience).

In the analysis of data from the Washington, D.C., sample, Kohn found that there are also differences between middle- and lower-SES parents in their behavior toward their children. These respondents were asked how they coped with a series of misdeeds ranging from fighting and playing wildly to disobedience and stealing. Most parents in both class subgroups said they tried to control their children's behavior first by such nonphysical means as ignoring them or asking them to stop. Only when misbehavior persisted despite parents' attempts to forestall it did they turn to physical punishment. At this point differences between lower- and middle-SES parents appear. Contrary to popular belief, the difference is not in the *extent* to which physical punishment is used—the middle-class mothers in the sample said they used it about as frequently as the working-class mothers—but rather in the conditions under which they choose it as opposed to alternative methods of control. Working-class mothers are most likely to punish severely when their children persist in physical aggression and severe fighting with siblings or other children, wild play that results in damage to the furniture and other kinds of physical aggression by the child. Middle-class mothers, on the other hand, are most likely to punish what they call "loss of temper" when this reflects a loss of self-control. That is, they judge aggression not in terms of its extremeness of direction (even when it is directed against the mother herself) but rather in terms of the child's presumed intent. As Kohn puts it, "For the working-class parents, the 'important but problematic' centers around qualities that assure *respectability;* for middle-class parents, it centers around *internalized standards of conduct.* In the first instance, desirable behavior consists, essentially, of not violating proscriptions; in the second, of acting according to the dictates of one's own principles. Here the act becomes less important than the actor's intent." (Kohn, 1959b: 364–365).

The overall impression left by Kohn's studies is that the higher-SES parent wants his child to understand the world around him and to come to grips with it through his own efforts, although control of his environment will require getting along with others; while the lower-SES parent is concerned mainly with avoiding trouble, by means of meeting the demands of those in authority. It has been suggested that the lesser emphasis by middle-class parents upon conformity to external authority does not mean that they do not value, and indeed expect, good behavior of the sort that will lead to success in school, but rather that they do not see these things as problematic. In the relatively secure environment of the middle-class home, it is more likely that cleanliness and orderly behavior can be taken for granted than in a lower-SES neighborhood, where simply keeping one's children and home neat and clean and trying to control children's behavior so that they will not get into trouble takes a strong commitment and continuous effort.

Recently some researchers have begun to cast doubts upon the strength of the relationship between social status and academic values. From reexamination of the data from earlier studies and from his own study of Los Angeles high school students, Ralph Turner (1964) concludes that the overall relationship is actually rather small. Turner also noted that more recent studies tended to show less class difference than earlier ones, raising the possibility that the stratification system or the value system or both are changing in our society. Some social commentators have claimed that America is becoming a middle-class society, and that middle-class values and life styles are spreading into lower-status levels. If this is so, one could expect a convergence in attitudes, including lessening of class differences in educational aspirations and expectations. This is the conclusion of Bronfenbrenner (1958), who in a review of studies of child-rearing practice in our country during the previous twenty-five-year period, noted changes in child-training techniques in both middle-class and working-class families, with middle-class parents, who were, at the beginning of the twenty-five-year period, relatively more "restrictive" than working-class parents, becoming more "permissive" and working-class parents moving toward less permissiveness. Although changes in child-rearing practices tended to occur sooner in the middle class than in the working class, Bronfenbrenner concludes that the overall pattern is one of a narrowing of the gap between social classes. Bronfenbrenner attributes some of this narrowing to the widespread influence of certain sources of expert opinion on child rearing, such as the books of Dr. Benjamin Spock, and the U.S. Children's Bureau bulletins.

Others would disagree that social status differences matter less than they used to. If stratification patterns in our society have changed, says Deutsch (1963), so have the other social and economic conditions which affect social mobility—in such a way that it actually may be harder for those of low status to get into the mainstream of American life. Granted that the poor and those of racial minority groups are no longer excluded from the "social elevator":

> the same elevator more frequently moves in two directions or stands still altogether . . . it also provides an observation window on what, at least superficially, appears to be a most affluent society. Television, movies, and other media continually expose the individual from the slum to the explicit assumption that the products of a consumer society are available to all—or, rather, as he sees it, to all but him. In effect, this means that the child from the disadvantaged neighborhood is an outsider and an observer—through his own eyes and those of his parents or neighbors (Deutsch, 1963: 165).

While the relationship between social status and success in school is a complex one, direct economic effects should not be overlooked. Not only do the costs of class dues, class rings, game tickets, prom tickets, clothes, yearbooks, and so on, keep the lower-income child from participating in extracurricular activities, but the lack of money to pay for basic school supplies (and even to rent required textbooks in some school districts) may raise the absentee rates of many children or keep them out of school altogether. In virtually every study of high school dropouts, a sizable portion give the need to take a job or other financial problems as the major reason for leaving school—the figures range from 11% of a 1961 sample of Maryland students (Millers, 1963) to 55% in a federal study of fourteen American cities (Segan and Schwarm, 1957). While a number of youngsters probably are motivated by the ready cash and the independence which a job seems to promise, a detailed study of dropouts from a large national sample indicated that for many of these young people "a job was really a matter of desperate necessity rather than just an excuse for getting away from a hated school" (Shaycroft *et al.,* 1963). And even with expansion of scholarship aid, the high costs of college tuition and other expenses (apart from class differentials in *access to information* about financial assistance) still keep lots of low-income students out of college.

Thus the limited income that is an integral part of low SES affects school participation and achievement directly, as well as through the cluster of variables that are a reflection of or related to SES. Severe poverty can account for children's failure even to get to school, let alone learn anything there. The congressional investigations following the urban riots of the mid-1960's have highlighted the powerful correlation between poverty and such indicators of health as infant mortality rates, the prevalence of nutritional deficiencies, disease and mental retardation among children— not to mention the probability of being bitten by rats! The immobilizing effects or severe poverty are presented by a writer who established residence in a New York City slum neighborhood and who argues that:

> It does not help matters to picture the slum child as the repository of a whole set of special cultural resources, generated by his poverty, which only need to be tapped by an understanding teacher. . . . Such resources, as listed by Hersey, include the "Closeness and warmth of the extended family, humor, easiness, fluidity of feeling, freedom from parental overprotection and from inner guilt, the enjoyment of sports, music, acting, a physical mode of existence, a delight in doing." Freedom from parental overprotection indeed! To imply that children deafened, immobilized and orphaned by poverty have acquired such assets in the process contributes to the sentimental impression that somehow life in the deep city ghetto can be character building and can develop a healthy toughness lacking in middle-class children. This view of the very poor, whatever its relevance to people of the ethnic slums of the past, minimizes the murderous quality of modern poverty and all the diseases associated with it, and paves the way for easy assumptions that all any slum child needs is the right educational formula and a teacher who "cares" (Lyford, 1966, 183).

Race

No other characteristic which the child acquires at birth has been the subject of more educational argument, analysis, and soul-searching than race. Recent research has focused upon the differences in school success between black and other minority group children and their white counterparts, and the extent to which such differences are a function of differential opportunities and experiences in and outside of school. In Chapter 6, we shall examine the arguments and evidence on interracial differences in intelligence and other abilities. Differences in the schools attended by minority group children and the neighborhoods in which they are located will be examined in Chapters 10 and 12. What we shall examine here is the effect of being a black (or some other racial minority) upon the adequacy of one's preparation for the student role and the ultimate likelihood of "making it" in school.

The most comprehensive survey on this topic is the landmark *Equality of Educational Opportunity*—already mentioned in Chapter 2. The sample of about 625,000 (all the students at grades 1, 3, 6, 9, and 12 in about five per cent of the public schools in the United States) included children from six racial and ethnic groups: Negroes, American Indians, Oriental Americans, Puerto Ricans, Mexican Americans, and whites other than Mexican Americans and Puerto Ricans (referred to as "majority" or simply "white"). Coleman and his colleagues make clear in the introduction to the report that "These terms of identification are not used in the anthropological sense, but reflect social categories by which people in the United States identify themselves and are identified by others" (Coleman, Campbell, *et al.*, 1966: iii).

Using as his major dependent variable scores on a set of standard tests, Coleman found substantial differences among the various racial-ethnic groups:

> With some exceptions—notably Oriental Americans—the average minority pupil scores distinctly lower on these tests at every level than the average white pupil. The minority pupils' scores are as much as one standard deviation[4] below the majority pupils' scores in the first grade. At the 12th grade, results of tests in the same verbal and nonverbal skills show that, in every case, the minority scores are *farther below* the majority than are the 1st graders'. For some groups, the relative decline is negligible; for others it is large. . . . Thus, by this measure, the deficiency in achievement is progressively greater for the minority pupils at progressively higher grade levels.
>
> For most minority groups, then, and most particularly the Negro, schools provide no opportunity at all for them to overcome this initial deficiency; in fact, they fall farther behind the white majority in the development of several skills which are critical to making a living and participating fully in modern society. Whatever may be the combination of nonschool factors—poverty, community attitudes, low educational level of parents—which put minority children at a disadvantage in verbal and non verbal skills when they enter the first grade, the fact is the schools have not overcome it (Coleman, Campbell, *et al.*, 1966: 21).

Having established the substantial and consistent test score differences among the various racial-ethnic subgroups in their sample, Coleman and his colleagues turned to the task of trying to account for these differences. They first examined the orientations of students themselves, including their academic motivations, and their future educational and occupational aspirations as well as their feelings about themselves. Exhibit 3–1 compares the responses of whites and nonwhites in two areas of the United States with large black populations and where race relations and the differential opportunities related to race are exceptionally problematic. (Coleman's full analysis, which subdivided the sample into eight geographical regions as well as into the six racial-ethnic categories, is too extensive to reproduce here—the general pattern of results shown in Exhibit 3–1 is essentially the same in the regions not shown.) In addition to Negroes, ethnic minority groups included in the analysis are Puerto Ricans, the group which is similar to Negroes in educational disabilities, and Oriental Americans who have unusually *high* levels of academic achievement.

On attitudes toward school and academic work generally, black-white differences are negligible or even indicate a higher valuation of school and achievement by blacks. The black twelfth graders in these two areas of the country are as likely as their peers to want to stay in school now and to continue their education beyond high school, and to spend relatively great amounts of time outside of school studying and reading books. They are even more likely to want to be the best students in their class and less likely to be truants from school. Where the black and white students do differ is in taking concrete steps to implement their educational aspirations. Not only do relatively fewer of the black respondents have definite plans to attend college *next year,* but also fewer have gone through the necessary preliminary phase of consulting college catalogs or officials. In sum, the black students approaching the end of their high school careers have essentially the same (generally high) valuation of academic achievement and higher education, but they are less likely to *do* the things that will translate their aspirations into reality.[5]

By contrast to the blacks' pattern of responses, the Puerto Rican students have the lowest percentage of positive responses on almost every item on Exhibit 3–1. They display lower aspirations, do less reading and studying, and are even less likely than blacks to be taking steps to continue their schooling beyond high school. The Oriental Americans, on the other hand showed a pattern of aspiration and activity that almost mirrored that of the white majority group students.

Another set of attitudinal items that showed interesting racial-ethnic differences was respondents' sense of control of their environment. The figures in the bottom three rows of Exhibit 3–1 show that both Negroes and Puerto Ricans are more likely than whites to agree that "Good luck is more important than hard work for success," that "Every time I try to get ahead, something or somebody stops me," or that "People like me don't have much of a chance to be successful in life," items which reflect a lack of confidence in the individual's ability to control events in their lives. These differences are more impressive when considered in conjunction with the related finding that sense of control of environment is also among the most powerful predictors of test scores. In a multiple regression analysis designed to determine the relative contribution of students' family backgrounds, their attitudes, the characteristics of their teachers and of their

Exhibit 3-1

Attitudes Toward School and Academic Work, by Race and Region

% Respondents Who	White		Negro			
	Northeast Metro-politan	South Rural	Northeast Metro-politan	South Rural	Puerto Rican	Oriental American
Would "do almost anything" to stay in school	47	50	47	49	35	44
Want to be among the best students	36	46	48	69	36	46
Spend two or more hours on homework (daily)	51	47	57	54	41	64
Have not missed any school because of truancy	61	75	68	84	53	76
Read six or more books during previous summer	29	31	32	35	30	31
Want to get education beyond high school	86	83	86	85	66	93
Plan to go to college next year	46	35	31	30	26	53
Have read a college catalogue	73	58	59	49	45	70
Have talked to a college official	46	38	32	22	25	33
Plan to have a professional occupation	46	31	31	25	21	43
% Respondents Who Agree						
"Good luck is more important than hard work for success"	4	4	9	15	19	8
"Every time I try to get ahead, something or somebody stops me"	13	16	21	22	30	18
"People like me don't have much of a chance to be successful in life"	5	6	12	11	19	9

Data assembled from Coleman, Campbell, *et al.*, 1966: Chapter 3.

schools to variations in test scores,[6] the researchers found that for black children, sense of control of environment accounted for more test score variation than any other variable. Black children who did exhibit relatively strong sense of control had considerably higher achievement than those with low sense of control. The control dimension was less strongly related to achievement for whites, whose *self-concept*—their confidence in their own ability to learn—was a more powerful predictor of test scores. The authors conclude that there is a:

> ... different set of predispositional factors operating to create low or high achievement for children from disadvantaged groups than for children from advantaged groups. For children from advantaged groups, achievement or lack of it appears closely related to their self-concept; what they believe about themselves. For children from disadvantaged groups, achievement or lack of achievement appears closely related to what they believe about their environment: whether they believe the environment will respond to reasonable efforts, or whether they believe it is, instead, merely random or immovable. In different words, it appears that children from advantaged groups assume that the environment will respond if they are able to affect it; children from disadvantaged groups do not make this assumption, but in many cases assume that nothing they will do can affect the environment—it will give benefits or withhold them but not as a consequence of their own action (Coleman, Campbell, *et al.,* 1966: 320–321).

The relationships between the variables of race, academic achievement, and sense of control of environment may be summarized as follows:

Minority group children (in particular blacks and Puerto Ricans) are less likely than white majority group children to be good students (even if they value education and achievement).

Minority group children are less likely to have a sense of control of their own environment.

Children with low sense of control of environment are less likely to be good students.

Throughout the Coleman study, one ethnic minority group did not fit the pattern of lower scholastic achievement. On virtually every variable of intellectual value, aspiration, or achievement, the Oriental American children were equal to, or even outperformed their white majority group peers. On the sense of control variables, they stood between the white students and the blacks and Puerto Ricans, perhaps reflecting a realistic awareness of lingering racial prejudice (or, as we shall see in the study to be considered next, the restrictions of an authoritarian family system), but on any measures of academic achievement or steps toward higher education, they excelled. Is there anything in the background of the Oriental American child that explains his subsequent academic and occupational success?

Some clues are offered in a study by Caudill and De Vos of Japanese Americans who migrated to Chicago from relocation camps at the end of World War II. Longitudinal comparisons of a group of first and second generation Japanese Americans (Issei and Nisei respectively) with a sample of middle- and lower-SES nonOrientals on a variety of educational and occupational achievement measures showed that the Japanese Americans "achieved more in the space of four years in Chicago than other groups who had long been in the city, and who appear far less handicapped by racial and cultural differences" (Caudill and De Vos, 1966, p. 218).

The heart of the Caudill-De Vos study was an intensive clinical analysis of test, interview, and psychotherapeutic data from a subgroup of the total study sample. These clinical data suggest that the source of the Japanese American phenomenon lies in "a significant compatibility (but by no means identity) between the value system found in the culture of Japan and the value system found in American middle class culture." Both groups valued politeness, respect for authority and parental wishes, diligence, and personal achievement of long-range goals. These shared values, plus a common "adaptive mechanism of being highly sensitive to cues coming from the external world as to how they should act," even to the extent of suppressing many of their true feelings, assured that the Japanese Americans, while acting in terms of the values and adaptive mechanisms of their own ethnic heritage, would at the same time project an image that would be favorably evaluated by Americans. "What has happened here is that the peers, teachers, employers, and fellow workers of the Nisei have projected their own values onto the neat, well-dressed, and efficient Nisei in whom they saw mirrored many of their own ideals" (Caudill and De Vos, 1966: 214–215; 226). Thus was built up a set of role expectations which both reinforce and produce achievement behavior. Teachers and others in important role relationships with Japanese Americans came to expect high levels of performance from them, and they in turn fulfilled these expectations by actually obtaining relatively high-level jobs, which in turn reinforced the expectations of those around them, and so on.

The authors also point out that communication of achievement oriented values and skills was facilitated by the family structure of Oriental Americans, who "formed tight, self-contained communities controlled by parental authority and strong social sanctions." (Ironically, the very family structure which was so conducive to success in American society was also a source of strain for the second-generation [Nisei] Japanese Americans, making it difficult for them to break free from their families. In other words, what may be very functional for success in certain social institutions, such as the school or office, may be less functional at the individual level, where it may hinder personal satisfaction and development.)

Although Caudill's sample is small and uniracial, his findings suggest that a cohesive form of family life combined with strong positive expectations from persons outside the family can produce a level of actual achievement high enough to allow a minority group to break out of the cycle of disadvantage. (Of course, the recent formation of Yellow Power groups and programs and the general unrest among the young in big city China-towns indicate that the breakthrough is not complete.)

Although race has a clear impact upon school success or failure, and at least part of the effect is due to the systematic discrimination practiced against certain racial minorities, the exact extent of the purely racial effect is difficult to specify because race is itself related to other family charac-teristics. Probably the strongest relationship is between race and SES, and before turning to the third family characteristic of religion, let us consider the simultaneous or interactive effect of the first two.

That blacks are more likely than whites to have low income and low educational and occupational status is well documented, but many studies of racial effects upon academic success do not take account of this rela-tionship. For example, a study of child rearing (Radin and Kamii, 1965), based upon responses to questionnaires administered to forty-four low-income Negro mothers and fifty middle-income white mothers, found the former more protective of their children and more disturbed by any evi-dence of sexuality and aggressiveness. However, there is no way of know-ing whether the attitudinal differences obtained were related to differences in race, differences in SES, or a combination of the two.

A better choice of sample was made for a laboratory study by Hess, Shipman, and Jackson (1965). Subjects consisted of 160 black mothers of four-year-olds, selected from four social status levels ranging from college-educated professionals and managers to unskilled or semiskilled levels to families with fathers absent and family support from public welfare. While the study does not allow interracial comparisons, it does allow us to see whether the effect of race is uniform or whether it varies across status lines.

The study was conducted in a university laboratory setting, where the mothers were interviewed and were taught three simple learning tasks which they were then asked to teach to their own children. The tasks were: sorting a number of plastic toys by color and function; sorting eight blocks by two characteristics simultaneously; and copying five designs on a toy called an Etch-a-Sketch. The interaction between mother and child was observed and recorded by the research staff with the objective of relating "the behavior and performance of individual mothers to the cognitive and scholastic behavior of their own children" (p. 224). The results showed that the middle-income mothers were more skilled in planning the tasks and in communicating to their children how to carry them out. They were more likely to praise the child's efforts, although they gave just as much criticism as the lower-income mothers. There was little difference between the groups in the amount of affection expressed toward the child. In re-sponse to an interview question concerning how the mothers would prepare their children to go to school for the first time, the middle-income mothers

emphasized the child as an active learner, with a positive personal relationship between teacher and child, while the lower-income mothers
stressed the need for good behavior, for doing what the teacher said rather
than for active seeking of information. In sum:

> . . . the mothers differed relatively little in the affective elements of their
> interaction with the children. The gross differences appeared in *verbal*
> and *cognitive* environments which they presented. The significance of the
> maternal environment lies not only in the lack of verbal exchange but
> in the structure of the interaction between learner and teacher. The work-
> ing class mothers appear to be socializing impassive learning styles on the
> part of the child, teaching him to be docile in such learning situations, in
> contrast to the more active, initiatory behavior of the child from a mid-
> dle class home (Hess *et al.,* 1965: 226).

Although one cannot draw conclusions about racial influences from
a uniracial sample, the above findings suggest that the interaction between
race and SES—with blacks, Puerto Ricans, and other racial minorities
more likely to be of lower SES—rather than race alone, explains differential academic performance. In the multistatus sample studied by Hess
et al., the middle-SES Negro mothers, like middle-SES mothers in general,
had both the attitudes toward goal achievement and the kind of interactive
relationship with their children which facilitated learning.

To conclude this section, we shall describe some of the findings from a
carefully designed study which not only controls on race and SES, but also
breaks the dependent variable of test performance into several components.
Working on the premise that "social-class and ethnic influences differ not
only in degree but in kind, with the consequence that different kinds of
intellectual skills are fostered or hindered in different environments,"
Stodolsky and Lesser (1967) tested a specially selected sample of 320
first graders, evenly distributed by sex and social class, in four different
ability areas: verbal, reasoning, number, and space conceptualization.
Since the researchers wanted tasks which did not require transfer from
previous learning, they constructed tests which included only objects and
experiences common to all social and ethnic groups in an urban area. Thus,
they used pictures of buses, fire hydrants, police cars, and other objects
to which all urban children are exposed, rather than the conventional
giraffes, xylophones and other objects which middle-class children are
more likely to encounter in picture books, family excursions, and so on.
Stodolsky and Lesser also controlled for "examiner bias" by having each
child tested by a person of his own ethnic group and by extensive video-
tape training of the examiners.

Exhibit 3–2 shows the average test scores in the four intellectual areas
for the four ethnic subsamples. Children in these four groups differed both
in the absolute level of each mental ability and in the pattern among these
abilities. For example, on verbal ability, the Jewish children rank way
above the others, and this was also their area of most outstanding per-

Exhibit 3-2

Pattern of Normalized Mental-Ability Scores for Each Ethnic Group

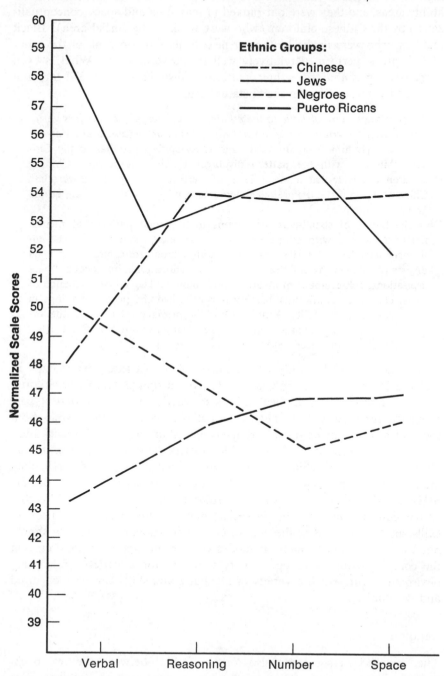

Ethnic Groups:
- – – – Chinese
- ——— Jews
- - - - - Negroes
- – · – · Puerto Ricans

Stodolsky-Lesser, 1967.

formance. Although the overall pattern of Jewish children was relatively high, their average scores were considerably lower in the other three ability areas, and they were out-ranked in reasoning and space conceptualization by the Chinese children (who were weak in the verbal area). Black children, who were in the bottom or next to the bottom rank in three out of four areas, performed relatively well in the verbal area. What is even more striking is that the ethnic patterns shown in Exhibit 3–2 are not changed by introducing the social status factor:

> *... once the pattern specific to the ethnic group emerges, social-class variations within the ethnic group do not alter this basic organization.* For example . . . [Exhibit 3–3] shows the mentality pattern peculiar to the Chinese children—with the pattern displayed by the middle-class Chinese children duplicated at a lower level of performance by the lower-class Chinese children. . . . Parallel statements can be made for each ethnic group.
>
> The failure of social-class conditions to transcend patterns of mental ability associated with ethnic influences was unexpected. Social-class influences have been described as superceding ethnic group effects for such diverse phenomena as child-rearing practices, educational and occupational aspirations, achievement motivation, and anomie. The greater salience of social class over ethnic membership is reversed in the present findings in patterns of mental ability. Ethnicity has the primary effect upon the organization of mental abilities, and the organization is not modified further by social-class influences (Stodolsky and Lesser, 1967: 567, 570).

A replication of the study by the same authors (a rare phenomenon in social research, as we saw in Chapter 2), with a similar sample of children but in a different city, duplicated almost exactly the pattern of test performance reported above. Thus, the authors conclude that while both social class and ethnical-racial group membership affect the level of intellectual performance, it is ethnicity which fosters the development of unique ability patterns, with children from higher social classes simply reflecting the same ability pattern at higher levels of performance than their lower-SES racial-ethnic peers. Thus an important implication of this study is that certain cultural subgroups in our society may nurture special attributes and skills, and that pursuit of the goal of equal educational opportunity should not lead us to impose uniform modes of learning upon all children. On the contrary, equality of opportunity may call for a variety of learning environments, in which a variety of attributes and skills can be recognized and developed.

Religion

The Stodolsky-Lesser study also forms a bridge between the two background characteristics of race and religion, since Jewish children were included in this study ostensibly focusing upon ethnic differences. As we

Exhibit 3-3

Patterns of Normalized Mental-Ability Scores for Middle- and Lower-Income Chinese Children

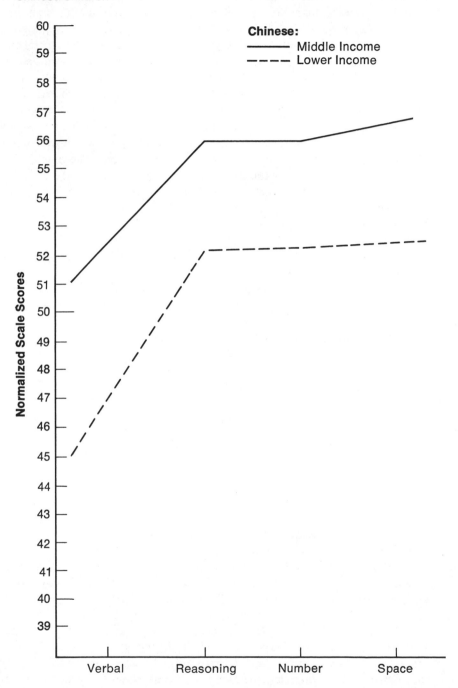

noted at the beginning of the chapter, it is not always clear whether Jewish identity is an ethnic or religious one. What *is* consistent is the general phenomenon of high achievement among Jewish subjects. As early as the 1940's, Terman's longitudinal studies of gifted children (Terman and Oden, 1947) showed that their Jewish subjects, while not differing significantly in mean IQ scores from the group as a whole, went on to receive higher grades in college, higher incomes, and to concentrate more heavily in professional occupations. The Stodolsky-Lesser data showed overall high performance by the Jewish children in the sample, with extremely high test scores in the verbal area. While the consistently high achievement points to the likelihood of factors specific to the Jewish culture which encourage and facilitate achievement, the first study in which systematic efforts to specify and measure these factors were made is the comparison of a sample of Jewish with Italian Catholic families carried out by Strodtbeck in the early 1950's. These two groups were chosen because they had similar periods of residence in this country and it was possible to locate adequate numbers of second-generation families with early adolescent sons in the particular school system studied (New Haven), but their socioeconomic attainments and their rates of mobility *as groups* in American society differed markedly.

A sample of 1151 boys between the ages of 14 and 17 in the New Haven public and parochial schools completed a questionnaire asking about their values, educational and occupational aspirations, parental expectations and control, and the balance of power within their family. The researchers also gathered information on the boys' school performance and the SES of their families. From this sample, Strodtbeck selected the following stratified group of Italian Catholic and Jewish boys for intensive study:

	Italian Boys School Achievement		Jewish Boys School Achievement	
Family SES	"Over"	"Under"	"Over"	"Under"
High	4	4	4	4
Medium	4	4	4	4
Low	4	4	4	4

Total = 48

Achievement was determined by the extent to which the boys' school grades were higher or lower than would be predicted on the basis of performance on intelligence tests. Note that the sample makes no pretensions at being representative. In the context of New Haven as a whole, Strodtbeck "oversampled" for Italians of high SES. Note also that Strodtbeck's group contains a religious-ethnic combination. That is, his Catholic boys are Catholics of one specific ethnic background. Since there is considerable evidence that family structure, styles of life, residence, and even achievement vary among American Catholics of different national backgrounds (see Greeley and Rossi, 1966), one cannot specify in Strodtbeck's study which differences are due to the religious and which are due to the ethnic factor.

(Recognizing the biases of his sample, Strodtbeck felt that "the stratification served our theoretical curiosity about effects of combinations of classificatory factors rather than the straightforward description objective of efficiently estimating parameters of incidence for particular populations" Strodtbeck, 1958: 160–161.)

The data were collected by Strodtbeck and an assistant in the respondents' homes, using a technique called "revealed differences." This technique involved interviewing the boy and both his parents, and then having the family as a group resolve disagreements in opinion which had been expressed in the individual interviews. Recordings of the interviews were scored both in terms of the content of the attitudes expressed and the structure of the interaction (the number of acts by each family member, and the proportion of decisions "won" by each).

From an analysis of both questionnaire and interview data, Strodtbeck found that the Jewish families were more likely to hold three values postulated as important for achievement in the United States:

the belief that the world is orderly and amenable to rational mastery, and that the individual can and should make systematic plans for controlling his destiny (this is a close parallel to the sense of control of destiny items which Coleman *et al.* found to be strongly related both to race and to scholastic performance);

willingness to leave home to make one's way in life;

preference for individual rather than collective credit for work accomplished.

Examination of the data on resolution of family disagreements indicated more equalitarian relations in the Jewish than in the Italian Catholic families. In comparison with the boys of Italian background, the Jewish boys were encouraged to express their opinions and to be independent. This autonomy, coupled with the Jewish parents' willingness for their sons to leave home to make their own way in life, meant that these boys could move out of the formal family setting and establish ties with other systems without having to rupture family ties altogether, as was the case in the traditional, authoritarian Italian families.

Notice that the picture of the Jewish family constructed by Strodtbeck is very different from that of the Japanese American families studied by Caudill and De Vos. While the Japanese Americans' impressive performance in school and in the occupational world paralleled the Jewish pattern, their authoritarian family structure was closer to the Italian Catholic model. The two studies are not really comparable because of differences in conceptual formulation and data-gathering methods, as well as geographical and other differences, but they do indicate that no single dimension can predict the achievement propensity of all religious or ethnic groups. Valuation of achievement is not a satisfactory predictor, because it appears to be a necessary but not sufficient condition for academic achievement. That is, if one took a cross-section of racial-ethnic-religious groups in our society, one would find some groups which had both relatively lower achievement orientation and lower academic achievement as a group (the Puerto Ricans in the Coleman *et al.* sample, the Italian Catholics in the Strodtbeck sample). However, there would also be groups which had reached the stage of recognizing the value of education and desiring it for themselves or their children but which had not yet learned the strategies for successful performance in formal educational settings (the Negroes in the Coleman *et al.* sample).

Every since Max Weber's classic work on the influence of religious beliefs upon social activity, *The Protestant Ethic and the Spirit of Capitalism,* there has been general acceptance of the notion that the set of concepts, values, and structures constituting a religious dogma has impact upon the believer's view of the world and his activity in it, in particular the extent to which he is concerned about and actually achieves worldly success. Weber's thesis was that Protestantism, especially the Calvinist sects, emphasized the value of hard work, coupled with an asceticism which denied any kind of sensual pleasure in the fruits of one's labor but hinted that success in worldly affairs might be an indication of God's grace. In contrast with Catholic dogma, with its emphasis upon the imperfectibility of man and his constant exposure to sin and moral conflict, Calvinist dogma was congruent with the development of both competitive capitalism and modern science. Analysis of historical materials by Weber and later researchers did in fact show a disproportionate number of scientists and successful businessmen among Protestant individuals and countries.

More recent studies, including Strodtbeck's, have found Catholics less oriented toward educational and occupational mobility generally, less likely to attend college, and less likely to go into scientific careers if they do attend college. David McClelland, whose *n* Achievement scale will be discussed in the next chapter, has found that Protestant parents tend to set earlier standards of independence for their children and has inferred that this would produce higher achievement motivation (McClelland, Rindlishbacker, and de Charms, 1955). In a study of the educational expectations of a national sample of white teenagers, Rhodes and Nam (1970) found that the proportion planning to attend college was related to the religious identification of the respondent's mother, with the following rank ordering:

	% Planning College
Jewish	86
Large Protestant denominations (except Baptist)	58
Roman Catholic	55
Baptist and smaller Protestant denominations and sects	42

However, the relationship between religious background and academic success is not as simple as the theoretical arguments and some of the empirical findings suggest. In the same study, Rhodes and Nam found that the religious context of the school, as well as the religious identity of the individual student, made a difference. Catholics attending Catholic schools were more likely than Catholics attending public schools to plan college, though whether this is because parochial schools have an option of selectivity of students which public schools do not have, or because students in parochial schools are pressured not just to attend college but to attend a Catholic college (the motive being to produce more good Catholics rather than more good students), cannot be explained with the study data.

Findings from a national sample survey, which, unlike Rhodes and Nam's, controlled for several socioeconomic favors, indicate that the achievement orientation of some subgroups of Catholics is as great or greater than that of comparable Protestants (Veroff *et al.*, 1962). As part of a larger study of mental health, 1620 men and women were given a thematic apperceptive test of achievement motivation, similar to McClelland's *n* Achievement scale, in which imaginative stories told in response to a set of pictures were scored for references to indicants of achievement motivation. The proportions of men in each of the three religion categories who had scores above the median for the entire male population were as follows: Protestant, 48%; Catholic, 57%; Jewish, 68%. The finding that relatively more Jewish men had high achievement scores than either of the other religious groups was anticipated (and is consistent with, say, the Strodtbeck findings). What was unexpected was that the Catholic men's scores were higher than the Protestants'.

Further analyses designed to interpret this unexpected result showed that the motivation of Catholic men is more directly related to economic factors. Thus for the Catholics, the lower the income and the greater the number of children in the family, the higher the achievement motivation; for Protestants, the scores showed a slight positive association with income and none with family size. The effect of religious identity was also dependent upon place of residence, including geographical region and the extent to which one's religion was a minority religion in a given area. For example, Veroff and his associates found that the Protestants living in the relatively higher income areas of the industrial Northeast had higher motivation scores than Protestants in other regions of the country, and they point out that most researchers who have reported higher achievement among Protestants have also been studying this one area. While they concede that religious doctrine undoubtedly influences the way a child is socialized, including his orientation to academic and other kinds of success, they conclude that the effect of religion, like that of race, also depends upon other attributes of the individual and upon the social environment in which he is located. Thus:

> . . . the situational effects that the social milieu has on these dispositions —region, socioeconomic status, education, income, size of family—may be so large as to cancel out any real differences between the personality dispositions of Catholics and Protestants which may be there. . . . Our im-

pression is that the Protestant Ethic hypothesis when used to contrast achievement motivated Protestants and Catholics has many new facets to be considered within certain social conditions. The hypothesis does seem to work simply only at the upper status positions of a well integrated, fairly prosperous, economic structure, in the established Northeastern parts of the United States. Perhaps this region is more typical of the European structure Weber originally observed. Change in the tempo of capitalism in America, change in the Calvinistic ideology in Protestant groups, changes in direction to Catholic living in a highly mobile society, may all contribute to making the Protestant Ethic less generally discernible and outstanding as a way of life geared to achievement in modern America (Veroff *et al.,* 1962: 217).

Conclusions

The weight of evidence examined in this chapter has clearly indicated that the social characteristics of a child's family affect his chances of success at school. Children whose parents are outside the cultural "mainstream" (althought the exact "mainstream" boundaries are not clear, and may vary from one part of society to another, those who are poor and of racial or religious minority groups tend to be excluded from it) are less likely to have the kind of school career that in turn enables them to succeed in the adult world.

Each era has its own words for groups which contain high proportions of social failures. "Underprivileged" was fashionable a few years ago; more recent favorites are "culturally deprived" or "disadvantaged." The concept of cultural disadvantage was extensively developed in Riessman's influential book, *The Culturally Deprived Child* (1962), which characterized these children as having a unique set of beliefs and customs—a "culture of the underprivileged" or "culture of poverty"—transmitted through the family and other neighborhood groups. This culture includes such characteristics as fatalism, feelings of frustration and alienation with respect to the larger society, and emphasis upon the physical rather than the intellectual—manifesting itself both in a love of excitement and in a love of personal comforts. All of this is the antithesis of the conventional middle-class orientation. Riessman argues that the schools need to develop a positive new approach toward these children and teaching methods that suit their particular view of the world and learning style.

Criticism of Riessman's work has centered around the notion of a separate culture of poverty. Not only is this a form of social stereotyping, argue the critics, but by allowing us to believe that minority group children are somehow "different" from other children, it provides us with an unjustified alibi for their failure in school and other social institutions. The disadvantaged:

> do not need to be taught middle-class values. By and large they hold these values already. Instead, they need only the same chances that the middle class has to realize their aspirations (Furstenberg, 1970: 52).

Kenneth Clark, the Negro sociologist whose *Dark Ghetto* (1965) is in part a response to the culture of poverty theory, claims that the poor academic records of poor black children should not be blamed upon inadequacies in the children's families but upon inadequacies in their schools, especially in the attitudes of educators who use the culture of poverty theory to absolve themselves from responsibility to teach well.

This argument cannot be resolved here. Assuming that different subgroups in our society are differentially able to communicate to their children the attitudes and skills necessary to playing the student role successfully, *how* they do so has been only hinted at. In the next chapter we shall examine what goes on within the family which produces differential success in school.

Notes

1. Of course, socioeconomic status and religion can have visible manifestations, such as clothing style or quality. The very poor may have poverty-connected health problems connected which affect their physical appearance. But these are mainly things that could be changed. With the proper "costume" an individual can pass for almost any social class, and in industrialized Western countries, mass production has given the majority of citizens access to clothing styles formerly available only to the upper strata. One cannot "do something" about one's race in this respect. With the exception of a handful of individuals whose physical features are ambiguous enough to allow them to "pass" from one group to another, one's race at birth is a lifetime attribute.

2. See for example, Clark, 1962; Sewell *et al.,* 1957; Hieronymus, 1951.

3. The extent to which one is affected by situations where one's performance can be judged. Note that achievement motivation is only an *indirect* measure of learning (see Chapter 2) and is itself often used to explain differences in actual achievement (see Chapter 4).

4. A statistic which measures the extent of dispersion of scores around some central value or score. In this case the measure of central tendency was the *median* or midpoint score, above which fell half of the scores and below which fell the other half, for each test at each grade level in the sample. In most samples about two-thirds of the cases fall within one standard deviation on either side of the central value and almost all cases fall within two standard deviations. For a fuller discussion of measures of central tendency and dispersion, see Riley, 1963: Volume II, Section 3.

5. Another perspective on racial differences is presented by U.S. Census statistics on educational attainment. Comparison of the median years of schooling completed by age-groups of young adults, between 1940 and 1966, shows that the most impressive gains were made by black men. During this twenty-six-year period, the median years of school completed almost doubled, from 6.5 to 12.1 years (the comparable figures for white males were 10.6 and 12.6). The four-year gap which existed between black and white men in 1940 was closed to two years in 1961 and to only one-half year in 1966. There was a

similar though less extreme pattern of "catching up" for black females. It should also be noted that, by 1966, the median for black males had for the first time surpassed that for females of the same race (Faltermayer, 1968: 145). Thus black-white differences in *quantity* of education are now very slight, but this same report also shows, parallel to the *Equality of Educational Opportunity* findings, that the *quality* of black education still lags far behind.

6. Regression analysis is a statistical technique by which the researcher tries to describe the nature of the relationship between two variables so that he can predict the value of one from the other. In the multiple regression which was used in the *Equality of Education Opportunity* study, the objective was to understand the *combination* of independent variables that would best predict the values of the response variable (verbal achievement)—and the relative contribution of each. The design of this part of the analysis is described in a Technical Appendix, Coleman, Campbell, *et al.,* 1966: 325–330. For a more general discussion of regression analysis, see Blalock, 1960: Chapters 17–19.

Family Interrelationships and Structure

Chapter 4

A

Mother: Hold on tight to your seat [a bus seat].
Child: Why?
Mother: Hold on tight.
Child: Why?
Mother: You'll fall.
Child: Why?
Mother: I told you to hold on tight, didn't I?

B

Mother: Hold on tight, darling.
Child: Why?
Mother: If you don't, you will be thrown forward and then you'll fall.
Child: Why?
*Mother: Because if the bus stops suddenly you'll jerk forward and bump
against the seat in front.*
Child: Why?
Mother: Now hold on tightly, darling, and don't make such a fuss.

Robert Havighurst

*Books and college courses too often say jolly things about the family hearth,
but sometimes home and family life are plain hell, and the chief obstruction to
education. . . . Home influence is overriding.*   Abraham Bernstein

In this chapter we turn to the internal life of the family, and we shall consider the kinds of parental expectations, modes of communication, distribution of power, and child-rearing practices which contribute to academic
achievement.

This is a more difficult task than the one we faced in Chapter 3. First,
for obvious ethical reasons, most of the available data on child rearing in

America is based upon parents' or children's reports of their home life rather than upon actual observation within homes.[1] Second, most of the social psychological research on family socialization does not link the family and school systems. There are, for example, many studies on the various modes of socialization and on the individual motives which are the product of socialization.[2] However, the particular combination of social motives most conducive to high achievement and the particular patterns of socialization most likely to produce them have not been clearly established. Thus some of the following discussion is based on studies which deal only indirectly with the relationship between family dynamics and school success—and also on pure conjecture.

Third, the topic of family effects upon school performance is one in which the dangers of experimenter effects, as described in Chapter 2, are great. Since family experiences are such an important, and emotion-laden, part of everyone's life (indeed, it is difficult to separate our feelings from our theories), the probabilities are high that the researcher will "find" his personal view of the best kind of family life to be related to desirable learning outcomes. Thus in reading research reports, one must be sensitive to the possible effects of the researcher's personal ideology upon his research design and his interpretation of results—not to mention the extent to which our own feelings color our reading of the work of others.

Parental Aspirations

It is clear that high-achieving children tend to come from families who have high expectations for them, and who consequently are likely to "set standards" and to make greater demands at an earlier age. Generally, success is held in high esteem in our society, and while most people recognize the hard work and sacrifice involved in attaining it, parents differ in the degree to which they set these as specific goals for themselves and their children. Turner, whose reservations about the strength of the direct relationship between SES and academic success were mentioned in the last chapter, found, among the boys in his sample, greater class differences on items that required endorsement of achievement values "as applicable to themselves as goals for their own striving" than on items which simply reflected impersonal acceptance of the value of achievement (Turner, 1964: 80–84). We also saw in the preceding chapter that groups differ in their estimates of the relative importance of personal intiative as against fate or luck as the source of success.

A study which illustrates the power of parental aspirations, but which at the same time shows that they are not synonymous with socioeconomic status, is Kahl's often-cited analysis of a sample of Boston high school boys (1953). Kahl's objective was to explain the educational commitment of students subject to educational "cross pressures"—who had some characteristics that would lead one to expect high academic commitment and performance and some that would lead to the opposite prediction. The two variables he chose to control were individual academic ability (IQ scores) and family SES.

Past analyses have shown that it is quite safe to predict that boys with high IQ's and fathers in white-collar or higher-SES occupations will go to college (cell *a* in Exhibit 4–1) and that boys with low IQ's and fathers in low-SES occupations will not (cell *d*). Kahl focused upon cell *b,* one of the two cells where prediction is problematic. He selected a sample of

Exhibit 4–1
Property-Space for Predicting College Attendance

		Socioeconomic Status	
		High	Low
IQ	High	a	b
Score	Low	c	d

twenty-four boys, from a larger survey known as the "Boston-Harvard Mobility Study." All of the boys tested in the top three IQ deciles in their schools. All of their fathers held low-level white-collar or skilled to semi-skilled labor jobs. Half of the boys were taking a college prep course and planning to go on to college; the other half were not. Kahl conducted intensive interviews with all twenty-four boys to find out what influenced the decisions of students whose abilities and environments could lead them in two different directions. His conclusion: their parents. Unlike boys without college aspirations, those who planned to continue their education had parents who were not satisfied with their own status and who had applied steady pressure on their sons to do better. In other words, it was not class per se that explained differential behavior, but the degree to which families retained the values and outlook of their own class or instead looked to a higher class as a reference group.

Once students acquire the motivation to achieve, their social background does not seem to hold them back. Although the Kahl data stopped with academic aspirations, data from Rosen's achievement syndrome study (1956) show the translation of achievement motive into school performance. In a comparison of sixty middle-class and sixty working-class high school boys, Rosen found that achievement motivation tends to be stronger among middle-class students (38 of the 60 middle-class students in the sample, but only 16 of the 60 working-class students, had high motivation), but that working-class boys who were strongly motivated to achieve did as well academically as their middle-class counterparts (75% of the working-class boys with high motivation had B averages or better, compared with 66% of the middle-class boys with high achievement motive). While Rosen's results are based upon an admittedly small sample (which, like Kahl's, did not contain students from truly low SES backgrounds), they do suggest that lower-SES children whose physical and mental facilities have not been seriously impaired by their surroundings are no less capable of high academic achievement than their higher-SES schoolmates.

Kahl's objective was to show that different kinds of socialization to the student role could occur within a single social class, and he did not compare the boys in his sample with boys from any of the other cells in Exhibit 4–1. His findings also suggest, however, that the mechanisms for inducing educational commitment may be different in different classes. He found, for example, that *none* of the boys in his sample, college-oriented or not, valued learning itself. All viewed education purely as a means of achieving socioeconomic mobility; what distinguished the high and low aspirers was that only the former had internalized the success-achievement ethic as a goal for themselves. Learning for its own sake is a luxury that these working-class boys could not afford.[3]

Recent evidence of the power of parental aspirations comes from a reanalysis of part of the data from the *Equality of Educational Opportunity* survey conducted by Chad Gordon.[4] Gordon constructed an index of perceived parental aspiration from four items, asking respondents: how good, as students, their mothers wanted them to be; how good, their fathers wanted them to be; their mothers' educational desires for them; and their fathers' educational desires. Exhibit 4–2 shows the relationships between scores on this index and ninth-graders' (N = 1663) own aspirations and academic performance, both totals and controlling for SES and race.

The totals show a strong positive relationship for each of the four items. For example, the first set of underlined figures show that only 15.3% of the respondents with low perceived parental aspirations wanted to be among the best students in their school, while 46.8% of the middle group and 74.5% of those with high parental aspirations wanted to be top students. The figures above the underlined rows show the effects on that item of parental aspiration controlling simultaneously for race and SES. Reading from left to right across the various rows shows a fairly consistent and substantial pattern of increases. Almost without exception, the higher the parental aspiration, the higher the proportion of students within a given race-SES subgroup with high performance or aspirations.[5]

Interaction

A second important contribution to academic success is a high level of parent-child interaction, especially in the form of positive adult response to the mastery of approved tasks. Achievement behavior is believed to originate in the desire of the very young child to get response from those around him: "only later, and for some children, does approval from others for good performance become unnecessary and feelings of pride or self-approval constitute sufficient reinforcement to maintain or increase their achievement behaviors" (Crandall, 1964: 78).

Exhibit 4–2

The Effects of Parental Aspirations Upon Student Performance and Aspiration Controlling for SES and Race

% Respondents Who	Race	SES	Parental Aspiration		
			Low	Medium	High
Want to be among the best students	black	low	30.2	71.9	71.0
		working class	17.6	59.0	77.4
		middle	20.8	58.3	79.7
	white	low	14.3	56.4	57.9
		working class	12.0	41.3	66.2
		middle	11.3	35.1	79.2
		TOTALS	**15.3**	**46.8**	**74.5**
Have overall grade averages of A or B	black	low	26.8	44.8	40.0
		working class	38.9	48.2	62.1
		middle	17.9	63.2	53.9
	white	low	33.3	50.0	60.0
		working class	42.9	64.7	73.0
		middle	48.0	65.2	73.4
		TOTALS	**38.6**	**59.4**	**71.2**
Are in college preparatory courses	black	low	8.5	18.4	25.7
		working class	12.5	15.7	28.7
		middle	7.1	44.7	41.5
	white	low	9.7	12.5	50.0
		working class	16.9	37.3	57.2
		middle	18.0	54.2	66.4
		TOTALS	**13.9**	**36.1**	**52.8**
Want a BA or more education	black	low	22.5	34.2	62.9
		working class	19.4	38.6	81.6
		middle	25.0	57.9	90.8
	white	low	12.5	32.5	60.0
		working class	8.7	54.2	80.9
		middle	16.0	74.2	92.7
		TOTALS	**14.6**	**54.5**	**84.8**

While the communication of high expectations and clear definitions of appropriate behavior are a necessary antecedent to high academic achievement, researchers disagree about the degree of intrafamily closeness and warmth which constitutes the most effective socialization climate. One view is that the families of high achievers are characterized by relatively greater warmth, closer primary relationships, a greater amount and depth of intra-communication, and many shared activities (Rosen and D'Andrade, 1959; Cervantes, 1965). An opposing view is that striving for achievement is most frequent among children whose relationship with their parents is more reserved, even unsatisfying (for instance, the review of studies conducted by Strodtbeck [1958] as background for his need-for-achievement research).

Both views oversimplify a complicated and controversial subject. Insofar as the Rosen position suggests that warmth and acceptance are unconditionally functional for achievement, it is misleading. Unconditional love from parents provides no motivation for the child to achieve (since he will receive love whether or not he achieves). Only when the power of the parent to withdraw or withhold love and approval is felt by the child does parental closeness itself promote achievement. Moreover, the assumption that the child feels a need for parental approval is not always justified. Studies such as Arnold Green's classic comparison of middle-class American families with Polish immigrant families (1946) have demonstrated that the need varies from one cultural subgroup to another.

On the other hand, for the more reserved parent-child relationship to promote high achievement, there must be clear definitions clearly communicated, as mentioned above. A child may perform very well for parents who maintain their emotional distance, but only if they effectively communicate high expectations to him.

The relationship between parental warmth and children's achievement is also conditional upon the sex of child and parent. A review of sex differences in intellectual development (Maccoby, 1966) found that a high level of "nurturance" or supportive behavior on the part of the mother during the preschool years was negatively related to subsequent academic performance among girls but postively related for boys (although the latter effect tended to disappear after a few years of school). What girls benefited from was *freedom* from maternal restrictions, plus supportive behavior from their *fathers*. A parallel for boys is Strodtbeck's finding that the fathers of boys with the strongest academic orientation were not only reserved with their sons but were also relatively nonassertive about achievement values or about their own position within the family:

> Oddly enough, the more the father subscribes to achievement values, the less the son's power appears to be—perhaps because the father is himself so energetic that the son assumes a reciprocal, passive role . . . the less the mother and son are dominated by the father in the power area, the greater the disposition of both to believe that the world can be rationally mastered and that a son should risk separation from his family. Apparently for a

boy lack of potency in the family might well lead him to infer that he could never control his destiny anywhere (Strodtbeck, 1958: 182–183).

The pattern suggested is that high academic performance is a product of a relatively close relationship with the parent of the opposite sex, but reserve or autonomy with respect to the same-sex parent. (This point will be taken up again the next chapter when we consider the effects of sex on school success.)

An often-stated platitude is that middle-class children learn faster because their surroundings are more "stimulating." Like many platitudes, this one is partly true but also misleading. There is a large body of evidence on the prevalence of mental and social retardation among children raised in orphanages or hospitals where the ratio of adults to children is low and there is little adult-child interaction. The importance of interaction with adults is underscored by the dramatic gains often made by institutionalized children when they received nurturance from substitute mothers, even if the substitutes were severely retarded themselves.

Institutionalization is not, however, a good analogy for the life of most lower-class children. Anyone who has spent much time in an urban slum can testify to the barrage of noises, smells, and activity that is a constant part of their environment. The point is that only certain kinds of "noise" are linked directly to the developmental needs of children and the demands of the school system. The middle-class family is usually better able to provide the books, play materials, trips to zoos and farms, and other stimuli which fall into the "school-functional" category—and to protect their children from stimuli that are excessive or nonfunctional. In the crowded apartments of the urban poor, the child is surrounded by noise, but the noise is seldom directed at him in a meaningful way and is often of a stressful sort. As one analyst puts it, "the situation is ideal for the child to learn inattention" (Deutsch, 1963: 171).

The excursions of the middle-class family provide experiences which can be used in the classroom situation; the constant moving of poor children from one apartment to another, from one school to another, do not. While mobility is not generally related to achievement, low-SES children who have the highest mobility have the poorest school records. In a study of over nine hundred New York City children drawn from the third and sixth grades of schools located in low-income areas, Miller (1967) found that the greater the number of moves from school to school, the lower the scores on intelligence and reading tests. Students in these same schools who had low mobility scored at or near average on the same tests. In a world of often excessive stimulation, it may be that "uninterrupted school experience is an important element in the school performance of disadvantaged pupils" (Miller, 1967: 23).

That the interaction of middle-class parents with their children often goes beyond mere cultural "enrichment" is suggested by a dissertation by

Dave (1963), which reported that a third of the students in one algebra class in a middle-class high school received tutorial help at home equal in time to the time they spent in class. Moreover, the students who received help from their families had generally higher grades in the course than those who received no instruction outside of class. Another difference was that the relationship between math aptitude scores at the beginning of the course and test scores and grades at the end of the course was very high (+ .90) for the untutored students but was almost zero for those who received home tutoring. Although this was a small study, it merits replication, since it indicates that parents can, and do, provide concrete assistance with academic work as well as help in mastering the external characteristics of the good student role.

Some of the recent private and public programs to raise the scholastic level of the culturally deprived are based largely upon providing an intellectually enriched environment like the ideal middle-class home, either within the home (research programs in which low-income mothers are taught how to "play" with their preschool children) or by getting children into the school system and by implication out of "inadequate" homes sooner (Head Start nursery schools). There is also anecdotal evidence that low-income mothers with high aspirations for their children often use a strategy of keeping them inside the home almost all the time they are not in school, thus protecting them from stimuli that might fault the good student role. The general point is that an "impoverished" home environment is not so much characterized by lack of stimuli as by stimuli that are either irrelevant to the school experience (when not actually dangerous to the child) or are not organized for the child so that he can make use of them in school.

It is in the family that most children acquire language, both a product of social interaction and the central pivot for all other forms of socialization. Because speech is one of the few immediately identifiable clues to a person's social position (class used to be readily identifiable by dress also, but the differences between type and quality of clothing worn by members of high and low social classes have steadily decreased), a child's life chances are directly shaped by the way he speaks. Thus:

> if his speech identifies him as a member of an out-group, when tagged as a member of that group he may be endowed with all the other modal qualities of that group—relatively low economic status, low educational status, values that emphasize immediate rather than delayed gratifications, relatively low power in the social hierarchy, or even having certain political leanings (Entwisle, 1970a: 3).

And since language is a threshold skill for all basic school work (and for the standard tests which are used to determine a child's place in the school system), children whose parents have facility in the "standard English" used by teachers, who encourage their children to express themselves verbally, and who have time to talk and listen to them are at a distinct advantage in the typical American classroom. As already indicated above, this is more likely to occur in middle-income than lower-income homes.[6]

A series of studies on children's linguistic development conducted by Entwisle have shown, however, that "disadvantaged" children actually may begin school with greater linguistic sophistication than their more advantaged age peers. Entwisle's studies concern the word associations of elementary school children. Most of the experiments involved administering a list of 96 stimulus words chosen to represent the different form-classes (nouns, adjectives, and so forth) and frequencies of standard English. Each stimulus word on the list was said aloud by an adult interviewer, and the child was asked to say "the first word you can think of." In order to make the young subjects comfortable, the test was administered in an informal, game-like fashion, and both black and white interviewers were used.

While the experimental task obviously covers only a small part of the total range of verbal skills, word associations have a tendency to fall into fairly clear patterns according to the age of the child. Preschool children tend to respond to all words with a noun or with a syntagmatic response (a word which is related to the stimulus word in a meaningful sense, and which usually directly precedes or follows it in a sentence, for instance, table-brown, or table-break). Between kindergarten and fifth grade there is a marked increase in *paradigmatic* responses (matching of words with their own form class, for instance, table-chair, responding to a verb with another verb, an adjective with an adjective, and so on). Because of these developmental patterns among children in general, individual subjects can be classified according to their level of verbal development. In addition, word associations have been found to be closely related to general linguistic competence and verbal comprehension. And they have the advantage of being easily obtained in large numbers from many children and of being easily analyzed by computers.

Comparison of a sample of black and white children of the same IQ range and from both high- and low-income areas of a large city showed:

> contrary to expectation, that slum children are apparently more advanced
> linguistically than suburban children at first grade. . . . While first grade
> slum children of average IQ give paradigmatic responses to about the same
> extent as gifted (IQ 130) suburban children, and although inner city black
> first graders of average IQ lag behind inner city white first graders, they
> give *more* paradigmatic responses than white suburban first graders of
> average IQ. Thus, at first grade the white child is slightly ahead of the
> black child when both are reared in the inner city, but the black slum child
> exceeds the white suburban child. The superiority is short-lived, however,
> for by third grade, suburban children, whether blue collar or upper middle
> class, have surpassed the inner city children, whether black or white
> (Entwisle, 1970a: 14).

These findings were unexpected, so unexpected in fact that the researcher replicated the basic study in a number of settings and has re-analyzed her data in various ways in order to be sure that the findings were not the result of sampling biases or some artifacts in the statistical analysis.[7] In addition to the differences in numbers of paradigmatic responses, Entwisle found differences between the semantic systems of black and white, middle- and lower-SES children. Analysis of the three most common responses for each stimulus word showed, for example, that black children were more likely than white children to give nonsense responses and less likely to give a "primary" or high frequency response (for example, "hot" in response to "cold"). For eight high frequency adjectives, the percentage of primary responses ranged from 46 to 71% for white children, from 34 to 58% for black children. In sum, even by the early elementary grades, black and white children were, to a certain degree, not talking the same language.

Entwisle's research underscores that the semantic differences between disadvantaged and advantaged children do *not* mean that the former are less competent in language. Similar conclusions have been reached by other researchers. Exhibit 3–2 in the last chapter showed that black children perform well in the verbal area relative to children from other minority groups. In a comparison of white preschoolers from very low-income families with white children in a private nursery school, Shriner (1968) found no differences among the groups in knowledge of basic language forms and rules. Finally, it has been pointed out that if proficiency in more than one language is used as the indicator of linguistic development, the black inner-city child—who lives in a kind of subcultural enclave and who must adapt to a different kind of language or "linguistic code" (standard English) when he ventures out into the larger white society—is linguistically advanced compared to the white middle-class child who hears the same language in his home and at school (Baratz, 1968).

While Entwisle's data do not provide any direct evidence about what accounts for the greater linguistic sophistication of "disadvantaged" children when they start school, it is interesting to speculate on the potential effects of certain already documented characteristics of their social environment. One is the virtually unrestricted exposure to television common to urban slum children (virtually all of whom lived in homes with TV sets by the mid-1960's). Although there is disagreement on the effects of television upon children's intellectual and social development, research evidence has indicated that while excessive television viewing has negative effects upon the academic performance of older children (both because it cuts into the time they might otherwise spend on homework and reading and because the intellectual level of most of the popular programs is below that of an intelligent adolescent), television serves a truly educational function for young children, introducing the kind of vocabulary and range of situations and experiences characteristic of the middle-class culture children

(Schramm *et al.*, 1961). Thus, in the slum household, where the television may be turned on most of the time, and where there is no middle-class mother to monitor the selection of programs or the number of viewing hours, the preschool child is exposed to a steady stream of spoken words (it is perhaps not insignificant that the tests on which the urban slum children outperformed their suburban counterparts were oral).

Other clues may lie in the position of the slum child in the family and the nature of communication between children and adults. In the suburban home, children are "taken care of" for a longer time. Adults not only take time to talk with children (or at least feel guilty if they don't), but they also make genuine efforts to *understand* what the young child needs. When he cannot express his needs in readily understandable language, adults are likely to help him. Among the urban poor, children do many things for themselves at an earlier age—cross busy streets, use money, get their own meals, take care of young siblings. Adults do not have or do not take the time to interpret or translate requests formulated in childish syntax. If the child is to survive in his environment, he has to be able to express his needs in the language of the adult world, whatever may be the language or dialect of his particular home or neighborhood.

These interpretations are congruent with the findings from another Entwisle experiment, which compared the word association patterns of Baltimore city children with those of a matched sample of rural Maryland children and a group of Amish children who lived on very isolated farms without electricity (and thus without television and radio), with few books and magazines, and with limited interpersonal relations (contacts with non-Amish persons are discouraged by subcultural norms). The scores for the urban children were substantially higher. Entwisle concludes that:

> rural residence impedes language development somewhat during the preschool period, so that first graders who live in the country are slightly retarded compared to first graders who live in the city. This is true irrespective of IQ level. Rural children of superior endowment quickly compensate, and by third-grade the difference is abolished. Rural children of lesser endowment still lag at third-grade, and it is not until fifth-grade that they are able to compensate fully (Entwisle, 1966: 76).

The Amish children, moreover, lagged even further behind the other rural children at all levels. In summary, the more the child's place of residence isolates him from exposure to the mass media and to other persons—both kinds of exposure are plentiful in the urban child's environment—the more likely he is to be retarded in verbal skills, although the school experience does eventually compensate for these disadvantages, more quickly for the bright than for the slower child.

The implications of this research are ironic as well as important. For the linguistic advantage that "disadvantaged" children hold when they enter school is not recognized and is lost within a few years. While their social environment equips them rather well for learning in certain areas, either the failure of this same environment to train children for the role of student in the formal school setting or the way they are perceived and treated by the school itself manages to neutralize any initial advantage these children may possess!

Perhaps a more significant, if subtle, implication is that in our desire to explain, we tend to categorize children as "successes" or "failures" before examining all the evidence. This may occasionally work to the advantage of a minority group. In Chapter 3 we saw how Japanese Americans were apparently able to break out of the cycle of disadvantage because they fit the image of the kind of person who was highly valued in post-World War II in America. In Chapter 7, we shall discuss a study which suggests how high expectations can be created experimentally which can in turn raise academic performance. However, too often in our effort to form a consistent picture of a child or a subcultural group, we overlook the very strengths which could be used to help children overcome learning difficulties. Simply by holding simplistic views, moreover, we may be contributing to their academic failure, by presenting to them an image of themselves as intellectually inadequate, which in turn has a depressant effect upon their actual learning. That the stereotypes of the larger society can shape the self-image of minority group children is indicated in a study of Jewish and Negro youth groups (Cahman, 1949). Questionnaire and interview data indicated that Jewish adolescents saw themselves as clannish, competitive, defensive, inhibited, and insecure; the black self-image stressed such weaknesses as drinking, fighting, carelessness, and lack of foresight. Although Cahman's sample was small and the findings may be somewhat dated by now, they do suggest that it may be the subleties of interpersonal expectations and interactions among groups, rather than gross aggregate differences in potentialities, that constitute the real source of inequality of educational opportunity.

Entwisle has some suggestions for restructuring the encounter of the disadvantaged child with the formal learning system (Entwisle, 1969: 1970a). One is to provide reading materials that, on the one hand, use the linguistic strengths with which these children enter school and, on the other hand, devote more attention to semantic areas which are not emphasized in the slum child's linguistic code (for instance, verbs and adverbs). Entwisle currently is developing some instructional games which provide drill in these areas in a play-like atmosphere. A more powerful remedy, in her opinion, is to speed up the desegregation of schools (on both race and class lines):

> Different semantic systems are no doubt a direct consequence of residential and educational segregation. With more mixing of students the semantic systems of all groups would tend to converge. This convergence would occur as a result of changes in all groups, not just the minority groups, and and would thereby pose less of a burden for the underprivileged child (Entwisle, 1970a: 25).

Family Structure

Related to the dynamics of intrafamily relations is the position of family members with respect to one another. Although the evidence is limited, there seems to be a positive relationship between academic achievement and a relatively equalitarian family structure. The Strodtbeck study indicated that parental authoritarianism was related both to religious-ethnic background and (negatively) to achievement orientation. A crosscultural study relating family structure with educational attainment in five different countries showed that parental dominance was negatively associated with the probability of reaching secondary school, both between and within countries (Elder, 1965).

A common explanation for the failure of disadvantaged children is that they are likely to come from "broken" homes. Indeed the theme of a controversial report on the black family (Moynihan, 1965) is that the matriarchal lower-SES black family structure, often with no legal husband-father present, is a pathological environment for the rearing of children. Actually the findings on the effects of broken homes are contradictory. Although Moynihan does present data showing that children from father-absent homes do have poorer school records, other studies show no such relationship.[8]

That the physical presence of both parents may be less important to the child's welfare than the degree to which the parents are meeting their role expectations is suggested by Gordon's analysis of the variables affecting academic output, introduced earlier in this chapter. As part of this analysis, Gordon constructed a measure of family structure based upon (1) the presence or absence of both parents and (2) their employment status. Some of the results of crosstabulating this family structure measure with a variety of dependent variables are shown in Exhibit 4–3.

The most positive attitudes and highest performances are found in families with both parents present and the father working (columns 1 and 2 of Exhibit 4–3). Whether the mother was working did not seem to make much difference (columns 1 and 2 alternate between first and second rank for almost all of the positive attitude and performance measures), as long as the father is employed. The most damaging family situations were those where the father was present but not working (columns 3 and 4), again regardless of whether or not the mother worked, and where the father is absent and the mother unemployed (column 6). Families with only one parent but where that parent is employed are in the middle (columns 5 and 7).

These results suggest that it is the relative economic security attached to alternative family structures that explains variations in children's self-image and success in school, and that the children who are least successful in the student role are from families where the major breadwinner is not fulfilling the major requirement of that role (this includes families where the father is present but unemployed, even if the mother is bringing in some income). The data also indicate that the employment of women is not

Exhibit 4–3

The Effects of Family Structure Upon Student Performance and Attitudes

	Both Parents Present				Mother Only		Father Only
Father employed?	(1) yes	(2) yes	(3) no	(4) no	(5) —	(6) —	(7) yes
Mother employed?	yes	no	yes	no	yes	no	—
% Respondents Who							
Say their parents have high aspirations for them	41.4	42.2	24.7	21.9	28.1	21.8	36.0
Say they are among the brightest in their grade	17.1	14.6	15.4	12.8	12.2	9.6	12.5
Say they are below average in their grade	2.1	3.0	9.2	6.4	6.5	8.5	4.2
Have a high grade average (A or B)	26.2	29.4	9.1	12.8	27.7	17.6	17.4
Have high overall competence	13.6	11.0	11.1	7.7	10.7	8.1	13.0
Have high self-acceptance	53.7	55.6	31.7	43.6	54.1	48.8	50.0
Have high self-esteem	26.2	30.4	13.4	12.3	26.2	13.8	26.1
Have high self-determinism	24.2	29.1	19.7	16.7	20.2	16.3	30.4
Have high verbal ability	60.7	63.0	16.9	19.8	37.8	29.1	60.0

detrimental to their children's self-confidence or achievement. Students do well when the father is present and employed, regardless of the mother's employment status; and if he is present and unemployed, her employment does not noticeably help or hinder the situation (with the exception of especially low self-acceptance among children with working mothers and unemployed fathers). If the mother is raising the children alone, it is apparently to their advantage if she works (compare columns 5 and 6).

Behavior Standards

In the process of socialization, the individual acquires, in addition to language, the standards of behavior which will determine how he will act in subsequent social situations, including the school classroom. These behavior standards consist of a set of motives with their associated activities and habits. The social motives most studied by social psychologists are dependency, aggression, and achievement, but while we know quite a bit about how these motives are produced in the family, their linkages with academic learning are still ambiguous.

Independence has often been noted as a characteristic of high-achieving children, but as in the case of environmental stimulation and family closeness, its components and consequences are complex. The nature of this complexity is indicated in several studies of young children (Crandall *et al.,* 1960; Crandall, 1964; Haggard, 1957) which found that high achievers are at the same time less dependent than other children upon parents and teachers for emotional support and instrumental help in carrying out intellectual tasks *and* more sensitive to adult expectations. "It would appear, then, that achieving children, in contrast to peers who perform less well, do not need to depend upon adults but are somewhat compliant and conforming to their demands and accept and incorporate adults' high evaluations of the importance of achievement. They are also able to work without being immediately rewarded for their efforts, show initiative, self-reliance, and emotional control" (Crandall *et al.,* 1964: 81).

By contrast, observers in inner-city classrooms have commented upon what seems to be excessive dependence upon the teacher. Severely disadvantaged children are, in fact, often so "hyper-alert" to the teacher's whereabouts and actions that they fail to respond to the learning materials and activities provided for them (see, for example, Miller, 1967: 58ff; and Moore, 1967).

In the language of social psychology, the high achieving child has internalized adult values and expectations. The process of identification is a subtle one, the trick being not only to provide appropriate role models but also to create the right degree of dependency in the child by providing attention and affection which are linked to the child's performance, with the underlying threat of withdrawal of the attention and affection if the behavior is unsatisfactory. The properly socialized child looks to the parent for values and guides to behavior but is capable of operating without constant parental supervision. As Rosen puts it, the ideal is for the child "to act appropriately not because his parents tell him to but because he wants to." The word "appropriate" is a clue to a subtle but important point about the value of independence. What the success-oriented parent wants for his child is not true independence of judgment—which would, of course, leave the child free to choose goals other than achievement and success—but rather internalization of the success goals of the parent by the child, so that he appears to strive for these goals under his own volition.

Achievement motivation is the individual's response to situations where some standard of excellence can be applied to their behavior. "At one extreme, persons set high standards for themselves, strive very hard to achieve them, and respond with considerable feeling to their success or failure in meeting them. At the other extreme, persons are unlikely to set such standards, exert little effort, and feel relatively indifferent about achieving the standards" (Second and Backman, 1964: 568). It is difficult to separate the child-rearing practices which produce high achievement motivation from those which produce the combination of dependency and independence just described. Both seem to be adopted by parents who combine considerable interest and concern with approval and disapproval conditional upon the child's behavior. The achievement syndrome posited by Rosen (1961) contains the impetus to behave in a self-directed way. It has also been found that the parents of children with high achievement expect them to be active and energetic, to know their way around their neighborhood, and to make friends for themselves at a relatively early age (Winterbottom, 1953). The unique component of socialization for high achievement motivation seems to be a kind of "coaching" of the child in the skills of problem solving (which may reach the point of actual tutoring in course work as described in the Dave study).

It seems almost a truism that high achievement motivation will lead directly to high achievement itself. Indeed educational innovations or curricular changes are often justified with claims that they will raise student motivation—and teachers and teaching methods generally are believed to be incapable of producing learning unless they also produce high student morale. The available evidence, however, casts some doubt on these assumptions.

The most widely used measure of achievement motivation is the *n* Achievement scale developed by McClelland and his colleagues (1953), based upon the number and type of references to achievement elicited by a series of stimulus pictures. (On the level of the total society, McClelland's Achievement Imagery technique can be applied to the myths and folk tales most commonly told to children—research using this kind of indicator will be discussed in Chapter 13.) The number of studies using McClelland's measure or some variation of it runs into the thousands. In a recent review of this literature, however, Entwisle (1970b) concludes that, despite its popularity, the scale has neither high test reliability nor strong correlations with grades or any other measure of school performance. Her own analysis suggested that the few statistically significant positive relationships between *n* Achievement and performance scores could be explained by the verbal productivity or the general intelligence of the subjects—that is, their high *n* Achievement score seemed to be a consequence of their having produced more intelligent verbalization in response to the picture, and this linguistic facility rather than the test as a whole was related to academic performance.

In sum, little of the variance in educational performance seems to be explained by current modes of measuring the motivation to achieve, although this lack of relationship may be due to weaknesses in the measures used, including lack of internal consistency and failure to separate out the unique motivational component from the other components which are related to academic performance.

The relationship between aggression and learning is even less clear. Any effects it does have are probably indirect or interactive with other individual or societal attributes. For example, the discouragement of aggressive—even active—behavior in any part of the school except the gym may explain why boys (for whom aggressive behavior is more likely to be tolerated, indeed encouraged) or children from inner-city ghetto neighborhoods where interpersonal aggression is an everyday occurrence have a hard time adapting to the aspects of classroom life that call for sitting quietly, following instructions, and so on. On the other hand, since academic success is at least partly based upon actual performance, girls who have been taught to equate femininity with passivity are also unlikely to have high achievement. The sex relationship will be developed further in the next chapter.

Conclusions

The theme of Part Two is that being a student is in large part a role-playing activity. The child's initial view of the world is furnished by his family. The last two chapters have reinforced the commonsense belief that the position of the family within the larger society and the way in which children are socialized within the family have a powerful effect upon the way children play the student role. Although our understanding of the interrelationships among various families related to academic success is still incomplete, the findings we have assembled fit the general model diagrammed in Exhibit 4–4.

The empirical evidence has indicated that there is relatively little difference among families in their valuation of achievement. Most children and their parents value success and recognize formal education as an important ingredient. What differs is the degree to which a general yearning is translated into a workable set of life goals and strategies for reaching them.

Exhibit 4-4
Model of the Relationship of Family Variables and School Performance

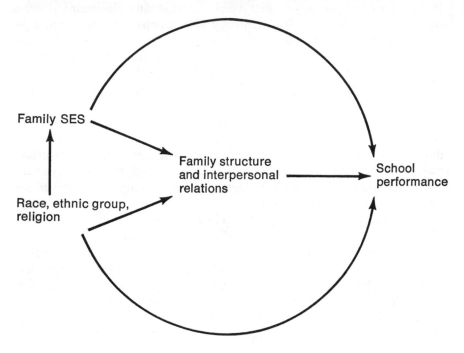

Parents of school achievers not only expect more and communicate this to their children, but they also teach them the *behavior* needed to fulfill their expectations. In sum, *what children who fail to "make it" in school lack is role-playing skill, not the desire to succeed, and because they do not know how to play the role of student, they are less likely to do the things that will lead to success.*

Thus by the time they enter school, children are already differentiated in terms of their academic success. In particular, the disadvantaged child already has entered a vicious cycle. The specifics of his home life have been documented here and elsewhere. Its inadequacies can be summarized by Miller's image of the disadvantaged home as a combination of the desert and the jungle:

> By "desert" we mean the barren wasteland of unmet, neglected needs in their family and social lives which constitute *deprivation*. By "jungle" we mean the confusing, untamed family and neighborhood world of impulsivity, excess and asocial patterning which constitutes *real external danger* (Miller, 1967: 58).

Arriving at school without the speech patterns, the self-control and good manners, and the familiarity with books and other educational paraphernalia of his better prepared peers, the disadvantaged child will probably draw more inexperienced or incompetent teachers.[9] Consequently he will perform poorly (and his performance will get lower relative to his middle-class age mates the longer he stays in school), get into more, and more serious trouble, and leave school earlier, thus fulfilling teachers' and society's expectations for him—and guaranteeing that he will remain at the bottom of the social ladder.

Notes

1. It is interesting that most of the "inside" studies of American families were done by anthropologists, and they were usually done to provide comparative data with families in more "primitive" societies (Whiting, 1963). Close observation of family life is a standard operating procedure in anthropology—and we do not seem to worry so much about invading the privacy of the home in other people's cultures!

2. For a good general discussion, see Secord and Backman, 1965: Chapter 18.

3. Actually, to value learning for its own sake is rare in *any* social class, according to a study by Douvan (1962) on the motivational factors affecting college entrance. To go to college does, however, have different meanings for students from different backgrounds: "For many youngsters from upper- and upper-middle-class homes, the question of going or not going to college probably never arises. Continuing in school beyond high school involves no conscious decision; the child from his earliest years is taught that following high school comes college. . . . In this setting, a decision *not* to go to college is the major and highly individual one, and undoubtedly requires unusual and intense motivation and a deviant personal integration. Most middle class parents see college serving several purposes; it is to provide the young person vocational preparation, a general intellectual broadening, and an opportunity to grow and develop for another four years, to grow in knowledge and skill, and also in emotional stability and autonomy. The children share many of these expectations, but their vision of college has additional dimensions (e.g., a gay and glamorous social life and release from parental control).

"To young people of lower social status, the decision for college may be a more conscious and problematic one. On the borderline of economic ease, one expects to find motivational factors most clearly distinguishing those who do and do not enter college. We have seen that for many of these less privileged youngsters, college represents the golden path to social mobility, the chance to increase their share of social and economic rewards" (Douvan, 1962: 200–201).

The implications of the Kahl and Douvan findings taken together are that we can motivate students from a great range of social backgrounds to achieve academically, but that this requires taking account of the view of themselves and the world which they have acquired as a result of their socialization.

4. The discussion of Gordon's findings here and elsewhere in this book is taken from an unpublished manuscript (Gordon, 1969) plus additional statistical data furnished by him.

5. Race and SES also were related to the dependent variables. High social class was consistently related to high aspiration and achievement. Blacks tended to have higher aspirations than whites, but were less likely to be in the college preparatory program and to get high grades. Status was also positively related to parental aspiration for both races; but while lower-class and working-class blacks were more likely to report high parental aspirations than whites of the same status, there were no racial differences at the middle-class level. As Exhibit 4–2 shows, however, the effects of race and SES tend to decrease or disappear when they are controlled simultaneously with the aspiration index.

One must, of course, be extremely cautious about making casual interpretations, since these data are cross-sectional rather than longitudinal, and since the parents' aspiration measure was based solely upon student reports.

6. See also Nisbet, 1961; Bernstein, 1961.

7. For full details see Entwisle 1968; 1969; 1970a.

8. Recent reviews are contained in Herzog, 1970; and Miller, 1967.

9. See, for instance Herriott and St. John, 1966. Among other things, "good" teachers are often rewarded by being transferred to schools in "better" neighborhoods.

In light of the social expectations about women, it is not surprising that women end up where society expects them to; the surprise is that little girls don't get the message that they are supposed to be stupid until they get into high school. It is no use to talk about women being different-but-equal; all the sex-difference tests I can think of have a "good" outcome and a "bad" outcome. Women usually end up with the bad outcome.   Naomi Weisstein

An attribute which is given to the child at birth, which is visible and permanent, and which is related to the way an individual perceives and plays the student role, is sex. At the same time, sex constitutes an important role in all known societies. It must be learned like any other role, and there is extensive literature, in clinical as well as experimental and survey research, on what is expected of males and females in different cultures and how they are socialized to their sex roles.

A general question which surfaces in most discussions of behavioral differences between the sexes is whether these differences are a consequence of "natural" or biological differences between males and females, or whether they can be better explained by differences in socialization. We are less concerned here with trying to answer this question conclusively[1] than with understanding the sociology of sex differences. Whatever the exact origins, boys and girls have different patterns of performance in school, and their experiences outside of school also differ in ways that would seem to affect academic motivation and achievement.

After a comparison of performance at various age levels and in different content areas, we shall examine some of the ability and personality characteristics which are related both to sex and to academic performance, and then the modes of socialization of boys and girls with respect to achievement in general and school behavior in particular. We shall also include some multivariate analysis in which the effects of sex will be examined simultaneously with some other sociological variables.

The ideal data for studying the sociological effects of sex upon learning would be standardized or otherwise comparable ability and achievement measures for a sizable sample of boys and girls at different age levels, preferably measuring the same children at various points in their school career (a longitudinal study). The closest recent approximation to this is the *Educational Opportunity* survey, but to date these data have been analyzed by sex only for a subsample of the ninth graders. We are, therefore, dependent upon the inference strategy described at the end of Chapter 2, hoping that the accumulation of evidence from a number of not-strictly-comparable studies will point to meaningful patterns.

Performance

In our country, sex contributes to a unique educational phenomenon—a switch in the relative academic performance of boys and girls during the course of the educational career of an age group. Starting out ahead of boys in almost all academic areas, girls begin to fall behind in certain areas during the later high school years, and beyond high school academic productivity and accomplishment of women drop off even more sharply. Evidence for the higher performance of girls in high school was described in a 1957 report by the National Manpower Council:

> It is not clear why girls achieve, on the average, better grades in high school than boys. But on the basis of the measures used, there is no question that they do. Up to college . . . girls outdistance boys in the number of years of schooling achieved. Those who replied to the National Manpower Council's questionnaire also reported that girls earn better grades than boys; that a smaller proportion fails; that they constitute a majority of the honor roll and scholarship society students; and that their grades, in relation to their intellectual ability, are higher than is the case with boys. . . .
>
> The recently developed National Merit Scholarship testing program also indicates that girls, on the average, do better than boys in high school. The first step in the program involved the screening of students in all the high schools of the nation in order to select those qualified to compete for a National Merit Scholarship. On the basis of the standards used—grades and class standing—girls made up 55 per cent of the total selected to compete (National Manpower Council, 1957: 183).

More recent reports have been consistent with the above picture. Gordon's reanalysis of data from the *Educational Opportunity* survey has found higher overall grades among girls than boys. Maccoby's review of sex differences in intellectual functioning (1966) included five studies of school grades published between 1958 and 1965, all of which showed higher achievement among girls. Kagan (1969) reports that at the elementary level, girls tend to outproduce boys in nearly all academic areas, and that boys are six times as likely to have reading problems. In fact, the apparent learning disadvantage of boys in the early elementary years has led to serious proposals that the sexes be separated for the first few grades and that systematic attempts be made to recruit more male teachers at this level.

The reversal that occurs in high school is also documented in the National Manpower Council study, which points to the following trends:

Although girls made up the majority of those selected to *take* the National Merit Scholarship exams, boys accounted for 69% of the scholarships actually awarded (on the basis of test results).

More boys than girls quality for college entrance and for scholarship aid on the basis of College Entrance Examination Board tests, which ostensibly measure ability to do college work.

More boys than girls enroll in a college prep curriculum, as a proportion of both the total high school population and the subgroup who rank highest in academic ability.

The latter finding was replicated in Gordon's analysis, which found a statistically significant sex difference in definite college plans even by the ninth grade.

Finally, if one breaks down performance into different substantial areas, there are some male advantages right from the beginning. Mathematics is one such area. Boys have higher interest and achievement in math from the beginning of school, and the sex difference increases with age. This pattern shows up with special clarity in an international comparison of mathematics achievement among adolescents at two age levels in twelve countries, including the United States (Husen, 1967). Almost without exception, male students in these countries showed a greater predilection for math—the ratio of males to females specializing in or taking advanced math courses varies from 2/1 to 7/1—and higher achievement scores, even when the level of instruction was held constant and regardless of the type of problem.

In sum, each sex tends to outperform the other at some phase of the school career, and there also seem to be substantive areas of sexual "specialty" from the beginning school years.

Abilities and Personality Characteristics

Is the thinking of males different from the thinking of females? The evidence suggests that it is, at least by the time both are old enough to be tested. One explanation for differential academic performance is that abilities are differentially distributed between the sexes. Studies comparing sex differences in intelligence tend to show negligible overall differences but substantial differences in specific ability areas. The findings are generally consistent with popular stereotypes; males outperform females on mathematical reasoning, judgment and manipulation of spatial relations, and mechanical aptitudes, while females excel at vocabulary and verbal fluency and tasks involving straight memory (see Maccoby, 1966; Wechsler, 1958). Test scores also indicate, however, that superior or highly developed ability is more or less equally distributed among boys and girls, and on all measures there is considerable overlap between the distribution of scores for the two sexes.

As in performance, "ability" development over time seems to favor boys. The Manpower Council survey unearthed data showing that by the end of high school, boys were doing somewhat better on "intelligence" as well as achievement tests, even though the girls, on the average, were still getting better grades. Apart from the question of whether so-called aptitude tests are really measuring aptitude or learning (which will be discussed in the next chapter), the argument for innate sex differences is weakened by the fact that much of the empirical evidence that is available in any quantity is on older students (the Wechsler data are for individuals sixteen and older; the studies surveyed by the Manpower Council are all on the high school level). Where test score data are available on younger children, many of the results show no significant sex differences, even on such sex-typed aptitudes as mathematical reasoning and spatial relations (Maccoby, 1966: 338ff), and by the time such differences do clearly emerge, the child has received a considerable amount of sex role training, such that original biological differences have been shaped by social expectations and experiences.

Another explanation for differential academic performance is that some types of individual personality traits which are related to achievement are differentially distributed among boys and girls. Three such traits are anxiety, dependency, and aggressiveness (or activity and impulsiveness as opposed to passivity). Social psychological research has indicated that the first two traits are stronger in girls than boys, the third stronger in boys than girls.[2]

Maccoby's review indicates that the relationship of these characteristics with intellectual performance is different for boys and girls. One longitudinal study shows that timidity, caution, and other components of anxiety are positively related to IQ and intellectual interests for boys but not for girls. On the other hand, impulsiveness and aggressiveness, which are negatively correlated with a number of aptitude and achievement measures for boys actually may be productive of achievement among girls.

One of Maccoby's major contribtuions is a model which encompasses and explains this whole set of findings. Her model postulates a relationship as shown in Exhibit 5–1. For the dimension of passivity-activity, the model postulates that:

> both the very inhibited and the very bold will perform less well, while those who occupy the intermediate positions on the inhibited-impulsiveness dimension will perform optimally. We further suggest that boys and girls, on the average, occupy different positions on the dimension we have described. There is reason to believe that boys are more aggressive, more

active, and less passive than girls. . . . If the hypothesis holds, it would follow that for optimum intellectual performance, most girls need to become less passive and inhibited, while most boys need to become less impulsive. However, for those girls who do happen to be highly impulsive (as much as the average boy, or even more so), impulsiveness should be a negative factor, as timidity should be for those boys at the passive end of the scale.

A parallel analysis may be made of anxiety as it affects intellectual performance in the two sexes. There is substantial evidence . . . that the relation of anxiety to performance is curvilinear. Either very high or very low

Exhibit 5-1

Maccoby Model of Sex Differences in Personality Traits and Intellectual Performance

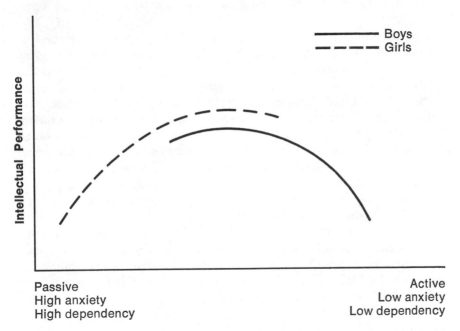

levels of anxiety interfere with performance on a variety of tasks; intermediate levels facilitate performance. If women and girls have a high base level of anxiety, then increases in anxiety above their base level will frequently carry them past the optimum point of the curve, and result in inhibition or disorganization of performance. If boys and men have a low base level of anxiety, increases in anxiety will more often either improve performance, or move them through the middle portions of the curve where changes in performance would not be found (Maccoby) 1966: 47–48).

In sum, because the two sexes appear to have somewhat different intellectual strengths and weaknesses, the interpersonal tactics aimed at counteracting the weaknesses or augmenting the strengths of boys and girls also should be different.

Most of the research with McClelland's *n* Achievement scale has been with male subjects, and the reason for this limitation tells us something about sex differences on this dimension. Many studies have involved manipulation of the subjects' environment by means of introducing the task in a manner varying from "relaxed" to "aroused."[3] These conditional variations or cues had a distinct effect upon the performance of male subjects, independently of their individual differences in *n* Achievement, but early experiments showed that girls' scores did not increase significantly from relaxed to aroused conditions. For this and other reasons, there were few studies with female subjects until the 1950's, when research by Field (1951) showed that while girls' need-to-achieve was not whetted by such arousal stimuli as talk about intelligence and leadership, increases in female scores could be produced by substituting such terms as popularity and social acceptance.

Another possible explanation for the failure of girls to respond to achievement-oriented cues is that the stimulus pictures are not attractive. During her review of the literature on *n* Achievement, Entwisle noted that in most of the pictures portraying achievement-oriented activities, the women are physically unappealing (they have glasses, heavy shoes, unattractive hair styles, and so on). They are seldom portrayed in positions of real status (women office workers usually are engaged in clerical rather than managerial activities). Because of her strong doubts about the overall reliability and validity of the *n* Achievement scale, Entwisle has not pursued this idea further, but she has suggested that some new stimulus pictures showing attractive young women in a variety of updated occupational settings might produce quite different responses from girls.

Thus while we cannot conclude that girls have more, less, or the same achievement needs as boys, the evidence we have suggests (1) that if past testing has been biased, it has been in the direction of underestimating female need-achievement, and (2) that girls and boys may be responsive to different kinds of motivational stimuli.

Socialization

A recent formulation of psychosexual development (Simon and Gagnon, 1969) refers to sexual behavior as "scripted" behavior, underscoring its sociocultural, learned components as opposed to its biological ones. This view is based upon the observation that in all known societies, the sex role is one of the first and most important in the child's repertory, and that, in most, boys and girls are socialized differently. What we are interested in are the socialization differences that lead to differences in the way boys and girls perceive and play the student role.

Sociological analysts of the family often refer to a basic sex-role division along what they term the instrumental-expressive dimension, a division which they see as universal. Instrumental functions include "direct responsibility for the solution of group tasks, for the skills and information prerequisite to the role in its adaptive aspects, and for the authority required to make binding managerial decisions." Within the family, when both parents are present, instrumental leadership is typically assumed by the husband-father, who is thus boss-manager of the family as well as of any economic or political units encompassed within it. As such, he is the "final court of appeals, final judge and executor of punishment, discipline, and control over the children of the family." Complementary to the instrumental role is the expressive role, which includes "responsibility for the maintenance of solidarity and management of tension" and care and emotional support of children. The expressive leader, normally the wife-mother, is the family mediator or conciliator. She is "affectionate, solicitous, warm, emotional to the children of the family," and by contrast with the instrumental leader, is indulgent and unpunishing (Parsons and Bales, 1955: 317–318).

Evidence for early sex role differentiation and training is found in twenty-nine out of the thirty-two studies reviewed by Maccoby (1966: 349ff). An example is research conducted by Pitcher, who concluded that by age two or three, boys and girls have strikingly different interests and attitudes, which their parents influence and strengthen. In a simple experiment in which preschoolers were allowed to play freely with brightly colored chips and the researchers recorded everything said by their young subjects for ten-minute intervals:

> The forms and problems the game presented seemed to fascinate the boys, so that they kept talking about the chips, wondering about their use, how they could be arranged, where they had come from. . . . The whole business intrigued the girls much less. Like women bored by men's conversations, after a few minutes they would look up and say, "I'm going to a party tomorrow," or, "We have blue wastebaskets at our cottage at the beach." Their digressions included comments about planting seeds, birthday parties, Christmas, friends, gifts, clothing, visits to doctors, pictures on the wall, quarrels with brothers, conversations with mothers (Pitcher, 1963: 87).

In a second experiment, children were asked to draw something and to explain their pictures. Over half the girls, but only about fifteen per cent of the boys, said they had drawn persons. There was a marked interest among the girls in the family, babies, clothing, and domestic activities. By contrast, the boys drew a disproportionate number of *things*—cars, benches, trains, and so on. Similar patterns were found in stories the children made up. (Similar results from parallel analyses of children's pictures and stories were obtained by Omark and Edelman, reported in Freedman, 1969. For data on the further development of children's concepts of male and female roles, based upon interviews with eight to eleven-year-olds, see Hartley, 1960, 1959, 1964.)

To understand how boys and girls had come to think so differently at such an early age, Pitcher questioned their parents, and she concluded that the children were from infancy subject to influences to develop sex-appropriate social characteristics. Both parents, but especially fathers, discouraged any evidences of femininity in their sons; an interest in dolls or putting on feminine clothing or cosmetics was taboo. Parents were more tolerant of tomboyishness in girls, although they fostered their daughters' interest in clothes and family-oriented activities, and expected a girl to be "more social, more interested in herself and in other people than a boy would be." Again, it was the fathers who were more interested in accentuating sex-appropriate characteristics; half of the fathers in this sample "pointed out their daughters' coquetry in a way to show that they were themselves personally intrigued" (Pitcher, 1963: 91).[4]

A study by Brim (1960) explored the behaviors encouraged in young boys and girls within the general framework of the instrumental-expressive dimension. The following list compares the personality traits which were classified by Brim as instrumental or expressive and which were also differentially encouraged in five- and six-year-olds:

instrumental-masculine	*expressive-feminine*
tenacity	kindness
aggressiveness	cheerfulness
curiosity	friendliness
ambition	obedience
planfulness	affection
responsibility	
originality	
competitiveness	

Brim's list suggests clues both to girls' greater success in school in the early years *and* to boys' greater success over the long haul. Such "feminine" traits as obedience and friendliness are apparently functional at the elementary level, or at least they are better understood by the typical female teacher than the active but as-yet-unfocused curiosity, originality, and aggressiveness displayed by young boys. Indeed, it has been reported in another study (Kagan, 1964) that young children view school as a feminine place; given a variety of stimuli to classify, they consistently labeled books, blackboards, desks, and other school paraphernalia as feminine.

However, the characteristics that foster true intellectual growth are in the left-hand list. As school becomes less dominated by the female element, and as boys approach adulthood and the assuming of the instrumental leader role, the student role becomes more congruent with a boy's other roles. Moreover, among adolescent girls studied by Kagan (1969), intellectual striving comes to be seen as a form of aggressive behavior (probably partly because in our schools success usually requires competition with peers, a theme that will be elaborated in Part Three). Thus to the extent that girls are socialized not to be competitive, they tend to inhibit intellectual activities that might be defined as unfeminine. They may still want to get good grades, where this reflects obedience and the desire to please people, but not to perform at such a high level as to appear aggressive.

Kohn's research on class differences in child-rearing practices also contains some data on differences related to the sex of the child—data which partially support Brim's findings, or indicate the conditions under which Brim's findings are most applicable. The middle-class parents in Kohn's sample made little distinction between boys and girls with regard to what was regarded as desirable and what was punished—"the issue for both sexes being whether or not the child acts in accord with internalized principles." Working-class parents, however, were more likely to punish daughters than sons for fighting, stealing, and especially for refusing to do as they were told; boys often were allowed to get away with defiance to parents. Kohn interprets these differences as follows:

> The answer seems to lie in different conceptions of what is right and proper for boys and for girls. What may be taken as acceptable behavior (perhaps even as an assertion of manliness) in a preadolescent boy may be thought thoroughly unladylike in a young girl. Working-class parents differentiate quite clearly between the qualities they regard as desirable for their daughters (happiness, manners, neatness, and cleanliness) and those they hold out for their sons (dependability, being a good student, and ambition). . . .
> This being the case, the criteria of disobedience are necessarily different for boys and for girls (Kohn, 1959b: 365).

The differential expectations introduced early in the family are strengthened over time and are reinforced by other reference groups. Moreover, the linkage between sex-role and student-role becomes ever more direct. The Gordon analysis of *Educational Opportunity* survey data showed that the variable most strongly correlated with sex for ninth graders was the parental aspiration index and that boys were more likely than girls to see their parents as holding high educational expectations for them, even though these same girls were achieving higher grades, a difference that was also statistically significant.

The adolescent peer culture reinforces the differentiation process begun in the family. Among the Chicago-area high school students who were the subjects of Coleman's *Adolescent Society* (1961), high status for boys could be reached by *doing* things. Athletic success was the most direct path, but having a car (again something that could be achieved through the boy's own efforts) and even academic success were possible alternatives. "There are fewer solid barriers, such as family background, and fewer criteria that can be twisted at the whim of the in-group, than there are for girls. To be sure, achievement must be in the right area—chiefly athletics—but achievement *can* in most of these schools bring a boy into the leading crowd, which is more than it can do in many instances for girls" (Coleman, 1961: 42).

Girls do not have these kinds of opportunities. The qualities contributing to female status are, according to Coleman, "all of a piece":

they express the fact that being born into the right family is a great help to a girl in getting into the leading crowd. It is expressed differently in different schools and by different girls—sometimes as "parents having money," sometimes as "coming from the right neighborhood," sometimes as "expensive clothes." These qualities differ sharply from some of those discussed (for boys), for they are not something a girl can *change*. [There is, moreover], the suggestion that the girls' culture derives in some fashion from the boys'. . . . She must cultivate her looks, be vivacious and attractive, wear the right clothes, but then wait—until the football player, whose status is determined by his specific achievements, comes along to choose her (Coleman, 1961: 38, 42).

The result: girls were less likely than boys to want to be remembered as a "brilliant student," more likely to want to be remembered as "most popular." Moreover, girls who were named by their peers as top students had lower IQ scores than boys so named, even though girls in this sample had higher *average* IQ scores. Coleman suggests that the girls are caught in a "double bind." They want to meet their parents' and teachers' expectations for good performance, but also fear that conspicuous achievement will make them unpopular with boys. As a result of the cross pressures, bright girls may do less than their best in school, while bright boys, who do not fear that academic achievement will interfere with peer acceptance, are more likely to be top students.

One of the classic studies of the socialization of girls to lower their achievement goals is Mirra Komarovsky's *Women in the Modern World* (1953). It contains, for example, a number of reports by college girls describing advice received by parents, brothers, and friends, all urging the girls not to set their sights too high and not to reveal their intellectual abilities or achievement-oriented goals (say, to go to medical school) to potential boy friends, at least until they knew them well enough to judge whether such an admission would be offensive. The general process that is set in motion is a circular one, by which certain activities (getting outstanding grades, going on for graduate or professional training) and certain subjects (math) are identified as masculine, which means that girls who might otherwise have the interest, and the potential, for such activities and subjects never cultivate them, which in turn reinforces the unfeminine image of such activities and subjects. This phenomenon has been popularized in recent years as the "feminine mystique" or the "woman-as-nigger" syndrome—the premise of which is that women in our society get talked out of and/or talk themselves out of high educational and occupational achievement.

Again Maccoby provides a formulation which incorporates a number of individual empirical findings and explains the puzzling shift in performance of boys and girls relative to each other. Pointing to the evidence that girls who are underachievers (that is, girls whose school performance is markedly below their measured abilities) usually begin to be so at about the onset of puberty, while boy underachievers usually appear much earlier, along with the other performance differences and shifts we have noted above, Maccoby suggests that the evidence fits a model of differential social pressures for boys and girls, with a reverse time sequence for the two sexes:

> As noted above, the pressures on bright girls not to do as well as they can tend to be augmented in adolescence, so that correlations between ability and achievement ought to be higher during the early school years. By contrast, peer-group pressures on boys in the early school years are often (though not always) in the direction of achievement in sports and other nonacademic pursuits; and boys of this age are frequently engaged in efforts to achieve autonomy, especially in relation to their mothers, with the result that they are less willing than girls to accede to the demands of their predominantly female teachers. In adolescence, however, especially for middle-class boys, the pressures for college entrance and professional preparation begin to be felt, with the result that the more intelligent boys begin to buckle down at this time. Even in high school, however, the boys' more autonomous approach to their school work is indicated in the greater selectivity of their efforts; boys are likely to do well in subjects that interest them and poorly in subjects that bore them, while girls tend to perform uniformly in all their school subjects (Maccoby, 1966: 31–32).[5]

In addition to family and peer group influences, pressures to behave in school in accordance with sex-role definitions can come from other levels of the learning system. While there is little sociological research in this area, two studies suggest the possibilities of cultural influences. In a comparison of schools classified as "modern" and "traditional" (on the basis of curriculum and general school philosophy), Minuchin (1964) found not only more sex-typed play behavior in the traditional school, but also greater sex differences in the performance of problem-solving and coding tasks. In a theoretical paper on crosscultural differences in educational systems, Livingstone (1968) postulates that the structure of a society as a social system as well as the differences in educational opportunities provided by different cultures serve as conditional variables explaining some of the variation in educational attainment by sex. Among his hypotheses are the following:

The greater the enrollment ratio within the compulsory age limits, the greater the percentage of females enrolled.

The greater the educational expenditure per capita, the greater the percentage of female students.

The greater the pupil/teacher ratio, the lower the percentage of female students.

The more advanced the educational research procedures adopted by the system, the greater the percentage of female students.

The greater the proportion of urban students, the greater the percentage of female students.

The greater the percentage of female teachers at respective levels, the greater the percentage of female students at those levels.

The greater the religious homogeneity of enrollment at a given level, the lower the percentage of female students at that level.

The general theme of Livingstone's model is that girls benefit from an urban (or urbanizing), secular society which makes a substantial investment in a modern education system.

The Simultaneous Effect of Sex and Other Independent Variables

We have already seen that parents' social status has an impact upon children's sex-role training (for instance, in the Kohn studies showing that working-class and middle-class parents differed not only in their primary expectations, but also in the degree to which they treated boys and girls differently). A similar pattern has been shown with respect to the probability of entering college, although at this older age level, SES effects seem to reflect mainly differences in economic resources. In a comparison of 76,015 boys and 51,110 girls, controlling for father's occupation and student's high school grade average, Werts (1966) found that the college entrance rates of boys and girls whose fathers had high-status jobs were similar, but that among low-SES students, boys were much more likely than girls to go to college. A similar pattern was found with respect to previous academic achievement; high ability boys and girls were equally likely to enter college, but among students with low high school grade averages, boys were more likely to go than girls. The independent variables were, moreover, interactively related:

> There were more girls than boys in the A−, A, A+ grade category for all four groups of fathers' occupations (ratio < 1.0), and the ratios were not much different in the four groups. . . . Since previously cited studies show that among able, upper SES students girls attend college as often as boys, the similarity of the ratios across the father's occupation groups at this highest grade level suggests that very bright, lower SES girls are as likely to attend college as their brothers. Low-SES boys with low grades outnumber low-SES low-grade girls to a greater extent than high-SES boys with low grades outnumber high-SES low-grade girls. This suggests that low grades are a greater deterrent to college attendance for low-SES girls than for high-SES girls (Werts, 1966: 5, 7).

What Werts' data indicate is that when the resources needed for high education—whether they be the student's own academic capacity or his parents' ability to pay—are freely available, sex does not make much difference in determining college attendance, but when such resources are in short supply, boys get first choice at higher education.

Several of the findings reported in this chapter raise parallels between race and sex—girls seem to have many of the same disadvantages as Negroes with respect to school success. On the other hand, recent discussions of the educational problems of the culturally "disadvantaged" have suggested that the black *boy* has special problems in "making it" at school and in the larger society. While there is still more conjecturing than hard data, the Gordon re-analysis of the *Educational Opportunity* survey data sheds some light on this debate. When he studied the simultaneous effect of sex and race upon various indicants of school success, Gordon found that while whites were generally more likely to have college aspiration at the ninth grade level, controlling for sex showed that this racial difference existed only for the boys. At the ninth grade level there were no differences between black and white girls in their desire for college or graduate education. Similarly, race did not appear to be related to girls' self-acceptance and general academic competence, although white boys were stronger than their black counterparts in these areas. Black girls were also stronger than black boys in self-acceptance and general academic competence, and in a measure of self-esteem.

Special motivation and achievement problems for black boys also are reported in a study by Green and Farguar (1965), which found a positive correlation between academic motivation and academic achievement in all race-sex subgroups and a similar correlation between verbal aptitude and achievement in all but one—for black males, unlike white males and females and black females, there was no significant relationship between their general aptitude for school work and their performance. Their performance was explained only by their motivation to achieve. In sum, the combination of forces working against school success seems to be especially powerful for black boys; these include the feminine, middle-class image of school, the prominence of females in the home,[6] the economic disadvantage and the prejudice that go with membership in a racial minority group. For black girls, the negative effects of SES disadvantage and racial prejudice may be at least partly offset by the availability of adult female role models who incorporate leadership of the household with employment on a fairly regular basis. The general point is that the social characteristics and position of the family may affect sex-role and student-role identity differently for boys and girls.

Conclusions

The argument about the relative weight of biological and sociocultural effects upon sex-role behavior has not been resolved in this chapter, but there is little doubt that a sizable amount of the variation in the way children play the student role is related to their socialization to their sex role. The relationship of sex and school performance can be summarized by some of the most recently published findings of an ongoing study on the academic careers of a large sample of high school students (Center for Research and Development in Higher Education, 1969). The project known as SCOPE is a seven-year study of some 90,000 students in four states, sponsored jointly by the Center for Research and Development in Higher Education (at the University of California, Berkeley) and the College Entrance Exam-

Exhibit 5–2
Boys' and Girls' Educational Attitudes and Performance in Four States

% Respondents Who Say	California		Illinois		Massachusetts		No. Carolina	
	Boys	Girls	Boys	Girls	Boys	Girls	Boys	Girls
They get A or B grades	42.9	54.3	37.1	49.5	39.4	50.1	31.8	45.8
They try to get A or B grades	70.7	78.4	64.8	75.1	70.7	79.4	62.6	77.1
They spend more than 10 hours a week on homework	13.0	18.3	15.1	22.4	18.8	27.9	11.6	23.1
They definitely feel they can do college work	29.0	22.5	28.9	21.4	31.7	23.2	25.0	17.4
They save money regularly for college	16.3	8.9	23.9	15.1	27.3	16.8	18.9	9.1
The following influence their college decisions:								
parents don't have enough money	12.5	16.4	14.7	22.1	12.7	16.3	14.9	20.9
not given the right advice on courses	12.5	11.0	11.7	13.5	12.0	13.2	12.3	12.8
wanting to get married	10.2	22.8	9.1	22.4	10.2	18.1	11.2	20.8
not able to earn enough money	22.8	27.0	22.9	28.8	19.3	21.5	18.7	22.4
not getting enough encouragement to go	9.2	10.2	8.9	11.3	8.3	11.1	11.1	13.8
grades not good enough	19.8	24.9	23.5	30.0	24.2	28.8	28.7	32.1
afraid of not making it	12.7	18.6	16.7	24.8	15.4	21.2	19.4	27.8

It is very important:

to be a leader	29.0	20.0	36.0	25.0	34.3	21.9	44.0	33.3
to get good grades	65.8	66.9	68.5	74.5	71.9	76.0	74.6	83.2
to learn a maximum	68.9	70.2	71.9	74.9	72.4	73.7	76.1	83.6
to be liked by girls	50.9	57.5	50.7	70.5	50.6	67.9	60.8	70.2
to be liked by boys	34.6	65.1	44.3	69.6	42.7	70.0	47.0	71.4
They have visited a college	31.2	34.3	28.0	29.2	20.9	23.3	28.9	28.5
They have looked at college catalogues	47.0	52.1	53.5	59.1	60.2	67.0	55.3	62.6
They have discussed college with:								
teachers	49.2	53.6	53.7	55.5	55.1	58.3	52.3	53.9
counselors	51.5	53.6	56.2	62.0	59.4	62.5	43.0	45.0
someone who attends	65.5	74.8	68.2	71.8	68.4	73.6	65.2	71.3
Their most interesting course this year is:								
science	18.0	13.4	15.1	9.0	21.5	10.9	12.6	6.5
math	9.2	3.6	13.7	7.1	14.0	10.1	12.0	6.7
English	9.1	16.0	10.4	16.3	10.0	17.7	12.0	20.5
foreign language	2.8	5.3	4.1	7.7	3.9	11.1	3.6	8.1
The teacher of their most interesting course is a man	83.4	46.0	83.8	38.9	76.4	38.1	60.2	27.3
The teacher they like best this year is a man	79.6	48.0	81.3	40.7	75.4	40.7	54.1	28.4

Data taken from Center for Research and Development in Higher Education, 1969.

ination Board. The study focuses upon the progression of students through high school and into the first years of college. The research design is longitudinal and the sample large enough to allow multivariate analyses at the end of the seven-year period (the goal was to end up with about 4000 students in each of the four states, which meant starting with samples of up to three times that number).

The selection of SCOPE data presented in Exhibit 5–2 mirrors the major patterns which have emerged from the combination of studies considered in this chapter. In all four states, girls are more likely than boys to report *getting* good grades and *trying* to get them, although, in trying, the differences are not quite so great. Girls are also more likely to report spending a relatively large amount of time on homework. Boys, however, express greater confidence in their ability to do college work (even though their performance thus far has not been as good as their female classmates'). Furthermore, boys are more likely to be saving money for college, and are less likely to see financial and other impediments blocking their path to higher education. (The boy-girl differences in the set of items on influences upon college decisions are not large, with the exception of the marriage items, but the overall pattern is consistent.)

In addition to perceived influence upon whether to continue their education, these boys and girls also placed rather different emphasis upon various high school roles or statuses. We have seen that the girls ascribe greater importance to being a good student. They are, however, also much more concerned about being liked. Popularity with their own sex is considerably more important to girls than boys (in the California group, 57.5% of the girls said it was very important for them to be liked by other girls, while only 34.6% of the boys said being liked by boys was very important); and girls are more concerned about popularity with boys than the boys are themselves (65.1% of the California girls admitted to the importance of being liked by boys, as compared to 34.6% of the boys). Although girls still are managing to outshine the boys slightly in grades, their concern with success in interpersonal relations, especially with boys (in some cases reaching the point of wanting to get married), is probably deflecting the attention and energies of many girls from intellectual pursuits. The one item in this group on which the boys are more likely to respond positively is the desire to be a leader, a role calling for the qualities of ambition, aggressiveness, competitiveness, and so on which are increasingly likely to be rejected by girls as they continue their school careers. On the other hand, leadership is a role congruent with the ambitions and status reflected in achievement at the college and graduate level, where boys overtake girls.

Parallels between the effects of sex and race roles have been suggested in this chapter, and in Chapter 3 we saw that while black students were as eager as whites to do well in school and to go to college, they were less likely to take the practical steps that would lead to ultimate college admission. By contrast, Exhibit 5–2 shows that girls are as likely or slightly more likely to visit colleges, look at catalogs, and discuss college plans with adults. Girls' educational problems, then, are not simply a mirror of those of a racial minority group, and, as we have also seen, sex and race themselves are interactively related to school success.

Finally, a few words about intellectual preferences. The SCOPE data illustrate the division-of-interest in substantive fields, with the boys more likely to cite a science or math course as their most interesting, the girls relatively more interested in the verbally oriented areas of English and foreign languages. The second preference is for teachers of one's own sex. The predominantly female composition of most elementary school faculties has been suggested as a source of young boys' negative attitudes toward school and their lower performance in the early years; these data indicate that a preference for teachers of one's own sex holds through adolescence.

In sum, the structure of the student role and the educational system in general is in some important respects incongruent with sex-role expectations and performance, *for both boys and girls*. For boys, the feminine atmosphere of the school and the emphasis upon obedience and conformity, instead of upon more active learning, overshadows their first years in school, and they do not catch up with the girls in performance until the clear linkages of academic achievement with occupational and other kinds of adult success make school and learning more relevant. For girls, intellectual interests and potentialities are increasingly repressed as they come to represent unfeminine competitiveness.

There are, however, changes in the air. A basic goal of the Women's Liberation Movement is a basic redefinition of sex roles, which, it is hoped, will increase intellectual independence and reduce anxiety about competition among girls. Other trends focus upon making the structure of the learning system more congruent with socialization to sex roles. For example, a project in Akron, Ohio, aims to increase the number of male teachers in the elementary schools, and thereby reduce the incidence of reading and other learning difficulties among boys. Whether the new trends will succeed in making sex roles more congruent with the student role, and whether changes will be extensive enough to have any real impact upon learning, remains to be seen.

Notes

1. The best evidence indicates that both kinds of factors play a part, and that the exact contribution of each is not known and probably depends upon other characteristics of the person and the situation.

2. Not only is the question of whether these traits, like intelligence, are innate or learned still an open one, but the studies as a whole reveal many "no significant difference" results when the measure of the personality characteristic is based upon observation or rating by others. It is only on *self*-report studies

that girls are consistently higher. That is, we do not have conclusive evidence that boys *have* less anxiety or dependence than girls, only that they consistently *report* less. The point, however, is that whether the differences are "real" or not, they may have real consequences for learning in school.

3. In the relaxed situation, the test administrator affected a conspicuously easygoing manner, introducing himself as a graduate student who simply wanted to "try out" some tests on them. In the aroused condition, the administrator introduced himself and the tests in a brisk, formal manner, and told the subjects that the tests measured both their general level of intelligence and their capacity for leadership.

4. There has been considerable research on which parent is most responsible for the child's psychosexual and sociosexual development and what type of parent-child relationship is most conducive to satisfactory development. While the findings are mixed, the weight of evidence is in the direction of stronger effects of same-sex parent and the advantages of a relatively warm relationship. On the other hand, we noted in Chapter 4 that academic achievement seems to go with a relatively reserved or autonomous relationship with the same-sex parent and warmth and support from the opposite-sex parent. These differences may reflect the fact that sex-role and student-role identity are quite distinct, that, in fact, as suggested in the Maccoby model and other findings reported in this chapter, strong academic achievement may be synonymous with a form of deviance in terms of sex role expectations *for both boys and girls* (although for different reasons, and more or less at different age levels).

5. The latter finding was also reported in Coleman's *Adolescent Society* (1961: Chapter IX).

6. "The lower-class Negro family pattern commonly consists of a female-dominated household, with either the mother or the grandmother acting as the mainstay of the family unit. The husband, if present, is often an ineffective family leader. The boy growing up in a Negro family frequently perceives his father as a person with a low-status job, who is regarded with indifference or varying degrees of hostility by members of the out-group. In short, the lower-class Negro adult male is seldom regarded as a worthwhile model for the boy to emulate" (Woronoff, 1966: 293).

American children are given IQ tests, American adults are impressed (or depressed) by the results, and children are treated accordingly. This means that a high IQ score, like a white skin, will be an asset even if IQ itself is no more intrinsically important than skin color.   Christopher Jencks

No one has yet produced any evidence based on a properly controlled study to show that representative samples of Negro and white children can be equalized in intellectual ability through statistical control of environment and education.   A. R. Jensen

Individual potential is one of the most unmarketable properties if the child acquires no means for its development, or if no means exist for measuring it objectively.   Martin Deutsch

To teach rigor while preserving imagination is an unsolved challenge to education.   R. W. Gerard

The view of the child formulated in Chapter 1 postulated that one characteristic which almost all children have in common is a curiosity about their environment and a desire to master it. The chapters immediately preceding have shown, however, that children differ greatly in their ability to translate this apparently universal motive into a capacity to learn in a formal educational setting, and that a child's family resources and experiences contribute to such differences. In this chapter we shall consider another type of individual differentiation, that of individual abilities. Although it seems reasonable, indeed self-evident, that those children with the greatest mental abilities will be most successful at school, neither the source of innate ability differences nor the processes by which they are nurtured and channeled into actual learning are fully understood.

First, the distinction between ability and achievement is not clear cut. This is partly because "pure" ability is virtually impossible to abstract, even in a very young child, from the life experiences that may have nurtured or failed to nurture talents. Ability tests have been challenged on the grounds that they do not control for external influences, but this is probably an unreasonable demand. What distinguishes ability from achievement tests is not the presence or absence of external influence but the nature of the influence.

> Intelligence tests must now be thought of as samples of learning based on general experiences. A child's score may be thought of as an indication of the richness of the milieu in which he functions and the extent to which he has been able to profit from that milieu. In contradistinction, school achievement tests assume deliberate instruction oriented to the outcomes measured in the tests (Stodolsky and Lesser, 1967: 548).

In addition to distinguishing between ability and achievement, it is also important to distinguish between the ability itself and the test used to measure it. So-called intelligence tests are not the same thing as intelligence but are rather a sampling of responses or behaviors which are believed to reflect intelligence. Thus in following the discussion in this chapter, it will be important to keep in mind the differences between: (1) the mental ability itself; (2) performance or score on the test being used as a measure of (1); and (3) performance on academic tasks or tests (academic achievement).

Second, mental ability is multidimensional, a composite of a number of different talents which are differentially related to success in conventional learning tasks and only some of which have been subjected to rigorous psychological scrutiny. In Project Talent, an extensive survey conducted during the early 1960's for the purpose of estimating the range and levels of ability among American high school students, each subject in a national sample took two full days of tests measuring over fifty different kinds of abilities and information (Flanagan *et al.,* 1962). The mental ability most strongly related to academic achievement is intelligence, which has come to be used almost interchangeably with IQ score.[1] There are, however, many different IQ tests. Furthermore, behavioral scientists are coming to believe that most IQ tests measure only one kind of intelligence.

Finally, while measured intelligence is the best single predictor of scholastic performance, it does not explain everything. Even if the estimated upper limit is the true one, there is still a lot of difference to be explained by other factors. (Even if intelligence accounted for 100% of the performance *variation* among students, other variables might affect the level for performance of *all* students in a given class or school.) Moreover, while students cannot perform above their ability levels, they can and often do perform well below them. And there is also the possibility that the relationship between ability and performance in one social context might not be the same in another.

The meaning and measurement of ability and its relationship to achievement have been the subject of much recent controversy. Ability tests and testing have been accused of perpetuating—perhaps even producing—the gaps in achievement between disadvantaged and nondisadvantaged children. For example, the National Advisory Committee on Mexican-American Education has called for a halt to ability testing in the public schools, charging that all the tests now in use discriminate against bilingual children, whose test scores determine their placement in school and their ultimate career and socioeconomic position. A scholarly article aimed at clearing up some of the confusion about intelligence and its measurement (Jensen, 1969) has instead unloosed a flood of controversy, carried on in newspapers and news magazines as well as in professional journals and has made its author, in the words of one observer, "the most publicized (and vilified) figure in psychology today" (Jencks, 1969: 21).

The controversy over Jensen's paper is of sociological interest in itself, illustrating some of the dynamic features of the school's environment to be discussed in Chapter 12. In this chapter, we shall examine it and other pieces of research in terms of what they say about the sociology of mental ability, in particular the social factors which contribute to the development and use of mental ability. We shall first focus upon intelligence, since it is the ability most strongly related to success in school, and since the twin problems of accurate measurement and understanding of origins are well illustrated in the current arguments over intelligence testing. Then we shall consider rather more briefly two other aspects or types of individual ability that have sociological ramifications. One is cognitive style, or the way a student approaches and attacks a learning task; the other is creativity, or the extent to which he handles learning tasks in a novel or imaginative fashion.

Measurement of Intelligence

Although IQ has come to be almost synonymous with the term intelligence, the IQ test is a relatively recent "invention." (Binet and Simon's Metrical Scale of Intelligence, the ancestor of present-day IQ tests, was devised in 1905.) IQ tests vary in content and design, but all of the tests currently in wide use contain items having to do with the recognition, retention, and manipulation of verbal and numerical symbols, which have been found to be strongly related to each other both within and between tests. Perhaps the most accurate way to describe what it is that IQ tests measure is to say it is the capacity for abstract reasoning and problem solving. When the tests are administered on a group basis, or when individuals' responses are scored against the averages or "norms" of some larger population, an individual's score also indicates his aptitude for, or his likelihood of success in, traditional school subjects.

It should also be noted that an IQ is a measure of *relative* brightness; an individual's intelligence "quotient" is obtained by dividing his *mental* age (that is, the age in the general population at which his score is the statistical average) by his *chronological* age, and then multiplying by 100 to eliminate decimal points. The particular score established as the norm for a given age depends, of course, upon the population or class of subjects upon which the test is standardized. Since most IQ tests have been standardized on groups containing high proportions of middle-class subjects, their validity as accurate indicators of the intelligence of low SES children, or children from nonEnglish-speaking homes, has been justifiably questioned. Thus while the tests do not themselves *cause* the initial discrepancies between students (as the attacks of certain social scientists and ethnic groups have implied), by reflecting the lack of learning opportunities caused by poverty and discrimination, they are in a sense unfair to disadvantaged groups. Moreover, to the extent that test scores are used to place children in school tracks or programs, they themselves may lead to subsequent differences in academic achievement.

Like school achievement, IQ scores are related to social background. The relationship between IQ and socioeconomic status is a worldwide phenomenon documented by an extensive crosscultural literature. Similarly, differences averaging about fifteen points have been found in a number of statistical comparisons between Negro and white school children (Shuey, 1966).

Individual scores are not fixed but tend to shift over time in some predictable directions. For example, children's scores tend to move closer to those of their natural parents, regardless of whether or not they are raised by them (Jensen, 1969.) The scores of students in inner-city schools tend to decrease the longer they stay in school. In addition to social background, two other variables of sociological interest seem to explain between-group IQ differences or changes in scores.

1. *The child's attitudes.* While motivation has long been postulated as a necessary, though not sufficient, cause for academic achievement, it has been assumed that it is, if related to ability, an intervening variable between intelligence and performance. In a study of Los Angeles high school boys, Turner (1964) proposes a different sequence, one in which desire to do well affects aptitude as well as ultimate achievement:

> In any causal chain we must assume that influences which are extraneous for our purposes play upon each link. The effect of the extraneous influences is to reduce the observed correlations. So long as the causation with which we are concerned follows a simple chain pattern, the effects of these extraneous variables will become relatively greater as the number of intervening links in the chain increases. Consequently, so long as the extraneous factors are constant, the correlations between variables which are separated by one or more intervening variables will be less than the correlations between variables which operate directly upon one another. When

this logic is applied, the hypothesis that background determines ambition indirectly through the intervening variable of intelligence leads to the prediction that correlations of both ambition and background with IQ should be larger than the correlation between ambition and background (Turner, 1964: 51).

Or, if intelligence were prior to ambition in the causal chain, the relationship between ambition and background should diminish when the variable of intelligence is introduced.

Turner's analysis, a series of correlations and partial correlations between family background, IQ scores, and educational-occupational ambitions, did not produce such a pattern. Not only was the correlation between background and ambition greater than the correlation between background and IQ, but it was only slightly reduced when IQ was held constant. That is, if one gets along with Turner's use of correlational data to make causal connections, his findings suggest that students' attitudes with respect to their future education and occupation, at least by the time they reach adolescence, have an effect upon their performance on intelligence tests rather than the reverse. Turner's interpretation of this causal sequence is that students "who have the motivations and attitudes which lead to high ambition may be those who are accordingly motivated to make their best performance in the test" (Turner, 1964: 52. Note that Turner's use of the intelligence variable certainly implies that he sees the tests taken by his teenage subjects as measuring something which is learned rather than innate).

2. *The social situation in which the tests are given.* That disadvantaged children can often raise their scores dramatically if the test is administered in a friendly atmosphere where they are both expected and helped to do well is illustrated in the following description of some experiments by Haggard:

> Haggard reasoned that although deprived children may have taken many IQ tests, they really did not know how to take these tests properly: they lacked meaningful, directed practice. They also lacked motivation, and their relationship to the examiner was typically distant and beset by fears.
>
> Haggard decided to control each of these factors. He gave both deprived and non-deprived children three one-hour training periods in taking IQ tests. These practice periods included careful explanation of what was involved in each of the different types of problems found on the IQ tests. The explanations were given in words that were familiar to both groups. Haggard also offered special rewards for doing well, and he trained his examiners to be responsive to the deprived children as well as to the middle class youngsters, thus greatly enhancing the rapport.
>
> Under these conditions the IQ's of the disadvantaged children improved sharply. *This occurred with only three hours of practice.* And it occurred even on the old IQ tests with the middle-class-biased items. Apparently more important than the content of the test items was the attitude of the children toward the test situation and the examiner (Reissman, 1962: 53).

Jensen reports that in his own experience in a psychological clinic, disadvantaged children regularly boosted their IQ scores 8 to 10 points when a repeat test was given after two or more play sessions during which the young subjects became familiar with the clinic setting and the examiner. He argues that this slight though uniform increase simply represents the more accurate score obtained by testing under optimal conditions rather than any change in ability. In terms of school success, however, the point is that when these scores determine a child's class placement and the kind of counseling he receives about his future educational and occupational goals, every little boost in score helps.

That the social climate effect can be at the level of the entire school or school system, as well as at that of the class or small group, is indicated by the wide variations in test score means and ranges between schools—beyond what would be expected by difference in the characteristics of the student bodies, and the tendencies for some group scores to increase or decrease consistently over time. A depressing example is the regular drop in IQ scores of children in Harlem schools. As Paul Goodman puts it, "The combined efforts of home influence and school education, a powerful combination, succeeded in making the children significantly stupider year by year" (Goodman, 1960: 79).

Although attitudes and setting have been discussed separately, their effect upon test performance is probably interactive. That is, the setting can affect the attitudes (self-confidence, desire to succeed, and so on) which in turn affect performance. For example, the studies of *n* Achievement reported in Chapter 5 showed that, for boys at least, achievement motivation could be changed by manipulation of the test atmosphere.

The shifts in IQ scores that seem to be explained by sociological variables (for instance, the IQ drops in ghetto schools) and the relationship between IQ scores and the social characteristics that, as we found in Chapter 3, explain much of the variation in school performance have led to much of the criticism of school testing programs. They also have led to attempts to develop "culture-free" or "culture-fair" tests which do not depend upon verbal facility or life experiences that middle-class white children as a group are more likely to have had. There are to date few serious alternatives to the classical IQ test, and the findings of research based on them are mixed. On the positive side, scores on a test based upon matching random forms (as opposed to circles, squares and other geometric shapes) have been found to be closely correlated with standard IQ scores for a sample of middle-class white children but not for a comparable sample of Negro slum children (Rosenberg, 1966). Furthermore, the difference between the average scores on the new test for the two groups was negligible. One can, however, argue whether such a test is truly culture-free, since an affinity for forms in general, whether or not they are randomly generated, might be subject to cultural influence. (Another argument against the cultural "freedom" of such tests will be presented later in this chapter.)

On the negative side, the results of culture-free tests generally have been found to be weakly correlated with school achievement as well as with verbal ability.[2] Moreover, Jensen reports that on some supposedly culture-free tests, minority children have scored even lower than they do on such conventional IQ tests as the Stanford-Binet and the Wechsler, although he does not identify the new tests nor describe their content (Jensen, 1969: 81). On the other hand, he is quick to point out that the particular kind of intelligence measured by IQ tests is not the only kind and that there are other kinds at which black children often excel. An example is *associative* ability, which includes the facility for learning quickly names, game rules, and the fine points of informal social interaction. Such talents should, in Jensen's opinion, be recognized and rewarded by the school system, since they could be channeled into improved classroom learning.

Origin of Intelligence

Almost all biological and behavioral scientists agree that the intelligence of any individual is a combination of genetic mechanisms established at birth and the environmental influences experienced during childhood. Environmental influences can be both physical (say, adequacy of diet) and social (the way a child is treated by others). The argument is over the *relative* contribution of heredity and environment. Throughout most of the 1960's, the trend in the behavioral sciences was to play down the former and play up the latter. The Stodolsky and Lesser passage quoted earlier in this chapter illustrates the experiential view of intelligence (at least of measured intelligence) and some recent reviews estimated the genetic component of intelligence as less than fifty per cent (for instance, Mayr, 1967) as compared to Jensen's estimate of about eighty per cent.

A major proponent of the power of the learner's environment and the potentialities of environmental manipulation is J. M. Hunt, whose influential work, *Intelligence and Experience* (1961), contains an excellent synthesis of the important psychological and neuropsychological research on intelligence and a discussion of the implications of work in the area of information processing using electronic computers. Hunt dismisses the view of genetically fixed inherited capacity destined to develop in a biologically predetermined fashion. He argues that both the initial establishment and the subsequent development of the child's mental capacities are the result of interaction between his hereditary potential and his experiences in the world around him, his "encounter with the environment," as Hunt puts it.

Hunt marshals evidence in support of his view from studies of humans and nonhumans. While one must always use caution in drawing conclusions about humans from studies of laboratory animals, evidence of the sort shown in Exhibit 6–1 is suggestive of the effects of environment upon learning, and it also shows the kinds of experimental controls which are feasible in work with laboratory animals but which cannot be applied to humans.

Exhibit 6–1

Maze Error Scores for Genetically Bright and Dull Rats in Three Environments

| | Environment | | |
	Enriched	Natural	Restricted
Bright Strain	111.2	117.0	169.7
Dull Strain	119.7	164.0	169.5

From an experiment by Cooper and Zubch in Pettigrew, 1966.

Exhibit 6–1 shows how hereditary and environment combine to produce variation in "intelligent behavior" in rats. The animals used were carefully bred for *thirteen generations* (a heredity control which would be impossible in terms of time even if we did not have moral strictures against genetic manipulation of human beings). Animals from the extremes of the genetic continuum were distributed to one of three kinds of environment: (1) *enriched,* in which ramps, swings, slides, balls, tunnels, and other kinds of equipment were added to the animal's cage; (2) *natural,* the usual cage used in laboratory work—natural in the sense of being not manipulated, not in the sense of being identified with the animals' noncaptive environment; and (3) *restricted,* an empty cage with the minimum food and water requirements and no contact with humans or other animals. The figures in the table show the mean error scores on a test involving running a maze for each of the six subgroups produced by the combination of two hereditary and three environmental categories. Thus the lower the score, the more "intelligent" the average performance in a group.

Within each genetic category, the more enriched the environment, the better the test performance, although among the genetically brightest rats the biggest gap is between the natural and restricted environments (117.0 and 169.7), while among the dullest rats the biggest gap is between the enriched and the neutral (119.7 and 164.0). Controlling the environment, on the other hand, shows that the performance of bright and dull rats differs only in the natural environment (117.0 and 164.0). When the environment was manipulated in either direction, it masked the genetic potential of the animals to a point at which there was little difference in performance between the bright and dull groups. Indeed the genetically dull perform almost as well in an enriched environment as the bright in a natural one. Apparently the enriched environment can have a sizable impact upon the least able animals, while for the genetically able, it is enough simply not to be in a severely restrictive environment.

Hunt also cites research on the intellectually damaging effects of deprived environments upon children, including on the one hand extremely isolated environments (such as isolated farms or canal boats), and on the other hand, environments where there may be many other children but too few adults and resources to provide environmental stimulation (such as orphanages). That such children have consistently lower measured intelligence seems to result from a combination of (1) lower intelligence among people who abandon or isolate children or who have extremely large families (the very poor) and (2) an environment in which there are relatively few adults and/or the available adults have relatively little time to spend with each child (in orphanages or large families where all the adults must work).

The implications of this view of intellectual origins and development are great. As Hunt summarizes:

It is no longer unreasonable to consider that it might be feasible to discover ways to govern the encounters that children have with their environments, especially during the early years of their development, to achieve a substantially higher adult level of intellectual capacity. Moreover, inasmuch as the optimum rate of intellectual development would mean also self-directing interest and curiosity and genuine pleasure in intellectual activity, promoting intellectual development properly need imply nothing like the grim urgency which has been associated with "pushing" children (Hunt, 1961: 363).

Hunt does, however, caution that constructing educational environments which maximized each child's intellectual potential would probably increase rather than decrease individual differences in performance, and the first major argument in Jensen's paper is that behavioral scientists have, for a variety of professional, sociopolitical, and ideological reasons, underestimated both the great spread in natural intelligence and the impact of genetic factors, to the detriment of educational theory and policy-making. "The belief in the almost infinite plasticity of intelligence, the ostrich-like denial of biological factors in individual differences, and the slighting of the role of genetics in the study of intelligence can only hinder investigation and understanding of the conditions, processes, and limits through which the social environment influences human behavior" (Jensen, 1969: 29).[3]

Like Hunt, Jensen cites evidence from studies of selectively bred laboratory animals, but he uses the same data to argue that the ability of rats to behave "intelligently" (to get through mazes quickly without making errors) can be markedly influenced by selective breeding, and that the dull and bright rats do not respond in the same way to the same kinds of environmental manipulation—that is, how the animals respond to their environment depends upon their genetic constitution (Jensen, 1969: 40–41).

Jensen's evidence on human intelligence is drawn heavily from studies of kinship IQ correlations. For example, the correlation between IQ scores of natural siblings reared apart is considerably higher than that of unrelated children reared together in the same home and not a great deal lower than the correlation for siblings reared together. Identical twins have the highest correlations of any sibling combinations. The correlation between the IQ scores of children with those of their natural parents increases steadily over time to a value of about .50 between ages 5 and 6, "and this is true whether the child is reared by his parents or not" (Jensen, 1969: 48–52).

Jensen argues that one cannot deduce from studies of extremely isolated or deprived children that large increases in IQ can generally be induced by environmental enrichment. Unlike the extremely isolated child, urban poor children in general are free to move about in their environment and to interact with great numbers of people. (As we saw in Chapter 3, the problem of the urban ghetto is not lack of stimulation, but lack of articulation between the home and neighborhood experiences and life in school.) This important difference is reflected in test score differences between extremely isolated children and children of the urban poor generally. The latter tend to show a slight gain in IQ after their first few months in school, but unlike children brought from isolated life situations, this initial gain is soon lost, after which there is a gradual but continuous decline in IQ throughout the remaining years of schooling. Thus Jensen is pessimistic about the chances of producing large and permanent increases in the IQ scores of poor children by means of environmental manipulation (Jensen, 1969: 59–60).

If this had been the sum of Jensen's paper, it probably would have attracted little attention outside of scholarly circles. After all, both Hunt and Jensen conceptualize intelligence as formed by a combination of genetic factors and environmental experiences; they differ mainly in the relative weight they assign to these two influences and in the extent to which they believe environmental effects can be meaningfully manipulated. Both sides of the debate have been based upon interpretation of data from small and rather special samples (orphans, twins), and there is no way of knowing whether the cases which have come to the attention of social scientists are typical of even the special subgroups of children which they represent. The best one can say is that we still lack the evidence to decide conclusively which side of the argument is closer to the truth.

Jensen, however, moved on to argue, as the passage quoted at the beginning of this chapter indicates, that the lower IQ scores of disadvantaged racial-ethnic and socioeconomic *groups* could also involve genetic as well as environmental components—that heredity is a major factor in explaining IQ differences *between* as well as *within* social groups. One of the arguments for a genetic explanation of the relationship between SES and IQ is that of "assortive mating," which claims that young people tend to select dates and mates not only from similar social backgrounds (which, given the strong relationship between SES and IQ, tends to bring together persons of relatively similar intelligence), but also of IQ (bright people being attracted to other bright people). While this seems true among certain groups in our society (among university students and graduates), the extensiveness of such a pattern (among black Americans) is simply not known. An even more circuitous argument is based upon the correlation between intelligence and occupational status. The educational and occupational systems operate as "screening" mechanisms, and over the generations, individuals get "sorted" into occupational and status categories commensurate with their abilities. It is, argues Jensen, "most unlikely that groups differing in SES would not also differ, on the average, in their genetic endowment of intelligence" (Jensen, 1969: 75).

Jensen's empirical claim for hereditary racial differences seems to rest upon the fact that no one has yet established *statistical* equality of Negro and white IQ scores, even when the variables which are supposed to "explain" the differences (such as, inequalities in income or in educational level or quality) are controlled. In Jensen's view, the hypothesis that "the lower average intelligence and scholastic performance of Negro children could involve not only environmental, but also genetic, factors," is consistent with the "preponderance of the evidence," although he realizes that such a hypothesis is "anathema to many social scientists" (Jensen, 1969: 82–83).

That such a view is "anathema" is an understatement in view of the clamor that has arisen in response to Jensen's paper. The more dispassionate arguments against innate interracial ability differences usually point out that while interracial comparisons of mean IQ scores consistently have shown that white children on the average score higher than comparable samples of black children, there is considerable overlap in the IQ distributions of the two groups. A few blacks will score higher than almost all Caucasians, and many blacks will score higher than most Caucasians. (Pettigrew, 1964: Chapter 5.) Indeed Jensen points out that in no group is there a sizable proportion of children with IQ scores below 75, or the "educability" level.) Individual differences *within* any racial group greatly exceed between-group differences.

The core of the argument, however, is that there really is no way to test Jensen's hypothesis (or its reverse) in our society. A true test of innate intelligence must compare subjects and groups of equivalent backgrounds, a requirement which simply cannot be met in a society in which there is a high level of racial segregation and discrimination and gross differential poverty between racial groups (see Pettigrew, 1966. Pettigrew also argues that the effect of "pure race" on intelligence cannot be tested in America because of the high proportion of American Negroes of mixed blood). One can, with the available evidence, construct an equally strong explanation of between-group difference in IQ scores based upon differences in child-rearing and other socialization factors, since we know that the way children are treated both within and outside the family does differ by race and socio-economic status (see Chapters 3 and 4).

In sum, one can conclude only that differences in measured intelligence do exist both within and between cultural subgroups; that the within-group differences are greater than the between-group differences; that the extent to which differences are genetic as opposed to environmental in origin is still unknown, but that genetic effects would seem to explain more of the within-group than of the between-group differences.

Finally, Jensen turns to the question asked in the title of his paper—can intelligence be raised substantially by intervention in the child's environment? Jensen's answer is no, given the high genetic component of intelligence. He draws two kinds of implications from his answer: one seems unduly pessimistic because it misses the basic point about society's needs and the schools' functions; the other offers a sensible sequence of strategic priorities.

On the pessimistic side, Jensen comments that, "while you can teach almost anyone to play chess, or the piano, or to conduct an orchestra, or to write prose, you cannot teach everyone to be a . . . Paderewski, a Toscanini, or a Bernard Shaw" (Jensen, 1969: 76). Granted that neither our patterns of reproduction nor our available modes of environmental intervention have to date produced a large supply of geniuses, the more important part of Jensen's observation seems to be the first. He himself admits that in no cultural subgroup are there many children below the "educability" level. Even among the most socially disadvantaged, most children are capable of learning the basic skills required by the educational and occupational world.[4] Jensen is also worried that our rapidly automating technological society is pushing up the mental ability requirement too rapidly, but this does not cancel out the argument that many children would be *capable* of learning much more than they do if the school environment were redesigned to enable them to learn.

Jensen's other argument is that scholastic *achievement* is much less tied to genetic factors than is intelligence. Thus educational reform programs should be aimed at the first rather than the second:

> This means that there is potentially much more we can do to improve school performance through environmental means than we can do to change intelligence per se. Thus it seems likely that if compensatory education programs are to have a beneficial effect on achievement, it will be through their influence on motivation, values, and other environmentally conditioned habits that play an important part in scholastic performance, rather than through any marked direct influence on intelligence per se. The proper evaluation of such programs should therefore be sought in their effects on actual scholarship performance rather than in how much they raise the child's IQ (Jensen, 1969: 59).

In a review of the compensatory programs that have been initiated in recent years, mainly under the aegis of the federal antipoverty program, Jensen concludes that the few instances where the results have been truly encouraging have been in projects which focused upon teaching the specific skills which are linked to school learning rather than attempting all-round enrichment of the child's environment and experience. An example is the Bereiter-Engelman program at the University of Illinois, which is built upon brief but intensive periods of drill in language, reading, and arithmetic skills, using almost militaristic procedures which demand a high and continuous level of participation from all the children. The now-famous opening sentence in Jensen's paper—"Compensatory education has been tried and it apparently has failed"—is not only inflammatory, but also misleading. Jensen's statement does not mean that compensatory education *cannot* succeed, but rather that most of the programs to date have focused upon the wrong things.[5]

Cognitive Style

To complicate the issue of ability still further, behavioral scientists are coming to realize that children differ not only in types and levels of intelligence (which are themselves differentially recognized and rewarded by the educational system), but also in the way in which they approach and handle academic tasks, in particular their modes of selecting, classifying, and generalizing from the information in a given stimulus or situation. The term used to describe individuals' methods of selecting and processing information is *cognitive,* or conceptual, *style.* Cognitive style is of interest to educational sociologists because of the way in which it links the expectations of the school system and the characteristics brought to the school by children from various social backgrounds.

Pioneering work in the development and definition of cognitive style categories was done by Kagan, Moss, and Sigel (1960 and 1963). Their scheme includes two major dimensions. One dimension defines three conceptual categories by which the individual organizes or groups a series of objects. At one extreme is the *descriptive,* sometimes referred to as the analytic, or analytic-descriptive, mode. Groupings in this category are made on the basis of some shared physical attribute—a lamp post, door, and hammer are all "hard" objects; a radio, television, and telephone all "make noise." At the other extreme is the *relational* mode, by which objects are grouped in terms of their meaning or functional relationship to each other or to a total concept encompassing them all. For example, a comb, lipstick, pocketbook, and door might be grouped together under the conceptual umbrella of "getting ready to go out." Note that in this cognitive mode, no single object is an example of the label than envelopes it; each has meaning only in connection with the other objects in the set. There is also a middle category in Kagan's original scheme—the inferential, or categorical-inferential, mode, by which groupings are made on the basis of some shared characteristics, but what is shared is not inherent in the physical nature of the objects (spoon, cup, and glass are "for eating." Note that these same stimuli could also be grouped according to the descriptive mode (using the "hardness" theme given in the example above.) The inferential category has not been used much, most research being based upon a descriptive-relational continuum.

The second major dimension is the individual's orientation toward objects. Here Kagan distinguishes between an *egocentric,* or personalized, affective response to stimuli, and a *stimulus-centered* orientation, in which the individual's focus is upon the aspects of the stimulus itself rather than upon his personal feelings about it.

A typical test of cognitive style involves a series of figure-sorting tasks, where, for example, the subject is asked to say which pair of pictures out of a set of three are most "alike" and how he came to this decision. Kagan and his associates have found some correlations between the analytic-descriptive mode of conceptualization and high scores on IQ and other intellectual measures, though the relationships are not large or consistent, and they are greater for boys than for girls. Their assumption is that the analytic-cognitive style is the more desirable one, since it involves a more active approach to intellectual tasks and indicates a sensitivity to the less obvious aspects of grouped stimuli. Because the relational style implies a more "passive acceptance of the whole stimulus," it is intellectually inferior to the analytic mode.

Another important body of research on cognitive style, which questions some of Kagan's assumptions about the relative superiority of different cognitive styles, is being produced at the Learning Research and Development Center at the University of Pittsburgh. Rosalie Cohen is interested in the differences in cognitive style between children from low-income and higher-income homes, and in the extent of congruency between the learning styles children bring to school and the cognitive requirements of the formal school system. To get at the latter, Cohen did a content analysis of ten widely used standardized intelligence and achievement tests. Three general types of cognitive requirements were identified:

breadth and depth of general information;

analytic abstraction;

field articulation, or the ability to extract salient information from the embedding context.

In general, achievement tests are weighted toward the first kind of skill, intelligence tests toward the second and third (the "logical" skills). Reading comprehension tests also measure skill in field articulation, as do arithmetic "word problems." "Thus the school requires improvement in analytic abstraction and field articulation skills in increasingly measured amounts at each higher grade level, as well as a demonstration of growth in pupils' information priorities" (Cohen, 1968: 3). This combination of skills, or the mode of thinking which allows an individual to perform well on conventional school tasks and standardized tests, combines the descriptive-analytic form of conceptualization and the stimulus-centered orientation defined in Kagan's scheme. Cohen terms this combination of categories the analytic-cognitive style and contrasts it with the relational style, which is characterized as "self-centered in its orientation to reality" plus incorporating a conceptual strategy in which "only the global characteristics of a stimulus have meaning to its users, and these only in reference to some total context" (Cohen, 1968: 4)—that is, it combines the relational conceptual mode and the egocentric orientation of Kagan's scheme. In Cohen's opinion, "So discrepant are the analytic and relational frames of reference that a pupil whose preferred mode of cognitive organization is emphatically relational is unlikely to be rewarded in the school setting, either socially or by grades, regardless of his native abilities, and even if his information repertoire and background of experience are adequate" (Cohen, 1968: 4–5). In fact a child who has high intelligence or other abilities but a relational cognitive style may be in a particularly unhappy position since his talents are not of a sort which allow him to play the student role successfully. Cohen speculates, though she does not have empirical evidence to test her speculations, that such students are the source of the "greatest behavior problems in school, as well as the leaders of delinquent gangs" (Cohen, 1968: 11).

Cohen does have data showing that cognitive style is related both to the child's likelihood of meeting the behavioral expectations of the student role (for instance, having an attention span of the required length and intensity) and to socioeconomic status, with children from low-income homes being more likely to demonstrate a relational approach to cognitive problems as well as to the behavioral correlates of this style. These findings lead her to cast doubt upon the rationale underlying the construction of most "culture-free" tests as described earlier in this chapter. Cohen argues that by substituting manipulation of nonverbal forms and symbols for the direct experience and information components of conventional intelligence tests, the newer tests discriminate even more strongly against the child with a relational cognitive style, who is also likely to be of low SES:

> Traditional attempts at the development of culture-free tests have, thus, eliminated the information components of such tests of ability in the belief that it is their experience components which are culture-bound. However, the *most* culture-bound characteristics of these tests appear not in their information components, but in the analytic logical sequences which they require. They concentrate wholly on the stimulus centered, parts-specific analytic mode of abstraction and the field articulation skills which define the analytic mode of cognitive organization. In addition, in using contentless symbols, the *level* of analytic abstraction which is required focuses on the most extreme level on which these analytic skills can be demonstrated. Thus, both in the mode of abstraction which these nonverbal tests require, and in the level of abstraction in which the items are couched, nonverbal tests of intelligence are much more discriminatory against relational pupils than are conventional instruments which test, in part, for information growth (Cohen, 1968: 12).

Cohen's interpretation offers an explanation for Jensen's earlier-reported finding that culturally deprived children do even poorer on supposedly culture-free tests than on standard IQ tests. Also like Jensen, she offers a plea for school environments designed to allow more kinds of students to succeed. As she sees it, any child who does not approach classroom tasks with the one cognitive style "approved" by the school system is automatically in conflict with the school and foredoomed to failure. Teaching innovations geared toward learning via alternative kinds of mental abilities and modes of thinking might thus have a significant, and immediate, impact upon the proportions of children who succeed in the role of student.

Creativity

We have seen that intelligence can be distinguished from the mode by which an individual attacks an intellectual task, although the kinds of intelligence called for by most school tasks and tests favor one cognitive style over another, and the kind of intelligence and cognitive style related to school success are both related to students' social backgrounds. Intelligence also can be distinguished from the dimension of creativity, which is the quality of inventiveness and imagination, the ability to produce new or novel ideas—or linkages between ideas, insights, and solutions, as opposed to the logical selection and combination of cognitive components. While intelligence includes such components as "a person's memory storage capacities, his skill in solving problems, his dexterity in manipulating and dealing with concepts," creativity has to do with his facility in producing fresh or unique associations, ideas, or solutions to problems (Wallach and Kogan, 1967: 38).

Although behavioral scientists have long felt that creativity and intelligence are different psychological dimensions, proof of such differentiation rests upon developing a set of creativity assessment devices, parallel to the IQ tests of intelligence, which are highly interrelated among themselves but are independent of or from measures of other mental abilities.[6] Most creativity tests judge the extent to which an individual *differs* from or exceeds some group norm or standard. One kind of task is to name all the uses one can think of for some common object (for instance, a key, shoe, chair, or newspaper). Responses are judged both for quantity and originality. Another procedure is to give a simple ambiguous stimulus and, again, to judge the number and uniqueness of the responses: for example, for a triangle with three circles around it, "three mice eating a piece of cheese" was a unique response, while "three people sitting around a table" was not; for two half-circles over a straight line, "two haystacks on a flying carpet" was a unique response, "two igloos" was not (Wallach and Kogan, 1967: 40). Another technique is to analyze children's own stories or drawings on the basis of originality of theme and execution.

Both of the major published studies of creativity in children (Getzels and Jackson, 1962; Wallach and Kogan, 1965 and 1967) identify children on both creativity and intelligence, make some comparisons between them, and draw some conclusions about how differing combinations of these two mental dimensions relate to success in school. The sample for the Getzels and Jackson study consisted of over 500 students, the upper six grades of one private school. The major portion of their reports is a comparison of students who scored high on creativity but not on IQ with students who scored high on IQ but not creativity (cells b and c respectively of Exhibit 6–2).[7] Data consisted of responses to a series of ability, achievement, and attitude tests. The creativity battery included measures of the ability to devise mathematical problems, to compose endings for incomplete stories,

Exhibit 6–2
Combinations of Mental Characteristics Used in Creativity Studies

		Intelligence	
		High	**Low**
Creativity	**High**	a	b
	Low	c	d

to think up word definitions, and to imagine uses for an object. Some of the students' own stories and pictures were also analyzed for theme and originality. In addition, the parents of some of the subjects were questioned.

The researchers found that the high creativity and high IQ students differed on a number of attitudinal and family experience variables. First, the parents of the latter were more "vigilant" about their children's behavior, their academic performance, and their choice of friends. They also tended to be more critical of their children and of the education the school was providing. The qualities they especially valued were the conventional (and visible) virtues of cleanliness, good manners, and studiousness. In contrast, the parents of the high creativity students focused less on the conventional virtues, more on such things as the child's "openness to experience" and "interests and enthusiasm for life" (Getzels and Jackson, 1962: 68–75).

Second, while both groups of students agreed on the types of personal characteristics which would contribute to success in school and in later life, only the high IQ group wanted these characteristics for themselves. Subjects were asked to rank thirteen hypothetical children, each exemplifying a desirable personal quality (for instance, one child was described as the brightest student in the school, another as the best athlete, another as having outstanding social skills), in three ways—as to (1) which would be the most successful in adult life; (2) which ones their teachers would like best; and (3) which they themselves would like to be like. The rankings of the high IQ and high creativity groups were almost identical for the first two categories:

> The high creatives and the high IQ's agree on what qualities make for adult success in our society and on what qualities teachers prefer in their students. However, as compared with these correlations of 1.00 and .98 respectively, the correlation between the self-ideal rankings—the qualities the adolescents in the two groups want for themselves—is but .41 . . .

A more detailed analysis compared students' preferred self-image with the perceived preferences of the adult world:

> By comparing "self-ideal" ranking with "success-image" ranking, we may elicit an answer to the question: how success-oriented are the students? Are the qualities they value highly for themselves the same as those they believe make for "success" as adults? And by comparing the "self-ideal"

ranking with the "teacher-perception" ranking, we may in effect obtain an answer to the question: how teacher-oriented are the students? The comparisons yielded the rank-order correlation coefficients presented . . . in (Exhibit 6–3).

The results are again rather clear-cut. For the high IQ students the relationship between the qualities they value for themselves and those they believe lead to "success" as adults is quite close. That is, these students appear to be highly success oriented. For the high creativity students the relationship between the qualities *they* value and those they believe lead to "success" as adults is virtually *nil*. These students appear *not* to be highly success oriented (at least not by conventional standards of adult success) (Getzels and Jackson, 1962: 34–35).

Third, the in-school experiences and behavior of the two types of students differed. Both groups had high achievement motivation and high actual achievement, suggesting either that IQ tests do measure something other than pure scholastic aptitude, or that the highly creative student has other qualities which compensate for a lesser amount of "pure" intelligence. They differ, however, in their approach to intellectual tasks. By comparison with their high IQ classmates, the high creativity students' work was characterized by a certain playfulness. Their stories were "significantly higher than the high IQ adolescents'" in *stimulus-free themes, unexpected endings, humor, incongruities, and playfulness* and showed a marked tendency toward more *violence*" (Getzels and Jackson, 1962: 38). The less methodical, more playful approach of these children may also explain another empirical finding—the teachers in this school preferred the high IQ to the high creativity students (Getzels and Jackson, 1962: 33).

The "playful" component of creativity is even more strongly emphasized by Wallach and Kogan. They deduced (1) from the number of references made to "playing with ideas," "letting things happen," "freedom of expression," and the like in memoires and interviews with writers, scientists; and other highly creative individuals; and (2) from the inability to separate creativity from IQ when it is measured in a test-like situation, that creativity,

Exhibit 6–3
Rank Order Correlations Among Subsections of the Outstanding Traits Test

	Subjects	
Components of Correlations	**High IQ** **(N = 28)**	**High Creative** **(N = 26)**
"Personal traits preferred for oneself × personal traits believed predictive of adult success"	.81	.10
"Personal traits preferred for oneself × personal traits believed favored by teachers"	.67	—.25

From Getzels and Jackson, 1967: 35.

"if it is to reveal itself most clearly, requires a frame of reference which is relatively free from the coercion of time limits and relatively free from stress of knowing that one's behavior is under close evaluation" (Wallach and Kogan, 1965a: 24). Thus, as researchers, they took great pains to construct a "permissive" atmosphere for the administration of their research instruments. The administrators got to know the children, by observing and playing with them before the actual testing; subjects were tested individually rather than in groups; the tasks were introduced as part of a study of children's games for the purpose of developing new games that children would like, *not* as a test or as anything directly related to their regular school work; and there was no time limit on any of the procedures.

The 151 children in Wallach and Kogan's samples were all fifth graders, the entire fifth-grade population of one suburban New England public school system. Thus they were younger than the subjects of the Getzels and Jackson study, but like them were mainly of middle-class background (the 6% of the children's fathers who did not have professional or managerial occupations were nearly all in upper level blue-collar occupations—electricians or carpenters).

The ten creativity indicators—a uniqueness and a productivity measure for each of five types of association tasks (including naming uses for common objects and responses to ambiguous doodle pictures)—were found to be highly intercorrelated and to have only low correlations with the intelligence. Thus Wallach and Kogan succeeded, where Getzels and Jackson did not, in producing a clear distinction between measures of the two concepts. The Wallach and Kogan study is also an extension of Getzel and Jackson's work in that they compared children in all four cells of Exhibit 6–2.

Exhibit 6–4 summarizes the results of an analysis of the classroom behavior of the four subgroups of female subjects. (The behavior variables were derived from a series of nine rating scales, completed during a two-week observation period preceeding the administration of the creativity tasks, by two judges who worked independently both of each other and of the administrators of the other tests and tasks. For a full discussion of the scales and the rating procedures, see Wallach and Kogan, 1965a: 35–38.) As Exhibit 6–4 indicates, children high in creativity *and* intelligence combined academic bent with successful peer relationships. They displayed the "highest level of self-confidence, the least tendency toward deprecation of oneself and one's work, the strongest tendency to seek out others for companionship, the strongest tendency to be sought by others, the highest levels of attention span and concentration for academic work" (Wallach and Kogan, 1965b: 115). The only negative aspect of their behavior is a tendency to engage in "disruptive" behavior (in particular, attention-seeking acts such as speaking out of turn or making noise), a tendency which in the authors' opinion is congruent with their positive self-image and high (and healthy) level of interest. As they put it, "It's as if they are bursting through the typical behavioral molds that the society has constructed" (Wallach and Kogan, 1967: 41).

Exhibit 6–4
Girls' Classroom Behavior
by Intelligence and Creativity Levels

Creativity	Intelligence: High	Intelligence: Low
High	Self-evaluation: high Concentration and attention span: high Tendency to seek and be sought by peers: high Disruptive behavior: high	Self-evaluation: low Concentration and attention span: low Tendency to seek and be sought by peers: low Disruptive behavior: high
Low	Self-evaluation: high Concentration and attention span: high Tendency to seek and be sought by peers: low on seeking, high on being sought Disruptive behavior: low	Self-evaluation: medium Concentration and attention span: low Tendency to seek and be sought by peers: medium Disruptive behavior: low to medium

Adapted from findings in Wallach and Kogan, 1965a and 1965b.

Examination of the other three cells of Exhibit 6–4 shows that:

Those high in creativity but low in intelligence, in contrast, were the most cautious and hesitant of all the groups, the least confident, the most self-deprecatory, the least sought after by others, the least able to concentrate and maintain attention, and in addition they were quite avoidant of others. The one characteristic they shared with the high-high group was the presence of disruptive behavior. Turning next to the group low in both creativity and intelligence, these girls were more confident, and self-assured, less hesitant, and more extroverted socially than were the high creativity-low intelligence girls. Finally, the group of high intelligence but low creativity was least likely to engage in disruptive behavior, was reasonably hesitant about expressing opinions, was sought out socially by others but tended not to seek out others in return, and was high in attention span and concentration. In sum, the high creativity-low intelligence group seems to be the maximally disadvantaged group in the classroom, and the high intelligence-low creativity group seems to be characterized by a basic reserve and an unwillingness to take chances (Wallach and Kogan, 1965b: 115–116).

For boys, the relationship between the *intelligence* dimension and classroom behavior was similar to the girls' pattern, but creativity had no observable behavioral consequences (Wallach and Kogan, 1965a: 89–94). Although their data do not explain these sex differences, the authors speculate that they may be a function of the differential role expectations explored in the previous chapter. Since achievement is highly valued in boys (and the boys in this sample were more achievement oriented than the girls), the intelligence needed to perform well in classroom tasks was all that was needed for approval and self-confidence.

However, a further analysis which brought in the additional dimension of cognitive style (using Kagan's basic test) showed that adding this mental variable did not affect the girls' results in any consistent way but that it did bring out an effect of creativity among boys that did not show up when only intelligence and creativity were controlled. The highly creative boys seemed able to switch rather flexibly among the different cognitive modes. By contrast, boys high on intelligence but low on creativity concentrated on the "conceptual common elements" (the analytic mode) and displayed an "avoidance" of thematic-relational categorizing, and boys low on both dimensions seemed "locked" into relational modes of responding and relatively incapable of analytical thinking (Wallach and Kogan, 1965a: Chapter 4). Thus the most general implications of Wallach and Kogan's research are: (1) that one can design an appropriate learning program for a child only by taking into account the combination of his abilities and modes of thinking; and (2) that boys and girls respond to the classroom and to intellectual stimuli differently, which may be explained by "differential normative expectations for boys and girls in the achievement and affiliation areas" (Wallach and Kogan, 1965a: 94).

Conclusions

In this brief analysis of individual ability, we have seen that it is not a single dimension but rather a complex of dimensions, only some of which are linearly related to each other. Psychologists have given more attention to intelligence than to any other kind of mental ability, but few are satisfied with our present measuring instruments. A low score on an IQ test may reflect lack of interest in verbal and numerical symbols, lack of motivation to do well on tests, lack of practice in taking tests, and lack of real-life experiences related to the content of the tests, as well as a low level of natural intelligence, and it is often difficult to sort out which factors are operating in a particular case. While it seems clear that intelligence combines genetic and environmental components, neither the relative strength of the two nor the way in which one may affect or limit the power of the other has been decisively determined. And while intelligence, like school performance, is strongly related to the background variables of SES and race, the extent to which social subgroup differences are also genetically determined is also unknown, and interpretation of what empirical evidence exists is clouded by political and ideological biases.

What does seem clear is that a child's learning in school is not simply a function of his total or composite level of natural abilities. It is affected by the extent to which the particular combination of mental abilities he possesses meshes with the structure and expectations of the school. Thus a child who has a well developed imagination but a low interest in or limited experience with verbal and numerical symbols, or a child who analyzes problems in their total relational context rather than in a logical, analytical fashion abstracted from their larger meaning, is not likely to receive much encouragement from his teachers; on the contrary, he may be defined as stupid or even troublemaking. To look at it another way, the conventional classroom is structured to build up ever greater repertoires of factual information and analytic skills but not to encourage the "playful contemplation" that is conducive to creativity. The social structure and dynamics of the school will be the subject of Part Three of this book, after which we should be better able to determine the best interface between what the individual student brings with him to school and what he confronts when he gets there. In the final chapter of the book, we shall consider some proposed changes in the structure of learning environments which might increase the productivity of certain kinds of children.

A child's learning also is dependent upon the extent to which his total experience outside of school has prepared him to play the student role in accordance with the expectations of school personnel. A synthesis of the findings of the past four chapters suggests, as indicated in Exhibit 6–5, that social background and experiences shape the individual's abilities to some degree (there is probably some reverse effect also, but the impact of children's ability upon the family itself is less well understood and is probably much smaller), which in turn affects his academic attitudes and performance, and that these variables have both interactive and independent effects upon school success. This kind of model is illustrated in the recent work of William Sewell and associates at the University of Wisconsin, who have been analyzing the educational achievement and aspirations of Wisconsin high school students using path analysis, a technique which allows the researcher to make inferences about causal sequence. Analysis of a randomly selected group of over 10,000 high school seniors showed that family socioeconomic status, family attitudes (educational aspirations and encouragement), and intelligence all have *substantial* and *independent* relationships with the college plans of both boys and girls, that no pair of these three variables can completely account for the differences explained by the third variable. They are also related to each other—ability tends to accentuate social class differences in educational plans. Finally, the path model indicates that parental encouragement is a powerful intervening variable between SES, intelligence, and educational aspirations (Sewell and Shah, 1968. For a discussion of the technique of path analysis, see Borgatta, 1969; Wright, 1934 and 1960).

A final observation is that Part Two has made it abundantly clear that, whatever the exact contribution of hereditary, environmental, ability, and social background factors, children enter school with a tremendous range

Exhibit 6-5
*Characteristics of Individual Students Which are Related to School
Performance*

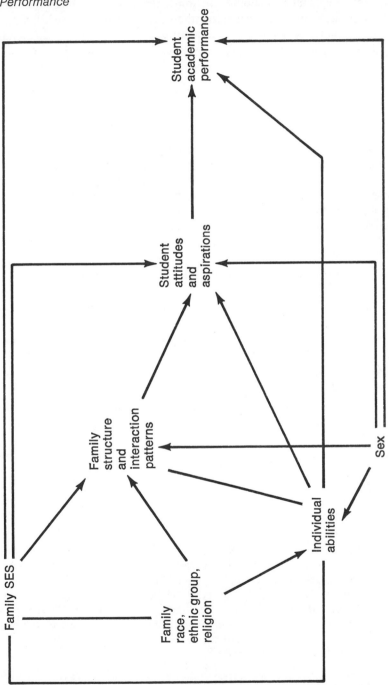

of difference in their facility to benefit from it. The very humane efforts to develop measures that assess fairly the true potentialities of deprived and minority group children should not mask the fact that children in certain social subgroups perform well below their peers on the tests predicting aptitude for school learning, and, subsequently, on school work itself. And that efforts at "compensatory" education have not, to date, gone far toward closing the gap.

Notes

1. A review of evidence on the relationship between IQ and achievement by Rossi (1961) concludes that the former accounts for between forty and sixty per cent of the variation in student performance. While the twenty percentage point range shows that our best quantitative estimates are still far from precise, even the lowest estimate indicates the potency of IQ as a predictor. Moreover, if IQ is held constant, relationships between achievement and other variables are nearly always reduced. The second most powerful predictor of achievement is *past* achievement.

2. See, for example, Miller, 1967: 74ff.

3. This is also the view of some sociologists (for instance, Eckland, 1967) who have pointed to the necessity of integrating environmental and genetic principles in the study of intelligence. Like Jensen, Eckland feels an understanding of genetic factors is necessary in understanding social class differences.

4. As noted earlier, one educated guess is that over 90% of the children now in school are capable of mastering most subjects, given sufficient time and appropriate types of help (Bloom, 1968: 4).

5. On compensatory education programs, see also McDill *et al.*, 1969.

6. Some recent developments in biological research suggest that creativity or imagination may have a different biological basis from more "logical" forms of mental ability and activity—that is, that creative thinking emanates from a separate "territory" of the brain and nervous system from reasoning and abstract thinking. One suggestive piece of evidence is that individuals with certain kinds of brain injuries may perform as well as previously on IQ tests but decline on tests requiring imagination. For a brief discussion of the biological basis of creativity, see Gerard, 1952.

7. It should be noted that while Getzels and Jackson focused upon the subjects who were high on only one of the two ability dimensions, such cases were in the minority. All of the creativity tests in the test batteries administered correlated significantly with IQ for the boys, all but one for the girls. In fact, the individual creativity test scores were as highly correlated with IQ as they were among themselves, a point taken by Wallach and Kogan as one of the starting points for their research and one of the reasons why they took special pains with the setting of their test administration.

PART THREE

The School

Classroom Role Structure and Role Relationships

Now, the class is a small society. It is therefore both natural and necessary that it have its own morality corresponding to its size, the character of its elements, and its function. Discipline is this morality. . . . On the other hand, the schoolroom society is much closer to the society of adults than it is to that of the family. For, aside from the fact that it is larger, the individuals—teachers and students—who make it up are not brought together by personal feelings or preferences but for altogether general and abstract reasons, that is to say, because of the social functions to be performed by the teacher, and the immature mental condition of the students. For all these reasons, the rule of the classroom cannot bend or give with the same flexibility as that of the family in all kinds and combinations of circumstances. It cannot accommodate itself to given temperaments. . . . It is a first initiation into the austerity of duty. Serious life has now begun. Emile Durkheim

Although the details of physical structure vary from school to school, most schools are broken up into a series of classrooms, and it is here that students presumably do their learning. Our first task is to examine this assumption. If differential classroom productivity can be explained, on the one hand, by differences in individual students' backgrounds and personal characteristics, or, on the other hand, by differences between schools as total social systems, then innovation and reform focused at the classroom level are not likely to have any real effects upon learning.

Two recent studies present evidence on the subject of such differences. The first is a study of New York City fifth and sixth graders (Goldberg *et al.,* 1966), in which eighty-six classes were organized to represent fifteen different patterns of student ability level and ability spread. All students were given a series of tests measuring achievement, interests, and attitudes at the beginning of the fifth grade and end of the sixth. The findings pertaining to the authors' major concern—the effects of ability grouping upon academic and social success—will be discussed in the next chapter. What is of interest here is the amount of variance between classes which is *not* explained by differences in students' ability. An analysis of variance[1] comparing class average test scores in three subjects showed that, with one exception, the differences between class means *within* a given ability grouping pattern were as great or greater than the mean differences *among different patterns.* Moreover, the between-class differences within individual *schools* were greater than the range among schools (Goldberg *et al.,* 1966: 61). That is, membership in a particular class did seem to make a difference, a difference which the authors attribute to the "personality" or "syntality" of the classroom unit.

A second study supporting the importance of the classroom is a reanalysis of *Equality of Educational Opportunity* survey data conducted by one of the coauthors of the report. McPartland (1967) was interested in comparing the relative influence of desegregation at the level of the school and the classroom upon the academic performance of Negro students. Using a subsample of some 5000 ninth graders from metropolitan areas of the New England and Middle Atlantic states, McPartland crosstabulated scores from the verbal tests with the following three independent variables: (1) percentage of white students in the ninth grade of the respondent's school; (2) percentage of white classmates;[2] and (3) family background, based upon the respondent's report of his mother's education and his responses on a nine-item check list of possessions in his home.

Exhibit 7–1 shows the results of McPartland's analysis. The figures show the "average increment in achievement between successive categories of the racial composition variables for students who are matched on categories of other variables. For example, the first value in Exhibit 7–1, +.16, is an estimate of the average number of units of achievement gained by moving from one category of 'proportion white classmates' to the next higher category" (McPartland, 1967: 2–3). This influence of racial composition upon achievement holds even when family background is controlled (the "effect parameter" is only slightly reduced, from +.16 to +.13). There is a similarly small reduction when the proportion of white students in the school as a whole is controlled (also to +.13), which means that, "regardless of the racial composition of the school, the average achievement of Negro students increases with the proportion of their classmates who are white." On the other hand, the effect of *school* racial composition upon verbal achievement (+.13) almost disappears when the degree of integration at the classroom level is controlled (+.02). School level racial composition does have a contingency effect, however. The figures .07, .16, .19, and .34 indicate that the effect of classroom integration is increasingly strong as the proportion of white students in the school as a whole increases, perhaps reflecting the advantages of mostly white over mostly black schools in other respects. McPartland's general conclusion is that:

Taken together, the above results strongly suggest that it is desegregation at the classroom level which encompasses the factors having important influences on Negro student academic performance. No matter what the racial composition of the school, increases in Negro student achievement accompany increases in the proportion of their classmates who are white. The only students who appear to derive benefit from attendance at mostly white schools are those in predominantly white classes within the school. As far as differences in their achievement are concerned, the students in segregated classes may as well be in segregated schools as desegregated ones (McPartland, 1967:5).

Thus both the McPartland and the Goldberg *et al.* studies support the premise that the classroom is of central importance, although McPartland's analysis focuses upon the influence of the students' peers, "who form the immediate environment for an individual," while Goldberg notes two characteristics that vary from class to class: the "syntality" of the classroom unit and the teacher.

Exhibit 7–1

Weighted Parameters of Main Effects on Ninth-Grade Negro Student Verbal Achievement, Under Different Control Conditions*

	Effect Parameter	
Proportion white classmates (3 comparisons)	+.16	
Proportion white classmates, controlling family background (18)	+.13	
Proportion white classmates, controlling family background and per cent white in school (72)	+.13	
0–19% white in school (18)		+.07
20–49% white in school (18)		+.16
50–69% white in school (18)		+.19
70–99% white in school (18)		+.34
Per cent white in school (3)	+.13	
Per cent white in school, controlling family background (18)	+.11	
Per cent white in school, controlling family background and proportion white classmates (72)	+.02	
No white classmates (18)		—.03
Less than half white classmates (18)		—.02
About half white classmates (18)		+.03
More than half white classmates (18)		+.09

* The numbers in parentheses are the number of comparisons which were combined in the weighted average of achievement increments. Each value in this table is based on 5,075 cases.
From McPartland, 1967: 12.

The Role Structure: Teachers and Students

The two crucial roles in the classroom are those of the teacher and the student, and life in the classroom is largely based upon the interaction between them. Perhaps the distinguishing characteristic of the student role in most schools is passivity. The "good" student listens to the teacher, follows instructions, does not disturb the class by talking too much or out of turn or by unnecessary physical movement, and is otherwise receptive to *being taught*. Some forty years ago, John Dewey noted, "Why is it, in spite of the fact that teaching by pouring in, learning by passive absorption, are universally condemned, that they are still intrenched in practice?" (Dewey, 1928:46), and the activities which set the early progressive schools apart from other schools—for example, experiments, individual and class projects, manipulation of "real" materials, field trips—were focused on making the student as well as the teacher an active participant in the learning process.

In an analysis of "life in classroom" that combines the author's own observations of several elementary classes with a synthesis of a number of empirical studies,⁴ Jackson (1968) concludes that the most useful quality for a student to possess is patience. The "daily grind" of classroom life contains great amounts of delay (waiting in line, waiting to get the teacher's attention, waiting for someone else to catch up, and so on); interruption (activities begin and end in accordance with the class schedule rather than with student interest and development); and distraction paired with denial (the student is surrounded by peers but is not allowed to talk with them during much of the school day). In addition to learning to live in a crowd, the successful student learns how to deal with authority, especially in his relationships with his teachers, and how to face constant evaluation of himself and his behavior (Jackson, 1968: Chapter 1). Small wonder that many students have ambivalent feelings about school. In a review of attitudinal studies, including a survey of some five hundred Chicago students that he himself conducted, Jackson found that from a fifth to over a half of the respondents expressed boredom, discontent, or mixed feelings about going to school. Few, however, expressed either strong love or hate. Perhaps because children really have no choice about going to school, most think of the academic side of school life as something to "put up with" rather than as something to have strong feelings about one way or the other (Jackson, 1968: Chapter 2).

In a social system as tightly organized as that of most classrooms, the position and activities of any role depend upon those of its role "mates." In this sense the student is dependent upon the teacher. One of the first sociologists to take an interest in the teacher role was Durkheim. In a series of lectures on pedagogy delivered just after the turn of the century (from which the excerpt at the beginning of this chapter was taken), Durkheim noted that the teacher role was characterized by its "indisputable authority," based upon the teacher's age and a certain "moral authority" attached to his vocation. Since the teacher was imbued with civilization and the students were subjects to be civilized, the relationship was in essence that between two populations of unequal culture. Moreover, because of the physical isolation of the classroom and the at-most superficial supervision of teachers, they were seldom subject to external discipline. Lacking access to any institutionalized form of legitimate power, the student was in no position to resist.

In addition to age and status differences and discrepancies in goals, other factors may contribute to disequilibrium in the teacher-student relationship. One is the teacher's social background. As we pointed out in the first chapter, the teacher, like the student, comes to the school with a social history which affects his attitudes toward and interaction with students and other persons in the school. Considerable research has been done on the kind of persons who go into teaching (for a review of studies up to the early 1960's, see Charters, 1963). A recent national survey of some five hundred public schools in forty-one American cities with populations of 50,000 or more has shown that the majority of teachers (over three-fourths) come from upper-blue-collar or lower-white-collar families (Herriot and Hoyt, 1966). This means that there is general teacher-student status congruency in schools of middle-range SES, but that teachers in schools of high SES are apt to be of lower status than their pupils, and teachers in low-SES schools are apt to be of higher status than their pupils (although teachers in higher SES schools were also of slightly higher social origins than teachers in lower SES schools). There is also a tendency for the proportion of nonwhite students to exceed the proportion of nonwhite teachers, but as in the case of SES, the incongruency is greatest at the lowest SES schools.

Thus schools with a high proportion of students from low-SES families may have some rather special problems with respect to the teacher-student relationship. Since it is in these schools that the teacher is most likely to have a higher social position than the students and since low-SES children are most likely to be subject to negative image and treatment, there is a need for strategies designed either to change teachers' perceptions of the kinds of students they now consider undesirable or to create new roles which can mediate between these children and the school system, perhaps helping them to change certain superficial but symbolic things about their appearance or behavior which will lead teachers to view and treat them differently.

A second set of variables has to do with the teacher's position *within* the school. The hierarchical structure of the school system will be discussed in Chapter 9, but it is worth noting that the teacher's generally low position on the system ladder and his lack of autonomy with respect to curriculum, class structure, and other basic issues affect his self-image and his subsequent treatment of students.

The structural defects inherent in the teacher-student relationship have been described in Waller's *Sociology of Teaching*—after some thirty-five years still the most vivid presentation of the social structure of schools.

As Waller formulates it:

> The teacher represents the established social order in the school, and his interest is in maintaining that order, whereas pupils have only a negative interest in that feudal superstructure. Teacher and pupil confront each other with attitudes from which the underlying hostility can never be altogether removed. Pupils are the material in which teachers are supposed to produce results. Pupils are human beings striving to realize themselves in their own spontaneous manner, striving to produce their own results in their own way. Each of these hostile parts stands in the way of the other; insofar as the aims of either are realized, it is at the sacrifice of the aims of the other.
>
> Authority is on the side of the teacher. The teacher nearly always wins. In fact, he must win, or he cannot remain a teacher. . . . Conflict between teachers and students therefore passes to the second level. All the externals of conflict and of authority having been settled, the matter chiefly at issue is the meaning of these externals. Whatever the rules that the teacher lays down, the tendency of the pupils is to empty them of meaning. By mechanization of conformity, by "laughing off" the teacher or hating him out of all existence as a person, by taking refuge in self-initiated activities that are always just beyond the teacher's reach, students attempt to neutralize teacher control (Waller, 1932: 195–196).

As Waller notes, students develop strategies to cope with the "institutionalized dominance and subordination" built into the classroom role structure. In addition to the neutralization tactics described in the preceding passage, there are "apple-polishing" tactics, by which the student gets around the teacher's authority by developing a separate set of "backstage" relationships with him; and at the other extreme, withdrawal tactics, by which the student relinquishes the possibility of getting any of the rewards of the learning system and invests minimal effort in classroom activities. Various kinds of student maneuvers are analyzed in a pair of books by John Holt: *How Children Fail* (1964), and *How Children Learn* (1967). In the following passage, Holt describes the elaborate strategems employed by one child who has figured out that with a student-teacher ratio of over twenty to one, the teacher cannot focus very long on any one student:

> She also knows the teacher's strategy of asking questions of students who seem confused, or not paying attention. She therefore feels safe waving her hand in the air, as if she were bursting to tell the answer, whether she really knows it or not. When someone else answers correctly, she nods her head in emphatic agreement. Sometimes she even adds a comment, though her expression and tone of voice show that she feels this is risky. It is also interesting to note that she does not raise her hand unless there are at least half a dozen other hands up.
>
> Sometimes she gets called on. The question arose the other day, "What is half of forty-eight?" Her hand was up; in the tiniest whisper she said, "Twenty-four." I asked her to repeat it. She said, loudly, "I said," then whispered, "twenty-four." I asked her to repeat it again, because many couldn't hear her. Her face showing tension, she said, very loudly, "I said

that one half of forty-eight is . . ." and then, very softly, "twenty-four."

Of course, this is a strategy that often pays off. A teacher who asks a question is tuned to the right answer, since it will tell him that his teaching is good and that he can go on to the next topic. (Holt, 1964: 12–13).

Holt's basic complaint is that schools squelch the child's natural need to know and to master things. Being a student involves a kind of play acting in which the player's aim is to escape embarrassment and pain by figuring out the "correct" answer the teacher wants. Although the author's arguments are based almost entirely upon his own teaching experience, they seem to ring true not only because of Holt's intense conviction but also because his observations are mainly of above-average students in private schools, supposedly the most favorable learning environments currently available in our society.

Teachers also can respond to the classroom role structure in a variety of ways. While many teachers seem unduly concerned with their own status and with "maintaining discipline," there is anecdotal evidence that many good teachers, especially at the elementary level, have devised ways to soften the dullness and harshness of the daily grind.[4] Alone with his own class for most of the school day, the teacher can if he chooses deal with his students in a less impersonal way than the formal dictates of his role would indicate, and can also act as a buffer between the students and the more abrasive aspects of the formal school system.

Teacher Effectiveness

Regardless of the structural defects in the student-teacher relationship, the notion persists that the teacher is important, and most readers can recall a teacher who had a distinct impact on his life for better or worse. In view of the almost universal importance attached to the teacher role, it is surprising how little can be said about the kind of teacher and teaching which produce the best learning results. Research has been done on the social background and status of teachers (some of which was reported in the preceding section), but very little is known about the relationships between what teachers *do* in the classroom and the subsequent behavior of their students.

A great deal of effort was expended during the 1940's and early 1950's in devising scales to measure teacher "effectiveness." (A number of these are described in reviews by Medley and Mitzel [1963] and Gordon and Adler [1963].) Most of these scales were developed in essentially the same way. Starting with a set of dimensions believed to be related to effectiveness, an observer visited classrooms for short intervals of time, coding the teacher's behavior with respect to the dimensions. Teachers were then designated as "good" or "poor" depending upon their classification on the scale.

Although the content of the scales varied considerably, they shared in an almost total lack of relationship to any measure of student achievement. Aside from the ridiculous categories used in many scales (for instance, "good" teachers are more likely to smile and gesture but less likely to snap their fingers or stamp their feet than poor teachers), they are based upon a fallacy "which says it is possible to judge a teacher's skill by watching him teach," that an intelligent observer "can recognize good teaching when he sees it" (Medley and Mitzel, 1963: 257).

A few clues about the kind of teacher or teaching conducive to certain kinds of learning can be pulled from scattered studies. There is some evidence that the type of training received by the teacher matters. In a study of science classes in fifty-six Minnesota high schools, Anderson (1950) found that the rate of individual student improvement (measured by comparisons of test scores at the beginning and end of the course, adjusted for students' IQ) was positively related to the teacher's having done his undergraduate work at some institution other than a teachers' college and having taken a relatively large number of science courses. Two studies have investigated the relationship between the teacher's classroom behavior as a reflection of his basic personality type and student productivity. Cogan (1958) asked students in five junior high schools to describe their teachers' control and organization of the subject matter and their degree of warmth and encouragement. Both types of variables were found to be significantly related to performance of required work and frequency of self-initiated (nonassigned) projects. Heil, Powell, and Feifer (1960) identified three teacher and four pupil personality types and then compared various teacher-student combinations. The "well-integrated, self-controlling" teacher was found most effective with all types of students. "Weakly-integrated, fearful" teachers were relatively ineffective with all types of students except "strivers." The "turbulent" type of teacher (defensively intellectual type) was effective with student "conformers" and "strivers," but not with "opposers" or "waverers," who needed a teacher equipped with greater interpersonal skills.

Strengthening the teacher-student relationship by providing teachers with information on their students' abilities, home environments, and emotional problems, and encouraging them to use this information in planning their class work, may have some positive effects. In a study by Ojemann and Wilkinson (1939), a sample of ninth graders was matched individually on IQ, home background, and past achievement, and then assigned randomly to experimental and control classes. In the experimental classes only, teachers were given comprehensive data on their students and participated in small group sessions at which student problems and possible solutions were discussed. The researchers' conclusion was that the experimental classes made greater academic gains as well as manifesting more positive attitudes toward school and fewer behavior problems. Several studies replicating the basic postulates of the Ojemann-Wilkinson study produced similar results.

There have been a number of studies in which students have been asked to describe their image of a good teacher and/or to rate their own teachers. For the most part, these studies do not add much to an understanding of teacher effectiveness, because the students' evaluations are not related to their academic performance. As a later discussion of value climates will suggest, whether the popular teacher is also the one who gets the best learning results may depend upon the extent to which such achievement is valued by the student body. In many schools the most popular teacher is simply the "easy" one.

Among the most influential research during the 1940's and 1950's were studies of leadership "style." Applied to education, the basic premise was that the teacher's quality as a leader, including how he or she sought to control the classroom situation, determined students' morale and performance. The pioneers in this research were Lewin, Lippitt, and their associates, who in the late 1930's began a series of experiments in which various leadership climates were artificially created.

In one of the best known experiments, four members of Lewin's research staff were trained in the following three leadership styles:

authoritarian. The general group goals, specific activities, and procedures for carrying them out are all dictated by the leader. However, the leader remains aloof from active participation except when demonstrating or assigning tasks;

democratic. All policies, activities, and work procedures are decided upon by the group as a whole. The leader takes an active part and tries to be a regular group member in spirit without doing too much of the work;

laissez-faire. There is complete freedom for group or individual decision-making, with a minimum of participation by the leader.

Each staff member was assigned to a club of ten-year-old boys, ostensibly to direct a variety of craft activities. In addition to selecting the groups so that they were initially comparable in the distribution of several personal and social characteristics, "The factor of personality differences in the boys was controlled by having each group pass through autocracy and then democracy, or vice versa. The factor of leader's personality was controlled by having each of the leaders play the role of autocrat and the role of democratic leader at least once." Thus, "every six weeks each group had a new leader with a different technique of leadership, each club having three leaders during the course of the five months of the experimental series" (Lewin *et al.,* 1939: 271–272, 298).

Discussions of the results of these experiments usually emphasize the higher levels of satisfaction and "group-mindedness" and the lower levels of aggression in the democratic groups (Lewin *et al.,* 1939: White and Lippitt, 1962). Less often reported is the finding that the quality of work produced was greater in the autocratic setting, although activity in this setting requires the presence of the leader—when the autocratic type of leader left the room, output tended to drop off. It is also an interesting and little reported finding that productivity in the laissez-faire setting, in which there was little formal structure and members were free to do as they pleased, went up in the absence of the leader. The authors attributed this to an observed tendency for one of the boys to assume a leadership role when the adult leader was absent. In sum, students may be happier and feel more positive toward the teacher and the other members of the group in a setting in which the adult acts essentially as one of the group and in which decisions are made via group discussion, but they may produce more when their leader tells them what to do and how to do it. And certain learning tasks may be handled effectively by giving students very little direction, forcing them to organize the situation themselves.

Recent experimental studies testing the Lewin thesis in classroom situations indicate that: (1) student productivity is not always greater, or as great, in democratic or "student-centered" classes; and (2) many students feel dissatisfied or anxious in this kind of setting. One review of forty-nine studies reported contradictory results; eleven found greater learning in student-centered groups, thirteen reported no difference, and eight found teacher-centered groups superior (Gordon and Adler, 1963). Another analysis of thirty-four such studies (Stern, 1962) found that of the eighteen in which student reaction was measured, nine were predominantly favorable, four unfavorable, and five mixed. Only two of the studies showed greater gains in cognitive knowledge of the subject matter in the democratic classes, as compared to five in which the cognitive gains were significantly less; in the rest of the studies there was no significant difference between the two types of classes. Some research based on the California F (authoritarianism) scale indicated that the type of student with high authoritarian needs is especially uncomfortable in an informal, equalitarian classroom atmosphere (Stern, 1962: 692–697).

If one can draw any conclusions from the mass of studies carried out during the past twenty-five years, they seem to be limited to the following:

there is no one "best" type of teacher or teaching for all students, probably not even one best way to teach any given student all subjects;

the focus of research should be upon the two-way interpersonal ties and interaction between teacher and student, as opposed to trying to deduce the components or effective teaching by studying the teacher alone;

some improvement in student performance as well as in the quality of student-teacher relationships might be produced by systematic efforts to match teachers more closely to the types of students and courses that fit their values, needs, and style of teaching;

full understanding of effective teacher behavior depends upon a comprehensive theory of the classroom as a social system.

During the 1960's, two promising avenues of research, each based upon at least the beginnings of a theory of the classroom, were opened. The first focuses upon the effects of the teacher's attitudes and expectations, with respect to specific students, upon the students' subsequent performance, and is best illustrated by the work of Robert Rosenthal and Lenore Jacobson. The second focuses upon the teacher's behavior, but, unlike earlier studies, relates the behavioral variables to the nature of the academic task and the type of student. There are two important studies in this area, one by Ned Flanders, the other by Wayne Gordon and Leta Adler. In each case, the translation of theory into operational definitions and research design has some flaws, so that the authors' claims cannot be said to have had a final test, but the interest and plausibility of the hypotheses, the sophistication of the design, and the relative consistency of the empirical findings make them worthy of serious consideration. The next section of this chapter will, then, be devoted to a fairly detailed examination of these three studies.

Three Classroom Studies

Rosenthal and Jacobson's experiment was designed to test the proposition that within a given classroom, "those children from whom the teacher expected greater intellectual growth would show such greater growth." The setting for the study was an elementary school in an older section of San Francisco, attended mainly by children from lower-SES, but not desperately poor, families. About one-sixth of the school's 650 students were of Mexican parentage. Students were organized into three ability tracks, based mainly upon reading performance. The lowest track classes contained disproportionate numbers of Mexican-American and lowest-income children. Another characteristic of the school was the relatively high proportion of transfers; about 30% of the school population transferred in or out during a given year.

As is appropriate in a study based upon a single school, Rosenthal makes no claims for the representativeness of his sample. Rather, by deliberately choosing a "difficult" sample—a school with a large proportion of students from subgroups whose school performance is normally lower than the population at large—he makes the findings of a limited sample seem more convincing than they might otherwise be.

The basic components of Rosenthal's research design are outlined in Exhibit 7–2. First, all children in grades one through six were given a nonverbal intelligence test, "disguised as a test designed to predict academic 'blooming' or intellectual gain." In each class, about twenty per cent of the students, *chosen by means of a table of random numbers,* were assigned to the "experimental" condition. "The names of these children were given to each teacher who was told that their scores on the 'test for intellectual blooming' indicated they would show unusual intellectual gains during the academic year. . . . The experimental treatment for these children, then, consisted of nothing more than being identified to their teachers as children

Exhibit 7–2

*Research Design of Rosenthal-Jacobson, Flanders,
and Gordon-Adler Classroom Studies*

	Rosenthal and Jacobson	Flanders: Laboratory Pre-test	Flanders: Final Classroom Test	Gordon and Adler
Sample	All children (N = 320) in grades 1–6 (18 classes) in 1 school.	1040 8th graders in 8 junior high schools.	38 8th-grade math classes; 37 7th grade social studies classes.	Pilot: 1400 7–8th graders in 38 classes. Final: 2700 6–8th graders in 79 classes in 30 schools.
Experimental and Control Groups	Exp. group = 20% of each class selected randomly. Control group = all others.	Groups of 20 each, balanced for sex and IQ, assigned randomly to one of four treatments.	Exp. classes = 8 highest + 8 lowest in "teacher direction." Control classes = all others.	No division into experimental and control groups.
Experimental Treatment	Tell teachers to expect unusual intellectual growth from children in experimental group.	40-minute lesson in one of these styles: Direct Influence / Indirect Influence. Goal Clear: Treatment I / Treatment II. Goal Ambiguous: Treatment III / Treatment IV.	2-week unit in math or geography. Observers record class interaction.	None.
Data Collected	Flanagan's TOGA (intelligence test) at beginning and end of school year.	Tests of lesson content perception of teacher influence, dependence proneness, and goal clarity before and during lesson.	Tests of course content, perception of teacher influence, dependence proneness at beginning and end of two-week unit.	STEP standardized achievement tests; questionnaires on teacher's behavior, class order, attitudes toward teacher, classmates, and school, at beginning and end of school year.

who would show unusual intellectual gains" (Rosenthal and Jacobson, 1966: 115–116). Eight months later all the children were given the same test again.

Exhibit 7–3 shows the mean gain in IQ points for experimental and control subjects at each grade level. For the school as a whole, the children from whom the teachers had been led to expect greater gain did show such gain (the difference between experimental and control group was statistically significant at the .02 level). This difference was greatest for the first and second graders; in fact, they accounted for most of the total difference, and the differences were nonexistent or even in the opposite direction for the older children.

In addition to grade level, Rosenthal controlled for ability track, sex, and ethnic group. The tendency was for the middle track—the more "average" children—to benefit most from the experimental treatment, but the differences were not statistically significant. Sex differences were similarly not large or clear. While girls who were expected to show an intellectual spurt had slightly greater gains in total IQ than boys similarly designated, the relationship was complicated in that girls were overrepresented in the higher ability track, and the sex differences were contingent upon the *types* of IQ. Rosenthal's summary of the findings involving subjects' sex was that "girls bloom more in the reasoning sphere of intellectual functioning when some kind of unspecified blooming is expected of them. Furthermore, these gains are more likely to occur to a dramatic degree in the lower grades" (Rosenthal and Jacobson, 1968: 81). In other words, high teacher expectations seem to allow children to increase their potential in the area that is not normally perceived as "natural" to their sex (reasoning for girls, verbal skills for boys), and the younger the child, the greater the chances of affecting these abilities (before the child has been rigidly socialized as to what is appropriate behavior for boys and girls—see Chapter 5).

Exhibit 7–3
Mean Gains in IQ
in Rosenthal's Experimental and Control Groups

Grade	Controls M	Controls σ	Experimentals M	Experimentals σ	Diff.	t	p†
1	12.0	16.6	27.4	12.5	15.4	2.97	.002
2	7.0	10.0	16.5	18.6	9.5	2.28	.02
3	5.0	11.9	5.0	9.3	0.0		
4	2.2	13.4	5.6	11.0	3.4		
5	17.5	13.1	17.4	17.8	—0.1		
6	10.7	10.0	10.0	6.5	—0.7		
Weighted M	8.4*	13.5	12.2**	15.0	3.8	2.15	.02

* Mean number of children per grade = 42.5   p† one-tailed
** Mean number of children per grade = 10.8   From Rosenthal and Jacobson, 1966: 116.

Among the most interesting findings were those relating to ethnic groups:

In total IQ, verbal IQ, and especially reasoning IQ, children of the minority group were more advantaged by favorable expectations than were the other children, though the differences were not statistically significant.

For each of the Mexican children the magnitude of expectancy advantage was computed by subtracting from his or her IQ gain the IQ gain made by the children of the control group in his or her classroom. The resulting magnitudes of expectancy advantage were then correlated with the "Mexican-ness" of the children's faces. . . . For total IQ and reasoning IQ, those Mexican boys who looked more Mexican benefitted more from teachers' favorable expectations than did the Mexican boys who looked less Mexican. There is no clear explanation for these findings, but we can speculate that the teachers' pre-experimental expectancies of the more Mexican-looking boys' intellectual performance were probably lowest of all. These children may have had the most to gain by the introduction of a more favorable expectation into the minds of their teachers (Rosenthal and Jacobson, 1968: 82).

In evaluating the results of Rosenthal's study, the first point is that while the findings are generally supportive of Rosenthal's hypothesis, the differences are neither consistently in the direction predicted, nor are they very large. We have noted already that in Exhibit 7–3, the difference for the school as a whole is mainly accounted for by large differences in two of the six grades tested. The multivariate analysis suggests complex patterns of interaction among such variables as sex, ability level, ethnicity, and grade in school, with no consistent overall effect of teacher expectations upon all student subgroups. If one takes these various subgroups as replications of the basic experiment, one can say only that the hypothesis is supported in some but not all cases. It should also be noted that in almost all the cases where the difference between experimental and control subjects was significant, the differences were about half a standard deviation or less in magnitude. Such a difference is moderately substantial but not dramatic.

A second type of objection has to do with Rosenthal's choice of measures. The dependent variable, performance on an intelligence test, can be criticized on the grounds that it was a single test and like all single tests limited in its range. It would have been useful to test also some of the more specific learning that took place. (Some data of this sort were undoubtedly available—for instance, results of standard achievement tests or grades in various subjects.)

Another objection about the dependent variable is procedural—that is, that in some cases, especially in the younger classes where the experimental treatment had the greatest effect, the post-test was given by the classroom teacher, who had been subjected to the experimental manipulation and who might thus, consciously or unconsciously, aid the children who were "supposed" to bloom. Rosenthal reports that retest results in groups tested by their own teacher did not differ significantly from groups tested by a school administrator who did not know which children were in the experimental group, but still one would like to see further testing controlled for possible teacher effects on the post-experimental instruments (note that this in itself would constitute a further test of the basic Rosenthal hypothesis).

With respect to the experimental variable, Rosenthal's manipulation of the teachers' expectations is dramatic, and his random selection of bloomers, by, in a sense holding constant the idiosyncracies of individual students, makes the point that this kind of treatment can produce results with virtually any kind of child and in the absence of any other stimuli to achieve. It does not, however, tell us anything about the normal selection process by which teachers come to hold different expectations for different students. A design alternative would be to manipulate the presentation of students to teachers. Given that certain kinds of children (white, middle-class, suburban) are preferred by many teachers, if one could coach students so that they more closely resembled those youngsters who are favored by the schools, this might lead to teachers' responding to these students differently. The success of researchers in prepping children for IQ and achievement tests, job interviews, and so on, an example of which was described in Chapter 6, indicates that this kind of strategy may not be as difficult as it initially appears, that, indeed, it may be easier to change the attitudes and behavior of children than those of adult educators!

Some of the weakness in the data and its interpretation arise from the unavoidable limitations of any single-school study. Because the total number of subjects was only about 320, of whom only about 65 were in the experimental group, the researchers could say little about the characteristics of children who are most affected by rising expectations. The analysis controlling in turn for sex, ethnic group, and ability group indicated complex patterns of effect, and Rosenthal did attempt to gather some clues from detailed case studies of a small subsample of his subjects. However, in the absence of enough cases to hold constant a number of variables simultaneously, understanding of the pattern of relationships is impossible. Similarly, the limited number of *classes* (18) allows little analysis of the kinds of teachers or teaching which are most responsive to manipulation of expectations.

Finally, Rosenthal himself raises an important missing element. As he puts it in the summary chapter of his book, "we can only speculate as to *how teachers brought about intellectual competence* simply by expecting it." A number of possibilities are suggested—paying more attention to these children, treating them in a pleasanter or more encouraging fashion, using new or different teaching techniques, evaluating them differently, demanding more of them. Even by "facial expression, posture, and perhaps by her touch, the teacher may have communicated to the children of the experimental group that she expected improved intellectual performance" (Rosenthal and Jacobson, 1968: 180; italics mine). The point is, though, that these are simply speculations, and that in order to learn how attitudes get translated into actual classroom behavior, the researcher needs to *be* in the classroom. An important characteristic of the next study is that the researcher did gather data, from observation of ongoing classroom sessions, about what teachers actually *do*.

Flanders' Study of Teacher Behavior

The first of the two studies on teacher behavior posits that student performance is a function of the simultaneous effects of teacher behavior, student needs, and the nature of the learning task. In a pair of experiments, the first a pre-test for the second (see Exhibit 7–2 for the design of the two parts), Flanders tested a set of hypotheses interrelating the following variables:

Teacher Influence. This behavioral variable included the relative amounts of teacher and student participation during a given segment of class time *plus* the quality of the teacher's behavior in terms of the degree to which he or she dominated the interaction rather than encouraging student contributions. Flanders' measure consists of ten categories of communication behavior. Seven are for various kinds of teacher talk; two for student talk; and one for pauses, short periods of silence, or simultaneous talk by several people. These ten categories are listed and described in Exhibit 7–4. The interaction is recorded by classroom observers who write down at three-second intervals the category which best describes the communication event(s) completed in that interval. The "data" thus consist of a list of numbers, which represent the sequence of events in the class.[5]

Student Perception of Teacher Behavior. This variable measured the degree to which students themselves agreed with the measures obtained for Variable 1. It was measured by a shortened version of the Minnesota Student Attitude Inventory.

Student Dependence. Students vary with respect to their need for regular supervision, response, or support from the teacher—with respect to their dependence "proneness." Flanders hypothesized that the effectiveness of given patterns of teacher behavior can be understood only in the context of the needs of the particular students with whom the teacher interacts. Students were classified on a scale constructed by Flanders, based upon their agreement or disagreement with forty-five statements such as the following:

> I hesitate to ask for help from others.
> It's fun to try out ideas that others think are crazy.
> What others think of me does not bother me.
> In class it is best to go along with the majority even when you disagree.

Student Learning. This was measured by content tests on curriculum units in math and geography. Both curriculum and tests were designed by the researchers.

Exhibit 7–4
Flanders' Catagories for Interaction Analysis

TEACHER TALK

Indirect Influence

1.* Accepts Feeling: accepts and clarifies the feeling tone of the students in a nonthreatening manner. Feelings may be positive or negative. Predicting or recalling feelings are included.
2.* Praises or Encourages: praises or encourages student action or behavior. Jokes that release tension, not at the expense of another individual, nodding head or saying, "um hm? or "go on" are included.
3.* Accepts or Uses Ideas of Student: clarifying, building, or developing ideas suggested by a student. As teacher brings more of his own ideas into play, shift to category five.
4.* Asks Questions: asking a question about content or procedure with intent that a student answer.

Direct Influence

5.* Lecturing: giving facts or opinions about content or procedure; expressing his own ideas, asking rhetorical questions.
6.* Giving Directions: directions, commands, or orders with which a student is expected to comply.
7.* Criticizing or Justifying Authority: statements intended to change student behavior from nonacceptable to acceptable pattern; bawling someone out; stating why the teacher is doing what he is doing; extreme self-reference.

STUDENT TALK

8.* Student Talk–Response: talk by students in response to teacher. Teacher initiates the contact or solicits student statement.
9.* Student Talk–Initiation: talk by students which they initiate. If "calling on" student is only to indicate who may talk next, observer must decide whether student wanted to talk. If he did, use this category.

10.* Silence or Confusion: pauses, short periods of silence, and periods of confusion in which communication cannot be understood by the observer.

---

* There is no scale implied by these numbers. Each number is classificatory; it designates a particular kind of communication event. To write these numbers down during observation is to enumerate, not to judge a position on a scale.   From Flanders, 1960: Appendix F.

Flanders' general hypothesis was that student learning will be greatest when the teacher's influence is relatively indirect, although the strength of this relationship will vary with the students' own dependency needs. A fifth variable having to do with the clarity of the task as perceived by the students was dropped from the second experiment after the pre-test revealed no difference in response to a series of questions asking how clearly students understood what they were doing, even though the explanation of the assignment was purposely varied in different groups. Apparently junior high students either will not admit it if they do not understand what they are told to do, or they will interpret the question in a very general way (in response to the question: "What are you doing?," one may answer: "I'm doing my geometry," without specifying the exact nature of one's activities).

The subjects for Flanders' study were eighth graders from a number of Minneapolis-St. Paul junior high schools. In the pre-test, a laboratory experiment, subjects were put into temporary groups balanced for sex and IQ distribution. Groups of twenty each were assigned to one of the four types shown in Exhibit 7–2 (there were six or seven groups in each of the four cells). An experimental session lasted about forty minutes, within which students were taught a lesson in either math or social studies and were given tests measuring dependency proneness, goal preception, and content learning. A trained member of the research team taught all the sessions of a given subject.

The post-test covered the same two content areas. However, here the population sampled was *classrooms* (rather than individual students of different types). The sampling procedure was quite complex but can be summarized roughly as follows: all students in thirty-eight math and thirty-seven social studies classes whose teachers had earlier indicated willingness to participate in the project filled out questionnaires about the kinds of social patterns existing in their classes (Variable 2). Class averages were calculated, and the eight classes in each subject ranking highest in teacher direct influence and the eight ranking highest in indirect influence were designated for use in the study.

The teachers designated as highest on direct and indirect teaching style taught a two-week unit to their regular classes. Teachers were free to use the materials prepared as they wished, but the units were more or less the same in all classes. During the two weeks, trained observers in the classroom recorded the interaction using the scheme described in connection with Variable 1. All students were given pre- and post-tests measuring the other major study variables.

On the basis of the observation, the teachers were classified on a simple "I/D ratio," which consisted of the total number of tallies in categories 1 through 3 divided by the total in categories 6 and 7 (see Exhibit 7–4). Categories 4 and 5 initially were included in the calculation of the I/D ratio, but later were eliminated in order to make the figure "more independent of the subject matter being taught." (Note that the I/D ratio also served as a kind of validator of the students' perception measure, which was used to select the classes for the study.)

The first experiment provided some but not very strong support for

Flanders' hypotheses. In the geometry sessions, there was a consistent tendency for indirect teacher influence to be related to higher student performance, but the relationship was statistically significant only for students of average IQ (students were divided into three IQ categories) and for those who were most dependent. In the social studies sessions, however, there were no significant effects of teacher influence, goal clarity, or any of the other variables. The data also indicated some trends toward lower levels of dependency resulting from the indirect teaching situation, but the results were not statistically significant.

The second year's field experiment, using a larger sample and revised research instruments and scoring system, produced more substantial support for Flanders' predicted interrelationships. Exhibit 7–5 shows that in general, students in classes whose teachers had a high proportion of indirect relative to direct acts gain more than classes whose teachers had more direct teaching styles. In the top half of Exhibit 7–5:

> . . . the achievement of the seven indirect classes is compared with the eight direct classes for social studies. The difference between a mean of 36.4 and 33.4 is significant beyond the 0.01 level. . . . [Similarly in the bottom half of the table] the difference between the mathematics means of the seven indirect and nine direct classes shows superior achievement in the indirect classes.
>
> In those mathematics and social studies classrooms in which the teacher had a higher I/D ratio, the students scored significantly higher on a measure of achievement controlled for initial ability. There is no evidence to support the notion that students of above average, average, or below average I.Q. respond differently to direct and indirect influence (Flanders, 1960: 89).

In a further analysis comparing only the five most direct with the five most indirect classes, this relationship was even more pronounced, although here the above average students were the ones most affected by teaching style (a finding at variance with the results of the pre-test). In addition to showing higher achievement, the students in the indirect classes tended to have more favorable attitudes toward the class.

One important prediction which was somewhat supported by the first experiment but not by the second was that students scoring high on the dependence proneness test would react differently to patterns of direct and indirect influence. There were no differences in achievement means between students with high and low dependence scores in either subject or either type of influence.

A more or less unanticipated finding was that *all* teachers used a great amount of direct influence. The difference was that "indirect" teachers were more likely to differentiate their type of influence in terms of the type of task or the stage within the two-week unit. That is, they were more flexible in their use of influence.[6]

Exhibit 7–5

Means and Variance of Adjusted Final Test by IQ Group

Teacher Style	Intelligence			Adjusted Final Test	
	IQ Group	Mean IQ	N	Mean	Variance
Social Studies Indirect N = 7	High	124.7	59	38.7	13.3
	Average	110.9	91	36.3	20.5
	Low	94.8	33	33.0	38.2
	All	112.4	183	36.4	34.2
Direct N = 8	High	123.3	38	35.7	18.9
	Average	109.2	101	33.8	31.2
	Low	93.8	59	31.1	38.4
	All	107.3	198	33.4	33.4
Mathematics Indirect N = 7	High	122.1	51	31.3	44.7
	Average	106.9	100	28.9	38.7
	Low	93.1	33	24.2	30.0
	All	108.7	184	28.7	43.5
Direct N = 9	High	122.9	42	29.3	40.1
	Average	107.1	77	27.3	38.8
	Low	91.6	60	23.3	23.7
	All	105.6	179	26.4	38.8

From Flanders, 1960: 90.

The great strength of Flanders' study is that it is based upon extensive but systematic observation of actual classroom behavior (not, as Medley and Mitzel justifiably criticized, upon simply "watching the teacher teach," but upon relating teacher behavior to the characteristics of the students and the learning tasks) and that the instrument for classifying the teacher's behavior was based upon a thorough review of previous work and a relatively sophisticated model of group behavior. The study is also unique in that the researchers tested their hypotheses in both a laboratory and a field setting.

As in the Rosenthal study, one can raise questions about the translation of concepts into operational variables, and about the statistical analysis. What is most disappointing about this report, however, is that Flanders does not really exploit the possibilities of his interaction analysis scheme. As he himself says: "Perhaps the most exciting part of this system of observation is the large number of interpretations that can be made from a matrix that are directly relevant to assessing teaching influence." Although the I/D ratio used in the main body of this report is "useful as a crude classifying procedure in the early phases of statistical analysis," such a simple measure does not begin to explore the analytical potentialities. In an appendix to the report, Flanders describes some interesting matrix patterns. One would hope to see more of this kind of analysis in the future.

Gordon and Adler's Study of Perceived Teacher Behavior

The Gordon and Adler study is in certain respects an extension of Lewin's attempts to define and test different modes of group leadership. Like Flanders, Gordon and Adler are indebted to Bales and, also like Flanders, Gordon and Adler studied the interrelationship among several behavioral and attitudinal variables, although, as the following description will show, these variables were conceptualized and measured quite differently.

Teacher Leadership. As we have just seen, Flanders measured teacher behavior in two ways, one by his Interaction Analysis scheme, the second by students' responses to questionnaire items about their teachers' behavior. The second measure was used mainly in the selection of the sample and as a validator of the first measure. Gordon and Adler's measures were based entirely upon student reports. Although their stated objective was to contribute to a theory of classroom leadership, "including necessary methodological accouterments such as systematic observation of teacher behavior within discreet categories over a long period of time," in both the pilot and final study, "pupils' perception of teacher behavior was chosen as the most appropriate means of observation to avoid the disturbance of the teacher's normal classroom style by outside observers, for reasons of administrative efficiency in conducting the study, but primarily because it was assumed that the pupils' observation was the most valid for the interest of the study, to predict the effect of teacher behavior on pupils" (Gordon and Adler, 1963: 115).

The three dimensions of teacher leadership reflect the influence of Bales:

task dimension: "the extent to which the teacher organized activity in the classroom in order to maximize specific goals in a program of learning." This scale is based upon 7 items, including: Does the teacher see to it that you complete all of the written assignments? What does this teacher most often do when he is teaching the class something new and pupils don't understand?

authority dimension: "the right of the teacher to control the actions of pupils in the classroom and to employ sanctions to enforce this control. . . . A teacher is considered high in the use of authority to the extent that he invokes the principle of uncritical acceptance as he initiates classroom activities and makes decisions." The nine-item scale used in the final study included: Do pupils have to get permission to leave their seats? When the class starts a new unit, who plans how you will do the work?

expressive dimension: the extent to which the teacher "acts to maximize the interests of pupils. . . . He may do this by himself using warmth and affection in his interaction with pupils, by being helpful and fair, by crediting pupils' ideas, effort, and feeling." The final scale contained 11 items, including: Does this teacher try to make the class enjoyable for the pupils? Does this teacher make sure you learn the facts or is he more interested in how pupils feel about things?

Pupil Productivity. This was measured by the gain (fall-to-spring difference) in scores on the reading, writing, and mathematics battery of the Sequential Test of Educational Progress (STEP).

Pupil Morale. Four kinds of satisfaction were measured: (1) school morale (I feel good about coming to school; I like to miss school); (2) work morale (I am making good progress in my school work for this class; My school work makes me feel nervous); (3) peer morale (Members of this class are friendly to me; I feel unhappy about the way I get along with the members of my class); and (4) teacher morale (I think this is an extremely good teacher; I dislike my teacher).

Pupil Compliance. This measure included questions asking respondents how often they *really* did various kinds of homework, how often they engaged in volunteer work (reading extra books, bringing things to school), and how orderly their classroom was (including their own conduct as well as the conduct of the class as a whole).

Like Flanders' study, Gordon and Adler's consisted of a pilot study, in which research instruments were tested and hypotheses formulated for a second larger study. In this case, however, the setting and data-gathering techniques were the same in both phases, the final study differing only in the size of sample (see Exhibit 7–2).

Findings. The first step in the data analysis was to examine the relationships among the three dimensions of teacher behavior.[7] Exhibit 7–6 shows the correlations between these dimensions in the pilot and final studies. (The scales in the final phase contained a few more items, and all items with affective content were eliminated or shifted to the expressive scale.)

Exhibit 7–6
Correlations Among Leadership Variables

	Pilot Study	Final Study
	(N = 38 Classes)	(N = 74 Classes)
Task X Authority	—.40	—.09
Authority X Expressive	—.46	—.47
Task X Expressive	.22	.32
Task X Authority, controlling for Expressive	—.40	.08
Authority X Expressive, controlling for Task	—.58	.20
Task X Expressive, controlling for Authority	—.04	.47

Data from Gordon and Adler, 1963: 23, 135–136.

Contrary to expectation, the task and authority dimensions were not positively correlated—a coefficient of −.40 was found in the pilot study and virtually no relationship in the final study. Another unexpected finding was that task orientation and expressive orientation were apparently not antithetical; they had a low but positive correlation. The negative correlation between the authority and expressive dimensions was as expected.

The bottom half of Exhibit 7–6 shows the partial correlations between each pair of dimensions with the third dimension controlled. The relationship between task and authority orientation did not change when the expressiveness scores were held constant. In the pilot study the negative relationship between authority and expressiveness was even greater with task orientation controlled, and the relationship between task and expressiveness was reduced almost to zero when authority was controlled. By contrast, in the final study the task-authority relationship was almost nonexistent, in both total and partial correlations. This was apparently the result of shifting all affective content into the expressive scale, which also accounted for the increased correlation between the task and expressive dimensions (Gordon and Adler, 1963: 136).

The major objective of the study, though, was to determine the effects of teacher leadership upon pupil productivity, and here Gordon and Adler hypothesized curvilinear relationships. In the case of the expressive and task dimensions, they predicted that higher scores would be positively related to learning up to a point, after which additional increments of expressive or task behavior would go with a leveling off in achievement. A reverse relationship was predicted for the authority dimension.

The technique used to test these predictions was regression analysis.[8] The regression line for the relationship between reading gain scores and teacher authority scale scores, shown in Exhibit 7–7, clearly supports the hypothesized curve. Increasing authority produced less and less gain until the middle range of gain scores, after which the line curved up again, with the most authoritarian teachers producing the highest reading gains. The same type of curve was found between teacher authority and all other types of learning and for a composite gain score combining all the learning measures. On the expressive dimension, the relationship was also curvilinear for reading score gains, but the curve was reversed—that is, increases in expressiveness produced greater gains until somewhat past the middle range of scores, after which it dropped sharply. None of the remaining expressiveness regressions and none of the regressions on the task dimension differed significantly from a linear regression, although all indicated some curve in the shape predicted.

Gordon and Adler also did regression analyses relating teacher style with morale and pupil compliance. Increases in the use of expressive behavior tended to go with higher morale, but expressive behavior contributed to classroom conformity only when it was supporting a task commitment or when it was used to activate compliance as an end in itself. Task-oriented behavior was positively related to compliance, and it initially contributed

Exhibit 7-7

Regression Line for Adjusted Reading Gain on Teacher Authority Scale Scores

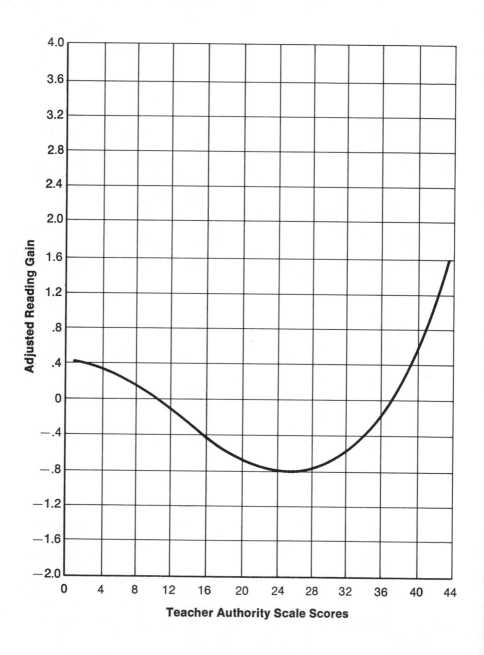

to morale, but the curve leveled off when the middle range of morale scores was reached. Increases in the use of authority had a negative effect on morale, though this curve also leveled off after a point. The relationship between authority and compliance was curvilinear, with middle authority producing the lowest morale as well as the lowest compliance.

The relating of all of the pupil effect variables showed that learning gain was positively correlated with compliance with assigned work and class order but not with high morale. As the Lewin studies already have suggested, learning productivity and group satisfaction apparently have different origins.

In order to synthesize all of the individual findings, the authors formed composite leadership "modes" by combining the scale scores between designated cutting points on the three leadership scales and assigning a letter to each of the modes thus obtained. The designation of modes and their relationship to student behavior is shown in Exhibit 7–8. This cross-classification of dimensions produced eighteen possible leadership modes (note that the task scale was cut into two segments and the authority and expressive dimensions into three segments each), although this sample of teachers was distributed into only twelve of the eighteen modes established, and some of these modes contained only one or a few cases.

The figures in each cell tell the rank of that leadership mode with respect to the various dependent variables. For example, Mode A, a teaching style which combines low scores on all three leadership dimensions, ranked low (11th place) on total learning gain, about in the middle (tied for fifth place) on class order, in ninth place for voluntary student work, tenth place for compliance, and last place for general morale.

The teacher style which came closest to maximizing all student effects was Mode G, which combined middle or high task orientation, middle expressiveness and low authority. Mode H, like G, except for greater emphasis on the expressive dimension, ranked high on everything except learning gain. Maximum learning was obtained when the teacher had high authority but low task orientation (Mode F), although this style produced low levels of class order and volunteer work. Moreover, what maximized student learning did not necessarily maximize morale. Modes D and H, which had the highest ranks on the latter both ranked low on the former. The lowest sets of student effects were produced by Modes A and C, both relatively low on all the leadership dimensions.

Exhibit 7–8 must be interpreted with caution, since the particular choice of cutting points on the three dimensions and the number of cells with few or no cases may well affect the rankings. And as the earlier analysis showed, the majority of relationships between teacher and student dimensions were curvilinear rather than linear. However, the overall pattern of the table does suggest that no single style clearly maximizes all desirable student effects. Though some are more effective than others, the best "mix" of dimensions depends upon what student effects one is most interested in. High academic

Exhibit 7–8 *Rank of Teacher Leadership Modes on Total Gain, General Class Order, Volunteer Work, Compliance, and General Morale*

Task	Authority		Low			Middle and High		
			Low	**Middle**	**High**	**Low**	**Middle**	**High**
	Low		Mode A	Mode C	Mode E		Mode I	Mode K
		Total gain	11	10	6		5	7
		Class order	5.5	10.5	8		10.5	4
		Volunteer work	9	10	8		12	7
		Compliance with assignments	10	11	1		8	4
		General morale	12	10	11		9	5
			Mode B	Mode D	Mode F	Mode G	Mode J	Mode L
Expressive	Middle	Total gain	3	12	1	2	9	4
		Class order	9	5.5	12	3	7	2
		Volunteer work	3	6	11	1	5	4
		Compliance with assignments	7	12	5	2	9	6
		General morale	7	1	4	3	8	6
	High					Mode H		
		Total gain				8		
		Class order				1		
		Volunteer work				2		
		Compliance with assignments				3		
		General morale				2		

From Gordon and Adler, 1963: 258.

gains were produced by teaching mixes containing both high and low levels of authority and task orientation (Modes F, G, and B), though in each case the levels of other kinds of student effects varied. And what produced the greatest gains in learning was seldom what produced the highest levels of student morale or classroom order.

Like the other two studies, this one has great strengths and some disappointing features. Of the three studies, this one involves the least manipulation of the classroom situation by the researchers, which has both advantages (the small likelihood of the kind of experimenter effects which bias data) and disadvantages (as in the Rosenthal study, we are frustrated by not knowing just what the teacher *does* to produce the student effects obtained). And to depend entirely upon the reports of junior high students for the measure of teacher behavior clearly introduces the possibility of additional bias. The comparability of the three studies is now limited, due to the differences in research design—for example, the samples varied in size, age, and geographical location, and the measures of learning varied from intelligence test scores (Rosenthal) to scores on standardized achievement tests (Gordon and Adler) to results on tests designed by the researcher to measure knowledge of the content of specially designed curriculum units (Flanders). All merit replication and further revision and variation, both to solve some of the measurement problems which still remained following these limited tests and to make possible a real synthesis of the various approaches and findings.

Student Effectiveness

While we are still far from a comprehensive sociological theory of what constitutes effective teaching, there is a great quantity of empirical research on the teaching role, and we have given considerable attention to three studies that combine at least a partial theory of the classroom with an intelligent research design. There is no comparable body of empirical research on the student role. Although the studies discussed in the previous sections have obvious implications, most experiments on the student role per se have been in the form of experimental schools built upon the ideology or personality of the founders rather than upon studies which systematically examine the effects of variations in the student role.

A myriad of experimental schools and courses have focused upon increasing student activity and autonomy with respect to learning. At the extreme in this direction is the Summerhill model (Neill, 1961), now having a revival in this country in the form of the "free school" movement. In a Summerhill or free school, children are viewed as capable of organizing themselves to achieve their own learning goals. The assumption is that if all adult controls are removed, children will direct their energies toward learning what truly interests them rather than toward resisting adult efforts to coerce them into learning what adults think is important. Thus students at a free school have a voice in the content and organization of classes—even the decision of whether or not to attend class is up to the individual student. Adult expertise and opinion are available and used when they contribute to the attainment of some specific project. Ideally, a variety of learning materials are available, but the emphasis is upon approaches that "make the student himself the content of his learning" (Portola Institute, 1970).

The effectiveness of the Summerhill model must still be considered hypothetical, since to date empirical evidence on the intellectual attainments (in creativity and pleasure as well as more conventional forms of achievement) of students in such schools is not available. Most literature on such schools focuses upon the effects upon personality development, but even here empirical evaluation has not been encouraged. Another barrier to evaluation is that most free schools enroll few students (the average is around fifty) and the free school "mortality rate" has been high (although the names of 800 new schools were added to the New Schools Exchange[9] in 1969, the average life span of free schools on the exchange list is only about eighteen months (Stretch, 1970: 78).

In a few experiments the notion of student self-responsibility has been operationalized more rigorously and the effects upon academic attainment measured. Under the Penn State Pyramid plan, for example, much of the class work in psychology courses is carried on in small groups composed of six freshmen, six sophomores, two juniors who are assistant leaders, and a senior group leader who has been trained by the faculty. Not only is the gap between teacher and taught narrowed in terms of age and status, but many students are put in the position of being teachers as well as learners so that they must "take in" the material covered in the course in such a way that they can pass it on to slightly younger students. Comparison of test data collected from "pyramid" classes and control classes has shown that students in the former are higher on "knowledge of the field of psychology, scientific thinking, use of the library for scholarly reading, intellectual orientation, and resourcefulness in problem solving." In addition, a higher proportion of these students continued as psychology majors (McKeachie, 1962: 333).

In between the carefully planned structure of the Penn State Pyramid plan and the purposeful lack of structure of the free school is the "open classroom," which depends for its effectiveness upon the richness of the environment planned and presented by the teacher, but which gives children fairly free choice within that environment and allows for "a little bit of chaos." The open classroom is probably the most influential and widely adopted innovation which emphasizes student activity and autonomy, and it will be discussed in some detail in the final chapter.[10]

Another dimension of potential change in the student role focuses upon his attitudes toward school and learning. The Jackson study showed that high proportions of students were bored or otherwise discontented with their current life in the classroom. One of the major goals of the free school is to promote joy in learning. (The assumption is that if the child has an absolutely free hand in the selection of classroom activities, he will both enjoy and master the tasks he has chosen.) The open classroom model also emphasizes the satisfactions of learning, but it does not assume that children know how to plan a course of study that is both enjoyable and profitable, nor that the choices provided by adults will necessarily be unattractive to children.

As in the case of achievement motivation, there is a common belief that children who are doing well in school are the happiest. Jackson's review of the data available on this subject[11] concluded, however, that the "best milk comes from contented cows" theory does not apply to academic learning. Only one out of over thirty correlations between attitudinal and achievement indicators was statistically significant. Moreover, Jackson found no relationships even when he removed the students with neutral or moderate attitudes from his analysis and recomputed the correlation coefficients with only students who strongly liked or disliked school. In sum, "such evidence as does exist points to an absence of a direct link between the way students view their school life and their relative mastery of academic objectives" (Jackson, 1968: 75).

Conclusions

The conventional classroom role structure is not conducive to the active involvement of most students in the learning process, but rather seems designed to promote distance and distrust between the roles of student and teacher. Early studies of teachers and teaching techniques tended to segment the characteristics and behavior of the teacher from the other elements of the classroom situation, and about all one could conclude was that there is no "best" way to teach all students and subjects. The most promising recent studies suggest that achievement can be raised if teachers expect a lot of their students[12] and if they conduct their classes in a relatively flexible fashion, using more indirect modes of communication and encouraging a greater amount of active student participation. A teaching style combining low authoritarianism with moderate to high task orientation and expressiveness seems to maximize the total range of positive effects (from learning gains to student morale to classroom orderliness), but various combinations of effects can also be obtained from very different modes of leadership. High learning gains, for example, can be obtained by relatively authoritarian modes of teaching. In general, a moderate position on any of the teaching dimensions studied produced greater learning gains than either extremely high or extremely low authoritarianism, expressiveness, or task orientation.

While the limited evidence available generally points to a higher degree of activity and autonomy for the student role, the lack of empirical studies designed to test student role alternatives and the small amount of well-documented applied research focused upon making students more responsible for their own learning testifies to our reluctance to make fundamental changes in the formal learning system. Part of this reluctance may be due to the conventional ways of viewing children in our society. Part may be due to the nature of the classroom itself. In the next chapter we shall continue our examination of the classroom by turning our attention from its role structure to its dynamics as a small social system.

Notes

1. A statistical technique for testing the significance of the differences among the means of more than two samples. Blalock, 1960: Chapter 16.

2. Measured by respondents' estimates of the percentage of white students in *all* of their classes. While this was the only measure of this variable available to McPartland, note its weaknesses, including dependence upon the accuracy of these students' estimates, and the fact that the estimate is made over *all* classes and thus conceals whether the proportion was relatively consistent over all or whether some classes contained a racial mixture and others were totally or mainly segregated, or whether most contained a mixture of integrated and segregated classes.

3. "Classroom life, in my judgement, is too complex an affair to be viewed or talked about from any single perspective. Accordingly, as we try to grasp the meaning of what school is like for students and teachers, we must not hesitate to use all the ways of knowing at our disposal. This means we must read and look, and listen, and count things, and talk to people, and even muse introspectively over the memories of our own childhood" (Jackson, 1968: vii–viii). Jackson admits frankly that some of the studies he includes in his book "would hardly pass muster in an undergraduate course on research design"—his justification being that they are about important topics not covered by more sophisticated research and researchers.

4. See, for example, Jackson, 1968: Chapter 4.

5. For a full description of the measure and the observer procedures, see Flanders, 1960: Appendix F. Flanders' measure is based upon a more elaborate and general scheme for the analysis of interaction in small groups developed by Bales and his colleagues at the Harvard Social Relations Laboratory—see, for example, Bales, 1952.

6. The relative flexibility of successful teachers is echoed in Jackson's finding that the teaching style of fifty elementary teachers identified by their superiors as "outstanding" was characterized by spontaneity, informality, and a deep concern for the well-being of individual students, and that they justified most of their actions on the grounds of feelings and intuition rather than general pedagogical theory. Since classrooms, especially at the elementary level, are busy places in which the interchange is fast and not very predictable, the best teachers are probably those who can respond in a flexible manner and can improvise to meet the needs of the moment rather than forcing an abstract model onto all events (Jackson, 1968: Chapter 4).

7. The researchers were able to form Guttman scales corresponding to the three leadership dimensions, using class medians for questionnaire items having to do with teacher behavior. The procedure for obtaining these scales is described in Gordon and Adler, 1963: 20–22. For a more general discussion of Guttman scaling, see Riley, 1963: Chapter 9; or Riley *et al.*, 1954.

8. See Chapter 3, footnote 3.

9. A clearing house for information on free schools, located in Santa Barbara, California.

10. See also Gross and Gross, 1970: Featherstone: 1967a.

11. The six studies reanalyzed by Jackson sampled over 3000 students in fifteen schools located in several regions of the United States. They cover a period of twenty-five years. Five different attitudinal measures and achievement measures ranging from grades to standard test scores were used.

12. Note that this parallels the findings in Chapter 4 that the *parents* of high achievers have high aspirations for their children and set high standards for their behavior.

The Class as a Social System   Chapter 8

*Only in schools do thirty or more people spend several hours each day liter-
ally side by side. Once we leave the classroom we seldom again are required
to have contact with so many people for so long a time.*   Philip Jackson

*I think that what we need is not to touch up or modernize classrooms but
rather to eliminate them. (Question from the audience: "Where would we
learn?" Answer: "We'd manage.")*   Jerry Farber

In this chapter we shall turn from the internal role structure of the classroom to its workings as a social system. As the Jackson quotation suggests,
the class is in some respects analogous to a crowd—in it, a fairly large
number of individuals are in close physical proximity. This may explain
partially why teachers often seem to be so obsessed with discipline and
control, with not letting students get "out of hand." One way to maintain
order in a crowd is to have a clear authority hierarchy with clearly institutionalized dominance and subordination. As we saw in the last chapter,
this is a characteristic of the traditional teacher-student relationship (and
we shall see in later chapters that it also describes the role structure of
the school and of the total educational system in a school district).

Another mechanism for maintaining order is to have a regular institutionalized sequence of events. As Jackson points out, one can enter a classroom almost anywhere in our country and recognize what is going on. This
is because:

there is a limited number of forms of classroom activity: seat work, teacher
lecture or demonstration, oral recitation, and group discussion almost
exhaust the repertoire. And most so-called educational innovations are
really a variation, often disguised by technological gadgetry, of one of
these basic tasks.

all activities are organized into a schedule—the pledge of allegiance is followed by reading at 8:30, which is followed by arithmetic at 9:00, which is followed by social studies. . . . The music teacher comes for an hour on Tuesday mornings, and the art teacher on Thursdays. And so on. There is an almost holy aura about the schedule, and it takes an event of crisis proportions to change it.

While the details and the order of events varies from one location to another, the basic structure of the "daily grind" is common to most. In addition to the rigidity of the schedule as a whole, each individual activity has its own rules—no loud talking during seat work, raise your hand to talk during discussion, keep your eyes on your own paper during tests. Note that the goal of much educational reform, including the free school and open classroom models, is to break up the ritualistic, cyclic quality of classroom life; in the latter by making a rich variety of materials and activities available from which the student can make a choice, and in the former by doing away with the schedule altogether and allowing the mass behavior of the crowd to develop freely—and occcasionally to erupt.

In the following sections, we shall take up some of the factors which affect how the class operates: its size and composition, in particular the degree of homogeneity and the structure of the communications system, and the reward system and structure of interpersonal attraction. For this discussion, we shall draw from diverse areas of sociology. For example, one way to analyze the classroom is in terms of the features it shares with small social groups generally, and for this many findings from the literature on small groups are relevant. Similarly the studies in industrial sociology having to do with productivity in factory and other work groups suggest many parallels to the classroom situation.

Size

The variable of group size illustrates the tendency to cling to an established pedogogical view despite persistent lack of evidence to support it. One of the basic tenets of our educational system is the value of the small classroom. Any report on a school or school system includes statistics on class size, and educators frequently use a small student-teacher ratio as one of the factors explaining a good school system and a large ratio as an excuse for a poor one. In virtually all of the recent teacher strikes and other confrontations between militant teacher groups and school administrations, one of the demands is for smaller classes. From the teacher's point of view, smaller classes are an obvious convenience. Fewer students mean fewer papers and tests to grade, fewer individuals with whom to communicate, a smaller probability of a classroom getting "out of control," and so on. The relevant question here, however—and the grounds upon which demands for smaller classes ostensibly are made—is whether size is meaningfully related to learning efficiency.

Research in this area has not been characterized by a high level of sophistication or rigor (possibly related to the education profession's vested interest in small classes, mentioned above), and it does not establish the superiority of either large or small classes. (See Watson, 1963, for some studies on the high school level; McKeachie, 1962; and Dubin and Taveggia, 1968, for studies on the college level.) The results of a recent experiment at the elementary level deal a devastating blow to the small class proponents. The first extensive evaluation of the New York City MES (More Effective Schools) program, which was designed to upgrade the academic performance of children in ghetto schools and which involved, among other changes, a substantial reduction in the student-teacher ratio, indicated that MES had, at most, a brief positive effect—one not maintained beyond the first two years of the program (Fox, 1968). Finally, in an elaborate crosscultural study comparing the mathematics achievement of children in the United States and eleven other countries (Husen, 1967), Japan, the country which consistently showed the highest achievement, also had the highest average class size (over 40).

When one considers the size differences which can actually be compared in most schools, the lack of effect of class size is not really surprising. The reduction of a class from, say, thirty-five to thirty students does not require any basic changes in the way it is organized and conducted. A reduction to ten or fifteen might make a difference, but from a practical point of view, this class size is unlikely in most of our public schools, even if found to be significantly more effective.

What seems more likely is that size alone is not a strong determining factor but rather is related to *other* factors which affect classroom productivity. For example, if one compares classes in a well-to-do suburb with those in the central city, the latter probably will be larger in size but lower in academic achievement—an indirect relationship between size and performance. But if one compares urban and rural schools, the latter will probably have smaller classes and lower achievement. In other words, size may be a causal factor, but it can be understood only when considered simultaneously with other factors.

Another possibility is that size affects different aspects of group functioning in different ways. McKeachie suggests that the apparent lack of relationship between class size and productivity may be due to two effects working in opposite directions. On the one hand, increasing size increases the resources of a group (the total pool of information available and the opportunities for feedback). On the other hand, it diminishes the possibility of getting the maximum contribution from all members.

Although the size of a class as a whole is not susceptible to manipulation in most school systems, it is possible to break down a class of any size into a number of smaller subgroups. At the subgroup level, research in the small groups area of school psychology offers clues about optimum group size.

One of the initial issues raised in small groups research was whether a group of *any* size had advantages over the individual. To put it another way —do individuals working together solve problems or learn faster or better than they would working alone? The answer seems to depend upon the nature of the learning task. For example, in a fairly early study, Shaw (1932) found that groups were more efficient than individuals at problems that had a single correct answer, especially if the final answer depended upon reaching correct solutions at several intermediate stages. Shaw's interpretation was that someone in a group was likely to catch a member's errors, and that individuals were prevented from pursuing unprofitable lines of reasoning. Other experiments have shown group performance to be superior to individual performance on a variety of tasks, although there seems to be a ceiling on the complexity of problems which a group can handle well, and groups are relatively better at solving specific problems than at more creative tasks (for instance, better at solving problems and puzzles than at designing them). One study (Perlmutter *et al.,* 1952) has indicated that individuals' productivity can be increased by placing them successively in group and individual situations; individuals who first had a group work experience performed better on a memorization task than individuals who did not have an initial group experience.

One might deduce from the above findings that increasing the size of the group would thereby increase problem-solving efficiency. However, a number of studies have shown little difference between groups of from two to five members, and in terms of "unit efficiency" (total time to reach a solution based upon the number of group members), Bales and Borgotta (1953) found a curvilinear rather than a linear relationship between size and efficiency. That is, there may be diminishing returns in simply increasing group size. At least one researcher (South, 1927) has found that smaller groups perform better than larger ones on more abstract problems.

Increasing group size has a number of different ramifications bearing on group efficiency. Bales' research has pointed to increasing role differentiation with increasing size, with the leaders taking over an ever greater share of the interaction. There is an extensive, though not consistent, literature on the unique characteristics of small groups of specific sizes, summarized in the following passage:

> The crucial transitions are those from one person to two, from two to three, from three to four, from four to seven, and from seven to nine. . . .
> The transition from one to two creates the basic unit of social behavior, the dyad. In a dyad there is interdependence, reciprocal behavior, and the necessity for accomodation to another person. The transition from two to three is significant because now there exists the possibility of an alliance between two members against the third one. The phenomena of control, cooperation *and* competition, and influence are produced by this transition. . . . The transition from three to four creates the possibility of two equal dyads or alliances, and this may perpetuate both the social unit and the problems of control. The significant feature of four is that an alliance be-

tween two members is not sufficient to gain control. . . . The jump from four to seven is crucial because just as individuals can form coalitions in the interest of control, so can groups. A seven-man group has the potential of splitting into two dyads and a triad. If the two dyads combine resources, they can gain some control over the larger triad. . . . Perfect symmetry with regard to all the processes we have described would be found in the nine-man group. Here there can exist three groups of three. This permits coalitions *within* a specified triad and coalitions *between* a pair of triads (Weick, 1969: 24–25).

Thus while teachers and school systems can probably do little to change the size of the class as a whole—and the available evidence shows that class size per se has little direct effect upon student learning—the small groups literature offers a number of suggestions on optimum group size which could be used in subdividing a class for various learning activities.

Group Homogeneity and Heterogeneity

A class of a particular size may be organized in a number of different ways. One of the issues which has been most hotly debated in recent years is ability grouping—the extent to which the students in a class are similar or homogeneous with respect to some measure(s) of ability or achievement. Like size, this is an issue which has been argued more on the basis of ideology or personal preference than on empirical evidence.

The pedagogical argument for homogeneous grouping is that less able students will not have to make invidious comparisons with their more able peers, that the brighter students will not be held back by the slower ones, and that the teacher will be able to adapt his teaching style to the needs of his students. The arguments against homogeneous grouping are that in a group composed of a cross-section of ability levels, the less able will have the example of the more able to spur them on; the brighter students, by helping their less able classmates, will gain a deeper understanding of the subject; and division into ability tracks or streams is inimical to egalitarian American values. Teachers generally prefer homogeneous grouping, although one suspects that they really prefer classes homogeneously high in ability and motivation and thus "easy" to teach.

Because of the factors discussed in Part Two of this book, children do come to school differentially prepared for learning. The conclusion of a compilation of achievement test profiles for a national sample of classrooms is that:

There are very few fourth-grade children in a so-called fourth-grade class when a fourth-grade child is defined as one who achieves at fourth-grade level in all subjects at approximately the mid-point of the school year. . . . A teacher, then, who considers himself a fourth-grade teacher is addressing himself to only three or four youngsters! (Moreover, an individual child is seldom at the same level in all subjects.) Most children in the intermediate grades vary in achievement from subject to subject by at least a full grade. That is, a sixth-grader may achieve at 8.1 in reading, 6.9 in arithmetic, 7.7 in spelling, 6.3 in science . . . some students vary from subject field to subject field by as many years as the number of the grade level (Goodlad, 1966: 34–35).

While there is no question of the great variations among children, the strategic question for the learning system is whether a wide or narrow range of student abilities is most effective in a classroom. The body of research on ability grouping is extensive, but comparability is difficult because of great variations in research design. There is no conclusive evidence in either direction; some study results favor homogeneous, others favor heterogeneous grouping. Moreover, the independent effects of grouping per se are difficult to sort out because grouping has become almost synonymous with separation by class and race.[1] Finally, the vacillating direction and lack of strong relationships, combined with the strong personal preferences of educators, suggest the likelihood of experimenter effects in many of the studies.

One of the most extensive recent studies is the experiment in New York City schools conducted by Goldberg and associates. The major objective of the study was to determine the extent to which a student's achievement increments over two academic years were affected by:

his ability level

the presence or absence of gifted children in his class

the presence or absence of slow learners in his class

the ability range in his class

his relative position within a given ability pattern.

As noted in Chapter 7, the sample consisted of 86 classes organized into fifteen different patterns of ability level and spread. Tests measuring achievement in several subjects, plus attitudinal questionnaires, were given at the beginning of the fifth and end of the sixth grade, and mean increments were computed for each class in each area of achievement.[2] Thus the study is a rare example of a relatively long-term longitudinal study of a relatively large sample.

While the sample size is large, it is not representative of the children of this age group in New York. In an attempt to obtain schools with broad ability ranges, the researchers included only schools which listed four or more fourth graders with IQ scores of 130 or higher and which were willing to cooperate. The sample thus excluded most schools from the low-income areas of the city. Moreover, schools which met the minimum requirement for students at the high end of the ability continuum tended to contain few students at the *low* end; there were only 206 students at ability level E (with IQ scores below 100). As the authors themselves point out, "conclusions can only be generalized to similar populations, and probably have little relevance for schools with predominantly low socioeconomic status or non-white pupil populations" (Goldberg *et al.,* 1966: 152).

It also should be noted that the experimental manipulation consisted only of setting up fifth-grade sections according to specified grouping patterns. Beyond alloting time for pre- and post-testing, there was no attempt to control what went on in the classroom. Thus we do not know how teachers were assigned to the various classes, nor anything about the content of various courses and the methods of teaching used during the period of the study.

To summarize some of the most important study results:

1. The presence of gifted children in a class had some upgrading effect upon the bright but not gifted students; less on the other students, in the area of science. In social studies, the upgrading effect was on the less able classmates. There were few effects in other subjects.

2. The presence of slow learners in a class does not appear to have any consistent effect.

3. Considering the *range* of ability within a class, the gifted students did best in a class of all gifted peers. Other students tended to do better in the broadest rather than narrowest range, but the overall differences were not large or consistent.

4. A student's *relative* ability position in a class had no consistent effect upon his test performance. "Neither for all three intermediate ability levels taken together or for each of them taken separately was any one position related to greater increments in all subjects" (Goldberg *et al.,* 1966: 56).

5. Comparisons of classes differing in range of ability (containing one, a few, or all ability levels) produced some statistically significant differences, but did not consistently favor broad or narrow patterns, and controlling for individual ability removed most of the significant differences. When each ability level was viewed in the separate subjects, with ability range also controlled, only eleven of the 105 comparisons were statistically significant, though nearly all favored a broad rather than a narrower range.

6. Differences between classes of the same ability distribution pattern were generally greater than differences between different ability patterns. (This was the finding reported at the beginning of Chapter 7—see also Goldberg *et al.,* 1966: 57–58, and Table III–8.)

The findings as a whole indicate that ability grouping alone does not have a strong impact upon the performance of most students. The presence of extremely gifted students in a class does seem to have some positive effects upon their classmates, although these children themselves did their best work in classes of their ability-equals. On the other hand, the presence of low-ability children, at least when they constitute a minority in a class, does not have a negative effect, a finding which speaks to the fear that racial integration and other kinds of school reorganization designed to assimilate low-SES children into white middle-class schools will "pull down" the more able students.[3]

A weakness of much ability group research, and a possible reason for the overall inconsistency of results, is that few studies are based upon a general model of classroom dynamics. A number of factors, none of which is controlled in the Goldberg study, may explain or specify the conditions under which certain patterns are stronger or weaker.

First are individual characteristics of students. Some experiments designed by Atkinson incorporate the personality variables of need-achievement and test anxiety. Using students of about the same age as those in the Goldberg study, Atkinson found that those who were high on need-achievement but low on anxiety showed greater interest and performed better on reading and arithmetic tests in homogeneous classes, regardless of their intelligence level. On the other hand, children with high anxiety relative to need achievement showed decrements in interest when placed in homogeneous ability classes, although their scholastic performance did not suffer (Atkinson, 1965).

Second is the extent to which students compare themselves with others of different ability levels—that is, use them as *reference groups* for themselves. The claim that less able students in heterogeneous classes will develop feelings of inferiority which will have negative effects upon their academic progress assumes that the low-ability students take their brighter classmates as a reference group. As Richer (1967) points out, this has never been substantiated or disproved by empirical research. Furthermore, the extent to which students of one ability level use those of a higher level as a reference group cannot be determined in any instance without taking into account additional factors. These include the similarity between the groups (Richer hypothesizes that the more similar two groups are in ability and other respects, the greater the likelihood that one will be taken as a reference group by the other); and the reward system (the more rewards are allocated on the basis of intellectual performance, the greater the likelihood that the ability subgroups in a class will be taken as reference groups).

A third kind of variable is the teacher's behavior. While Goldberg feels that the between-class variability reflected differential teacher competence, there was no systematic collection of data on what went on in the classrooms over the two-year period of the study. The authors do point out that although a common argument in favor of homogeneous grouping is that the teacher can adjust the content and method of teaching to the capacities of students, there is no evidence in this study that teachers did this when given the opportunity. On the contrary, it appeared that a narrowing of the range of ability for low-ability students simply led teachers to teach "less of the same" to their slower pupils, even though "pupils of comparable ability in the broad range appeared to benefit from exposure to the content probably intended for the brighter pupils as shown by the great increments of low ability students in science and vocabulary when in the broad range rather than the narrow range" (Goldberg *et al.,* 1966: 161). In other words, what seemed to operate in the homogeneous low-ability classes was a negative Rosenthal effect rather than a teaching approach especially oriented toward these students, and the potential advantages of the latter have yet to be tested.

Communication

A third structural characteristic of the classroom which merits examination is its communications structure. Since the goal of the formal learning system is to communicate information and skills, it is surprising how little systematic research has been done in this area. One thing known about classroom communication is that there is a lot of it. Jackson estimated from his own observations in several elementary classrooms that the teacher averages over two hundred interpersonal exchanges every hour of every working day! However, as earlier noted, the only consistently active communicator in most classroom interaction is the teacher, and much of the communication is one-way.

What systematic research there is on group communication is largely from the small groups field of social psychology, in particular the work of Bavelas, Leavitt, and their colleagues. Although most of this work is with groups much smaller than normal classroom size—and would thus apply directly to discussion groups or other sub-groups rather than to the class as a whole—it contains much that is relevant to a sociological theory of the classroom.

In a series of laboratory experiments in which the communication channels of five-man groups were controlled (the patterns are shown in Exhibit 8–1), both Bavelas and Leavitt found that communication patterns affected amount of activity, satisfaction, speed, and accuracy of performance on discovery problems, on both the individual and group level.[4] On the group level, groups arranged to afford a high degree of "centrality" (*Pattern 4* in Exhibit 8–1) tended to organize quickly to solve the problem with relatively few errors, although the total amount of group activity and satisfaction were not necessarily high. Leavitt attributed this to the position of the leader, which served as a kind of central office for receiving, organizing, and dispatching messages. When centrality was more evenly distributed *Pattern 1*), there was more activity and overall satisfaction, but fewer error-free solutions of the puzzle.

At the individual level, individuals in central positions were more likely to become active, more likely to become group leaders, and more satisfied with their group and their job. By contrast, where one position is low in centrality relative to the others, subjects in these more peripheral positions were likely to become "dependent on the leader, accepting his dictates,

Exhibit 8-1
Communication Patterns in Bavelas and Leavitt Experiments

Pattern 1   Pattern 2   Pattern 3   Pattern 4

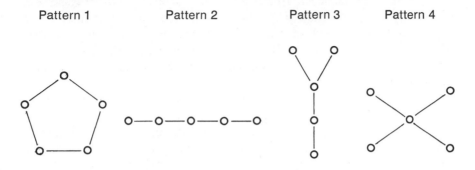

filling a role that allows little opportunity for prestige, activity, or self-ex-pression" (Leavitt, 1958: 563). Leavitt's summary of his own experi-ments would apply to both men's results:

> Patternwise, the picture formed by the results is of differences almost always in the order *circle, chain, Y, wheel* (or Patterns 1, 2, 3, 4, respec-tively in Exhibit 8–1).
> We may grossly characterize the kinds of differences that occur in this way: the circle, one extreme, is active, leaderless, unorganized, erratic, and yet is enjoyed by its members. The wheel, at the other extreme, is less active, has a distinct leader, is well and stably organized, is less erratic, and yet is unsatisfying to most of its members (Leavitt, 1958: 558).

To apply these findings to the school classroom, the communication structure of most classroom activities is an extension of *Pattern 4,* with the teacher in the central position and most of the communication consisting of a series of one-to-one exchanges between teacher and student. Such a crude diagram covers up much of the relevant detail of actual classroom situations—for instance, whether the communication is one-way from teacher to student, whether the teacher simply asks questions and indicates whether students answers are "correct," or whether there is anything like a true discussion between teacher and student (the sorts of variables ex-amined in the Flanders study). Even this oversimplified conceptualization, however, has suggestive implications. One is that the typical classroom communication structure is the one that is least gratifying to all group mem-bers except the member in the central position, although it is in a sense the most "well-organized" structure (which may explain its appeal to teachers). Second, while this type of group was found to be most productive of cor-rect answers to clearly structured tasks, this is really the result of the ac-tivity of the one central role—the productivity and contribution of other group members at the individual level was often greater in less "organized" types of structures where individuals were allowed to talk to members other than just the leader. Indeed, the highly centralized group seems to achieve its order and efficiency as a consequence of relatively passive behavior on the part of many members, a pattern which matches the typical classroom situation as described in the preceeding chapter. To put it another way, in a highly centralized system in which most members can communicate only with the leader, the person holding this position may learn a lot and be satisfied with the position and with the group, but this very activity limits the learning opportunities of other individuals.

Finally, although there experiments were not designed to bear directly on this point, both researchers speculated on the question of the degree of "insight" encouraged in and nurtured by varying patterns of communication. While every group in the Leavitt tests succeeded in forming at least some of the puzzle shapes:

> the ability to restructure the problem, to give up the partial successes, varied widely from pattern to pattern. If the indications of the few experimental runs that have been made to date are any guide, both occurrence and utilization of insight will be found to drop rapidly as centrality is more and more highly localized. In one group, the individual to whom the necessary insight occurred was "ordered" by the emergent leader to "forget it." Losses of productive potential, in this way, are probably very common in most working groups, and must be enormous in society at large (Bavelas, 1962: 681–682).

That is, once one moves beyond simply structured learning tasks to a more general understanding of some body of knowledge or to application of a skill or piece of information learned in one context to another context, more flexible classroom patterns, allowing more communication among students, may be more functional.

The Reward System

A feature of the learning system that has been blamed for student failure is the way in which rewards and punishments are structured and allocated. To many observers, the reward system of the classroom seems designed to produce anxiety, antagonism, and alienation in the teacher-student relationship. Three characteristics of the reward system are cited as especially nonfunctional in this respect:

the locus of rewards, which in most school systems is based upon grades. A dominant feature of grades is that they are external to the given learning activity. One carries out assignments in order to get a good grade or avoid a bad one, regardless of the intrinsic interest or usefulness of the activity involved. Such a locus obviously does not promote efforts to devise learning activities that are meaningful in themselves, nor does it make use of (nor trust) children's natural desire to know;

the structure of competition, which is mainly an individualistic contest for a scarce resource. High achievement by one student thus not only uses up or takes out of circulation one of a limited supply of good grades, but may punish the whole group by "raising the curve." Such a competitive structure discourages cooperative relationships among students and produces group sanctions against high achievement as a way of controlling the teacher's expectations;

the kind of student behavior which is encouraged. As Waller put it, the reward system fosters "docile assimilation and glib repetition," and discourages "fertile and rebellious creation." Those students who go along with the system for the sake of gaining its rewards concentrate on the kinds of behavior which are generally approved—say, reciting well and passing tests.

(It should be noted also that although the above outline has focused upon the reward system from the point of view of the student, there is also a system for the teacher, which will be described in the next chapter.)

Some sociologists have attempted to build mathematical models of school reward systems and to test them against empirical data. An example is Coleman's stochastic model of "situations in which one person's achievement takes away from another's success, and in turn the other person discourages efforts leading to such achievement." Coleman contrasts this model with situations where one person's achievement *contributes* to another's goals, and where, in turn, group pressure supports the efforts leading to such achievement. In an interscholastic athletic contest, "the achievements of one school's athletes contribute to the goals of all the members of the team and even of the school, who in turn cheer their team and accord the athletes high status and give them numerous other rewards" (Coleman, 1962: 120). Empirical data on the ways in which students react to and cope with the reward system will be discussed in Chapter 11, on the peer group.

The most serious attempt to change the reward system in a classroom is in applications of behavior modification, a rapidly developing field of social psychology which is essentially a strategy to restructure the child's environment so that he must change his behavior (or "learn") in order to gain the rewards of the system. A basic principle of behavior modification theory is that behavior can be changed in prespecified directions without extensive examination of the subject's underlying feelings and personality difficulties. Rather the social scientist analyzes the subject's physical and social environment in terms of its reward-punishment structure, and then "programs" it so that correct behavior, or moves toward correct behavior, is reinforced. The focus is upon the behavior itself and how to change it, whether or not one "cures"—or even understands—the child.

In an early classroom experiment, the disruptive behavior of a hyperactive child was reduced as follows: for every ten seconds of nondisruptive behavior, the child was given one point. Accumulated points could be converted into pennies and candy *which were shared with the child's classmates.* That is, the reward structure made the entire peer group depend upon the individual "problem" child, which both increased their pressure upon him to change his behavior and prevented them from dismissing him as a pest with whom they did not have to identify.[5]

Some of the most promising experiments currently are being carried out in experimental classrooms at the Central Midwestern Regional Educational Laboratory (CEMREL). All are based upon a simple cost-reward system in which plastic tokens are the major medium of exchange.

> A child who completes his arithmetic or reading may earn a dozen tokens, given one by one as he proceeds through the lessons. And at the end of the lesson period comes the reward.
>
> Often it is a movie. The price varies. For four tokens, a student can watch while sitting on the floor; for eight, he gets a chair; for 12 he can watch while sitting on the table. Perhaps the view is better from the table —anyway, the children almost always buy it if they have enough tokens. But if they dawdled so much that they earned fewer than four, they are "timed out" into the hall while the others see the movie. Throughout the morning, therefore, the children earn, then spend, then earn, then spend. . . .
>
> At the beginning the tokens are meaningless to the children; so to make them meaningful, we pair them with M&M candies, or something similar. As the child engages in the desired behavior (or a reasonable facsimile), the teacher gives him a "Thank you," an M&M, and a token. At first the children are motivated by the M&M's and have to be urged to hold on to the tokens; but then they find that the tokens can be used to buy admission to the movie, Playdoh, or other good things. The teacher tells them the price and asks them to count out the tokens. Increasingly, the teacher "forgets" the M&M's. In two or three days the children get no candy, just the approval and the tokens. By then, they have learned.
>
> There are problems in maintaining a token exchange. Children become disinterested in certain reinforcers if they are used too frequently, and therefore in the tokens that buy them. For instance, young children will work very hard to save up tokens to play with Playdoh once a week: if they are offered Playdoh every day, the charm quickly fades. Some activities—snacks, movies, walks outdoors—are powerful enough to be used every day (Hamblin *et al.*, 1969: 21).

With this basic token exchange system, CEMREL staff members have been conducting experiments with various kinds of "problem" learners, including a sample of ghetto children who arrived at school literally speechless, but who through a program of token exchanges worked up first to nonverbal communication (for example, pointing or headshaking), then to hesitant but spoken words and phrases, and finally to speaking in full sentences and initiating conversations with teachers and classmates (Hamblin *et al.*, 1969: 28–29).

The key to successful learning via behavior modification lies in discovering the most effective type of schedule of reinforcers for the student involved. In a series of verbal reinforcement, for example, Zigler and his associates found that reinforcers connoting praise—"good," "fine," and so on—produced the greatest improvements in performance among lower-SES children, while middle-class children were relatively more susceptible to reinforcers connoting correctness—for instance, "right"—(Krasner and Ullman, 1965). Another requirement is to reward learning frequently enough to reinforce desired behavior but not so frequently as to satiate. Finally, for a behavior change to be permanent, it must be reinforced by the persons and groups with whom the child interacts regularly or uses as reference groups. Hamblin felt that the children who learned to talk via behavior modification retained their verbal facility even several months after the end of the experiment because they were rewarded for doing so by their teachers, classmates, and families:

> Talking is important in our culture, and so is reading; therefore, they are reinforced. But other subjects—such as mathematics beyond simple arithmetic—are not for most people. For behavior to change permanently it must be reinforced at least intermittently (Hamblin *et al.*, 1969: 29–29).

Behavior modification is an approach which focuses upon the exchange relationship between teacher and student. The teacher still retains control over the giving and withholding of rewards, although the reward itself is made more relevant to the learner and its allocation is tied directly, and impersonally, to his performance. Punishment initiated by the teacher is eliminated as a control mechanism.

Another relationship which can be modified with respect to the reward system is that between students. As indicated at the beginning of this section, in the typical classroom situation students compete against each other to get approval, good grades, and other scarce rewards. To help another student not only does not increase one's chances of getting rewarded but may even be defined as "cheating." The fierce, individualistic competition characteristic of American classrooms has bothered many educators. Perhaps the best insights into the effects of a system's competitive structure upon the performance of individual members come from two well-known social psychological studies. The one which uses a classroom setting is Deutsch's study of artificially created climates in a college class.

Students in an introductory psychology course at the Massachusetts Institute of Technology were divided into two kinds of groups, cooperative or competitive, each given an assignment involving mental puzzles and discussion of some human relations case studies. In the cooperative groups, evaluation and grading was done by group, each member of a given group receiving the same grade and all members of the best group being excused from a term paper. In the competitive groups, individual members were ranked on their individual contributions, grading was on a curve within groups, and the highest ranking individual in each group was excused from the paper. As in the Lewin studies, the cooperative groups showed consistently higher coordination of efforts, attentiveness, friendliness toward each other, and a more favorable evaluation of the group. Also as in the Lewin studies, there was no evidence of superior output, in this case learning of the course content. There was also no greater interest or involvement in the subject matter of the course (Deutsch, 1949).

The effects of competition and cooperation are further explored in Blau's study of groups in a public employment agency (1955). Here the researcher did not create group atmospheres, but compared work units characterized by cooperative work norms (emphasis upon a "professional" code with a norm of service to clients rather than upon simply processing a large number of cases) with those in which members competed against each other for high productivity records, even to the extent of using such "illegal" tactics as hiding case records from each other. Blau found that while cooperative groups were more productive *as groups* (mean number of cases processed, or number of placements made), the highest levels of *individual* productivity were found in competitive groups.

These two studies have been very influential in many areas of sociology, but few if any replications or variations have been conducted in school classrooms. There is clearly a need for further experimentation with alternative modes of structuring academic competition.

Sociometric Structure

The aspect of student-student relationship which has received the most attention is their feelings toward each other. Although the topic of peer status and the relationship between students' sociometric status and their academic behavior will be discussed in Chapter 11, the sociometric structure of the class as a group is relevant to this chapter.[6]

Sociometry, a field which is largely the creation of Moreno and his followers, attempts to measure the "tele" relations—the positive or negative attractions—among the members of a group. The basic data-gathering technique is to ask all members to tell which other members they feel most strongly about (like, dislike, respect, want to work with, and so forth) or to identify the ones with high and low status in the group (the most popular, the smartest, or the best leader). Sociometric analysis had a brief vogue in teacher education, and during the 1950's American teachers produced sociograms (the diagrams consisting of circles, representing students, linked by arrowed lines, representing their likes and dislikes for each other) by the thousands. The basic postulate of the sociometry enthusiasts was:

(1)	(2)	(3)
Good	Satisfying	High individual motivation
sociometric $\longrightarrow$	intragroup $\longrightarrow$	and achievement
structure	relations	and
		High level of group
		performance

The exact definition of "good" sociometric relations is not specified in the literature. Presumably it includes a high rate of interpersonal contacts and no isolates or sharp cleavages between subgroups and identifiable leaders —since these are the kinds of things that are made visible by sociograms and matrices.[7]

The trouble with this formulation is that any empirical evidence that can be brought to bear on it—in particular findings from the field of industrial sociology on the factors contributing to worker productivity—indicate that it is not true. More specifically, studies of factory work groups suggest that while factor (1) does usually lead to factor (2), factor (3) does not necessarily follow. In the famous Hawthorne studies,[8] the girls in the Relay Assembly Room set a high productivity norm, the men in the Bank Wiring Room a low one, although both groups had the characteristics of "good" sociometric structure. Apparently cohesive groups do provide satisfying environments in which to work, but they do not guarantee a high level of achievement. Reviewing some of his own and other researchers' studies of the electrical industry, Kahn (1956) finds that some show direct, some inverse, and some no, relationship, and he concludes that group atmosphere measures are less powerful predictors than measures of individual goals and interests. His formulation is that a worker will have a high rate of production when he perceives high productivity as leading to or having some direct connection with his own individual interests, providing there are no serious barriers.

Translated into educational terms, this would say that a student "produces" when he sees that it is in his interest to do so (when getting good grades is highly rewarded by his peers, or when he is committed to getting into college or some vocational field that requires a good school record), providing there are no obstacles that seem impassable (low ability or parents with low income). A sociometrically integrated class thus will assure a high level of academic productivity only if this group sets a standard of high productivity, that is, if academic excellence is to the interest of the group members. Otherwise good group relations make no contribution to academic performance goals and may in fact work against such goals if the group is unified in its nonacceptance of achievement values. Probably the effect of sociometric structure upon academic achievement is interactive with other features of classroom organization. For example, it may be more important in classes with an open communications pattern than in classes in which most communication is from teacher to student and little student-to-student communication is allowed. Probably the reward structure is also a factor. The Coleman model described earlier suggests that in a system with an individualistic reward structure, such as is found in most high schools, those groups which are most highly integrated and satisfying to their members will be the ones in which productivity is most effectively held down! The general point is that satisfying group feelings, like particular forms of ability grouping, do not in themselves seem to produce high levels of learning.

Conclusions

The classroom is a system characterized by the close physical proximity of its young members for long intervals of time; and regulated by a relatively rigid authority pattern and schedule of activities, each of which has its own set of rules.

Class size and student achievement are not related, at least not in a simple linear fashion for the size range (20–40) normally found in our public schools. There are similarly, no clear-cut relationships between ability grouping and achievement. The presence of very gifted students may raise the performance of their classmates, though the gifted themselves seem to achieve at *their* highest levels in homogeneous classes. The presence of slow learners does not have any clearly negative effects upon other students.

The highly centralized communication system found in most classrooms may be satisfying to the person in the central position (usually the teacher). It is also an orderly system and an efficient way of reaching "correct" answers to well-defined problems, but less centralized structures are more conducive to the involvement of additional group members and encourage greater independence from the leader.

When talking about good "group dynamics," one must specify whether one is interested in a satisfying group situation or a productive one, since they are not necessarily synonymous. From what can be deduced from the evidence of studies in social psychology and industrial sociology, people produce when it is to their self-interest to do so and/or when the group standard (set by the group or by influential reference groups within or outside the group) is to achieve.

Most research on the classroom is weakened by lack of a model or theory of the classroom as a social system. There is a great need for more studies which combine a larger perspective with actual in-classroom observation or experimentation (the Jackson and Flanders studies are rare exceptions), replicated under a variety of "conditions" (types of students and schools as well as variations in size, homogeneity, and other classroom level variables). But the overview provided by Chapters 7 and 8 suggests that the conventional classroom represents a decidedly unnatural arrangement for the young and is not the most effective environment for effective learning. One could argue that in a situation involving a choice between teaching materials or methods that retained the conventional classroom structure and dynamics and methods that changed the classroom in some basic way, the burden of proof should be upon the former.

Notes

1. A finding which has been replicated crossculturally, in the Plowden Report on English education (Central Advisory Council on Education, 1967). The best summaries of the literature on ability grouping are in NEA (1968) and Goldberg *et al.* (1966). A "selective" bibliography at the end of the latter study cites over a hundred studies for the period from 1923 through 1964.

2. This reliance upon mean increments as indicators of learning or attitude change may introduce biases in interpretation, in that, for classes or subgroups which started out at a high level, further increments are "harder" than for groups with lower initial scores.

3. Note, however, that Goldberg's findings caution against a simplistic interpretation. In their sample, only the most gifted—those with IQ scores of 130 or higher—produce an upgrading effect in a heterogeneous class. This, in addition to the wide interclass variations found within a given school and ability pattern, indicate that it is not enough simply to place culturally deprived children in schools with higher-status age mates. It is how and in what number they are assimilated into a new learning environment that determine subsequent academic progress.

4. In a typical experiment, the task was to solve a puzzle in which 15 pieces had to be arranged to form 5 squares. In another, subjects were given cards with a number of different symbols, the task being to determine the one symbol common to all cards. In both experiments, subjects were allowed to communicate only via written messages, according to the particular communication structure assigned. Some of the experiments used a specially designed circular table, at which subjects were separated from each other by vertical partitions, with slots between pairs of subjects who were allowed to communicate with each other.

5. This experiment and others incorporating behavior modification techniques are discussed in Krasner and Ullman, 1965 and 1966.

6. The distinction between individual and group level sociometric measures is not always understood by researchers: For example, Buswell (1953) claims to be testing the null hypothesis that "there is no relationship between the social structure of a classroom and the achievement in some of the basic elementary school subjects," but her research design pulls students from several different classes in eight different schools and compares all the high-SES individuals (from all schools) with all the low-SES individuals.

7. See Gronlund, 1959, Chapter 7.

8. These studies have been extensively analyzed by Homans (1941 and 1950). For descriptions of the original research, see Roethlisberger and Dickson, 1939.

The school is a social organism. . . . As a social organism the school shows an organismic interdependence of its parts; it is not possible to affect a part of it without affecting the whole. Willard Waller

Schools should be places where people go to find out the things they want to find out and develop the skills they want to develop. . . . What is most shocking and horrifying about public education today is that in almost all schools the children are treated, most of the time, like convicts in jail. Like black men in South Africa, they cannot move without written permission. . . . And yet, on second thought, this is not what shocks me most. What shocks me most is that the students do not resist this, do not complain about it, do not mind it, even defend it as being necessary and for their own good. John Holt

In this chapter we shall move from the single classroom to the school as a whole. Although schools vary on many of the same dimensions as classrooms (size and social class homogeneity), schools also contain structural components other than classrooms,[1] and have dimensions which are unique to the school as a social system. Following a brief description of the distinguishing features of schools, we shall begin, as we did with the classroom, with an analysis of role structure. In the next chapter, we shall turn to the characteristic ways in which schools differ from one another, ranging from physical facilities to the social context formed by the system members, in an effort to understand what kinds of schools comprise the most favorable environments for learning.

Since Dewey, it has been fashionable to think of the school as a small community, ideally with some continuity between the learning experiences in school and those in the larger society (Dewey, 1928: 416ff). More recently, Katz, in a paper entitled "The School as a Complex Social Organization" (1964), pointed out that schools, like most complex organizations, are not self-sufficient communities, but rather specialized structures serving special functions and tightly interlocked with other structures. The special function of the school, according to Katz, is to prepare children for active participation in adult activities. Thus it must allow enough independent action to ensure adequate performance of adult activities without constant supervision, but it must be ever alert to activities, organizations, and opinions which are potentially dangerous to the carrying out of this function (For instance, serious questioning of the "American way of life". See also Zeigler and Peak, 1970).

Much sociological analysis of the school has consisted of specifying the similarities and differences between schools and other social systems, either ideal type system models or various types of real-life institutions. An example of the first kind of analysis is Bidwell's comparison of schools with the bureaucratic model. According to this analysis, schools as social systems have the following bureaucratic characteristics:

1. a functional division of labor (for instance, the allocation of instructional and coordinative tasks to the roles of teacher and administrator);
2. the definition of staff roles as offices, that is, in terms of recruitment according to merit and competence, legally based tenure, functional specificity of performance, and universalistic, affectively neutral interaction with clients;
3. a hierarchical ordering of offices, providing an authority structure based on the legally defined and circumscribed power of officers and regularized lines of communication;
4. operation according to rules of procedure, which set limits to the discretionary performance of officers by specifying both the aims and modes of official action (Bidwell, 1965: 974).

Although American public school systems in general are bureaucratized organizations, individual schools or school systems vary in degree or mode of bureaucratization. For a study of the effect of organizational structure upon teachers' attitudes, Moeller (1968) constructed an index of bureaucratization based upon the following eight characteristics:

uniform course of study

communication through established channels

uniform hiring and firing procedures

secure tenure for nonteaching personnel

explicit statement of school policies

clearly delimited areas of responsibility

specific lines of authority

standard salary policies for new teachers.

Each of twenty schools was rated by several judges, and it was found that the eight items formed a Guttman scale with a reproducibility of .93, with the items going from "hardest" to "easiest" in the order in which they are listed above.[2] For example, schools which passed on only one item were almost always plus on the item of standard salary policies; schools which passed all but one item (had a score of 7) usually had a minus only on the item of uniform course of study. The substantive results of Moeller's study, which challenge the prevalent emphasis upon the negative consequences of school bureaucratization, will be discussed later in this chapter.

Another general type of institution of which schools are one subtype is the service institution, in which one or more groups or categories of roles do their work *for* another group or category of roles. It is in their guise as service institutions that one can see most clearly the nature of the authority problems of the school. As one analyst puts it:

> One aspect of the institutional organization of activity is a division of authority, a set of shared understandings specifying the amount and kind of control each kind of person involved in the institution is to have over others; who is allowed to do what, and who may give orders to whom. This authority is subject to stresses and possible change to the degree that participants ignore the shared understandings and refuse to operate in terms of them. A chronic feature of service institutions is the indifference or ignorance of the client with regard to the authority system set up by institutional functionaires; this stems from the fact that he looks at the institution's operation from other perspectives and with other interests. In addition to the problems of authority which arise in the internal life of any organization, the service institution's functionaries must deal with such problems in the client relationship as well. One of their preoccupations tends to be the maintenance of their authority definitions over those of clients, in order to assure a stable and congenial work setting (Becker, 1968: 298).

Indeed the apparent fixation of many school personnel upon the authority problem has led some observers to draw parallels between schools and one particular kind of service institution—the *involuntary* institution. It is pointed out that in schools, as well as prisons, mental hospitals, and other institutions where the client is "serviced" regardless of his own wishes, a central focus is the maintenance of order and control. For this purpose the institution staff may develop elaborate rules and monitoring systems, which place severe limitations upon the autonomy of the client, even though students, prisoners, and mental patients constitute a sizable majority of the total population in their respective institutions.

Obviously such comparisons can be taken only so far. One important difference between schools and involuntary institutions is that most of the latter are also total institutions—the inmates are in residence twenty-four hours a day. However, it is also interesting to see that current trends may be narrowing this difference. The tendency in prisons and mental hospitals is toward greater amounts of time away from the institution—in the home, at a job, and so forth. On the other hand, the view of many persons working with "problem" students is that in order to overcome the adverse influences of family and neighborhood, the school should become more of a total institution. Some educational and child-rearing experiments built on this principle will be described in Chapters 13 and 14.

As Exhibit 9–1 indicates, the school is organized in a hierarchical, pyramidal pattern, with a single or small set of administrative roles at the top. The pattern moves down through several sets of adult roles, each set larger than the one just above it on the pyramid, to the "majority group" of students at the base. (Not included in Exhibit 9–1 are clerical and cus-

Exhibit 9-1
The Role Structure of the School

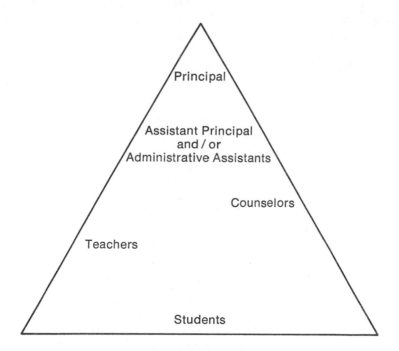

todial roles, which have to do with the organizational and physical maintenance rather than the educational functions of the school.) The pyramid form was chosen in preference to the organization chart form, commonly used to illustrate the structure of bureaucratic institutions, because while it oversimplifies in certain respects, it shows the relative quantitative strength as well as the relative position of the roles.

The Principal

At the top of the role hierarchy is the principal, the "boss" of the school. His or her duties encompass the general management of the school and its instructional program, dealing with students and teachers, and maintaining relations with social groups and system outside of the school, both professional (his superiors in the "central office") and nonprofessional (parents). That the principal is under a great deal of pressure because of the broad scope of his role is a recurring theme of the National Principalship Study, a national survey of principals, their administrative superiors, and a sample of teachers from their schools, in 490 elementary and secondary schools in 41 large American cities, conducted by Neal Gross and a large group of Harvard research colleagues. Data were collected in four-hour interviews, supplemented with extensive written questionnaires. At least half of the principal respondents reported exposure to each of forty potential conflict items in the questionnaire, with the conflicting demands of teachers and parents being the greatest source of pressures. Over half said they worked an average of two or more nights a week in addition to their regular work day, and the amount of off-duty time spent was directly related to respondents' Executive Professional Leadership (EPL) score,[3] —additional evidence of the demands of the job.

Further evidence of conflicting pressures is presented in a study of Oregon principals (McAbee, 1958), which compares respondents' actual use of their time with their opinions on how their time *should* be spent. On the average, the 204 principals in the sample would assign about 13% of their time to routine office work; in fact, they spent an average of 22.5% of their time at this type of task. Conversely, the type of activity to which they felt they should devote the most time—supervision of teachers and improvement of instruction, 22%—actually received about half that much time. In other words, practical realities force many principals to allocate their time in a way that is inconsistent with their own role expectations.

Although principals are recruited almost exclusively from the teaching ranks, they do not represent a random or representative sampling of teachers. Although they are similar to teachers as a whole in socioeconomic origins and religious affiliation, they are more likely to be male (about half the elementary principals in the National Principalship sample, as compared with less than one-fifth of the teachers), to be older, with more years of teaching experience, and to be white. (As we saw in Chapter 7, teachers themselves are more likely to be white than their students.) In the National Principalship Study, moreover: all schools with all-white faculties ($N = 8$) had white principals; all schools with all nonwhite faculties ($N = 8$) had nonwhite principals; nearly all of the 14 nonwhite principals were in schools where over 80% of the teachers were nonwhite; and all of the nonwhite principals were in lower-SES schools.

Do the characteristics and behavior of the principal have any impact on

Exhibit 9–2

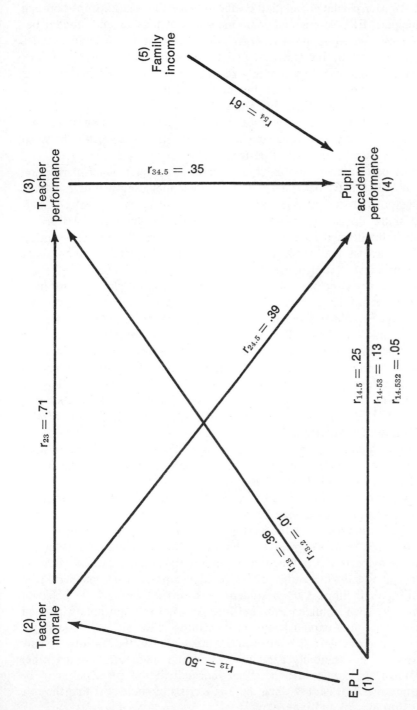

student productivity? Exhibit 9–2 summarizes relevant findings from the National Principalship Study. The figure, which gives the zero-order and some first-order partial correlation coefficients for the relationships between the principals' EPL scores and some measures of teacher and student behavior, shows a strong positive correlation between the principal's adequacy, as defined by his teachers, and the morale of his teachers ($r_{12} = .50$), which is in turn very strongly related to the teachers' performance ($r_{23} = .71$).[4] The direct relationship between EPL and teacher performance (r_{13}) is .36, but when this relationship is reexamined with teacher morale controlled, it virtually disappears ($r_{13.2} = .01$), suggesting that teacher morale may intervene and account for the relationship between EPL and teachers' professional performance.

Student performance in this study is measured by teacher perception of the overall achievement level in the school, including estimates of the percentage of the student body who are or are not mastering subject matter and skills, displaying interest in academic achievement, and working up to their intellectual capacities. Exhibit 9–2 shows that the relationship between principal and student behaviors is initially smaller than those between principal and teacher measures, and that it decreases with the addition of every control variable. Further analyses, not shown here, indicated that for any level of principal's EPL and parental income level, the latter always explained a much greater amount of the variation in student behavior, and that the EPL variable had a consistent relationship with academic performance only in the lowest income schools (where, presumably, weak parental influence left room for influence by another adult role.) The relationships of student academic performance with the two teacher variables are, on the other hand, fairly substantial, (.35 with teacher performance and .39 with teacher morale, *after* removing the effects of students' family income).

What the figure as a whole suggests is a chain type of relationships within the school, in keeping with the hierarchical position of the roles. While the principal's behavior has little direct effect upon students' academic performance when other variables are controlled, "both teachers' performance and morale *may* serve as links in a causal chain between the EPL of principals and the performance of their pupils" (Gross and Herriott, 1965: 57). To put it another way, the principal's impact upon student behavior is not a function of his interpersonal relations with the students themselves, but rather of his relationships with his teachers, who do have a direct impact upon student performance and whose behavior is affected by their confidence in and interpersonal relationships with their principal. This may explain why the literature on the principal—and the role itself—seems colorless relative to the other roles in the learning system. The principal is essentially a facilitator for and mediator between other roles. When the system is operating "normally," the principal may be almost unnoticed. It is only when there is a crisis of some sort that the role becomes prominent and interesting.

The Teachers

The teacher role already has been considered in its relation to the students (Chapter 7). Here we shall focus upon some of the consequences of the teacher's peculiar position in the role hierarchy of the school system. Henry Adams is credited with saying that no man can be a teacher for ten years and remain fit for anything else. Since Adams' time a number of works have dealt with the dilemmas of teacher status. Among the problems are the inconsistencies in attitude toward teaching as an occupation, including its lack of acceptance as a true profession (the salary levels of teachers are not commensurate with other professional ones, and the very fact that teachers and teacher organizations so stoutly defend their professionalism suggests that there is some question about it in their own minds); the continued preponderance of women teachers; the lower academic abilities of persons entering teaching as compared with other professions; and the high turn-over rates within the occupation. Concommitant with their low status in the school:

> Teachers have virtually no control over their standards of work. They have little control over the subjects to be taught; the materials to be used; the criteria for deciding who should be admitted, retained, and graduated . . . the qualifications for teacher training; the forms to be used in reporting pupil progress; school boundary lines and the criteria for permitting students to attend; and other matters that affect teaching (Corwin, 1965: 241).

The teacher's relationship with the principal is an ambiguous one. On the one hand, the teacher is dependent upon the principal and/or other administrators in much the same way as the student is dependent upon the teacher—as judge (the principal is generally in charge of teacher evaluation) and dispenser of rewards and punishments (assignment to classes, and recommendations for retention and promotion). As we have seen, it is not the type of relationship conducive to free and frank interpersonal communication. On the other hand, the teachers as a group have a direct effect upon the principal's behavior:

> Although the teachers are subordinate to the principal in the organization, they wield powerful sanctions. A principal who fails to meet the expectations of a majority of his teachers may find his authority severely undermined, if not openly flouted. Many teachers have tenure and can be dismissed or transferred only with difficulty. . . . At the secondary level the teacher is also a specialist in subject matter, often in an area unfamiliar to the principal. Lacking control in technical matters, the principal's authority is weakened and circumscribed. The "technical freedom" may exist even at the elementary level, since many elementary school principals have not taught at this level . . .
>
> An additional element of strength in the teacher's position is the definition of his role as a professional one. The control over professionals in a formal organization is a delicate matter, even more so than the control

over technical specialists. To the extent that the principal accepts the teacher as a professional person, he must also accept restrictions on his own authority (Dodd, 1965: 3.12–3.13).

In the last chapter we saw that the reward system for students did little to encourage motivation toward high levels of academic performance. Examination of the reward system for teachers reveals that teachers are for the most part not rewarded for increasing their students' learning. Pay raises are given for years of service rather than evidence of student improvement, or for obtaining additional course credits at a teachers' college or university department of education (shown in the Coleman report to be relatively unrelated to student in-school achievement). Teachers who experiment with new teaching materials usually do so on their own time and are seldom rewarded for even successful results. Of course, the reward of greater interest or achievement among their students can be a powerful inducement for many teachers, but the point is that the school system provides no formal means of recognizing this kind of activity. In fact, teachers who substitute materials of their own for the regular syllabus run the risk of being reprimanded or even losing their jobs, as the recent "memoires" of several classroom teachers testify (Holt, 1964; Kohl, 1967; Herndon, 1968).

In Part Two, we saw that a sense of control of one's destiny was an important factor in students' self-image and academic success. Moeller's study, introduced at the beginning of this chapter, focuses upon the relationship between the extent of school bureaucratization and the teacher's sense of ability to influence the organizational forces that shape his occupational destiny. His hypothesis was that "the general level of sense of power in a school system varies inversely to the degree of bureacratization in that system" (Moeller, 1968: 238).

The study sample consisted of twenty elementary and twenty secondary teachers from each of twenty selected school systems in the St. Louis metropolitan area. Moeller's measure for the independent variable, school bureaucratization, was described earlier in this chapter. The teachers' sense-of-power scale consisted of six items (for instance, "In the school system where I work, a teacher has little to say about important system-wide policies relating to teaching.").

The empirical results showed no support for Moeller's original hypothesis. Contrary to his expectations, teachers in bureaucratic systems were significantly higher in sense of power. In an effort to understand these unexpected findings, Moeller examined the effects of some other variables upon sense of control. Regardless of the structure of the school system, strong sense of control was positively related to: having a position of authority within the school; having organizational ties outside school but within the profession (say, membership in a teachers' union); coming from a family with relatively high occupational status; being male; and having taught more than three years. It was negatively related to working in a school system whose superintendent exercised restrictive or oppressive authority.

An additional variable which was related to sense of control and also interactively related to the degree-of-bureaucratization variable was "particularism" in the administrator-teacher relationship, defined as the extent to which school officials interacted with teachers in a personal, as opposed to an impartial, manner. Particularism was more prevalent in low bureaucratic systems, but teachers in highly bureaucratized systems who *did* have strong personal ties with administrators were significantly higher in sense of power than those without such ties, while there was no such relationship in the low bureaucratic systems. As the author sees it, in a nonbureaucratic system, close, informal relationships are more common and nearly everyone has access to the administrators: "This, in effect, tends to devalue this avenue, for if everyone has access, then all should benefit equally" (Moeller, 1968: 249).

The final portion of Moeller's paper is devoted to interpreting the unexpected finding that the apparently more rigid policy of the bureaucratic school enhances rather than reduces the teacher's sense of control. He concludes that one of his original assumptions about the bureaucracy dimension was incorrect; while he perceived it as promoting the personal and professional autonomy of the teacher, these teachers saw it as reflecting a lack of order and predictability:

> Without the stabilizing benefit of a comprehensive and uniform written set of rules for the school system, many decisions arise for which adequate policy is unavailable. This, it would seem, leads teachers in the low bureaucratic systems to be uncertain as to such decisions and the element of unpredictability inherent in the system tends to abrogate their sense of power . . .
>
> In systems characterized by firm policy, we may postulate that teachers' knowledge of that policy is, in itself, a form of power. When policy is applicable to all, then any individual who knows the rules by which the system is governed is able to predict how any particular situation will be handled. This factor enables the teachers in the bureaucratic school systems, by the expedient of learning the rules, to anticipate how the administration will act in most problems confronting it. More importantly, knowledge of policy enables teachers to know the most effective course of action to take in order to influence the policy-maker (Moeller, 1968: 248–249).

This theme is echoed in a recent study of 115 new teachers in a large California school district (Edgar and Warren, 1969), which found that while autonomy was desired in some areas (curriculum content and teaching methods), a common source of dissatisfaction was lack of sufficient administrative structure and guidance in such areas as discipline and clerical tasks.

It is further concluded that the usual unitary approach to the study of "autonomy" may be misleading and that the distinctions between active and inert tasks, delegation versus direction, authority rights and legitimacy feelings are more promising research tools than the broader and ambiguous concepts of professionalism and bureaucracy (Edgar and Warren, 1969: 399).

It should be noted that neither of these studies includes any measures of student performance. While we are making an assumption that the teacher's sense of control is related to his classroom performance and thus to student learning (an assumption which is to some degree supported by the Gross and Herriott model—see Exhibit 9–2), this assumption is not directly tested in the Moeller or the Edgar-Warren study.

Two alternative strategies are available for dealing with the strains and inconsistencies of the teacher's role. One is the formation of informal faculty peer groups within the school. Although teacher colleague groups have so far received little research attention, one place to begin would be the "faculty room," a refuge for teachers whenever they can escape from their classroom duties. Faculty room activities consist mainly of smoking and drinking coffee (generally forbidden elsewhere in the school), and gossiping about students (most faculty rooms are off-limits to students) and school personnel not present, with a high component of disrespectful references to those higher up on the role hierarchy.[5] While a faculty room is an almost universal feature of American schools, some observers question whether it symbolizes any real degree of teacher solidarity. They claim that public school teachers "are characterized less by solidarity and viable colleague controls than by isolation from colleagues and sentiments favoring personal autonomy in the classroom," a consequence of a "fragmentary work structure that minimizes formal and informal interaction with fellow teachers" (Bidwell, 1969: 1252). Definite conclusions about the nature and strength of teacher peer groups must, however, wait upon further empirical research.

A second alternative is teacher professionalism, which by contrast with informal faculty room interaction is a formal, interschool activity characterized by "front region" behavior in Goffman's terms. The general movement to upgrade the teacher's role via professionalism is not new; there are already some 700 state, regional, and national teachers' organizations. What is new about much recent activity is its militancy—teachers' strikes, competition among unions for membership and the right to represent whole school districts in bargaining—more akin to a working-class than a professional association. Whether increased organization across school boundaries will have positive effects upon teachers' classroom competence is still an unanswered question. To the extent that the movement focuses upon "benefits" (higher salaries, fringe benefits, shorter working hours), its impact upon learning will probably be slight. However, to the extent that it focuses upon improving the image of the teacher role, including gaining a greater degree of self-direction and a greater share in making the decisions about how schools should be run, professionalism could both improve the performance of persons already in the teaching profession and attract more able teachers in the future.

The Counselors

This is a relatively new and still somewhat ambiguous role in many schools, although the trend is clearly away from assigning counseling functions to classroom teachers and toward hiring full-time counselors (now about 32,000 in number) who have been trained in this educational specialty. The role is of interest here because it seems to be emerging as the authority for defining the child's capacities, deciding whether or not his achievement and behavior are satisfactory, and determining his educational, and even his occupational, future (including what course of study to follow, whether to apply for college, what careers to aim for). The growing power of the counselor with respect to differentiating the student population is a consequence of two trends:

the increasing complexity of the larger society, which means among other things that families no longer can provide occupational training, or even appropriate advice. Lower-SES parents can seldom guide even a talented child along the torturous path to upward mobility, and, to a growing degree, being middle-SES no longer assures automatic acceptance into the more prestigious educational and occupational positions;

the increasing specialization within the school, such that differentation of students is no longer done via informal decisions of the principal and teachers but is a separate task assigned to a special role.

The major proponents of this view of the counselor are Cicourel and Kitsuse (1963), who claim that parental status and peer group climate are no longer the only major determinants of student aspirations and achievements, and that "the distribution of students in such categories as college-qualified and non-college-qualified is to a large extent characteristic of the administrative organization of the high school and therefore can be explained in terms of that organization." (Cicourel and Kitsuse, 1963: 6–7). In the upper-income suburban school studied by Cicourel and Kitsuse, the counselors were responsible not only for administering standard ability and achievement tests, but also for deciding whether a student was achieving at a satisfactory level and what education program he should be assigned in the future. In the substantial number of cases in which there was discrepancy between tested ability and school achievement, the counselor had to make a judgment about the student's achievement type. From the data gathered in interviews with students and counselors, the authors conclude that these judgments were typically made under pressure of time and were weighted by the counselor's own biases. For example, out of a sample of eighty students, all but one classified by the counselor in the brightest achievement category also were identified by the counselor as being in the highest social class attending the school. As the authors conclude:

> Our materials suggest that the counselor's achievement-type classification of students is a product of a subtle fusion of "rational" and common-sense judgment. Belonging to the "in-group" may be given greater weight than grade-point average in classifying a student as an "excellent" student, or "getting into a lot of trouble" may be more important than "performing up to ability level" in deciding that a student is an "underachiever" Cicourel and Kitsuse, 1963: 71).

Although the counselor is gaining ever more power over the lives of students, there is also evidence that counseling "services" are not distributed equitably to the student body. Studies by Armor (1969) and by Weinberg and Skager (1966) showed a relationship between the extent of utilization of career guidance services by high school students and their family and school status. Students from middle- and upper-SES families, students in college preparatory courses, and students with high extracurricular participation were more likely to have discussed their future plans with a counselor; virtually none of the students who were from the lowest status families or who admitted to having been in some kind of trouble with the law had discussed their problems or plans with a counselor. Thus, "counselors are seeing, generally, the students who need help less. For counseling programs established on a self-referral basis, the students who may require assistance most may be using the facilities least" (Armor, 1969: 132). The fact that counselors were not communicating effectively with many students also was indicated by the large number of students who planned to go on to college but were not in the college prep program and/or were in the lower quarter of their class academically. Moreover, the proportion of students in this category did not substantially decrease if the student had gone to see a counselor (McNeely and Buck, 1967). In sum, there is a discrepancy between reality and aspiration for many students, and counselors do not seem to be clarifying the situation for many such students.[6]

The Students

Since an entire chapter (Chapter 11) will be devoted to the student peer group, here we shall only review the characteristics of the student body which describe its position in the total school role structure.

First, although students constitute the majority group in the school, they are at the bottom of the role hierarchy, and they are the only members of the system who have no choice about being there—at least until the legal school-leaving age, which is set by adults.

Second, although students are the school's "clients," and the major school decisions are made on the grounds of "the welfare of the students," they have little to say in these decisions. What is "good" for students is "defined by the adults (teacher, principal, or parent) and fulfilment of the students' expectations is not a necessary part of his welfare" (Dodd, 1965: 3.12).

Third, the increased role specialization in schools, which has produced new staff roles in addition to making the traditional ones more "professionalized," probably has contributed to increased separation of students from staff, and also may have intensified the development of distinct student peer groups, with their own activities and norms which are not always congruent with those of the formal learning system.

An entire literature, mainly evocative rather than grounded in empirical research, is growing up around the theme that students are being exploited by the very institution that was designed to serve them (see especially Farber, 1969). This "student-as-nigger" literature borrows much of the rhetoric of current "liberation" movements in general. It claims "coercion" and "exploitation" of students by the authoritarian educational "establishment," and calls for liberation via protest sit-ins, strikes, and other activities aimed toward achieving equality and self-determination of all system members. Although it is still too soon to say what ultimate impact the current unrest and demands of high school and college students will have upon the student role in its most general sense (it is also difficult to determine whether the so-called spokesmen of student liberation are accurately reflecting student opinion or are wistfully trying to recapture their own lost youth), there is little doubt that pressures for greater participation in the school decision-making process are growing in strength and that the proportion of students who have opinions on the subject of their own education is increasing.

The position of the student body in a school undoubtedly is related to its social class distribution. In the next chapter, we shall see how the social class composition of the student body affects the performance of individual students, but here it should be noted that the relations between student and other roles in the school system are also affected by this variable. Pertinent to this point is Armor's finding that both teachers and counselors were more important sources of advice for students in urban working-class high schools than in suburban middle-class ones, where parents were most often sought for advice (Armor, 1969: 122).

Conclusions

Like the classroom, the school has a hierarchical structure and a more or less continuous concern with problems of maintaining discipline—although this is often under the guise of what is good for the student.

At the top of the hierarchy is the principal, who usually comes to this role by way of teacher education and classroom experience but who is not typical of teachers in general. He is both superordinate to and dependent upon the teachers in his school, and his impact upon students is mainly indirect, through the direct effect of his personality and behavior upon teacher morale and competence.

The teacher's position in the school as a whole is an inconsistent one. On the one hand, he is in sole command of his classroom; on the other hand, he lacks the salary, prestige, and decision-making power of many other professionals. Teachers' lack of autonomy and their discontent with their position may partially explain what often seems to be an overemphasis upon classroom authority and resistance to any new teaching methods which appear to threaten such authority. (Of course, these are also explained by the school-wide focus upon the control aspects of system maintenance, to the extent that a teacher who is suspected of less than tight control of his classes automatically is defined as incompetent.)

Although the "student-as-nigger" image is more provocative than precise, it is true that the students' own interests and expectations have little force in shaping the organization and the curriculum of most schools. Moreover their classification as successes or failures and the other decisions that most vitally affect their future lives are increasingly concentrated in the hands of specialists whose judgments often are made with limited information and time and are weighted heavily by social and personal biases.

The characteristics and attitudes of the individuals whose roles comprise the school combine to form its social context or climate. In the next chapter we shall turn to these and other characteristics of schools as social systems —characteristics which explain their "productivity" or effectiveness as learning environments.

Notes

1. "Children do not live their school lives only in the classes they attend; they live, also, in the halls, in the assemblies, in the principal's office" (Barker *et al.*, 1962: 47).

2. For discussion of Guttman scaling, see Riley, 1963: Chapter 9; or Riley *et al.*, 1954.

3. The major measure of principal efficiency used in the study. EPL is defined as "the efforts of an executive of a professionally staff organization to conform to a definition of his role that stresses his obligation to improve the quality of staff performance." A principal's EPL score is based upon his rating by a subsample of the teachers in his school on 18 kinds of behavior, including the following:

Gives teachers the feeling that their work is an important activity

Gets teachers to upgrade their performance standards in their classes

Maximizes the different skills found in the principal's faculty.

Taken as a dependent variable, EPL was found to be positively related to the following independent variables:

a high level of academic achievement in college

a high degree of interpersonal skills

a motive of service in choosing an educational administration career, as opposed to making a good income or gaining social mobility

having a professional rather than a managerial image of their role

receiving satisfactory leadership and support from their immediate superior (say, the superintendent)

participation in evaluation of teacher applicants.

EPL scores were *not* related to age, experience, or salary. (Gross and Herriott, 1965).

4. Items in the teacher performance scale include the estimated per cent of co-teachers who "do textbook teaching only," who "do everything possible to motivate their students," and who "try new teaching methods."

5. Faculty room activities thus fall into the category of behavior which Goffman terms "backstage": "The backstage language consists of reciprocal first-naming, co-operative decision-making, profanity, open sexual remarks, elaborate griping, smoking, rough informal dress, 'sloppy' sitting and standing posture, use of dialect or sub-standard speech, mumbling and shouting, playful aggressivity and 'kidding,' inconsiderateness for the other in minor but potentially symbolic acts, minor physical self-involvements such as humming, whistling, chewing, nibbling, belching, and flatulence. The frontstage behavior language can be taken as the absence (and in some sense the opposite) of this. In general, then, backstage conduct is one which allows minor acts which might easily be taken as symbolic of intimacy and disrespect for others present" (Goffman, 1959: 128).

6. Armor suggests that counselor effectiveness may be hampered by the fact that the professional role was developed, in the early part of this century, "before the institutionalization and codification of the knowledge base." He would include in this base "detailed knowledge of the occupational structure and of the special requirements for each vocation," tools for the "assessment of such individual characteristics as may be required for each vocation (or class of vocations)," and, more recently, familiarity with colleges and their requirements (Armor, 1969: 45).

. . . the hypothesis is rather compelling that qualitative differences in the schools themselves account for much, if not all, of the variation in academic and vocational achievement between one school and another.   H. S. Dyer

Schools bring little influence to bear on a child's development that is independent of his background and general social context.
James S. Coleman, Ernest Q. Campbell, *et al.*

. . . a good school can't be described very clearly in advance. . . . In fact, there may not even be such a thing as a good school within our present conception of what "school" means.   Jerry Farber

How does one measure the "effectiveness" or "efficiency" of a school? In Chapters 7 and 8, we saw the difficulties of evaluating a single classroom, even though at that level we are limited to a relatively small group of students, who are about the same age, and engaged in studying, with one or at most a few teachers, a given course or curriculum. At the level of the school as a whole, the complexities of conceptualizing and measuring both independent and dependent variables are intensified.

Although any research design depends upon the researcher's resources and upon the particular questions he wants to answer, one can distinguish some general types of designs for analyzing school productivity. The studies to be discussed in the rest of this chapter can be classified, without gross distortion, into one of the following general research designs or strategies:

Design 1. Designate one or a small set of variables as affecting student performance. Draw a sample of schools which vary on this dimension(s) and compare them on some measure(s) of academic performance.

Design 2. Gather data on a large number of variables in one or more schools. Use analysis procedures designed to determine which variables are related to each other (for example, factor analysis) and which are related most strongly to academic performance (multivariate analysis).

Design 3. Select a sample of schools which vary on academic performance (sample on the dependent rather than independent variables). Compare these schools upon a variety of school characteristics.

Design 4. Build models of school systems in order to compare the effects on output of manipulating various combinations of system characteristics.

This chapter will be organized by substantive topics; at the same time, the studies discussed will follow roughly the order of design types just outlined.

Size

An example of a single-variable effect (Design 1) is that of school size, which like classroom size has been rather extensively studied with rather inconclusive results. School size became a national issue with the publication of Conant's report on the American high school (1959), and its plea for the large, "comprehensive" high school. Conant based his plea upon the greater opportunities for differentiation in the larger school—the point being that a school with a graduating class of fewer than one hundred cannot offer an adequate program for all kinds of students (including nonacademic training for the less gifted, as well as advanced courses in mathematics, science, and foreign languages for the brightest fifteen to twenty per cent). Conant, however, offered no empirical support for his contention —say, in the form of comparisons between large and small schools on measures of academic output.

By contrast, studies by Barker and associates at the University of Kansas, which compared thirteen Kansas high schools, ranging from 35 to almost 2300 in size, favor the smaller schools. The general finding of the Barker studies was that students in smaller schools and communities participated on the average in more nonclass "behavior settings," and held more responsible positions in these settings. (The authors defend their choice of extracurricular activities on technical grounds—the difficulties of assessing motivation and involvement in activities where attendance and participation are not voluntary—and on the grounds that the great amount of students' energies invested in extracurricular activities and the schools' extensive support of them put such activities within the boundaries of the total educational process.)

The bits of data on academic activity in these schools suggest, however, that the academic and nonacademic structures of a school are not necessarily parallel. There were, for example, fewer different kinds of subjects offered in the smaller schools, although these were the schools which provided richer extracurricular environments. And in a comparison of 28 juniors from small schools with 28 selected from the large schools—all with IQ scores above 110 and of the same sex, it was found that the total class enrollments for the bright students were higher in the small schools, but that this higher average was accounted for mainly by nonacademic electives such as music, home economics, and shop. The students from small schools were actually taking fewer academic courses (Barker *et al.,* 1962: appendix 12.1). Another finding is that more students in the small schools had taken some kind of musical instruction, but that the large schools contained higher proportions of students who could be considered expert in some area of music. The authors interpret these findings as indicating greater and more varied academic "participation" by bright students in small schools. However, a different interpretation is also possible: that the small school environment produces less motivation or pressure for the talented student to take the "tough" academic courses and to master a skill, such as playing a musical instrument, to the point of expertness.

The most extensive recent analysis of school size effects can be found in the Project Talent study (introduced in Chapter 6). A series of correlations between high school size (measured by number of seniors and average grade level size as well as total school size) and a variety of school outcome measures (from achievement test scores to dropout rates to per cent going on to college) thus far have failed to reveal any distinct patterns. While there may be optimum size ranges for elementary and secondary schools, they have not been shown in the research to date. As is the case at the classroom level (see Chapter 8), size per se does not seem to affect academic performance directly.

Vertical Organization

A second kind of single-variable model, about which there is almost no empirical data, describes the school's vertical organization, in particular the modes of assigning students to grade level. In Chapter 8, we examined data on the effects of grouping children in various ways *within* the classroom on a given grade level—the *horizontal* organization. The other mode of grouping is the vertical, which serves to move students up through the various levels and which must be studied in the context of the school as a whole. The predominant vertical arrangement is by grade levels (the years or positions within the school, not the marks given for a particular course). Each grade consists of a year of academic work in the set of subjects assigned to that level, typically in the form of a textbook, workbook, or some combination of these. At regular intervals, usually once a year, children who have finished the work or "passed" the subjects at one grade level move on to the next. Those who have not worked through the required sequence of books and tests are not promoted and usually are required to repeat the grade.

The grade level system has long been a target of educational reformers, and a variety of attempts have been made to change it. One modification is *multigrading,* in which each class contains two or more grades simultaneously. "Although grade labels are retained, children are permitted to work in several grades at once, depending on their progress in each subject. In a multigraded class containing grades three, four, and five, a child could be in grade three for arithmetic, grade four for social studies, and grade five for reading" (Goodlad, 1966: 23).

A more radical change is nongrading, theoretically the polar opposite of the traditional grading system, by which grade levels are removed altogether:

> . . . the sequence of content is determined by the inherent difficulty of the subject matter and the children's demonstrated ability to cope with it; materials are selected to match the spread of individual differences existing within the instructional group; and the children move upward according to their readiness to proceed. Promotion or non-promotion does not exist as such. An important goal is to provide continuous progress for each child (Goodlad, 1966: 24).

The available research data comparing students' attitudes and achievement in graded and multigraded or nongraded schools are inadequate in design and inconclusive in results. Among the difficulties pointed out in Goodlad's review is the lack of certainty that a school's vertical structure truly fulfills its name. "The removal of grade labels, for example, is no guarantee that teachers will take advantage of the opportunities nongrading is supposed to provide. A nongraded school with only grade labels removed remains a graded school, nonetheless" (Goodlad, 1966: 24). A further difficulty is that the schools compared often differ in several structural characteristics. For example, some of the studies reviewed by Goodlad made comparisons between nongraded schools which use ability grouping and graded schools with heterogeneous grouping. Thus it was impossible to determine whether differences in achievement were the result of the grading system (vertical structure) or the ability grouping (horizontal structure).

Contextual Effects

A mode of analysis which has aroused considerable interest among sociologists in recent years is the study of social "context" or "climate," which examines the extent to which an individual's attitudes and behavior are affected by the proportion of the total group who have a given attribute or attitude. The basic technique in contextual analysis consists of combining the attributes or attitudes of all the members of a social group or system to form a single measure by which the individual members may be identified.

Among the sociologists most skilled in contextual analysis is Alan

Wilson, two of whose studies will be discussed here. Both studies use contextual variables based upon background attributes, although one is concerned with the effect of a single contextual variable upon student aspirations (Design 1); the other, with the independent and joint effects of two such variables, plus some additional independent variables, upon test scores (Design 2).

In the first of the two Wilson studies, conducted in the late 1950's, eight high schools in the San Francisco-Oakland Bay area were classified into three groups according to the SES of the students' parents. That is, the combined SES characteristics of the student body as a whole was conceived as forming part of the climate or context of the school for a given student. Group A schools contained high proportions of students whose parents ranked high in occupational and educational status; Group B schools had relatively fewer families in the higher categories; and Group C schools had the fewest. More specifically, in Group A schools, 64% of the fathers were in professional or white-collar occupations, 65% of the fathers had some college or more education, and 56% of the mothers had some college or more; the comparable figures for Groups B and C respectively were: 37, 35 and 31%; and 27, 14 and 12%.

The question Wilson wanted to answer was whether differences in school social context influenced the educational aspirations of boys from varying social strata. "Concretely, are the sons of manual workers more likely to adhere to middle-class values and have high educational aspirations if they attend a predominantly middle-class school, and conversely, are the aspirations of the sons of professionals more modest if they attend a predominantly working-class school?" (Wilson, 1959: 837). The empirical findings indicated that the answer is yes: 80% of the students in the Group A schools, 57% in the Group B schools, and only 38% in the Group C schools had college plans. Moreover, while the status of a student's parents did have an independent effect upon educational aspirations (children of professional parents were more likely to have college plans than children of manual workers), this family effect was modified by the dominant class character of the school's student body. Thus 93% of the sons of professionals in the Group A schools wanted to go to college, compared to less than two-thirds of the sons of professionals in the Group C schools; similarly more than half of the sons of manual workers in the Group A schools planned to go on to college, compared to one-third in the Group C schools.

Wilson found similar relationships when he used the father's education and the mother's education as the independent variables, and also when he used academic grades as the dependent variable. In each case the combined attributes of the student body, which in Wilson's conceptualization produced the student norms, had a clear, consistent effect upon students' educational aspirations and performance—and effect in addition to students' individual family origins.

The second Wilson study, carried out under contract with the U.S. Commission on Civil Rights, at about the same time and concerned with many of the same questions as the Equality of Educational Opportunity survey, considers both the racial and socioeconomic context of schools. Again the sample is from the San Francisco Bay area, but ranges from elementary through high school. A major portion of the study is devoted to a comparison of the effects of school and neighborhood context upon the academic achievement of Negro and white children at different age levels. School composition is measured by the proportion of students who were black and the proportion who were of the lower class—or lower SES (whose family heads were unskilled laborers, domestics, unemployed, or welfare recipients). The neighborhood context measure was analogous to the school measure, except that the unit was the "enumeration district" in which the student's family lived. Enumeration district is a concept adopted from the 1960 Census breakdowns and consists of a small geographic area of about 200 households. By contrast with school context, the neighborhood:

> consists of the several blocks surrounding the home of each student— ignoring school boundaries. Students living at the periphery of an elementary school boundary may have as neighbors children who attend a different school. Also, if an elementary school covers areas with varying demographic characteristics, a student's school and immediate neighborhood may be quite different in composition (Wilson, 1967: 180).

Examination of the mean reading achievement scores for the sixth graders in the sample, controlling for one independent variable at a time, indicated that the greatest differences were produced by school context; the mean reading level of the sixth graders who had attended primary schools with populations of less than ten per cent lower-SES children was 7.4, compared with a mean of 4.9 for children in schools where a majority of their classmates were of lower SES. This was a greater difference than that produced by neighborhood context, or by individual family status or race (the mean reading scores of black and white sixth graders were 5.0 and 6.7, respectively).

The univariate comparisons do not, however, take into account the fact that many of these variables are themselves interrelated (for example, black students tend to live in predominantly black neighborhoods and to attend predominantly black schools). The multivariate analysis controlling simultaneously for school context, neighborhood context, individual SES, race, ability, parental supervision, and home atmosphere (number of objects in the home) is summarized in Exhibit 10–1, which shows that, except for primary school mental maturity, the greatest amount of variance in reading scores is explained by the social class composition of the primary school (effect $= -.12$). Moreover, neither the *racial* composition of the school nor the racial *or* class composition of the *neighborhood* had any independent effect on school performance over and above the social class composition of the school.

Exhibit 10–1

Sources of Variation of 6th-Grade Reading Test Scores

Source of Variation	Marginal Relations		Partial Regression Coefficients	
	Sample Number	Estimated Mean	Raw	Normalized
Lower-class primary school				—0.12
Negro primary school				+ .10*
Lower-class primary neighborhood				— .01*
Negro primary neighborhood				0.00*
Primary-grade mental maturity				+ .15
Lack of supervision by mother				— .04
Number of objects in home				+ .07
Family status				+ .08
Professional and managerial	282	7.4	+ .3	+ .03
White collar	504	6.8	+ .3	+ .04
Semi-skilled and skilled manual	558	6.1	— .2	— .02
Lower-class	734	5.4	— .3	— .04
Race				+ .01*
Negro	905	5.0	— .1	— .01
White	1,173	6.7	0.0	0.00
Total variance joint effect	2,078	6.3		

* Not statistically significant

From Wilson, 1967: 181.

These findings have considerable significance for educational theory and policy:

> Our continuing reservation about the relevance of proposals to alter the demographic composition of schools is the question as to whether continuing residential segregation might structure the effective environment of students so that their integration in schools makes no difference. These data are inconsistent with this reservation. On the contrary, these data suggest that the effect of neighborhood segregation upon achievement is entirely through the resulting segregation of neighborhood schools on social class lines. Restructuring the composition of schools, even in the absence of residential rearrangements, can be expected to have an effect upon the academic achievement of students . . .
>
> Finally the racial composition of the elementary school does not have any independent effect, over and above the social-class composition of the school, upon achievement (Wilson, 1967: 180–181).

One implication of this analysis is that strategies of school desegregation should be conducted along class rather than racial lines, although the data also show that because black students are disproportionately concentrated in lower-SES neighborhoods and schools, they are more likely than whites to be subject to adverse school contextual effects. Another implication is that a redistribution of students among schools can have positive effects upon achievement even if there are no parallel changes outside the schools. This is because of the importance of the school climate set by peer group attitudes and behavior. As Wilson puts it: "Variations in the modal socioeconomic composition of a school, and accompanying variation in cognitive development in the primary grades, generate norms of interpersonal behavior and role-expectations which acquire a force of their own and have a resounding impact upon the students in the situation" (Wilson, 1967, 181).[1]

Comparisons Among Multiple Independent Variables

An important feature of Wilson's second study is that it moves from a focus upon a single contextual variable to a comparison of the relative strength of two contextual variables (and two kinds of measures at each contextual level) and the way in which they interact with other independent variables to affect achievement. We shall now consider some other studies in which the objective is to understand the relative impact of a variety of school characteristics, or the total amount of variance in achievement which can be explained by a combined set of independent variables (Design 2). An underlying issue in all these studies is whether the school as a total system has effects on students independent of the effects of the students' individual characteristics or of the environment in which the school is located. Two of the major studies using this basic design already have been introduced: the Project Talent and the *Equality of Educational Opportunity* surveys. To these, we shall add two earlier studies which were concerned with some of the same issues and variables and which form a framework for recent and ongoing work. Since these studies involve relatively large number of variables and cases and rather elaborate data processing and analysis procedures and thus make comparisons difficult, some basic information about the research design and the data is summarized in Exhibit 10–2.

The first study was carried out by Mollenkopf and Melville (1956), and involved a sample of high schools (like the Shaycoft, but unlike the Goodman and Coleman samples, which included elementary and secondary school students). Unilke the other researchers, who sought a representative cross-section of schools, at either the national or state level, Mollenkopf and Melville tried to get as diverse a sample as possible "so that those characteristics of schools that are in fact related to pupil achievement would have the best possible chance of emerging from the data."

Exhibit 10–2 Design of Four Studies Comparing the Effects of Multiple School Characteristics

	Mollenkopf-Melville	Goodman	Shaycott	Coleman et al.
Sample	9600 9th graders, 8400 12th graders in 100 high schools chosen for diversity in size, region, staff, student body, financial support.	70,000 students in grades 4, 7, 10 in 103 school systems, representative of New York State.	Project Talent sample of 6583 9th graders in 1960 who were 12th graders in 1963, in 118 high schools, representative of U.S.	900,000 students in grades 1, 3, 6, 9, 12 in 3000 elementary, 1170 high schools (5% representative sample of U.S.
Year of Data Collection	1953	1957–1958	1960 and 1963	1965
Data	Cross-sectional. Students: 4-part aptitude and 3-part achievement tests. Principals: questionnaire on school, parent, and community characteristics.	Cross-sectional. Students: achievement and aptitude tests.	Longitudinal. 42 Project Talent tests, from abstract reasoning and conceptual development to subject—specific knowledge.	Cross-sectional. Students: verbal and math ability (all grades): reading and math; (grades 3–12); general information (grades 9–12). Teachers and administrators: questionnaire on 45 school characteristics.
Data Analysis	Regression analysis, of school test score averages on school, parent, and community characteristics.	Correlation of test scores with school factors.	Comparison of rates of student test score gains among different schools.	Regression analysis, to find proportion of test score variation explained by family vs. school vs. teacher vs. student body characteristics.

Like the Coleman *et al.* study, the Mollenkopf-Melville one used regression analysis, in which school averages on several sets of achievement and aptitude tests were correlated with—or regressed on—thirty-four different school characteristics derived from questionnaire data supplied by school principals. The four characteristics showing the strongest relationships were: geographical location (especially whether or not the school was in the South); per-pupil expenditure; whether the school was in an urban, suburban, or rural community; and the number of guidance counselors and other specialists on the school staff.

The report available on Goodman's analysis (1959) is based mainly upon the seventh graders in the sample. Although the Goodman results cannot be compared directly with the Mollenkopf-Melville results, it is interesting to note that both found the characteristics of per-pupil expenditure and size of special staff to be positively and significantly associated with achievement. On the other hand, the variable found to be most strongly related to student performance among the seventh graders in Goodman's sample was the amount of teacher experience, while this relationship is relatively small in the Mollenkopf-Melville and the Coleman studies. Whether this reflects differences in the samples, differences in the measures of independent or dependent variables, or some other nonrandom variations cannot be determined, since the three studies differ in so many respects.

The Shaycoft report (1967) is one of a series based upon Project Talent data.[2] Since Shaycoft's is the only one of the four studies we are considering here which examines the same students at two different points in their school career (grades 9 and 12), it is the only one which can measure directly the impact of schooling upon cognitive development. Shaycoft concludes that the impact is considerable. There were gains on all of the 42 tests she analyzed, the average increase on some being as much as a full standard deviation in terms of the ninth-grade distribution. Moreover, the greatest gains tended to be on tests of subjects actually taught in school— for example, literature, mathematics, and social studies, and such vocational fields as mechanics and accounting—rather than in areas of general information or skills that could be acquired outside of school. Further support for the effect of schools upon learning was that on 40 of the 42 gain scores there were statistically significant variations *among* schools. Shaycoft's interpretation was that "students in some schools learn more, or improve their ability more, than in other schools."

In startling contrast to Shaycoft's convictions regarding the differential effects of schools, the conclusion of the *Equality of Educational Opportunity* study is that schools per se have little independent influence upon children's intellectual achievements. The results of the survey are difficult to present concisely, since the analysis includes a host of dependent and independent variables. It is, moreover, carried out upon a sample broken down into a number of subgroups, by race, age, geographical region, and so on. The set of variables showing the strongest relationship to verbal ability scores, the major indicant of student achievement used in the report, are factors of the social composition of the student body—for example, the proportion who are in a college prep curriculum, the proportion who are white, and the proportion who have encyclopedias in their homes. Only a small amount of achievement variance is accounted for explicitly by variations in physical facilities and curriculum (say, enriched curriculum, foreign language programs, libraries, or science labs). Some teacher characteristics—race, verbal scores, and attitudes toward integration—were related to the achievement of some categories of students, but such characteristics as experience, academic degree, student-teacher ratio, and the availability of counselors were not correlated. In summarizing these results, the authors conclude that schools have little independent effect upon children, and, moreover, "that this very lack of an independent effect means that the inequalities imposed on children by their home, neighborhood, and peer environment are carried along to become the inequalities with which they confront adult life at the end of school" (Coleman, Campbell, *et al.,* 1966: 325).

An important qualification of this general conclusion is that schools *do* differ in the degree of impact they have on different groups:

> . . . improving the school of a minority pupil will increase his achievement more than will improving the school of a white child. Similarly, the average minority pupil's achievement will suffer more in a school of low quality than will the average white pupil's. In short, white, and to a lesser extent Oriental Americans, are less affected one way or the other by the quality of their schools than are minority pupils. This indicates that it is for the most disadvantaged children that improvements in school quality will make the most difference in achievement (Coleman *et al.,* 1966: 21).

The Coleman report has been subjected to the most searching analysis and criticism since its publication in July, 1966.[3] Some of the problems of using a verbal ability test as the major dependent variable have been discussed in an earlier chapter. If verbal ability is more likely to be a product of a child's home than of his school experience, it may not reflect fairly the full range of the school's influence. The high rates of nonresponse also have been criticized, although it should be noted that this is not a problem unique to this study (Mollenkopf, for example, got returns from less than half of the principals to whom he sent questionnaires), and that Coleman and his statistical advisors worked out an elaborate procedure for estimating missing data which is fully described in the report (Coleman, Campbell, *et al.,* 1966: 56ff) along with discussion of the possible effects on their results.

Other criticism has focused on the puzzlingly small relationship between school facilities and academic achievement, a conclusion which is in conflict with the conclusions of the Mollenkopf-Melville and the Goodman reports. One critic (Bowles, 1968) has argued that Coleman's method of analysis, in particular his heavy dependence upon regression analysis in which the order of controlling the variables affects the size of the co-efficients obtained, has led to an underestimate of the effects of school investment. When two independent variables in a multiple regression analysis are themselves related, controlling for the first will reduce the correlation of the second with the dependent variable (that is, reduce the amount of the variance it "explains"). This is the case with students' social class and the level of resources in their schools:

> When we control for the social class of the student, we implicitly control also for some part of the variation in school resources. The additional predictive power associated with the explicit addition of school resources to the analysis thus represents a downward-biased estimate of the real re-lationship between school resources and achievement. There is no rigorous statistical or compelling theoretical reason for controlling first for social background. In particular, it is not relevant that much of the effect of family background is felt first, prior to a child's entry into school, for the Coleman analysis is cross-sectional and does not take into account in any way the time sequence of the explanatory variables. By choosing to control first for social-background factors the authors of the Report inadvertently biased its analysis against finding school resources to be an important de-terminant of scholastic achievement (Bowles, 1968: 92–93).

In a reanalysis of this data, Bowles found that reversing the order in which the resource and social class coefficients were computed produced results different from Coleman's. For example: "the amount of variance in achievement scores of twelfth grade Negro students explained by the variable 'teachers' verbal ability' more than doubles if this variable is brought into the analysis first, rather than after the social background variables." Bowles concludes that "contrary to the Coleman conclusion, significant gains in Negro students' achievement levels can be made by directing additional resources to their education" (Bowles, 1968: 92, 94).[4]

The Bowles critique underscores how difficult it is to estimate the true effects of investment in school facilities and personnel. While school ex-penditures are partly a reflection of socioeconomic factors, which are strongly associated with achievement, the relationship is complicated by variations in income level, cost of living and other economic factors, and by variations in the proportion of the education budget that is really avail-able for programs and materials specifically oriented to raising the achieve-ment level of special subgroups of students. For example, although the per-pupil expenditure is often relatively high in the inner-city school sys-tems, a much larger amount must be spent on the upkeep of old buildings and replacement of equipment due to age or vandalism. The rigidity of school budgets, moreover, often means that individual principals and teachers have little to say about what is bought. In Baltimore, for instance, all schools are allocated for each category of materials a given sum, which may be spent only for that category. Thus a school overstocked with textbooks cannot use "textbook" money to buy, say, audiovisual equipment, but must either continue to stockpile unused textbooks or return the money.

Another criticism of *Equality of Educational Opportunity* is that the authors have not succeeded in distinguishing between true effects of the school as a learning environment and effects which are simply a function of the combination of the individuals who compromise the student body. It has been suggested that the reason the level of academic achievement in, say, the Newton, Massachusetts, school system is so high is because the individual students are disproportionately talented and motivated to begin with and, moreover, that the meeting of these students in one place produces an unusually high initial commitment to achievement, regardless of any features of the school itself. If these same students got together *anywhere,* runs the argument, in all likelihood their learning would be at a high level even in the absence of other environmental advantages. Certainly Wilson's findings show that the combination of individual family background and the distribution of family background among the student body explains much about a school's productivity.[5] Indeed, one researcher (Astin, 1961) has gone so far as to claim that if enough individual background characteristics were controlled, any effects of schools per se ultimately would disappear.

None of the contextual studies discussed so far answers the Astin claim directly, although both the Coleman-Campbell and the Wilson reports refer to the issue. Some support for the validity of school level effects is contained in the Bennington study findings that seniors held more liberal views than freshmen, even when some background variables were controlled, and that the attitudes measured in the follow-up study were related to length of residence (the longer the residence at Bennington, the more liberal a woman's attitudes remained after leaving). Perhaps the most depressing evidence of the impact of even poor schools can be seen in the sharp drops in all areas of achievement measured by the Stanford Achievement tests among the Negro children whose school careers were discontinued by the closing of the Prince Edward County, Virginia, public schools from 1959 to 1963 (see, for example, Green and Hofmann, 1965). Although the reintroduction of schooling in 1963 produced slight improvements in academic skills, the low over-all achievement at the last testing indicated that the "lost years" without formal education could not be made up entirely.

Individual and School Components of School Success

Perhaps the most carefully controlled analysis of school and individual effects is a study (McDill, Meyers, and Rigsby, 1967) which sampled on the *dependent* variable—that is, selected schools differing in aggregate academic performance were compared with respect to their structural characteristics (Design 3). Because the design of this study is quite complex and because it contains the most comprehensive examination to date of issues raised by contextual analysis, we shall devote a separate section to it.

The goal of this study was to explain why some schools are more productive than others. In each of ten different geographical areas of the United States, a pair of high schools was chosen, with distinctly higher and lower records of academic performance. The sample of schools was chosen by a three-stage procedure: first, by ranking all U.S. high schools in terms of their numbers of National Merit Scholars and the proportion of graduates who subsequently obtained PhD's, as a rough measure of "academic productivity"; next, by "selecting from the larger pool of institutions a limited number which varied on several demographic and social characteristics" (for instance, size and SES and ethnic composition of the school and of the community it served). The final choice was made after obtaining —from alumni and educators familiar with their educational programs— additional information on the schools selected in the first two stages (McDill *et al.,* 1967: 183).

The procedure used to obtain the climate measures was a factor analysis[6] of 39 school characteristics. Some characteristics were based upon a single questionnaire item (say, the percentage of students in a school who say it is extremely important to get high grades). Others were a composite of several items, many of them adaptations of the "student press" and "faculty press" scales developed by Pace and Stern (1958).[7] From the factor analysis of these single- and multiple-item characteristics, six constructs or factors emerged, each of which contained a number of characteristics which grouped together statistically and substantively. McDill titled the six factors as follows:

1. Academic Emulation: the degree to which academic excellence is valued by the student body. (This factor is the most important of the six statistically, accounting for a greater proportion of the total variance in achievement than any of the others.)

2. Student Perception of Intellectualism-Estheticism: the degree to which acquisition of knowledge is valued.

3. Cohesive and Egalitarian Estheticism: the extent to which the student social system emphasizes intellectual criteria for status as opposed to family background or other ascribed criteria. This factor also taps the degree of social integration among students.

4. Scientism: the degree of scientific interest and emphasis in the school.

5. Humanistic Excellence: parallel to Factor 4, but focusing upon art, humanities, social studies, and current social issues.

6. Academically Oriented Student Status System: the extent to which intellectual and academic performance is rewarded by student peers as compared to rewards for participation in extracurricular activities.

Although the obtaining of the school climate factors required research sophistication and a substantial expenditure of time and money, and although they are interesting, and controversial, in themselves, the real purpose of the study was to measure the effects of such dimensions upon student productivity relative to such a characteristic as the SES composition of the school. Measures of both SES and school context were obtained by ranking the schools on each measure. The data analysis using these rankings showed a positive relationship between high scores on each of the six climate dimensions and students' math achievement scores, and between this achievement measure and high SES context. In terms of *relative* effects, each of the climate dimensions except Factor 4 was more strongly related to achievement than was SES, with Factor 1 having an especially strong relationship. Each of the climate dimensions continued to exert an effect in the expected direction even when the individual factors of scholastic ability, personal values, family status, and the school SES context were controlled simultaneously. By contrast, the original effect of SES context almost disappeared when IQ scores and individual SES were controlled—that is, "the putative influence of SES context seems primarily due to family background and scholastic ability of students" (McDill *et al.,* 1967: 194. Compare with the conclusions reached by Wilson).

Since the publication of the paper quoted here, McDill has done a multivariate regression analysis of these four dimensions upon math achievement. The results are shown in Exhibit 10–3. The figure .110, in the top left cell of the table is the effect of the school contextual Factor 1 upon a student's math test score, controlling for his father's education, his own academic orientations, and his IQ score. Individual ability explains the greatest amount of variation (that is, the figures in the last vertical column of Exhibit 10–3 are the largest), with father's education and own values having about equal weight. None of the school climate dimensions accounts for a large proportion of the variation in achievement, but each makes some contribution toward explaining this variation beyond that jointly explained by the other three variables (all of which already have been shown in much previous research to be correlated with academic performance). Academic emulation has the strongest independent effect of the six climate measures, and is apparently the most comprehensive indicator of the academic quality of the school.

McDill's recent analysis also included correlations of math scores with a number of formal school characteristics deriving from the economic resources of the community, including teachers' starting salaries and per-pupil expenditure. McDill found these correlations to be negligible or negative, a result congruent with the conclusion of *Equality of Educational Opportunity.*

In summary, the results of this very thorough analysis support the existence of school effects independent of the personal characteristics of the student body (either individually or aggregated). They also suggest

Exhibit 10–3

*Unique Effects of Each of Six Climate Dimensions of Schools
and of Three Personal Attributes on Math Achievement*

Climate Dimensions	Weighted Effects of Climate Dimensions (controlling for all other variables)	Weighted Effects of Father's Education (controlling for all other variables)	Weighted Effects of Student's Academic Value (controlling for all other variables)	Weighted Effects of Student's Ability (controlling for all other variables)
1. Academic Emulation	.110*	.119	.137	.299
2. Intellectual Estheticism	.072	.130	.136	.305
3. Cohesive and Egalitarian Estheticism	.048	.132	.135	.307
4. Scientism	.033	.138	.136	.309
5. Humanistic Excellence	.042	.133	.136	.308
6. Academically Oriented Status System	.046	.134	.136	.308

* All effect estimates are standardized to dichotomous form and are significant at the .01 level.
Unpublished data supplied by McDill.

something about the way in which schools as learning environments produce or fail to produce achievement. "More specifically, the findings lead to the tentative conclusion that in those schools where academic competition, intellectualism and subject-matter competence are emphasized and rewarded by faculty and student bodies, individual students tend to conform to the scholastic norms of the majority and achieve at a higher level" (McDill *et al.,* 1967: 199). Such schools are more likely to contain high proportions of students from advantaged families, but, concludes McDill, the value climate that gets built up in a high school comes to exert an influence above and beyond what would be predicted on the basis of student body characteristics alone.

Systems Analysis

A relatively new, technologically oriented approach to educational evaluation is to compare alternative school policies, programs, and models of organization by rigorous comparisons of the relative costs and benefits of each. The underlying theory of systems analysis is not new:

Its best formulations are indistinguishable from descriptions of the scientific method and thus have roots reaching back through Roger Bacon to

Aristotle. . . . At its best, therefore, the systems approach can be used in conjunction with well developed and reliable research designs to solve problems far more satisfactorily than naked intuition (Oetinger, 1968: 77).

Systems analysis has been developed most extensively by mathematicians, economists, and engineers working in government agencies or research organizations engaged in government projects, particularly in the area of defense. A typical analysis involves determining the actual cost of various "inputs" (of various combinations of weapons systems, or of different methods of organizing and supplying armed service personnel), taking into account any interrelations which might affect total cost or functioning, and then judging which of the model systems will produce the "output" most consistent with the real-life system's goals and resources.

In the field of education, the technique seems to lend itself most naturally to the analysis of the school's use of its resources—money, teachers' time, teaching materials, and so forth. Systems analysis enthusiasts argue that although most school budgets show the state or the schools' financial resources and financial output, they seldom show the real educational output in terms of how much mathematics, history, or other subject matter is learned for a given investment of resources.

> Many things learned, presumably in school, can be and are being measured, and we should consider the results of these measurements in our model building. Even in those important and great areas of the child's mind where we cannot or do not measure, we can at least make a judgment as to the presence of these factors in each model. . . . *The point is that the building of models, the gathering of data, and the assignment of values brings us face to face with problems in such a way as to help us make better judgments* (Mauch, 1962: 160).

Mauch describes how systems analysis techniques might be applied to evaluating alternative mathematics programs:

> At one end of the scale we might build a model in which we loan each student a math book, tell him to study it, and give him tests at stated periods with course credit for those who pass. This would certainly be a cheap method to teach math, but the level of achievement is likely to be unacceptable to us. At the other end of the scale, we might provide a tutor for each child. Although the level of learning would likely be quite high, the cost would be unaccepable to us even though we say we want the best math instruction possible . . .
>
> Many of our models would be more conventional: we would consider the new Yale and Illinois programs in math instruction. Instead of (or in addition to) new programs, we might manipulate our capital expenditure (audio-visual aids, math teaching aids and games, self-instruction devices), or our salary expenditures (teacher-pupil ratio, teacher aids, teacher salaries). Most likely we would build systems or models which utilized several or all of these alternatives in different ratios. The costs of the alternative systems and the amount of output will depend on the quality and amount of input and the way they are combined (Mauch, 1962: 159–160).

We report on systems analysis as a potential rather than a fully developed tool for the analysis of school effectiveness. The Mauch passage quoted above describes how a systems analysis of a school mathematic program *could* be designed, but it does not present the parameters and/or results of an actual analysis of a particular school. A general model for the systems analysis of schools is one of the projects of the Center for the Study of Evaluation of Instructional Programs, at the University of California (Los Angeles), but it is still in the developmental stages (Alkin, 1967). The only published data on a completed analysis of actual school systems is by Burkhead, whose findings will be reported in Chapter 12.

Simulation or simulation gaming is a technique that parallels systems analysis in that it involves construction of a system model and the insertion of parameters to represent the operation of important system components. A group under the direction of Coleman (of which the author is a member) has been working since the early 1960's on a series of simulated social environments for use in research and teaching, among which is a simulation of a high school social system (including the pressures on students from different reference groups and the likely consequences of different investments in academic, extracurricular, and outside-of-school activities).

Whether these promising new techniques will in fact lead to more precise educational analysis and more intelligent educational decision-making depends in part upon whether solutions to their unique problems can be found. One problem is the tremendous expense of developing a usable model. Both the Burkhead systems analysis and the Coleman game models required several years of work and considerable computer time (the Defense Department analyses are the product of a decade of development of programs and techniques and the work of hundreds of specialists).

The kinds of problems to which systems analysis has been applied (for instance, weapons systems) also point to possible limitations in its application to education. First, the method depends upon the ability to specify what constitutes a satisfactory "output," and as we have already seen, there is little consensus about goals appropriate to our educational system. Second, the input is typically limited to variables that can be readily quantified, preferably in terms of dollar costs, which tends to make the researcher limit himself to problems and model components that can be so measured. That is, although the financial and technical problems alone are formidable, the real problem from the point of view of a sociology of learning is that "the educational system is much more complicated than any system yet devised by the military, and that we have much less understanding of the former's component parts" (Oettinger, 1968). Moreover, several of the studies discussed in this chapter (for example, Coleman *et al.,* McDill *et al.*) concluded that any real improvement in school productivity, especially in terms of raising the achievement of the disadvantaged, will require changes in the underlying structure of the school as a social system, including role positions and expectations, the composition of the student body, and modes of communication, not simply increasing the amount of financial investment or using current funds more "efficiently."

On the other hand, such an approach to educational problems, if properly used, could produce clearer, more rigorous evaluations. While acknowledging the complexities of the learning system, systems analysts and game developers argue that this should not deter us from trying to describe them more objectively.

Conclusions

In this chapter and the preceding one, we have studied the school as a social system, that is, as a complex of interrelated parts. One important question raised in these chapters is whether a school as a whole has any independent effects upon its students, or to put it another way, whether the output of a given student or group of students with a given teacher would be different if that student or class were in a different school.

Some educational researchers are convinced that any apparent effects of the school per se ultimately can be explained away by the characteristics of the individual students who comprise the student body. On the other hand, there is some convincing if not conclusive evidence—particularly in the studies by Wilson and by McDill and his associates—that certain characteristics of the school do matter. There is also evidence—notably in *Equality of Educational Opportunity*—that schools matter more for some students than others, and that disadvantaged children are especially susceptible to the quality of the schools they attend.

What school dimensions are the most important determinants of student performance? The more interesting studies are those which examine the joint and/or relative effects of a variety of school characteristics. Single-variable analyses, such as the effect of school size or of the vertical arrangement of grade levels, have been inconclusive, and it seems unlikely that any single structural characteristic of a system as complex as a school will explain much of the variance in schools' outputs.

The most powerful predictors of student achievement which have emerged from reviewing available multiple-variable studies are the composition and climate of the student body, and to a lesser degree of the faculty. A relatively high school status "context" and a climate of opinion that is favorable toward and supportive of intellectual achievement are both conducive to actual student performance. The most important teacher variables identified so far are teachers' measured verbal ability and the pressure teachers exert on students to achieve.

The impact of school resources, including financial expenditures, is still debatable. The conclusion of the *Equality of Educational Opportunity* study is that economic factors have little effect, but this has been contradicted by earlier studies and by some reanalysis of the *EEO* study data. The strength of economic effects seems to depend upon what actual indicators are used and the order in which they are brought into a multivariate analysis. Moreover, the strength is hard to determine precisely because resources are interrelated with other factors related to achievement—they tend to be unequally distributed among schools, and schools with the greatest financial and other resources are at the same time likely to be high on the other variables related to academic success.

In sum, it does seem to matter what goes on in schools, and what seems to matter most to a student's level of accomplishment in school is who he interacts with there.

However, we are still in the conjecturing stage as far as identifying the aspects of in-school experience and the kinds of in-school interaction which contribute most to academic success. And we shall probably not move out of this stage until we move away from the "plague of the cross-sectional study," as Wilson puts it. The only direct way to understand the process by which learning is affected by the school environment is to undertake detailed longitudinal studies "comparing children with similar measured abilities early in their school careers who are subsequently exposed to contrasting school experiences" (Wilson, 1968: 83).

A fresh approach to the analysis of school effectiveness is offered also by the techniques of systems analysis and simulation gaming, both relatively new to behavioral science and educational research. By forcing the researcher to be very specific about the inputs and outputs he is analyzing, such techniques may lead to more objective evaluations of schools and school programs. Neither, however, has been used widely enough in empirical research studies for us to pass judgment upon its worth.

Before turning to groups and institutions outside of the school, we shall consider the educational implications of a group which is in a sense both inside and outside the school—the student peer group in general and the "youth culture" or "adolescent society" in particular. On the one hand, such a group is not part of the formal organization of the school and it carries on many of its activities—and often has its origins—outside of school. On the other hand, this chapter has indicated that an important part of the student's learning environment consists of his fellow students and that the composition of the student body is among the most important characteristics of a school. We shall devote the next chapter to an examination of the structure and dynamics of the peer group as it affects students' academic attitudes and achievement.

Notes

1. Note that this conclusion contradicts the conclusions reached in some of the studies to be presented in Chapter 12, which indicate that the effects of schools' external environments so outweigh the effects of the schools themselves that only 'massive redistribution of community resources will produce noteworthy changes in achievement patterns.

2. The first major report on Project Talent (Flanagan *et al.*, 1962) had consisted mainly of a series of statistical intercorrelations of school characteristics with school means on various parts of the test batteries, unconnected by any kind of theoretical framework. The five factors found to be most strongly correlated with mean achievement scores were: (1) male teacher starting salary; (2) housing quality in the school's immediate neighborhood; (3) absentee rate; (4) per-pupil expenditure (though low-spending schools sometimes had very high achievement in one or a few academic areas); and (5) college attendance rate. The factors with very low correlations were: (1) senior class size (a finding at variance with Conant's claims about the advantages of large, comprehensive high schools); (2) dropout rate; (3) average class size; and (4) urban or rural location (although this dimension was correlated with other variables which were strongly related to achievement—for instance, teachers' starting salary).

3. For some of the best analysis and criticism, see the special issue of the *Harvard Educational Review,* on *Equal Educational Opportunity,* Winter, 1968.

4. The implications of Bowles' reanalysis also are applicable to the regression analysis used in the second of the two Wilson studies. The relative effects of SES and racial context might have been different if the order in which these coefficients were computed had been different.

5. Also suggested by Wilson's study is the possibility of a selection process which differentiates students of the same social class who attend different schools. That is, it may be that working-class parents—or professional parents— who send their children to primarily middle-class schools are more ambitious or are in some way more competent than those parents who send their children to primarily working-class schools. The existence of such a selection process is consistent with some of the findings reported in Chapter 4, in particular with Kahl's discovery of differences among working-class parents in terms of satisfaction with their own social position and of their ambitions for their children.

6. A statistical technique for reducing a large number of items, or sets of items, to a smaller number of common dimensions or "factors." Ideally, each factor contains a cluster of items or scales which have high correlations with each other and low correlations with all other items or clusters. Factor analysis is an extremely complicated procedure which requires such extensive mathematical calculations that it was not widely used in the social sciences until the development of factor analysis programs for computers. See McDill *et al.*, 1967, for a full discussion of their factors and the methodology used to obtain them. For a more general discussion of factor analysis, see Fruchter, 1954; Harman, 1967; or Henrysson, 1957.

7. "Press" refers to the demands or pressures of an environment as perceived by the aggregate of students in a school. For example one press scale consists of the following four items having to do with respondents' view of the pressures toward academic competition:

There is a lot of competition for grades here. (true)
Students here are very much aware of the competition to get into college. (true)
Few students try hard to get on the honor roll. (false)
A lot of students here are content just to get by. (false)

. . . at Madison Junior High School, if you cooperated with the teacher and did your homework, you were a "kook." At Levi Junior High School, if you don't cooperate with the teacher and don't do your homework, you are a "kook." . . . At Madison we asked a question, "Are you going to college?" At Brighton the question always is "What college are you going to?" . . .

What the pupils are learning from one another is probably just as important as what they are learning from the teachers. This is what I refer to as the hidden curriculum. It involves such things as how to think about themselves, how to think about other people, and how to get along with them. It involves such things as values, codes, and styles of behavior.

U.S. Commission on Civil Rights

In 1961, a landmark study in the sociology of education, James Coleman's *The Adolescent Society,* was published. After a decade of reanalysis and controversy, it seems appropriate to try to place the study in perspective, which includes reviewing not only the major themes of the study itself but also the implications drawn from it by educators and the further research stimulated by it.

In keeping with a claim of this book that the most "practical" solutions to real-life social problems, including educational problems, are often obtained from work carried out within a very general theoretical framework, it is interesting to note that Coleman turned to schools not primarily out of substantive interest or to argue a particular pedagogical creed, but because they provided a setting in which to test some of his more general theoretical and methodological concerns at that time. His major desire was to study the relation of the individual to society, in particular the "dilemma that confronts each society, on the one hand, to maintain social order and, on the other, not to restrict the freedom of the individuals within it" (Coleman, 1964: 184). Finding that the survey research techniques then used in most sociological research were not applicable to this sort of problem, and having become interested in the then developing methods of contextual analysis, Coleman began to look for social situations in which the system boundaries are clear and the individual members not involved in so many different social systems that identity and measurement of any one systemic influence becomes impossible. The idea of using high schools came to him as the result of a casual conversation with friends. In comparing experiences in schools varying from an academically elite high school in a large city to a basketball-oriented school in a small Midwestern town:

> It was difficult for each of us to understand the others' high schools, for the systems of status, the frames of reference they provided, were so different from our own. It suddenly struck us that the four of us had spent those years in four rather different worlds, and we were like Bushmen, aborigines, Moslems, and Mongols, trying to comprehend the others' customs and status structure and how it would feel to be in such a society.
>
> . . . Once the subject of high schools had arisen as a possibility, a number of other advantages were evident: they existed in abundance; they had a rapid and intense impact (the "life cycle" was only three or four years in length, and a new generation arrived each year); their members were old enough to look to each other for a large proportion of daily rewards, yet young enough to have some plasticity to the environment; the institution provided a boundary to the system, cutting its members off, in part, from the outside. . . . For my purpose and, indeed, for numerous problems in the functioning of social systems, high schools can constitute the sociologist's "fruit fly" for study (Coleman, 1964: 188).

The major thesis of *The Adolescent Society* is that there exists a strong student peer culture which is separate from, and often at variance with, the values and goals of adult society. Coleman sees the emergence of this culture as an almost inevitable consequence of our complex, highly industrialized society, in which the family is losing more and more of the functions which formerly made it a self-sufficient socioeconomic unit as well as the major source of emotional support and solidarity. In contrast to the family, the school has acquired more functions, both an extension of formal learning tasks (since there is more to be learned in a highly technical society, young people spend more years in school) and added responsibility for the teaching of values and morals—a function which used to be shared by the family and the church. As a formal institution, however, the school cannot provide the diffuse support and the particularistic treatment with which the family could infuse education. As a consequence, the student is "forced inward toward his own age group, made to carry out his whole social life with others his own age. With his fellows, he comes to constitute a small society, one that has most of its important interactions *within* itself, and maintains only a few threads of connection with the outside adult society" (Coleman, 1961: 3).

This conception of the youth-student within the learning system and the larger society is not unique to Coleman's work. A theoretical paper by Talcott Parsons, also written in the early 1960's, analyzes youth culture as a response to strains in contemporary American society, produced by massive changes in the structure of society without parallel adjustments in basic value patterns (which still stress active mastery of one's environment). Rising levels of expectations for children are combined with increased autonomy resulting from permissive child-rearing practices and progressive educational methods. As a consequence, there is a kind of "duality" of orientation among the young: on the one hand, an almost compulsive independence, a touchiness with respect to any adult expectations and demands; on the other hand, an equally compulsive conformity and loyalty to the peer group, with very literal observation of group norms and intolerance of deviance (Parsons, 1962).

While much of Parsons' (and Coleman's) argument would apply to Western industrial nations other than the United States, Parsons makes no claims for wider applicability. One of the most extensive studies of the formation of age groups in general and youth groups in particular is Eisenstadt's massive comparison of anthropological materials from primitive, historical, and modern societies. *From Generation to Generation,* which classifies the underlying value orientations of total societies and subgroups within them. Eisenstadt finds no society in which groupings of children are absent. "In all societies, children are drawn together for various reasons, play together—often at being adults—and thus learn the various types and rules of cooperative behavior and some universalistic norms" (Eisenstadt, 1956: 46). Similarly, the existence of adolescent groups seems to be universal, forming a transition group oriented toward the ultimate attainment of full adult status within the society. But the form and function which such groups take differs greatly. In modern industrial societies characterized by an emphasis upon achievement and regulated by "universalistic" criteria (that is, the individual is evaluated according to his own worth, by general or "universalistic" standards, rather than upon his position in a given family or some other basic societal unit), the youth group becomes more significant in the life of the adolescent and at the same time more isolated from the rest of society. This explains the "strong emotional interdependence and intensive mutual identification" in such groups—and also explains how such groups can "become nuclei of various rebellious and deviant movements and activities" (Eisenstadt, 1956: 227–228).

The implications of crosscultural differences for the structure of formal learning systems will be discussed more fully in Chapter 13. The point here is that the structure and value orientations of the larger society define the position of the youth and affect the nature of his relationships with his peers within as well as outside of school. And in societies like our own, the strength of the student peer group and its separation from other societal institutions is a response not only to the general value orientations of the larger society but also to the lack of fully institutionalized functions for the young within the productive life of their communities.

Coleman's Major Findings

The important elements of the high school system which are analyzed by Coleman are diagrammed in Exhibit 11–1. Coleman's study describes the content of adolescent values and attitudes (A), the way individuals' values and attitudes combine to form the value climate of a school (B), and the way in which the peer group, broken down into various subgroups varying in function and prestige (D) and operating within the context of the school (B and C), affects the performance of the individual students (E) and also reflects back upon their attitudes and aspirations (A).

The empirical data which Coleman used to support his argument of a separate and increasingly powerful peer influence come from the following sequence of questions:

> Let's say that you had always wanted to belong to a particular club in school, and then finally you were asked to join. But then you found out that your parents didn't approve of the group. Do you think you would . . .
> _____ definitely join anyway
> _____ probably join
> _____ probably not join
> _____ definitely not join
>
> What if your parents approved, but the teacher you like most disapproved of the group. Would you . . .
> _____ definitely join anyway
> _____ probably join
> _____ probably not join
> _____ definitely not join
>
> What if your parents and teachers approved of the group, but by joining the club you would break with your closest friend, who wasn't asked to join? Would you . . .
> _____ definitely join anyway
> _____ probably join
> _____ probably not join
> _____ definitely not join
>
> Which one of these things would be hardest for you to take—your parents' disapproval, your teacher's disapproval, or breaking with your friend?
> _____ parents' disapproval
> _____ teacher's disapproval
> _____ breaking with friend

In response to the last question in the sequence, Coleman found that while the largest percentage indicated parental disapproval as hardest to take, this was a bare majority (54% for boys, 52% for girls), and only about ten per cent higher than the proportion most concerned with their friend's reaction (43% for both boys and girls), with teacher disapproval amounting for only a small minority. As Coleman interprets these data: "The balance between parents and friends indicated the extent of the state of

Exhibit 11-1

Components of the High School Peer Culture

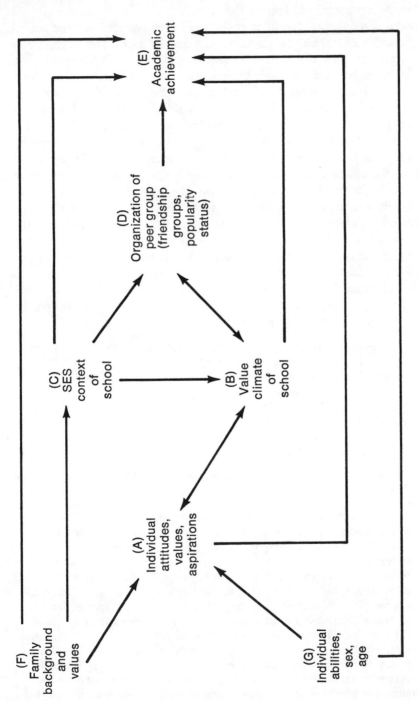

transition that adolescents experience—leaving one family, but not yet in another, they consequently look both forward to their peers and backward to their parents" (Coleman, 1961: 5).

Student responses to questions about their interests and favorite activities showed a deep concern about acceptance by peers and engaging in shared activities with them. Favored activities including dating, talking on the telephone, being in the same class and eating together with friends in school, and "hanging around together" or just "being with the group" outside of school. Esteem is gained by a combination of friendliness and popularity, an attractive appearance, physical and social maturity, and possession of skills and objects (cars, clothes, music, and so forth) valued by the culture. It is interesting to note that the latter are typically perceived as giving the owner an aura of sophistication, although the particular form they take is such as to set him apart from the adult world (for instance, rock music, teen styles in hair and clothes). Moreover, says Coleman, the attributes and activities most valued by students are discrepant with the central goals of the school as a formal learning system. As in his argument for the existence of powerful peer group pressures, Coleman's argument for the discrepancy between peer group and school system goals is based upon a small set of questions which posit a basic dilemma which the respondent must resolve. In this case it is a choice of roles within the school system, and the basic question is:

> If you could be remembered here at school for one of the three things below, which one would you want it to be?
> Boys: _____ Brilliant student
> _____ Athletic star
> _____ Most popular
> Girls: _____ Brilliant student
> _____ Leader in activities
> _____ Most popular

The responses, collected at the beginning and end of the school year, indicated that:

> For boys, not only is the athletic star's image more attractive at the beginning of the school year; the boys move even slightly further in that direction—at the expense of the popularity image—over the period of the school year.
> The girls are somewhat similar: at the beginning of the school year, the activities leader and most popular are about equally attractive images, both more often mentioned than the brilliant student. By spring, the activities leader image has gained slightly in attractiveness, at the expense of both the brilliant student and the most popular. These shifts, of course, are quite small, and there are differences from school to school, as later chapters will indicate. Nevertheless, the point is clear; the image of athletic star is most attractive for boys; the images of activities leader and most popular are more attractive to girls than brilliant student (Coleman, 1961: 30).

A parallel question asking which of the three kinds of ideal-type student they would like most to *date* revealed that the brilliant student, especially the brilliant girl student, fares poorly, and that the proportion of respondents naming the brilliant student as a dating choice declined even further during the course of the school year.

As he continues his search for an explanation of the low commitment to the basic goals of the school system, Coleman finds that when students were asked to speculate upon their *parents'* preferences for them, more thought their parents would be very proud of them if they made the basketball or cheer-leading team than if they were chosen by a science teacher to act as his assistant. "Thus, even the rewards a child gains from his parents may help reinforce the values of the adolescent culture—not because his parents hold these same values but because parents want their children to be successful and esteemed by their peers" (Coleman, 1961: 34).

Obviously related to what individual students want for themselves is the question of what gives an individual status with his peers (D in Exhibit 11–1). Coleman asked two kinds of questions about status: (1) an open-ended question, "What does it take to get in with the leading crowd in this school?"[1] and (2) a pair of questions asking respondents to rank the following six items in terms of their importance in making a student popular with their own sex and with the opposite sex:

Coming from the right family

Leader in activities

Having a nice car (for girls: clothes)

High grades, honor roll

Being an athletic star (for girls: being a cheer leader)

Being in the leading crowd.

Portions of the section reporting the responses to the first question were included in Chapter 5. For both sexes the emphasis was upon having a good personality, good looks, and good clothes. Averaging the rankings given to the lists of items showed that athletics was of primary importance in making a boy popular, with being in the leading crowd first in importance for girls and second for boys. Getting good grades was relatively unimportant for boys and even less so for girls, though it is worth noting that it is perceived as relatively more valuable for popularity with one's own sex. For girls especially, academic success is seen as contributing little to, and possibly even detracting from, popularity with the opposite sex. As we noted in Chapter 5, the tremendous importance of popularity with boys focused the attention of most girls upon projecting an image of personal attractiveness, and personal attractiveness required not appearing to care too much about academic success.

A major interest of Coleman's, and a major methodological and substantive contribution of *The Adolescent Society,* is the measurement of school value climates. As Coleman sees it, the attitudes of students at a given school form an important component of its social environment, and he wanted to show how they influenced individual students' status, attitudes, and achievement. The climate measure for each school in the sample is based upon the average rankings to the question of what it took to get to be important and looked up to by peers—the same question that was used to determine the components of individual popularity, but now combined and averaged within each school to get a composite index for the school as a social system. Coleman thus was able to locate each school in his sample in terms of its relative (that is, relative to the other schools) emphasis upon the three dimensions of scholastic achievement, family background, and athletic achievement (popularity and being a cheer leader for the girls).[2]

When Coleman compared the responses of students who received the greatest number of sociometric choices from their peers with the picture of the peer culture as a whole which he had already obtained, he found that no matter what the unique value climate of a school, the male elite was more oriented to the athletic image. In every school, boys identified as athletic stars received more sociometric status than those identified as top scholars, although the athlete-scholar usually received most of all, and the scholar who was not an athlete still received more choices than boys who were neither scholars nor athletes. Boys who were athletes or scholars or both made up almost half of the male leading crowds, although they constituted only about twelve per cent of the total population of the schools (Coleman, 1961: 148–149).

The elites were less favorable to the brilliant student value than the non-elites, although at the same time they tended to have higher grades than the student body as a whole.[3] Between-school comparisons revealed another interesting pattern, however, which was that the relative academic superiority of students in the leading crowd reflected the relative status of good grades in their schools. In schools in which the value climate incorporated a relatively high valuation of the brilliant student, elite students did even better relative to others (the standard deviation between grade averages for the leading crowd and for the total student body was greater); in schools with the lowest relative valuation of the brilliant student, the gap was smaller.[4] Although Coleman pointed out that his findings do not establish whether the grades of the leading crowds were a "source, consequence, or merely confirmation of the status system and its rewards for scholastic achievement," they do suggest a linkage between the value climate of a school and the level of scholastic performance of its students.[5]

The elites were also less adult-oriented than the rest of the student body. In the hypothetical decision about whether or not to join a club that their parents did not approve of, it was found that boys and girls identified as being in their school's leading crowd were even less likely than others to say that their parents' disapproval would be hardest to take (Coleman, 1961: 6). They were, on the other hand, more school oriented than the nonelites, although their commitment to the school was of a special sort. In yet another set of questions positing a conflict between various reference groups, this one having to do with attending a school pep rally or going riding with friends, the high status students were more likely to choose the rally.[6] They were, however, even *less* oriented than the student body as a whole toward doing what teachers wanted. As Coleman puts it, the elites are "selective in their overchoice of school-related activities."

Finally, Coleman's data throw light on the relationship between family status and peer status. Although there is a tendency toward control by the students from middle-class, relatively well-educated families, the strength of the effect of an individual student's family status upon his school status is mediated by the SES composition of the school he attends (the effects of components F and C upon D). This relationship is clarified by comparing two extreme cases, both schools in fairly homogeneous communities but at the opposite ends of the SES continuum (component C). At one extreme is Newlawn, "where students from well-educated families are very scarce," and where "they are scarcer yet among the leading crowd." At the other extreme, in Executive Heights, where most students are from well-educated families, middle-class students dominate the leading crowd. Colman's conclusion:

> The leading crowd of a school, and thus the norms which that crowd sets, is more than merely a reflection of the student body, with extra middle-class students thrown in. The leading crowd tends to accentuate those very background characteristics already dominant, whether they be upper- or lower-class. A boy or girl in such a system, then, finds it governed by an elite whose backgrounds exemplify, in the extreme, those of the dominant population group. In particular, a working-class boy or girl will be most left out in an upper-middle class school, least so in a school with few middle-class students (Coleman, 1961: 109).

Coleman's interpretation offers an explanation for a discrepancy between his view of one of the schools in his sample and the image presented by an earlier study of the same school, Hollingshead's *Elmtown's Youth* (1949). When Hollingshead studied Elmtown High School in the early 1940's, family status was the major determinant of school success. Over two-thirds of the children classified as coming from the top social classes were in the college prep curriculum, and grades were also strongly related to SES, partly, in Hollingshead's view, because of the teachers' sensitivity to the social position of their students. The working-class child had little opportunity in this school unless he possessed to an obvious degree one of the characteristics valued by the dominant middle-class culture (athletic talent in a boy, beauty in a girl), and few lower-SES students completed high school. By contrast, Coleman found that fewer than a third of the student leaders at Elmtown High School had college-educated fathers. Although this was a higher proportion than among the total student body, it indicated that by the later 1950's, the middle class no longer dominated the social life of the school. In addition to historical changes in the interval between the Hollingshead and Coleman studies (including the great increase in the proportion of the total age group who stays in school through high school), differences in the sampling framework (Coleman's was a comparative survey while Hollingshead's was an intensive study of a single case) and in the methods of collecting data and constructing measures may have contributed to the differences in results. This illustrates again the necessity—and the difficulty—of pooling findings from studies conducted at different times and using different kinds of research designs in order to understand the dynamics of the learning system.

The Adolescent Society has had strong supporters and vehement critics. Indeed one mark of its importance is the number of critiques and subsequent research studies which it has stimulated. We shall use Coleman's model as the framework for discussing other studies of the school peer group. Thus the studies will be grouped in terms of their general location in Exhibit 11–1, including:

studies which focus upon the conceptualization, measurement, and effects of value climate (B);

studies which focus upon the organization of the peer group (D), including the breakdown into friendship groups, cliques, elites, and other subgroups, and the way in which peer status is related to academic achievement;

studies which focus upon the *process* by which the peer group, influenced by individual and contextual factors, facilitates or hinders academic productivity (the linkages between A, B, C, D, and E);

studies which compare the strength of peer influence relative to that of parents and other possible reference groups, including the conditions under which and the areas in which peer influences are especially strong.

(Note that a few of these studies antedate *The Adolescent Society,* showing how Coleman's work incorporates or reflects some earlier work on social system structure and operation in general and schools in particular.)

Further Studies of Value Climate

As we saw in the last chapter, not all researchers acknowledge the existence of value climates as social "facts" separate from the combined personal characteristics of the individual system members. The McDill study discussed there is one of a number designed not only to refine certain of the techniques introduced in *The Adolescent Society,* but also to test the hypothesis of the reality of an independent normative climate. In support of this hypothesis, McDill and his colleagues found clusters of items, pertaining to composite student valuation of academic excellence, which accounted for a certain proportion of the variation in students' mathematics achievement even when (1) their *individual* abilities, values, and socio-economic status and (2) the SES *composition* of the school were held constant.

Although McDill developed multiple indices or factors of intellectual valuation, and each factor consisted of multiple items, his conceptualization of the value climate measure was essentially the same as Coleman's—a simple averaging of responses for a given school, with each student's response given equal weight. Other research has been directed toward developing more elaborate concepts and measures. One early study which offers some interesting insights into the nature of value climate is the Bennington College study (itself an influential and much-debated piece of research). The work of Newcomb and others in connection with this very atypical girls' college suggests that climate may be established and/or heavily influenced by certain subgroups within the total system. The original "tone" of Bennington was set by the New Deal, liberal attitudes of the faculty with respect to the controversial public issues of the time. Even after the college was in full operation, its atmosphere was influenced predominantly by the faculty and by those students who had internalized the faculty values (although many of those students came from families with conservative political and social views). For certain subgroups (entering freshmen), the perceived attitudes and expectations of the faculty, rather than the actual, often conservative, values of their immediate peers, provided the major point of reference—and the freshmen who adopted faculty attitudes were the ones who tended to be named by their classmates as "most worthy to represent the college."

At the same time, there was evidence that this influence was limited in range and time. For example, 62% of the freshmen voted for the Republican candidate in a mock election, and a follow-up study of a portion of the original sample indicated that for most students the liberal outlook was only temporary.

A more recent study of peer group influence at the college level, which supported some of the Bennington findings and also suggested further refinements of the measurement of climate, was conducted by Wallace (1965). When he compared the postgraduate aspirations of an entire freshman class of a midwestern college at three times during the school year, Wallace found that the proportion of freshmen wanting to go on to graduate or professional school rose at each subsequent measurement, bringing the freshman profile ever closer to the aspiration pattern of upper-classmen. Even with measures of previous academic achievement and future occupational ambition held constant, the aspiration climate created by the freshman's older peers seemed to account for an appreciable amount of his aspiration change.

There were also some interesting interaction effects among the three factors. For example, peer influence seemed to be most powerful among those students with the *lowest* past academic achievement. Wallace interprets this finding as suggesting that "the rise in low academic rank freshmen's graduate school aspirations may have had more to do with their social attitudes toward, and experiences in, college than with their expectations of graduate school success" (Wallace, 1965: 384), and that the student who is weaker academically is also the one most likely to be susceptible to and to conform to peer group pressures. A similar pattern was found in connection with socioeconomic ambition, with a greater rise in postgraduate study aspirations expressed among freshmen who chose relatively low-status occupations when they entered college.

A major distinction of the Wallace study is in the conceptualization of peer group influence. Unlike the Coleman measure, the Wallace technique computes an "interpersonal environment" score for each student by having the student check all the names he or she recognizes from a list of the entire student body. For each student, the measure "estimates that part of the total student-body with which he had direct or indirect contact sufficient to remember the names of its members" (Wallace, 1965: 378). This technique assumes that in a system as large as that of most colleges, there are likely to be several peer groups, each holding different values. Thus a student who seems to be a deviant from the student culture may simply be deviating from the most visible or "leading" clique, but may be well integrated into his own subgroup. And even if one can distinguish a single-value—or dominant-value—climate, Wallace's conceptualization suggests that it may affect different students differentially, depending upon the other members of the system with whom they have contact.

In summary, carefully designed studies provide enough evidence to allow us to retain the hypothesis of the reality of climatic or contextual effects, although some studies described here have suggested that the composition and influence of a school's value climate may not be exactly the same for all students. This leads us to the next set of studies, which have to do with internal differentiation within a given school.

The Components and Consequences of Peer Status

To support his hypothesis of the importance of peer group influence upon academic performance, Coleman showed that students within a given school grouped themselves into subgroups which varied in status as well as in favored activities, and that the elites tended (1) to represent the dominant social background of their school's student body and (2) to hold the dominant values of the larger peer group and to perform well at the activities most valued by the student body as a whole.

A study which predated *The Adolescent Society* and which foreshadowed it in certain respects is Wayne Gordon's *The Social System of the High School* (1957). In contrast to Coleman's multiple-school survey, Gordon's study is an intensive analysis of a single midwestern high school. The author was, moreover, a classroom teacher and the director of guidance at the school for ten years. Although he supplemented his regular contacts and day-to-day observations with some quite structured interviews and questionnaires, his presence in the school already was established when he began the formal study, and thus he was able to be a participant observer without introducing the usual bias of this role.

Gordon's general goal was "to develop a general framework for the analysis of adolescent behavior in the high school and to explore the crucial relationship between the social status and the behavior of adolescents" (Gordon, 1957: xi). His model described the adolescent's social system as composed of three subsystems. First was the "formal scheme of things," the curriculum, course work, teachers, rules, grades, and other aspects of school as a formal learning institution. Second was a "semi-formal set of sponsored organizations and activities," including athletics and clubs. Gordon saw these as arranged on a hierarchy of prestige, and among his research devices was a questionnaire in which students rated student organizations and the various positions within them. Third was the informal subsystem, the "half-world of usually non-recognized and non-approved cliques, factions, and fraternities." Like Coleman, Gordon measured interpersonal relations and peer status by asking students to designate which of their peers they liked best and held in the highest esteem, and he too carried out an extensive sociometric analysis of the entire student body.

Gordon's conclusions are very close to Coleman's. Success in non-academic areas contributes more than scholastic achievement to status, although "students showed an upward trend toward the fulfillment of the expectations for grade achievement with each additional year in school," and "conformity to classroom expectations[7] ran a cycle through lower to upper grade levels in the order of a maximum conformity to maximum nonconformity back toward increasing conformity among both boys and girls" (Gordon, 1957: 131). Successful participation in highly rated student activities—athletic teams, band, certain committees and clubs—is a better predictor of individual status. And the informal system of friendship groups and cliques is "especially powerful in controlling adolescent behavior, not only in such matters as dress and dating, but also in school achievement and deportment" (Gordon, 1957: viii).

A dissenting view of the relationship between academic achievement and peer status is registered in Turner's study of Los Angeles high schools (introduced in Chapter 6). Turner agrees that a youth culture exists, but he argues that it is "segmented and ritualistic, not necessarily in conflict with other kinds of behavior looked upon favorably by the adult world," and that it "does not penetrate deeply enough to require that solidarity takes precedence over pursuits related to long range success goals" (Turner, 1964: 146).

Turner's major variables were essentially the same as Gordon's—academic achievement, participation in school-sponsored extracurricular activities, and informal friendships with classmates—but while Gordon was interested in weighing the relative contribution of these three variables to an individual's overall status, Turner focuses upon the interrelation among the three. The differences in mode of analysis are indicated in the following diagram:

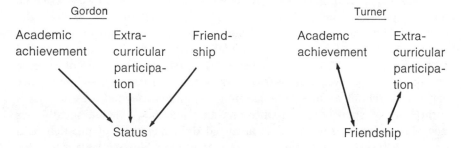

Also in contrast to Gordon, who obtained his data on the first two variables from school records and student self-reports, Turner measured all three by sociometric questionnaire items; respondents were asked to name their classmates who best fitted the categories of "brain," "big wheel," and "desired friend."

The results of Turner's analysis showed positive correlations among the three ratings. To be named good at schoolwork was related to being named both as a "desired friend" and as a "big wheel," with the relationship slightly stronger for girls than boys. That academic success is *not* seen as unattractive is suggested by the finding that virtually no one reputed to be a "brain" was not also named as a desired friend, although one could be named as a "desired friend" without being either a "brain" or a "wheel." While many students combined high "brain" with low "wheel" ratings, there were few cases of the reverse combination—low 'brain"-high "wheel." Turner attributes this to a possible halo effect, with "students overestimating the quality of school performance among their peer leaders," but he points out that "there could, however, be no halo effect unless students placed the same positive valuation upon both types of personal qualities." His conclusion is that his findings bely the notion of a youth culture "conspiracy" against academic excellence. On the contrary, individual students seem able to adhere to the central achievement values of the school while still enjoying the esteem of their peers, apparently embodying important peer standards while remaining somewhat detached from them (Turner, 1964: 153–154).

Turner's indicant of academic achievement was students' perceptions of their peers' performance. Some studies find similar, if slight, relationships when grades or achievement test scores are used as the dependent variable. In a review of studies of elementary school children, Gronlund (1959) found positive correlations between test scores and sociometric status ranging from .14 to .36, and these correlations tended to increase when comparisons were made between only the highest and lowest status groups. Ryan and Davie (1958) obtained similar results in a study of four classes (326 students) in a suburban Connecticut high school, and they concluded that social acceptance, at least in terms of their rather crude measure, accounted for at least a portion of grade variance. Buswell (1954) also found a small positive correlation, but it tended to disappear when he controlled for IQ. He attributed the small original correlation to a tendency for children to over-choose peers who were similar or slightly above them in achievement and intelligence rather than greatly superior.

The small size of their correlations led Gronlund and Ryan and Davie to conclude, as Coleman did, that the effect of social acceptance may differ from one school to another. "School achievement is probably most closely related to sociometric status where such achievement is highly valued by the group. . . . Thus, when the relation between school achievement and sociometric position is being considered, the level of achievement of the choosers as well as that of the chosen must be considered" (Gronlund, 1959: 195–196). The majority of the students in Ryan and Davie's sample were in the college prep program and thus would be expected to be positive toward academic achievement. Turner found that the relationships among the three kinds of status he examined varied throughout the ten schools in his sample (and, moreover, students of low-status and low-achievement subgroups were underrepresented in his sample). In sum, while status with one's peers does not necessarily detract from intellectual performance, and vice versa, the relationship depends also upon the social environment in which it occurs.

Processes of Peer Group Formation and Influence

We have seen that the particular subgroups to which a student belongs or with which he identifies have an impact upon his behavior in school, although there seems to be no simple, direct correlation between academic achievement and other kinds of school status. We have not, however, said much about *how* students get themselves into one or another of the subgroups into which a student body divides itself and *what* happens within the peer group to affect students' attitudes and efforts.

Two studies document the impact of peer contact upon academic aspirations and performance. One is a study of some 1400 male seniors in thirty North Carolina high schools, conducted by Campbell and Alexander (1964 and 1965), which attempts to test the effects of interpersonal relations as formulated by Newcomb and the balance theorists[8] and to synthesize these effects with the structural or contextual effects formulated by Wilson and others, as described in the previous chapter. As part of a larger study, Campbell and Alexander collected three kinds of information about their subjects:

status, determined by the educational attainment of respondents' parents;

friendship choices, obtained by asking each respondent, "What students here in school of your own sex do you go around with most often?";

educational aspirations, obtained by asking each respondent whether he wanted to and expected to go to college.

The data obtained showed a clear consistency between the educational plans of individual respondents and the plans of the students they named as their best friends, even controlling for SES and regardless of whether the friends named reciprocated the sociometric choice. That is, a student at a given status level is more likely to have college aspirations and expectations, and actually to attend college, when his best friend also has college plans. The relationship was even stronger when the friendship choices were reciprocated (Alexander and Campbell, 1964).

The authors were, however, interested in testing not only the relevance of balance theory but also in comparing or synthesizing this model with the structural-contextual model, and in the second of their two papers they postulate a two-step model incorporating both processes. Each respondent was scored (from 1 to 5) on each of three measures: his own status; his friends' status (the average of the fellow students named by the respondent); and his school status (the average status of all students in his school). Campbell and Alexander predict a positive correlation between the individual's aspiration and the status of both his school and his friends. However, they also predict that school status and the tendency of individuals to choose friends of high status are related in themselves and that "the influence of friends may be an intervening variable that mediates the association between average school status and college expectations." More concretely, they expect the relationship between school status and college plans to disappear when friends' status is held constant, but the relationship between college plans and friends' status *not* to disappear when school status is held constant (Campbell and Alexander, 1965: 287).

The statistical computations relevant to these predictions are presented in Exhibit 11–2. Columns 1, 2, and 3 show the correlations between the various pairs of variables in the three-variable model. For example, Column 1 shows that there is a slight positive correlation between average school status and college plans. The strongest two-variable relationship is between school status and friends' status (Column 3): "persons at every status level are more likely to choose high-status friends when there are relatively large numbers of high status persons in the system" (Campbell and Alexander, 1965: 287).

Columns 4 and 5, which show the relationships between pairs of variables with the third controlled, constitute the empirical test of the authors' predicted two-step model:

Exhibit 11–2

Correlations Among School Status, Friends' Status,
and College Plans of High School Seniors—by Parental Educational Level

Parental Educational Level	Zero-Order Correlations			Partial Correlations		
	School Status with College Plans (1)	Friends' Status with College Plans (2)	School Status with Friends' Status (3)	* (4)	** (5)	N (6)
Both parents—college	.10	.15	.49	.03	.12	172
One parent—college	.16	.29	.36	.06	.26	183
Both parents—high school	.15	.28	.50	.01	.24	147
One parent—high school	.07	.19	.34	.01	.18	178
Neither parent—high school	.14	.31	.40	.02	.28	295

* School status with college plans, holding friends' status constant
** Friends' status with college plans, holding school status constant
From Campbell and Alexander, 1965: 286.

Is there a relationship between school status and the college plans of individuals at each status level apart from the effects of interpersonal influence that are indicated by the status of friends? The answer to this question should be negative if our hypothesized two-step model is correct. In other words, we expect only negligible variation to be explained by school status when friendship status is held constant. The partial correlations presented in colum (4) of the table show that this is precisely what occurs. By contrast, when school status is held constant, the relationship between college plans and friends' status remains strong, as revealed in the partial correlation in column (5). . . . These two sets of partial-correlation coefficients support the inference that the structural effects of school status are best conceived of as due to the interpersonal influences of an individual's significant others (Campbell and Alexander, 1965: 287–288).

In summary, it is the interpersonal relationships with one's friends within the high school (D in Exhibit 11–1) that determine high or low academic aspirations, although the likelihood of having friends with a given set of attitudes toward school and learning is determined partially by the composition of the student body as a whole, which constitutes the pool from which one's friends may be drawn (Column 3 in Exhibit 11–2).

The significance of direct contact with peers was also the theme of the study by McPartland discussed at the beginning of Chapter 7, although here peers are viewed in the role of classmates rather than friends. McPartland's analysis indicated that for children of racial minority groups, the academic advantage of being in an integrated school depended upon *being in the same classes* with middle-class majority group students. That is, integration at the school level which does not include systematic means to prevent racial subdivision in different courses or academic tracks will not have much positive effect upon upgrading academic expectations and performance. Parallel to Campbell and Alexander's findings, McPartland's indicate that while the social (in this case racial) context of the school affects the likelihood of contact between students of different backgrounds, an individual student's academic gains are directly affected only by those students with whom he has direct interpersonal relations.

The most intensive recent examinations of peer influence upon academic commitment were the studies of Vassar College students, sponsored by the Mellon Foundation and directed by Nevitt Sanford (Sanford, 1956; Freedman, 1956; Sanford, 1959; Bushnell, 1962). Questionnaire data and diaries (in which respondents recorded all their activities for several one-week periods) were collected from all students over a five-year interval. In addition, a sample drawn from one class was intensively interviewed and tested; an anthropologist was a kind of participant observer of the student culture; and some studies of alumnae were conducted.

Sanford and his associates found peer group influences operating in much the same way as those described by Coleman. Although the pressures were more subtle, the fact that this was a residential school and that the girls spent a lot of time with roommates and other friends within the college made them even more intense. There was a distinct student culture, communicated largely via bull sessions and other informal interaction, although there were slightly differing emphases, attitudes, and "life styles" among different subgroups on the campus. These ranged from the "super-intellectuals" or "science-major types" to the sociability-oriented "debutantes" or "Yale weekend girls." The general theme of the student culture was pleasant campus life, with a minimum of individual soul-searching and interpersonal conflict, although the support of roommates and close friends was available to group members who were experiencing special strains, such as difficulty with a course or a professor, or a misunderstanding with a boy friend or with parents. Unlike their Bennington counterparts of an earlier era, most Vassar subgroups in the late 1950's resisted "acculturation" to faculty norms, not by rebelling against studying and achievement in general (good grades were, in fact, respected) but by refusing to be wholeheartedly committed to scholastic achievement at the cost of satisfactory social relations with peers. "If there is an ideal Vassar girl, she is the one who received consistently high grades without devoting her entire time to the endeavor. In fact, the emphasis on combining good marks with a reasonably full social life is so strong that some students who, in reality, have to work quite hard to maintain an impressive grade-point ratio will devote considerable effort to presenting an appearance of competency and freedom from academic harassment" (Bushnell, 1962: 507). Certain student norms—for instance, proscriptions against close relationships with professors or excessive amounts of study—helped to maintain the status quo that these students thought desirable. It is also interesting that the "scholar," one of several student types conceptualized by Sanford and a kind of clinical elaboration of Coleman's "brilliant student" role, tended to be found among girls who had suffered "early and persistent awkwardness in social relations with peers" (Sanford, 1959).

A study by Hughes, Becker, and Geer of student culture in a Kansas medical school acts as a kind of replication of the Vassar studies. Peer group effects showed up even more clearly in this setting because of the intense pressure placed on students by the formal requirements of medical training. The student culture was perceived to have two major functions: "first, to provide modes of adaptation that make the pressures of the school tolerable and not too upsetting to the individual student, and second, to provide support for patterns of behavior which, though they are in the interest of the students as they see it, may be at variance with what is desired by the faculty and administration" (Hughes *et al.,* 1962: 466). Thus students reached informal agreements on what *all* of them would learn in preparation for exams, and informal norms directed which and how many case summaries out of the total assigned by professors would actually be completed and turned in (Hughes *et al.,* 1962: 525–528).

One must, of course, be cautious in drawing generalizations about the learning system from studies of medical students or other near-adult students whose educational or occupational aspirations are stabilized. Such students "begin with similar interests, attitudes and goals; they are subjected to the same pressures—often intense ones—at the same time, and they work in close association with one another and in relative isolation from groups having different norms" (Sanford, 1962: 465). Although this setting provides the clearest possible view of the processes involved in the functioning of student groups, it leaves unanswered the applicability of this model to say the comprehensive high school. And we still know virtually nothing about the formation and influence of school peer groups among younger children—studies parallel to Coleman's and Sanford's at the elementary level are sorely needed.

There are, however, some parallel findings in noneducational settings, in particular in studies of factory work groups. One of the major outcomes of the Bank Wiring Room experiments which constituted part of the Hawthorne studies[9] was the formation of informal friendship groups which were not part of the formal system of the factory and which were in many cases unknown to the management. Like school peer groups, these work groups were characterized by close interpersonal ties of the "primary" sort, by resistance to "acculturation" by the superordinate levels of the system (management), and by procedures for controlling the productivity of group members so that the group would not be under pressure to work beyond a comfortable rate.

To round out our discussion of the internal structure of the school peer group, we shall turn to a study of subgroups which actively reject both the goals and the norms of the formal school system. Along with the culturally disadvantaged, the rebellious student provides a serious, and growing, dilemma for the schools, and the rebel is of particular relevance to this chapter since he is in some ways the "ideal type" of the adolescent society.

Like Gordon's study, Stinchcombe's *Rebellion in a High School* (1964) is an in-depth study of a single school, this one a predominantly working-class California school. The study also can be viewed as an elaboration of Coleman's point that the leading crowd of a school tends to accentuate the background characteristics and related norms that are already dominant, whether they are low-, middle-, or high-SES ones. Like the Newlawn school in Coleman's sample, the some 1600 students at this school were mainly of working-class background (component C of Exhibit 11–1), and high proportions of the boys expected to become manual workers. One-fourth of them wished for higher occupational status than they expected to achieve.

A major finding of the study, however, is that it was not SES per se that determined whether a student was rebellious.[10] On the contrary, the data showed no statistical association between boys' social class and rebellion, a finding which, in Stinchcombe's opinion, "is sufficient to refute any theory which sees a direct, unconditional chain of causes from birth in a class to deviant behavior in high school. . . . Social class will be a central variable in the analysis . . . but its role in causing rebellion depends on complex intervening processes" (Stinchcombe, 1964: 86). The key intervening process is the student's perceived linkage or "articulation" between his current school activities and his perceived future status and activities. As Stinchcombe formulates it, rebellion is more related to status *prospects* than to status *origins*.[11]

The hypothesis that "high school rebellion, and expressive alienation, occurs when future status is not clearly related to present performance" is supported by the finding that the percentage of respondents exhibiting rebellious behavior is particularly high among: boys aiming toward the lower sectors of the labor market; boys aiming for middle-class occupations but taking vocational or other nonacademic courses; and girls fully committed to marriage without any curricular interest to tie current schoolwork with even a temporary future in the labor market. These were also the subgroups which most often reported spending little or no time on homework.

The lack of association between SES and rebellion was partly explained by the unusually open opportunity structure in this school. Although the community was predominantly working-class, the school had a full college preparatory curriculum, and unlike the students of Hollingshead's Elmtown High, the majority of its students in the college prep course were working-class. Such a situation is atypical, and as Stinchcombe admits, creates a rather different set of success strains than say a predominantly black slum school. Since lower-SES students were not blocked by lack of access to the training which could lead to social mobility, the rebel had to reject the notion of mobility itself.

The patterns formed by the data in this study underscore the need for looking at the multiple levels of the learning system in order to understand the relationship between any pair of components. They show that a strategy of simply introducing more middle-class orientations, or peers, into a school will not necessarily have the desired effect upon certain subgroups of students, in particular those for whom perceived articulation between schoolwork and outside interests and commitments is lacking. Finally, Stinchcombe's study contributes a kind of conceptual model of a student type that is, according to some concerned observers, becoming more prevalent in our schools. Stinchcombe's rebel combines the attributes of "non-utilitarianism, negativism, short-run hedonism, and emphasis on group autonomy" (Hypothesis 1, page 4), with a simultaneous and strong identification with adult symbols (Hypothesis 3, page 7. Rebels are, among other things, more interested in cars and more likely to own one, more likely to smoke and to claim smoking as a right, than their non-rebellious peers). They are the ones most alienated from adult society at the same time that they highly value certain adult glamour symbols. In a sense, the rebel is the teenager who most purely personifies Coleman's adolescent society.

Of concern to many observers is what they see as a growing polarization not only between the adolescent-student and adult society but within student bodies themselves. Student subgroups are becoming differentiated not only on the traditional dimensions of class and race, but also according to the degree of integration into the culture of school success. On the one hand are those students who are reasonably compliant to the pressure for good grades and other indicants of achievement, the students who fit the Turner model of incorporating the demands of academic success into other school activities and the fun of youth culture without serious conflict. On the other hand are those who either engage in hedonistic forms of rebellion—such as Stinchcombe's working-class students or who withdraw from school altogether. We now turn to this question of the linkages of the youth culture with the larger society.

The Relative Strength of Peer Influence

In this final section we shall examine evidence relating to Coleman's claim that the young increasingly are turning to one another, rather than to adults, for their social cues and rewards. A work that predated *The Adolescent Society,* and is often cited in critiques of youth culture is Elkin and Wesley's "The Myth of Adolescent Culture" (1955). In the Montreal suburb chosen for study, the authors found little conflict between parents and children and little evidence of any kind of separate youth culture. On the contrary, the forty teenagers from whom interview or life history data were obtained claimed close but open relationships with their parents and many shared activities. This study has, however, been taken more seriously than its quality as empirical research would seem to warrant. The report does not tell enough about the kinds of questions asked and the classification of responses to draw any conclusions about their validity. Moreover, the sample contains a very small number of cases, drawn from a single upper middle-class suburban community, and as far as one can tell from the report, subjects were not asked to make any specific comparisons between parents and other kinds of reference group influences.

There are, however, a number of well-designed follow-ups or replications of certain aspects of *The Adolescent Society,* which focus upon getting accurate measures of the degree of parent and peer influence for different types of students or upon the substantive areas or the conditions under which students turn to adults and peers. Some of the "vital statistics" of the studies to be considered here are outlined in Exhibit 11–3.

Simpson's study was designed as a test of alternative hypotheses explaining social mobility of working-class students. One hypothesis explains mobility as the result of parental influence; the other, as a consequence of anticipatory socialization into middle-class values by middle-class peers. Simpson's data, shown in Exhibit 11–4, indicate that both influences have an effect, although the first may be rather more important than the second. In both classes students high in parental and also peer influence were most likely to have high occupational aspirations (81.9 and 71.4%); and those with low influence from those sources were least likely to have high aspirations (30.1 and 25.6%). For working-class boys, the parental influence measure seemed to be the more powerful one:

> Among the working-class boys high in peer influence, being high rather than low in parental influence brought the percentage of high-aspirers up from 35.7 per cent to twice this figure, 71.4 per cent; and among the working-class boys low in peer influence, high parental influence more than doubled the percentage of high aspirers, increasing it from 25.6 to 55.6 per cent. The effects of peer influence on working-class boys, with parental influence controlled, were substantially less than this. Among those high in parental influence, high peer influence increased the percentage of high-aspirers from 55.6 to 71.4. . . . The seemingly greater influence of par-

Exhibit 11-3

Design of Studies Comparing Parent and Peer Influence

	Simpson	Epperson	Kandel and Lesser	Musgrove	Riley and Riley
Sample	917 boys in 2 white Southern city high schools.	619 3–6th graders, 159 10–12th graders.	2327 students in 3 high schools; 1141 of their mothers.	778 students ages 9–15 in 2 areas of English Midlands.	2500 students in 8 New Jersey high schools.
Year of Data Collection	1960	1963	1965	1962	1950's
Indicants of Parental Influence	Father's occupation; whether parents had recommended professional occupation to subject.	% saying "I would be most unhappy" if parents disapproved of decisions.	Highest level of education desired for child.	% naming parent as preferred companion; social distance scales; sentence completion (Mothers can_____, Fathers can_____).	Topics and amount of communication; perceived expectations of parents.
Indicants of Peer Influence	Occupation of best friends' fathers; participation in extracurricular activities.	% saying "I would be most unhappy" if best friend disapproved of decisions.	Highest level of expected education of 3 best friends.	% naming friends as preferred companion; social distance scales; sentence completion (Boys, or Girls, can_____).	Topics and amount of communication; perceived expectations of peers.
Major Findings	Both groups' influence. Parent influence stronger, especially for working-class boys.	Concern for parental greater than concern for peer disapproval. Difference greater among older students.	Concordance with mother greater than with best friend, but high agreement with both.	Decline of choices to parent over time, but choice related to type of activity. No change in social distance.	Communication with and influence of parents and peers dependent upon topic. Division of labor between parents and peers.

ents than of peers is also evident when we compare the percentages of high-aspirers among working-class boys high in only one type of influence. Among those high in parental influence only, 55.6 per cent were high-aspirers, but this percentage dropped to 35.7 among those high in peer influence only (Simpson, 1962: 521).

Exhibit 11–4

*Per Cent of Working-Class and Middle-Class Boys
with High Occupational Aspirations,
by Extent of Parental and Peer Influence*

		Working-Class	
		Influence of Parents	
		High	Low
Influence of Peers	High	71.4 (28)	35.7 (70)
	Low	55.6 (45)	25.6 (168)

		Middle-Class	
		Influence of Parents	
		High	Low
Influence of Peers	High	81.9 (94)	72.5 (109)
	Low	78.0 (50)	30.1 (113)

Adapted from Simpson, 1962: 521.

The corresponding differences for middle-class boys were slight (for example, compare 72.5 and 78.0%), indicating that the relative influence of parents and peers as defined by Simpson was roughly equivalent.

Epperson's study contained a critique and revision of the questions used by Coleman to measure relative parent-peer influence. As he points out, the wording of the question upon which Coleman draws his conclusion about the growing strength of peer influence (see page 215) equates *breaking* with a friend with *disapproval* of parents. Epperson asked the same questions but used the same words for all reference groups. He found that 80% of his high school sample said it would make them most unhappy if their *parents* did not like what they did (Epperson, 1964: 94–95. Note that Epperson's revision still retains the assumption of conflict between adult and peer reference groups, an assumption not made in all the other studies discussed here).

A second question raised by Epperson is whether the figures obtained by Coleman are to be interpreted as evidence of strong and emerging peer influence. In the absence of figures with which to compare them, it is difficult to evaluate the size of the percentages—except that the parent figures were larger. To meet this problem, Epperson included elementary as well as secondary students in his sample, and he reasoned that if the hypothesis of a distinct adolescent subculture was true, he should find "a decided difference between elementary and secondary school pupils in the degree to which they are concerned over the disapproval of their parents," with the relationship in the direction of lesser concern among the older students. His data showed that, on the contrary:

> Secondary school pupils appear to be more, rather than less concerned about parental reactions. The elementary school pupils, however, appear to be more concerned over their teachers' disapproval, possibly because they spend more time with teachers than secondary school pupils spend with even their favorite teachers. Since opportunities for loyalties to develop are significantly different, these data provide no basis for saying that secondary school pupils are more estranged from the adult culture (Epperson, 1964: 95).

An important contribution of Epperson's study is the inclusion of pre-adolescent children. With the exception of the sociometric studies by Gronlund and Buswell reported earlier in this chapter, there are few systematic analyses of the organization and influence of the peer group among younger children, a gap that must be filled before we can answer many of the basic questions raised in this chapter. Epperson's conclusion—that, contrary to the fear of increasingly exclusive peer power, parental influence may be increased simultaneously in certain areas—could not have been drawn if he had not had comparative data from another age group.

Although the Kandel and Lesser analysis is in a sense the simplest—it compares the degree to which a student's own educational expectations agree with those of his closest friends and with those of his parent (mother) for him—it is also the only study in which the adult expectations were obtained from the parent herself. "Concordance," or agreement, of respondents' educational expectations with their mother's expectations for them: (1) was stronger than concordance with best friends, in or outside of school, although those who agreed most with their mothers also tended to have high agreement with their friends; (2) held when a variety of factors, from social class to course in school, were controlled; and (3) seemed to be independent of family structure and even of the closeness of the mother-adolescent child relationship:

> Thus we take exception to the "hydraulic" view taken by many investigators regarding the relative influence of adults and peers which assumes that the greater the influence of the one, the less the influence of the other. Our data lead to another view: in critical areas, interactions with peers support the values of the parents.
>
> The assumption is commonly made that peers provide a deterrent to intellectual development and educational aspirations during adolescence.

Our own data confirm that the climate of American high schools does not appear to reward intellectual achievement in school. But peers have less influence on adolescents than parents with regard to future educational goals (Kandel and Lesser, 1969a: 221–222).

Some additional insights into the parent versus peer question are provided by Musgrove's study, which, like Epperson's, allows comparisons of relationships at different ages. Musgrove is a British educational psychologist who feels that the "adolescent problem" is an invention of social scientists, or at best an elaboration of a notion originated by Rousseau. "Having invented the adolescent, society has been faced with two major problems: how and where to accommodate him in the social structure, and how to make his behavior accord with the specifications" (Musgrove, 1964: 33).[12]

Musgrove collected questionnaire data from 778 boys and girls between the ages of nine and fifteen, in two socially contrasted areas in the North Midlands. On questions asking respondents their preferred companions in a variety of activities and situations, Musgrove found that the proportion of choices to parents declined significantly each year except between ages ten and eleven, but that there was a relationship between the difficulty or seriousness of the activity and the choice of companion. For example, parents were more often chosen in a situation involving danger than as companions for a party, football game, or the movies. There were no relationships between responses to these questions and the IQ or SES of the respondents.

Analysis of responses to a set of social distance scales showed, like Epperson's results, no support for the view that younger children are "closer" to adults than teenagers. The difference was that the youngest children in the sample tended to perceive the same social distance between self and parents as between self and peers, while the fourteen- and fifteen-year-olds placed their parents at a greater distance than their peers. That is, as one enters adolescence, one moves closer to peers without necessarily getting farther away from parents.

A third set of questions, involving sentence-completion tasks (for instance, "Boys of my age can _____, Mothers can _____.") was given both to the students and to a subsample of their parents. The conclusion from these data was that even into adolescence, students not only turn to parents on the more serious issues confronting them, but they also have a more positive image of adults than the adults have of them:

> The picture which adults had of teenagers was widely different from the picture that adolescents had of themselves. The adults' picture was overwhelmingly negative, with scarcely any reference to teenagers' increasing social and technical competence . . . 29 per cent were generally disapproving in their remarks, and only 15 per cent appear to have been generally approving.

Although in some respects this study suggests important differences from American conditions, it is in line with those American investigations which have shown adolescents belittled by their elders, regarded as a separate, inferior, and even threatening population, exposed to contradictory expectations from the general body of adults, and consigned, as Hollingshead has said, to "an ill-defined no-man's land that lies between the protected dependency of childhood, where the parent is dominant, and the independent world of the adult, where the person is relatively free from parental controls" (Musgrove, 1964: 104–105).

Thus Musgrove seems to say that even if a separate youth period and subculture is not real or necessary in itself, it is real in its consequences. If the larger society defines adolescence as distinct and problematic, this will have implications for the way students see themselves and the way they behave.[13]

One of the richest sources of data on the linkages between teenagers and their major reference groups is the research carried out during the 1950's at Rutgers University, under the general direction of John and Matilda Riley (the author was connected with this research during the post-data-collection years). The sample of over 2500 high school students, in eight predominantly middle-class New Jersey communities, were questioned at two points in their high school career, first in 1952 when they were ninth- or tenth-graders, a second time two years later. A battery of questionnaires covered topics and patterns of communication with a variety of communication objects: respondents' self-image, present and future; and perceptions of the expectations of parents and peers concerning a wide range of attributes, skills, and activities. The number of reports and papers based on these data is prodigious, and the possible analyses still far from exhausted. (In addition to the high school years, a follow-up study, designed by the Rileys to study the continuing socialization of young adults, involved tracing a subsample of the original respondents, now mostly in their thirties.) We shall here mention only a few of the most significant findings.

Mothers and school friends, compared with fathers, teachers, siblings, and friends outside of school, were the most popular communication sources. On a list of ten topics, mother received the most or next to most choices on all but one topic, and friends in school received the most choices on half of the topics. Communication with fathers varied by topic—father was the person most often turned to for discussion of political questions, and was just behind mother on discussion of moral questions and school problems.

There was a clear pattern of specialization by topic. The topics high on parent communication included moral problems, school problems, and politics (the last the fathers' "speciality"). Communication with peers was low in all of these areas; their specialities included movies, whom to invite to a party, problems concerning the opposite sex, and "how you get along with the kids," all of which were rarely discussed with parents. Taking each topic individually, the Rutgers group found a negative relationship between the extent to which a topic was discussed with parents and the extent to which the same topic was discussed with peers. Graphs of response patterns revealed a clustering, which suggested an underlying structure of content specialization—one in which adolescent communication is directed predominantly to parents, another to peers. The first included the problems of present schoolwork and educational plans for the future, as well as general moral decisions and problems; the second included things having to do with interpersonal relations, popularity, and status with peers.

Although there was a division of labor between the two major reference groups on individual topics, there was no relationship between overall communication with parents and peers. That is, a student who talked with his parents on many topics was neither more nor less likely to have a high total communication score with his school friends. There was also very little change in communication scores or patterns in the two-year interval between the under- and upperclass high school years (Riley *et al.,* 1955).

Other important findings came from analysis of responses to a series of vignettes or brief descriptions of fictitious high school students, each embodying a particular value (say, academic achievement, good times, peer approval) found on the basis of preliminary interviewing to be of concern to adolescents (Riley *et al.,* 1961). Respondents were asked to rate each of the vignettes on the following questions:

Do I want to be just like them?

Do the well-liked kids in my grade want their friends to be like them?

Do my parents want me to be like them?

Would this help me later on when I am through school?

Comparison of responses to the whole set showed, for example, that the majority of respondents (79% of the boys, 83% of the girls) wanted to be like the following model:

Paul and Miriam are good students. Although they are not bookworms or grinds, they get good marks because they spend quite a bit of time studying and are always "on the beam" when it comes to their work.

This was almost as many as identified with the peer approval models of popularity and friendliness, and more than identified with the following:

Dottie and Ed have a great deal of fun with their friends. They spend a lot of time with the gang, going out, studying, playing all kinds of games, and just hanging around together.

That is, the majority of these boys and girls wanted to be successful students. What they wanted to avoid was the appearance of being too outstanding or of being a "grind" (which the Coleman "brilliant student" may imply).

As a whole, the respondents did see their parents and peers as placing rather different valuation upon many of the attributes and activities encompassed in the vignettes. As might be expected, parents were perceived as placing relatively greater emphasis upon school and success, peers upon having a good time. Their own preferred image fell between their perceived expectations of these two reference groups, a pattern that the Rileys interpret as forming a bridge between the two, but which could also be interpreted as placing many students in a position of cross-pressures or dissonance.[14] The bridging view is supported by the additional finding that the expectations these students had for themselves *as adults* were different from the way they perceived themselves at the moment, and that the future expectations were, in fact, very close to perceived parental expectations. That is, while sensitive to the demands of current peer relationships and anxious to avoid the appearance of deviation from the approved adolescent image (for instance, spending an excessive amount of time and effort to get top grades), these students could at the same time distinguish between values relevant to their current—and temporary—adolescent status and those relevant to the roles they expected to play in the future.

Many of the conclusions of the Rutgers project were partially replicated by a study carried out about ten years later. Brittain (1963) questioned some three hundred girls in seven Alabama and Georgia high schools, using a list of twelve situations in which there was conflict between parents' and peers' expectations (about which course to take in school, how to dress for a given event, a dating problem). Subjects were told which of two alternative resolutions of the conflict was favored by each of the two reference groups, and they were then asked to make their own choice. There were two versions of the questionnaire, with the alternative favored by parents and peers on the first version reversed on the second. The subjects were divided into "experimental" groups, who took the two different versions of the questionnaire, with an interval of one to two weeks in between, and "control" groups, who took the same version both times.

Brittain found a statistically significant difference between experimental and control groups on the amount of shifting. A higher proportion of girls changed their choices in the experimental classes on eleven out of the twelve items. The choices and changes were not, moreover, random, but depended upon the content of the dilemma and its alternatives. Subjects were more likely to shift toward the parent-favored alternative on such items as how to get chosen for a school honor, whether to report someone who had damaged school property, and which part-time job to take. Shifts toward the peer alternative were more likely on the items of how to dress for a football game or a party and which course to take in school (which Brittain interpreted as reflecting concern about separation from friends rather than with one's school career and educational plans in general). Although the comparability of stimuli in the Riley and Brittain studies is not exact, and there are some small inconsistencies on specific items, Brittain's conclusions that "responses of adolescents to parent-peer cross-pressures are a function of the content of the alternatives," that "peer-conformity in adolescence, rather than being diffuse, tends to vary systematically across situations," and that the responses "reflect the adolescent's perception of peers and parents as competent guides in different areas of judgment" could be applied to both studies (Brittain, 1963: 389).

Many of the issues raised in this and the preceding section are summarized in a review of the literature on adolescent socialization by the coauthor of *Equality of Educational Opportunity* and of the study comparing friends' status and school status effects described earlier in this chapter.

While acknowledging the strains endemic to young people in a society in which youth as a group has a kind of "pseudo-independence" but no functional significance in the productive life of the larger society, Campbell (1969) contends that most adolescents get along remarkably well with their parents and continue to be substantially influenced by them. To bolster his argument, Campbell points out that many parents welcome rather than resist adolescent demands for independence and extension of loyalties to persons and groups outside the family. As we saw in Chapter 4—and will see again in Chapter 13—the parents of successful students are the ones most likely to encourage these tendencies, and "it seems reasonable to interpret most parent-adolescent conflict as occurring not because the direction of the adolescent's quest for greater independence is illegitimate but because perfect congruence in the speed and circumstances under which new forms of expression are tolerable is not achieved" (Campbell, 1969: 830). Campbell also points out that many aspects of youth culture—especially those which demonstrate physical prowess and skill in getting along with others—are positively sanctioned by adults. The athletic star and student body president are heroes to their parents, teachers, and neighbors as well as to their peers, and "the mother who complains that her daughter spends too much time on the telephone and receives multiple requests for dates is not nearly so pained as the mother who complains that her daughter reads books endlessly and hardly goes outside the house" (Campbell, 1969: 851). Campbell goes on to state that the "ecology of adolescent behavior functions to reduce the probability of head-on clashes." The young are skillful at avoidance tactics, and since many of their activities are not under adult surveillance, they can simply "not emit clear signals" to adults concerning behavior that might be disapproved (Campbell, 1969: 831).[15]

Finally Campbell suggests that youth culture may fulfill an important function by virtue of being at variance with the goals of the school and adult world. During much of the school day, the student is engaged in activities "that are defended far less for their intrinsic worth or gratification than because they are qualificatory to a desired state in adulthood," and outside of school he is constantly reminded that his usefulness to society is still potential. "In the midst of such themes of impermanence, prepara-

tion, and transition, the activities and value of peer culture h
solid here-and-now quality about them" (Campbell, 1969: 84
help students to put up with the less satisfying aspects of schoo.

Conclusions

The notion of a youth culture is quite conclusively supported by the available empirical evidence and it is widely accepted by sociologists. In a "poll" of social scientists who have done major research on adolescent behavior, there was virtual consensus on the existence of a distinct adolescent subculture (Gottlieb and Reeves, 1963: 64–72). The few dissenters admit that the very notion of a youth culture may act as a self-fulfilling prophecy.

What is not agreed upon is the strength of the subculture and the extent to which it is separate from and in conflict with the school and the larger adult society. The studies we have examined here suggest that peer solidarity is a variable, affected by individual background (including SES, age, and sex), the school climate or context, and the nature of the surrounding environment. Several studies have also suggested that in many schools there may be more than one subculture, depending upon the breakdown of the student body into various cliques and subgroups.

With the exception of students who have rejected the basic goals of achievement and success, most young people use both parents and peers as reference groups. Parents are, in fact, more often turned to in connection with educational problems and plans, although the influence of peers in the academic area may operate to place limits upon investment in intellectual activities. Few students want to be known as "grinds," and they will often go out of their way to avoid giving the appearance of caring too much and trying too hard for good grades and other academic rewards.

Certain trends in our society as a whole (increased racial segregation in large metropolitan areas; and intergroup relations characterized either by hostile confrontations or by repulsion and withdrawal) point to a danger that students, even within the same school, may be increasingly divided into two separate "subsocieties"—one consisting of those who are reasonably compliant to the expectations of the learning system and who will move on through ever higher levels of education; the other consisting of active rebels, who disrupt the smooth functioning of the system and who are viewed in a very negative way by most school personnel, and of passive withdrawers, who simply mark time in school until they are old enough to drop out. While it is still too early to assess the results of the current unrest on high school and college campuses, the unrest does indicate that relatively fewer students are willing to accept the "compliant student" role. (It also indicates that the content of the youth culture is not uniform or fixed, since substantial subgroups among the young are shifting their attention from issues pertaining to their immediate gratification to the social and political issues of the larger society.)

In conclusion, while the true strength and nature of peer group influences are not yet known, it seems clear that educational programs that work against important peer values are doomed to failure. The best thing to do with such a potentially powerful force is to use it, and the search for areas of agreement between youth and adult culture and for methods of learning that retain the structure and channel the energies of student friendship groups seems a fruitful kind of research. In the final section of this book, some attempts to use the power of the peer group to further learning goals will be described.

Notes

1. The question of subdivisions of students in a given school into cliques, crowds, and so on—which may in some cases hold different values—will be taken up later in the chapter. Here it should be noted only that: "In every school, most students saw a leading crowd, and were willing to say what it took to get into it" (Coleman, 1961: 36).

2. For a description of each school and its classification in this three-dimensional property-space, see Coleman, 1961: 92–96. Keep in mind that the relative position of the three dimensions *with respect to each other* was similar in all schools—in particular, being an athlete always outranked being a top student.

3. Measured in standard deviations above the school grade average.

4. This finding is consistent with findings from studies of leadership in general, which have shown that persons with high group status are the ones most cognizant of the goals and reward structure of the group and most likely to shape their own behavior around them. See, for example, Cartwright and Zander, 1962: Part 5.

5. Further evidence of such a relationship is indicated in the finding that the schools where good grades were most often mentioned as a criterion for being in the leading crowd were also the ones in which the IQ scores of students with the highest scholastic averages exceeded the school mean IQ by the greatest number of standard deviations. In other words, if the climate of the school supports scholastic achievement, the brightest students, like those in the leading crowd, are most likely to invest their energies in intellectual achievement. Conversely, where intellectualism is least valued, those with the most intellectual ability are more likely to channel their energies into other, more highly rewarded activities, leaving the top student role to be filled by students who have lesser ability and who are willing to work at a relatively unrewarded activity. In such schools, the adolescent subculture acts as a real deterrent to achievement among the most able (Coleman, 1961: 262–265).

6. An activity which personifies the ambiguous relationship between the teen society and the high school. Although held under school auspices, pep rallies really have nothing to do with the school's formal learning goals—or even with the physical education program per se.

7. Operationally defined as regular attendance and punctuality, and not having a record of disturbing or breaking the disciplinary rules of the classroom.

8. In barest outline, balance theory (also known as consistency and dissonance theory, although there are variations among the three) posits a condition of balance or consistency in a person when he perceives agreement among his own attitudes or attributes or between his and those of another person. In the latter case, he is attracted to that person. Conversely, a condition of strain is produced when a person perceives discrepancies between his own and another person's views, a strain which motivates him to remove this "imbalance" or dissonance—by changing his own attitudes, by coming to perceive symmetry between his attitudes and the other person's, or by ceasing to be positively attracted to him. Newcomb, in his application of balance theory to his studies of college friendship patterns, hypothesizes that students who share common attitudes and interests, as well as physical proximity, are most likely to be attracted to one another and to group themselves together as a unit. And that the greater the number of attributes, attitudes, and activities shared by group members, and the greater the extent to which such sharing sets the group apart from other groups, the greater will be the group's attraction for and influence upon its members (Newcomb, 1962).

9. See Chapter 8, footnote 10.

10. Operationally defined by infractions of classroom rules which resulted in being sent out of class, or habitual absences or tardiness—the other side of the coin of Gordon's "conformity" measure.

11. Stinchcombe's focus upon future orientation rather than past status as the explanation for present behavior is echoed in Turner's hypothesis that boys from lower-class schools and neighborhoods were likely to display a "pattern of future orientation without anticipatory socialization" (Turner, 1964: 136). Such boys may value success and achievement, but they have not learned the student role well enough to attain them. Turner also found no strong correlations between differences in individual aspirations and differences in individual family background, but his explanation is that the important independent variable is the individual's larger social context, in particular the neighborhood in which his school is located.

12. For another argument for adolescence as an "invented" period, see Aries, 1962.

13. A similar point is made in an American review, which like Elkin and Wesley's paper plays upon the myth theme, but which admits that "in some instances the effects of visibility may well be to make the mythical stereotype based on it come true, owing to acceptance of a version of this stereotype by the very objects of the stereotyped perception" (Jahoda and Warren, 1965: 148).

14. The Rutgers data also contain some items on perceived strain, which would shed light on this issue but which to date have not been fully analyzed and integrated with the other findings.

15. This parallels Brittain's observation that adolescents "attempt to come to terms with parent-peer cross-pressures by simply not communicating with parents" (Brittain, 1963: 391).

PART FOUR

The School's Environment

. . . the things outside the schools matter even more than the things inside the schools, and govern and interpret the things inside.

M. E. Sadler (writing in 1900)

In many ways, the relationship of the school to the community is like that of a TV station that carries mostly network programs but that is largely dependent on local advertising for support. . . . The entertainment provided is frequently of high quality and shrewdly geared to the public taste. Concessions to the intellect and culture, provided as a public service, tend to be more ponderous, conventional, and unconvincing. . . . The commercials for the local way of life are interminable, boring, egregiously dishonest, and the audience knows it.

Edgar Z. Friedenberg

Were it not for their monopoly on educational opportunities for the poor, most big city school systems would probably go out of business.

Christopher Jencks

Almost any day's newspapers bring reports of crises in the school's external environment. School board elections or school bond referenda polarize a community. Superintendents resign under fire from their boards or from community interest groups. Parents storm school board meetings, demanding new schools, integrated schools, neighborhood schools, decentralized schools, or community-controlled schools. Indeed in much of the frenzied activity, the education of children seems all but forgotten, and the changes that do occur in the schools often seem to reflect a balancing of political pressures rather than any overall educational philosophy.

All this in an educational system supposedly designed for maximum sensitivity and efficiency, supposedly outside of—preferably above—politics!

In our initial description of the learning system in Chapter 1, the external environment was conceptualized as a series of surrounding layers, starting from the immediate neighborhood in which the school is located and moving out through the larger community (which may be anything from a large metropolis to a district combining small country towns and outlying farms) to a geographical region and finally to the total society. In Part Two we saw that the experiences of children in their families and in other groups outside of school affect their performance in school, a path of effects traced in Exhibit 12–1(a). In Part Three, although our focus was upon the internal structure and dynamics of schools, we saw evidence of the overlap of schools with outside groups and systems and the effects of external variables upon the school as a system as well as upon individual students. This interaction between the school and its environment will be the subject of Part Four.

Exhibit 12-1
The Relationship Between the School and Its Environment

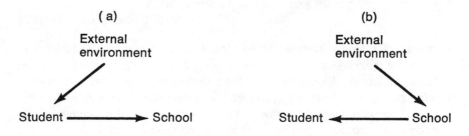

As indicated in Exhibit 12–1(b), we shall examine here influences of the external environment upon the school—which in turn affect student performance. Another way to view the "impinging" environment is in terms of the relationships of various individuals, groups, and systems with an interest in the schools. Following an evaluation of the strength of the external environment, we shall examine the formal educational bureaucracy, and some of the nonprofessional components, as these groups interact with —and often clash with—one another in the "arena" surrounding the schools.

The Community

In Part Two, we learned that a child's luck in his choice of parents was a deciding factor in his likelihood of "making it" at school. We explored the differences in family resources and life styles which lead to differences in the preparation children receive for playing the student role. A further difference between families is *where* they live insofar as this affects what schools their children attend. In this section, we shall study the effects of the first layer of the external environment—the neighborhood or community.

Some "vital statistics" of five important studies of community effects are presented in Exhibit 12–2. Four of the five argue that the effect is substantial. The earliest of these was carried out by Rogoff, who hypothesized that part of the differential achievement of children from the same kind of family background can be explained by community setting, that "the ecological environment leads to formal and informal arrangements within and outside the schools, affecting the educational attainment of residents" (Rogoff, 1961: 242). Using data collected by the Educational Testing Service, Rogoff classified the communities in which schools were located into nine categories based upon population size and relationship to a metropolitan area (small, independent towns of 3 sizes; suburbs of 3 sizes; and cities of 3 sizes). When she controlled for family SES (middle-class suburban children were compared with middle-class children in other kinds of communities) and corrected for school differences in retention rates, Rogoff found that the large suburban high school came off best on both college aspirations and scholastic aptitude test scores. High schools in the largest cities produced about the same proportions of high aspirers and achievers as those in small towns. Thus there was a relationship between the structure of the community and what went on in its schools, although the relationship was not a simple linear one.

Turner's study of social mobility patterns among Los Angeles high school students, already cited in Chapters 6 and 11, reaches similar conclusions. The ten schools in Turner's sample were selected as a more or less representative sample of socioeconomic areas of the city, by applying the Shevky index of social rank to census tract data. Thus each school was characterized in terms of the total community in which it was located.

Turner found that differences in educational values and aspirations were related to the status of the neighborhood, a relationship which held when factors of *individual* SES, IQ, and peer group pressures were controlled:

> Schools that draw their students disproportionately from higher family backgrounds tend to be more middle class in values than the individual backgrounds warrant. Schools which draw their students disproportionately from lower family backgrounds are less middle class in values than the individual backgrounds of their students warrant. The impact of neighborhood . . . is to accentuate the predominant tendencies (Turner, 1964: 104).

There were also differences in school average IQ scores—differences which seemed to be explained by influences external to the school and to individual characteristics. For example, the correlation coefficients for the relation between IQ scores and school attended were .20 for boys and

Exhibit 12–2
Design of Five Studies on Community Effects

	Rogoff	Turner	Boyle	Burkhead	Wilson
Sample	35,000 seniors in 500 high schools (national probability sample).	All boys in 10 L.A. high schools (representing SES areas of city).	1700 girls in 70 Canadian high schools.	Chicago and Atlanta systems plus 206 schools in small communities (Project Talent sample).	5500 students in 11 junior and senior high schools in 1 California county.
Study Published	1961	1964	1966	1967	1967
Dependent Variables	College plans; SAT scores.	College plans and aspirations; school average IQ.	College plans, scholastic ability.	Standard reading and other test scores; % dropouts; college plans.	IQ, reading achievement, reasoning, and other standard test scores.
Community Variable	Community type: size and relationship to metropolitan area.	Community SES.	Community size and type.	Median family income of city or area of city in which school is located.	SES of child's immediate neighborhood.
Other Independent Variables	Family SES.	Individual SES; individual IQ; peer status and pressures.	SES context of school.	Ed. expenditures; school size and age; teacher experience and education; teacher-student ratio.	School racial and SES composition; individual race; SES and mental maturity.

.23 for girls even when the effect of individual family background was partialed out. And values that reflected upward mobility ambitions were most common among students attending schools in neighborhoods where the dominant SES was higher than in their own (Turner, 1964: 59–61). Finally, the neighborhood factor seemed to affect the interrelationship of individual background, IQ, and aspirations. The linear multiple correlation for aspiration with the other two variables together was .54 for boys in high SES schools but only .34 for boys in low SES schools. Turner's conclusion that ambition may be a "more loosely determined or fortuitous matter for men in low neighborhoods than elsewhere," ties in with the earlier mentioned finding that boys from low-SES neighborhoods were more likely to have high aspirations without the concrete values and plans needed to implement them.

Turner rejects the notion that peer group pressures explain away or are the mechanism through which the neighborhood influences aspirations. Contrary to the common notion that the peer group in low-SES areas has a depressant effect upon the ambitions and performance of able individuals, students in low-SES neighborhoods were as likely as other students to prefer friends with reputations for academic performance. Whatever it is in such neighborhoods that lowers academic ambitions and achievement, it is not a uniform negative pressure from peers.

A study focusing upon the effect of community size was carried out with Canadian data by Boyle (1966). Beginning with a review of previous work (including Rogoff's, Turner's, and Wilson's), Boyle pointed out that although each study showed that a school's student body composition had a considerable effect upon individual aspirations or performance, each also showed an external environment effect, and that this effect was stronger in larger than in small communities.

Canada was chosen as the setting for Boyle's study because, unlike the United States, it has a highly centralized educational system, a structure which produces relative uniformity in standards and practices. By thus providing a kind of control for within-school difference which would not be possible in most American school systems, Boyle could be more confident that differences in output would be related to factors outside of the school.

The results indicated that even in a learning system designed to play down interschool differences, a student's place of residence still partially determined his school experience. Comparison of schools differing in SES composition, without taking into account their community environment, did show fewer differences than one would predict using United States data. There were slightly higher proportions of students in high status schools planning on college, but almost no differences between medium-SES and low-SES schools. However, the introduction of community size (whether the school was located in or outside of a metropolitan area) changed the picture. Controlling for both SES context and community size showed that:

The relationship between community size and population composition is so pronounced that *all* of the high-status schools, but *none* of the low-status schools, were located in metropolitan areas. As a consequence, the only comparison possible among metropolitan schools is between high- and medium-status categories, while the only comparison possible between non-metropolitan schools is between medium- and low-status categories. Among the former, the effect of population composition is quite strong ($a_1 = 0.25$), while among the latter the effect is minimal ($a_1 = 0.01$). This finding is consistent with the interpretation that more centralized administration in Canada will discourage divergence among non-metropolitan high schools but that residential segregation in metropolitan areas will create even stronger pressures toward divergence (Boyle, 1966: 636).

This relationship is reduced somewhat, but does not disappear, when scholastic ability (performance on province-wide examinations) is controlled. The ability variable is related to the other two, in that the highest ability students are the ones more likely to attend high-status metropolitan schools.

Thus both the population composition and the location of a school affect academic output, but these two variables are themselves interactively related, so that the size of the SES contextual effect is dependent upon the structure of the larger community. A certain amount of self-selection of students is also likely, with the more able and ambitious more apt to attend some schools than to attend others. Differences in societal structure in general as well as educational structure in particular necessitate caution in applying findings from one society to the somewhat different situation in another society. In addition to differences between Canada and the United States in the extent of educational centralization and uniformity of standards, the very small number of low-SES schools in the metropolitan areas in Boyle's sample suggest that Canadian cities do not yet contain the inner-city ghetto schools which create some of the thorniest problems in our educational system. "However, what is important is that the somewhat diverse findings of five independent pieces of research do fit together in a consistent pattern. The present framework thus provides an explicit target for future research" (Boyle, 1966: 638).

The most extensive evidence on the effects of the external social environment is contained in Burkhead's study of two large city school systems and a sample of small ones. This study represents one of the few available examples of the application of systems analysis techniques to the problems of learning systems (see Chapter 10). Burkhead's model relates a variety of input variables (for example, personnel time, expenditures for buildings and materials); process variables (class and school size); and status variables (in particular the median family income of the area of the city in which a school is located) to a variety of output or dependent variables (in particular standardized test scores and dropout rates). While not all of the variables are strictly comparable from one city to another—illustrating the difficulty of doing comparative analysis in a large society without national standards and measures—the careful definition and large number of variables used justifies confidence in the results. Within each city, a regression analysis was done to see which of the independent variables explained the greatest portion of variation in outputs.

The major finding is that in all the cities in the sample, the external variable of community average income explained a great deal more of the variance in test scores than any of the within-school variables, such as expenditures or class size. In the two large cities, variance in student output was almost wholly explained by the school's socioeconomic environment. To put it in the cost-benefit language of systems analysis:

> In Chicago an increase in median family income of $1,000 from the mean is associated with an increase of 21 per cent in the proportion of students scoring average or better in 11th grade reading. In Atlanta an increase of $1,000 in median family income is associated with an 8.5 per cent improvement in 10th grade reading scores (Burkhead, 1967: 88).

That this effect is a matter of the social context created by the residents of an area rather than of a simple translation of high income into a more "expensive" educational system is indicated by the lack of relationship between current expenditures and school outputs. Furthermore, an analysis of resource allocation patterns (comparing the expenditure for textbooks and other materials, staff, buildings, and so on among school attendance areas differing in median family income) produced a slight U-shaped curve. That is, expenditures were slightly higher in the lowest and highest income areas, dipping slightly in the middle.

Although median area income was the most powerful single predictor of student output in every community studied, there was a major division between large and small communities. For example, community income level accounted for 86% of the variance in eleventh-grade reading scores and IQ scores in Chicago, and 85% of the tenth-grade verbal scores in Atlanta, but only 45% of the twelfth-grade reading scores for the 206 small-town public schools taken from the Project Talent survey sample. Even taking into account differences in age or grade level or in the particular tests used in the different cities, the magnitude of the difference is clear, and it holds up consistently in every comparison between the two big cities and the sample of small ones. Income level alone has less impact, or less exclusive impact, in smaller communities than in large cities. This difference is partly explained by the different meaning of the income level variable for large and small communities:

> The deviations around the mean of family income are likely to be much greater in the smaller community than in the school attendance area of the large city. To make the data comparable it would be necessary to collect data on the family income, or other socioeconomic variables, for each student in the small community and thus to analyze the effect of school resource allocation policies on the educational outcomes of students with a similar background (Burkhead, 1967: 85).

Burkhead also admits that his output variables are probably affected by factors not included in his analysis, such as the educational and occupational opportunities in the surrounding area, and differences in school-leaving laws and practices.

A dissenting view of community effect was expressed in the second of the two Wilson studies discussed in Chapter 10. To recapitulate, Wilson found that although children who lived in primarily lower-SES and primarily black neighborhoods during their elementary school years did achieve lower test scores at the beginning of junior high, these differences disappeared in the multivariate analysis which controlled for *school* composition. Wilson concluded that "the effect of neighborhood segregation upon achievement is entirely through the resulting segregation of neighborhood schools on social-class lines" (Wilson, 1967: 180. For complete passage and supporting data, see Chapter 10).

Reexamination of the Wilson study shows that it differs from the others in several aspects—not only in its conclusions. First, the subjects were relatively younger. Not only was Wilson's the only sample drawn from junior as well as senior high schools, but the analysis comparing the relative effects of neighborhood and other variables uses respondents' residence *during their primary school years* on their *sixth-grade* reading scores. This raises the possibility that neighborhood impact is different at different age levels, but the *direction* of differences in this case (less effect when children first enter school than later) is the reverse of what one would expect.

A difference which makes more sense substantively concerns the measure of community which is used. Unlike Turner and Burkhead, whose measure was based upon the SES of the total area served by the school (including both families who did and who did not have children in school), and Boyle and Rogoff, who controlled for total community size and position with respect to the nearest large metropolitan area, Wilson's "neighborhood" consists of "the several blocks surrounding the home of each student —ignoring school boundaries" (Wilson, 1967: 180). That is, the first four studies all focus upon the overall climate and resources of the total area which supports a school, while the latter focuses upon the immediate surroundings of the individual students. The combined findings suggest that it is the total community environment which affects the productivity of the school as a whole. Although Rogoff's data did not deal directly with the processes by which structural differences between communities lead to differential school outputs, she speculates that they may be a combination of differential formal arrangements and resources—such as community cultural facilities and events—and informal mechanisms, such as normative climate and opportunities for informal socializing which affect *all* members of the community to some extent regardless of age and status (Rogoff, 1961: 242–243). Burkhead's conclusions also suggested a number of things that could vary from one community to another which were not included in his regression equation.

If there is an influence of residence at the level of the small neighborhood that is independent of family effects, it is apparently offset by students' relationships with significant others within the school. Thus Turner's findings imply that if there is a peer group influence upon educational aspiration and performance, it operates within the school rather than in the neighborhood, a conclusion also reached by Wilson ("While peers may have an influence, it is their behavior in the school setting—not their generalized attitudes as expressed out of school—which we should focus upon to illuminate the process of influence"—Wilson, 1967: 181). A related point is that, although assignment to schools is still largely in the hands of the professional education bureaucracy and still most strongly determined by proximity of residence, some families *choose* their residence in accordance with their aspirations for their children's education. Lower-SES children who attend schools where the general social level is higher often have parents who are training them for upward mobility, like the families of the college-bound boys studied by Kahl (Chapter 4). This trend is empirically supported by findings from a study of San Francisco Bay area high schools carried out shortly before Wilson's second study, which found that working-class students with college aspirations were more likely to be attending a predominantly middle-class than a predominantly working-class school, and, moreover, that they were more likely to have friends with college plans and to be participating in school extracurricular activities, which provide opportunities for association with middle-class peers (Kraus, 1964).

This complicated set of relationships is summarized in Exhibit 12–3, which shows that the community as a whole, but not the small primary neighborhood, affects both school context and student performance. The neighborhood is related to academic performance only insofar as it constitutes the environment for family life and attracts families who share personal characteristics and attitudes toward education. Conversely, the peer group influence works within the context of the school but not of the neighborhood (further support for the model of high schools as "adolescent societies").

When we move out from the local community or school district to the larger subdivisions of our society, the difficulties of understanding the effect of any single environmental variable are magnified. In one sense, it is true that: "There is no American school system, only a multitude of different systems, each with its own concerns, its own problems, its own needs and its own internal kind of perfection" (Schrag, 1965: 1). The author of this statement spent several months visiting school systems from Newton, Massachusetts, to rural Kentucky to the suburbs of Los Angeles, and his journalistic account stresses the uniqueness of each. On the other hand, there is a certain pattern to regional variations, for which we shall turn once again to the *Equality of Educational Opportunity* survey, which contains the most comprehensive data available on the effects of the larger social environment.

We have seen (in Chapter 3) that membership in minority ethnic groups

Exhibit 12-3

Relationship of External Environmental Variables to School Structure and Climate and Student Performance

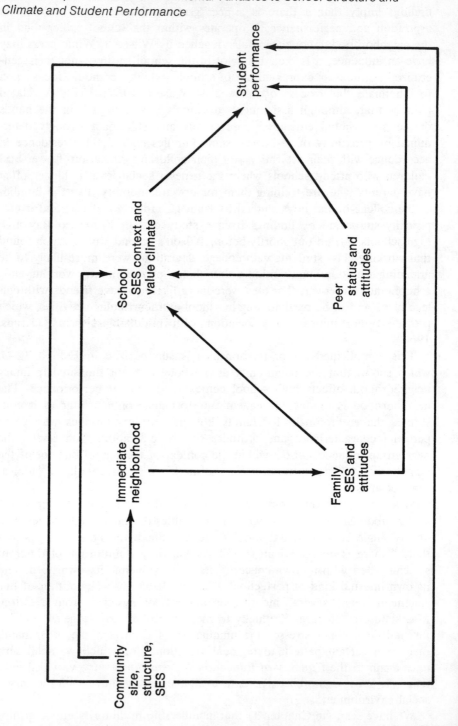

is related to lower test performance (with the exception of Oriental Americans). Since the survey sample was designed to represent major geographical regions of the United States and variations in urban-rural location as well as ethnic background, one can compare the effects of all three.

Achievement is lower in the South and Southwest than in the North, West, and Midwest, and it is also lower outside metropolitan areas than within them (Coleman, Campbell, *et al.,* 1966: 219–220). The interesting part of the analysis, however, is the simultaneous analysis of region, community size, and ethnicity, which are shown to be related to each other and to achievement. While achievement for all racial-ethnic groups is higher in the North and West and in metropolitan areas, the regional variation is greater for Negroes than whites, and the blacks' educational handicap is intensified by going to schools in areas that combine regional and community size disadvantages. To put this handicap in quantitative terms:

> The achievement disadvantage suffered by whites as a result of living in the rural South compared to the urban North is 3 or 4 points in the standard scores, or about 15 percentile points in the distribution of white scores. The achievement disadvantage suffered by 12th grade Negroes as a result of living in the rural South compared to the urban North is 7 or 8 points in the standard scores, or about 30 percentile points in the distribution of Negro scores. Or to make a different comparison, the achievement disadvantage suffered by Negroes in comparison to whites is about 9 points in the standard scores in the metropolitan North, but about 12 points in the rural South (Coleman, Campbell, *et al.,* 1966: 219–220).

Moreover, differences in the test scores of Negro children by region are very slight in the first grade but increase as they proceed through school, with the largest decline (about 5 points on the tests or a 20% percentile drop) in southern and southwestern nonmetropolitan areas.

The regional environment also specifies the conditions under which certain other independent variables affect achievement. For example, the relative importance of student background characteristics as opposed to student attitudes, as these form a social climate within a school, varies by region, with the effect of background characteristics being strongest in the South (it is also stronger for minority group children). Another interactive relationship concerns student turnover, which has a negative effect on achievement in the North, for both blacks and whites, but a positive effect in the South. The authors' interpretation is that in cities the poverty areas have the highest residential mobility and student turnover, and that this is part of a whole complex of factors which reflect general instability and limit the ability of schools to produce achievement. In rural areas, where mobility in general is much lower, lack of turnover reflects stagnancy rather than positive stability, and schools which have a very stable student body are usually schools where no one is learning much because no one is going anywhere! (Coleman, Campbell, *et al.,* 1966: 305).

Finally, location also may explain the ambiguous findings with respect to the effects of *school* size that were reported in Chapter 10. An analysis controlling for region, community size, race, and school size simultaneously shows that the effects of the latter may differ in different places:

> In urban areas, school size expresses the difference in location between city and suburb; outside urban areas, it expresses the difference in location between rural, small town, and larger town locations. For both Negroes and whites this variable is positively related to achievement in the South, where the difference is principally the difference between rural and small or larger town, but it is not positively related to achievement in the North, where the variable difference measures principally suburb versus city. This again suggests that quite apart from facilities and curriculum, the smallest and most rural schools have lower achievement than larger schools, but the largest and most urban do not have higher achievement than those of middle size and again, that this is most true for Negroes (Coleman, Campbell, *et al.*, 1966: 313–314).

Given the relationships between community type and school productivity, it should be noted that the school's external environment is, increasingly, a city or some part of a large metropolitan area. That is, in the United States and elsewhere in the world, the problems of schools are increasingly the problems of urban schools. As Schrag points out in the introduction to a study of the Boston school system, two out of every three American children attend school in a city or a suburb of a city. The twenty largest central cities alone account for one child in ten. "New York City alone educates more children than Delaware, Montana, Nevada, New Hampshire, New Mexico, North Dakota, Rhode Island, Utah, and Vermont combined, and even a relatively small city like Boston runs a school establishment as large as that of the state of Idaho" (Schrag, 1967: 1).

Urban school systems also contain a disproportionate share of the most disadvantaged students and of financial problems. While every city has unique characteristics and problems (some comparisons between the educational systems in several large cities will be described later in the chapter), certain trends can be noted to some degree in all metropolitan areas. The following were cited in testimony before congressional committees in support of the Elementary and Secondary Act of 1965 (Meranto, 1967: 36ff):

1. Well-educated and occupationally skilled people are moving out of the city, especially to the suburbs at the outer edges of a metropolitan area (which may or may not be within the city limits, but which are often independent municipalities with their own school and taxing systems).
2. People who remain in the city and incoming residents are increasingly from the lowest income and minority racial-ethnic groups, with a disproportionate number of the newcomers from the rural South.
3. Low-income and minority group families, who typically have little education and limited vocational skills, are heavily concentrated in particular neighborhoods of the city.

4. Site and construction costs are higher in large or central cities than on the outskirts or in smaller communities, and a larger portion of the tax dollar is required for non-school governmental services. Local support of education, however, still comes largely from local property taxes.

In sum, there is evidence that educational opportunities are not equally distributed in our society, and furthermore, that the areas of greatest need for educational and other services are often the areas with the most inadequate resources. Having seen that it does matter *where* children go to school, we shall turn to the question of *who* runs the schools or determines how they shall be run.

Professional Leadership

To go outside of the school itself does not mean leaving the formal educational system. Individual schools are grouped in school districts, political-educational units directed by a superintendent and his staff. In large districts, particularly in large cities, the professional staff takes the form of a complex hierarchical web of administrators and supervisors, curricular and other specialists, spilling out from the central office into a series of field offices. The growing size, power, and inertia of large city educational bureaucracies has in recent years received much of the blame for the "troubles" in the schools.

Although it seems obvious that professional leadership has a major impact upon what goes on in schools (one reviewer of the Coleman Report criticizes it for excluding this variable, on the grounds that, "differences in the quality of school administration—holding pupil backgrounds constant —should account for as much of the difference in student achievement as does peer environment" [Dentler, 1966a: 29]), good measures of educational leadeship which are in turn related to student output are still lacking. Studies of the superintendent tend to be limited to delineation of his role functions and the cross-pressures to which he is subject.[1] The sum of what has been written boils down to two basic points. First, the function of the role is basically a mediatory one. The superintendent's task is not only to coordinate educational activities within his district, but also "to serve as a liaison between the central administration on the one hand and the schools, parents and other community groups on the other." In particular, superintendents "act as a buffer protecting the central staff from parental dissatisfaction" (Gittell and Hollander, 1968: 76). Second, since many groups, with many differing interests, have access to the superintendent, most superintendents are relatively powerless to make major changes in the existing educational system. Indeed, their tenure is to a great extent determined by their avoidance of activities and programs which would "rock the boat" and their skill in avoiding or resolving conflict. An excellent illustration of this point is contained in the case studies of "Jackson County" conducted by the Center for the Advanced Study of Educational Adminis-

tration, at the University of Oregon. A man who took on the superintendency of the Jackson County schools pledged to bring about massive
changes. He introduced nongraded elementary schools, innovative foreign
language classes, a new reading program, and a general climate of experimentation and evaluation—and had his contract renewed only once. He
was replaced by a man from within the system who was described as
"more pragmatist than idealist," who "assessed every situation which con-
fronted him, weighed the possibilities, and then took his stand on the basis
of professionally accepted principles and upon a realistic assessment of
what could be attained," who did not take sides or become personally
involved with the liberal or conservative element on the school board
(whose relative strength fluctuated from one election year to another), who
"maintained close liaison with the teachers' groups and attempted to steer
a course of moderation between them and the board, avoiding insofar as
possible actions which would involve the teachers in the political and
ideological controversies created by the division of the board," who allowed
the curricular innovations initiated by his predecessor to die quietly—
and who, at last report, had secure tenure in his job! (Goldhammer and
Farner, 1964; Goldhammer and Pellegrin, 1968).

The insecurity of many superintendents may be the consequence of
inconsistencies between past and present status. In a study of decision-
making with respect to the school integration issue, Crain (1968) found
that most of the large city superintendents for whom he could obtain background material were upwardly mobile men from small-town or rural
backgrounds. Men who major in education, traditionally a "woman's field,"
tend to be of lower status than college men generally, and a man who rises
to a superintendency usually has come a long way from his social as well
as geographical origins. In Crain's view, the double strain—status inconsistencies plus the conflicting demands of groups inside and outside the
formal education system—result in a defensiveness about the schools and
an intolerance of lay "interference," especially from groups who make
aggressive demands for policy changes on grounds other than strictly educational ones (for instance, civil rights groups). As Crain puts it, the superintendent and many of the groups which confront him "literally do not speak
the same language."

Most studies of the operation of the school district as a whole have
focused upon what one observer (Jencks, 1966) has termed the "organizational schlerosis" of large urban school systems. Good case studies of
a single system, which make lively reading in a grim sort of way, are
Schrag's study of the Boston schools (1967) and Rogers' equally bleak
view of 110 Livingston Street (the address of the New York City Board
of Education and the title of Roger's 1968 book). Both describe in depressing detail the resistance of an entrenched bureaucracy to change in
general and to schemes designed to produce greater equality of educational
opportunity in particular.

A major comparative study of urban school systems was conducted by Gittell and Hollander, whose original examination of the New York City system was extended, under a federal grant, to include five other systems.[2] These additional cases provided a kind of replication of the general pattern found in New York and also allowed comparison of the outputs of systems that varied in structure as well as geography. What the researchers wanted to explain was the extent of innovation within the system (which is, of course, not the same dependent variable as student achievement, but which will be taken to be an intervening variable which determines whether a school has the flexibility to adapt to student needs). The empirical indicants of innovation included: (1) special programs for the disadvantaged; (2) reorganization of the administrative structure (including decentralization, and changes in recruitment, budgeting, and planning procedures); and (3) school reorganization (for example, educational parks). The major input or independent variables were also three: (1) present administrative organization (for example, the current extent of centralization, the relative power of the superintendent, top administrative staff, and school board, and the strength of teachers' associations); (2) the fiscal status and allocation of funds within the district; and (3) extent of "participation" (for instance, the percentage of votes on school issues relative to the total votes cast for the head of the ticket, amount of public participation at school board hearings, and activities of special educational and general interest groups). Data were collected from study reports, from legal documents, from newspaper accounts, and from interviews with persons actively involved in school affairs (the number of interviews per city ranged from thirteen to thirty-two).

A general conclusion of the study is that decision-making was controlled by a small core of professionals, who successfully insulated themselves from public officials and organizations (on the grounds of freedom from "political interference") or from parents and other private citizens (on the grounds of lack of professional "expertise"). "The insulation of public education is twofold: bureaucratic centralization (or more accurately over-centralization) which is a product of size, reinforced by an ideological rationale of professionalization, which is a product of the vested interests of the educationists. The result is a static, internalized, isolated system which has been unable to respond to vastly changing needs and demands of large city populations" (Gittell and Hollander, 1968: 197).

Of the six cities in the sample, two were relatively less ossified. In Detroit, public school officials at least gave lip service to the "community school" concept, and a variety of public interest groups were involved in citizens' committees. Philadelphia is currently in a period of transition and reform (following a long period of public inaction) which has produced change in the school system's structure and top personnel. These differences are, however, only relative. Indeed, one of the major points made by the study is the lack of meaningful change in curriculum, teacher recruitment and administrative organization in *all* large urban school systems.

The monopoly of decision-making by a few professionals is the more disturbing in that the extent of participation by individuals and groups outside of the formal school establishment is the only one of the three independent variables clearly related to the dependent variable of within-school innovation. Although certain modes of organization were hypothesized as representing a more open system (say, willingness to select a superintendent from outside), the two relatively innovative school systems did not differ from the others in this respect. Similarly, whether a system was financially independent or dependent for funds upon city or state did not seem to account for willingness to make changes in the system. The authors conclude that if there is a relationship, it is probably in the reverse direction—that is, a school system truly committed to educational innovations will find some way to finance them.

The School Board

The school board is the component of the external environment charged with the making of public school policy of a given district and with liaison between the formal school system and the community. Gross's work also includes analyses of school boards (1965), and as in his studies of the principal and the superintendent, he is concerned mainly with pinpointing the focal dimensions of the role. The dependent variable which he proposes as an indicant of role competence is educational "progressivism," a multi-item measure parallel to Gittell and Hollander's innovativeness concept at the formal school system level. Also, like Gittell and Hollander, Gross does not link progressivism to any measure of student or school output, although he did try to discover the background factors that would explain it. At the individual level, the only explanatory background factor was amount of education. Income, religion, age, number of children, and length of residence in the community were all unrelated, as was previous activity in politics or community affairs.

Gross was interested also in the degree of "professionalism" with which a school board member perceived and played his role. At one end of a continuum were individuals who took on the job as a civic responsibility, whose overriding goal was to achieve "quality" education for their community (however they defined quality). On the other end were those whose motivation was political, who saw the job as a stepping-stone to other higher political positions and who therefore used it to gain political experience and visibility. For example, nonprofessional members would be less likely to treat teacher appointments or budget recommendations in the context of an educational philosophy, more likely to use them as a means of balancing the demands of or placating constituent interest groups.

Gross admits bias in favor of the professional orientation, and using his own scheme he found that 64% of the board members in his sample could be placed at this end of the continuum. On the other hand, he did not find a strong relationship between a professional motivation for seeking election to the school board and a progressive attitude toward educational innovation. A constituency-oriented focus per se does not impede change. What apparently does matter, and more so for the politically than the professionally oriented, is the sociopolitical context from which the board member is elected or appointed and within which he must operate.

This conclusion was the starting point for a study of two northern suburban school districts—a study which focuses upon the way in which school board members become socialized to their role (Kerr, 1964). Kerr's explanation for the lack of relationship between a board member's background and his subsequent behavior is that any potential effect is nullified by pressures exerted by the superintendent and veteran board members. The two boards which Kerr studied acted mainly to legitimatize the decisions made by the superintendent and his staff, and most board meeting time was spent on discussion of noneducational topics, such as financing new buildings or improving the bus system.

One factor in this abdication of control over the educational program was the appalling ignorance of most board members about education in general and their local school system in particular, as illustrated by the following reply of one school board candidate to a question about her views of the school's needs:

> I'm not an educator. I feel it's a good system, but there's room for improvement. I'm willing to learn about the operations of the school board. I don't have any ideas about changes because I don't know enough about the operations of the system. I would love to serve; I would have to learn. I've been reading about it in the papers is all (Kerr, 1964: 42).

The Crain study mentioned earlier in this chapter presents a rather different view of the school board. In all but one of the school systems studied,[3] the board rather than the superintendent made the major decisions about school desegregation. Whether the differences between Crain's study and Gross's and Kerr's reflect differences in setting (Crain's cases were all large metropolitan school systems), differences in the issues before the boards (Crain's study focuses upon the single issue of desegregation), or biases in sampling and data gathering cannot be determined from the available data.

Unlike superintendents, says Crain, one cannot easily characterize the typical school board member. Variations in background, motivations, and educational opinions were great, within as well as between cities. There are also various paths to becoming a school board member (in addition to, although related to, the differences between appointed and elected school boards). The three major paths are achievement of high status in a business or profession which leads to (and allows) involvement in prestigious civic activities; activity in political party work; and activity as a representative of some special interest group (say, organized labor or an ethnic group). Other kinds of credentials are personal wealth, educational expertise (some boards reserve a slot for a representative of a local college), or some special skill such as finance or architecture.

The key dimension, though, for Crain as for Gross, is the choice between a civic and a political orientation.[4] Boards in which members shared a common orientation, *whether civic or political,* were found to operate most smoothly, while boards with a fairly even distribution between the two orientations tended to suffer lack of cohesion and difficulties in reaching decisions. The major determinants of school board receptiveness to the demands of civil rights groups are, on the *individual* level, high SES and liberal attitudes toward racial problems and the civil rights movement; on the level of the *board as a whole,* a high degree of group cohesion, a condition most often found in homogeneous boards that have a clear hierarchical structure and are relatively large in size; and on the level of the *total community,* the interaction of city SES and elite suburbanization (the boards which moved most readily and positively were in cities with a dominant blue-collar population, a relatively small middle class, and elites still living in the central city, Crain, 1968: Chapter 11 and 12).

An interesting construct developed by Crain is level of "conflict-tolerance," made up of three attitudinal variables which Crain interprets as having a common theme: (1) civil rights liberalism; (2) degree of acceptance of disagreement as inherent in school affairs (more specifically, whether or not one agrees with the statement, "If people really understood the issues, there would be no disagreement over school policy"); and (3) a civic orientation toward educational issues. The conflict-tolerant person avoids what Crain terms the "search for simplicity":

> Anyone who thinks that there are only two kinds of people—those who agree with them and those who misunderstand the issues—and who further believes that the task of a public official is simply to poll the public and vote as directed by the results, has an extremely simplistic view of life. . . . These attitudes also reflect an intolerance of the difficult decision, of the ambiguous issue, of the irreconcilable difference of opinion, of the possibility of being wrong (Crain, 1968: 174).

One encouraging bit of evidence is that the board members rated as most involved and influential by the study interviewers were more likely to be conflict-tolerant than conflict-resistant.

Although Crain pictures the school board as relatively strong and active, he admits that much school board activity is a response to crisis and is taken in the absence of any guiding education policy or philosophy:

> The typical school board is not closely knit. It ordinarily meets to handle the legal paperwork of the schools; at irregular intervals it makes specific decisions about a particular school or on a particular policy. But it can be thought of as making school policy only in a fire-fighting fashion. If an issue comes up, it acts; otherwise it does not. It may not take a position at all on some of the most fundamental issues of school policy, simply because those particular policies have not been made salient by community

discussion. The result is that the school board members do not, either as individuals or as a group, have a highly articulated educational policy. Almost every time they oppose the superintendent, or the superintendent comes to them for guidance, the board has some difficulty making a decision. Every issue is different and every decision can take a good deal of time (Crain, 1968: 125).

The Public

Finally there are the individuals and groups who are not part of the formal school system but who have a direct stake in it. The most important of these are the parents of school-age children. While we know a great deal about the effects of families upon individual children's academic success (Part II), the direct effect of parents as a group upon the productivity of schools as social systems has received scant research attention.[5] There are two conflicting hypotheses about the relationship between parental activity in school affairs and school outputs. One hypothesis predicts a positive relationship. Based upon a balance or dissonance theory model, this argument is that a high level of parental interest and involvement would be consonant with feelings of control of environment, and that parents who had such positive feelings would be most likely to communicate to their children the academic motivation and role-playing skills needed for school success. The alternative hypothesis, that parental activity is negatively related to school productivity, is based upon a model of role specialization. What teachers and schools need, runs this argument, is autonomy—release from the pressures of the external environment.

To date, these hypotheses have been supported more on the basis of personal biases than empirical evidence. What limited evidence there is favors the first model. The Gittell and Hollander study showed a relationship between indicants of community participation and educational innovativeness, although the link between innovativeness at the system level and actual student achievement was implied rather than documented. In an extension of his study of school value climates, McDill added several community level variables, and he found that the only one related to achievement was parental involvement in the schools. A simple scale of parental involvement was constructed from teachers' responses to the following three items:

Most parents in this school are apathetic to school politics. (false)

Parents of students here seem interested in their children's progress (true)

Parents often ask for appointments with teachers to discuss their children's school work. (true)

Each teacher was given an individual score from 0 to 3, and schools were ranked by the average of individual teacher scores. The index is admittedly crude, and it is based upon the perception of one subgroup in the learning system (parents) by another subgroup (teachers) with the latter having not only a strong professional involvement but also a potentially biased view of the appropriate behavior of parents in connection with the schools. Still the relationships of the scale with several measures of aspiration and achievement were consistently positive; Spearman rank order correlations with all but one of the six intellectual climate dimensions, with math achievement scores, and with college plans were all in the direction predicted and statistically significant at the .01 level. (Contrary to Rogoff's suggestion, McDill found no effects of any of his measures of cultural and other facilities, although he points out that his information is only on the *availability* of such facilities and does not include any indication as to their utilization.)

Another set of findings on participation come from the National Principalship study. Here also parental involvement is from a school's-eye view, with both teachers and principals being asked whether the principal (1) should and (2) does engage in a variety of activities ranging from encouraging parental attendance at school assemblies to using parents as part-time teacher helpers to allowing parental advice on curriculum and school practices. School rankings, based upon the averaged perceived parental involvement scores, were positively correlated with both teacher morale and teacher "efforts" (the latter was a measure of teachers' perception of their colleagues' commitment to their jobs). The correlation of perceived parental involvement with perceived academic achievement (based upon teachers' reports of the proportion of students in their school who had efficient study habits, had mastered subject matter fundamentals, were free of serious disciplinary problems, and so forth), controlling for school SES, was positive at the junior high but not at the elementary and senior high levels. The meaning of these results is not entirely clear. The authors hypothesized that parental involvement would be differentially encouraged by the school at different levels, with the greatest encouragement at especially problematic phases of the education process. In this view the two key points would come at the entry into elementary school, when the child has the combined strain of leaving home and coping with the new pressures to learn and to meet new standards of behavior, and again at the entry to secondary school, where the approach of entry into higher education or the job market would bring new academic demands and more impersonal, universalistic standards for judging the worth of individual students (Dreeben and Gross, 1965).

All that can be concluded from the research to date is that there is no empirical evidence that a high level of activity by a broad range of groups in the school's external environment has harmful effects upon the climate and performance within the school. This interpretation may seem excessively cautious, but we have no measures of involvement that are not based upon the view of persons with a personal stake in school-community relations. Also, as it stands, the model is too simple an explanation of a complex subject. For example, in the Dreeben and Gross study, high parental involvement was also positively correlated with the SES level of the school. This indicates that families differ in their propensity to take an active role in school affairs, or that schools are more receptive to the involvement of some parents than others, or both. It also suggests that level of participation may be one of the intervening variables which explain the exceptionally strong relationship between the socioeconomic level of a community and the output of its schools.

The relationship between external participation and internal productivity may also be affected by the overall quality of educational leadership. Dreeben and Gross found a positive correlation between parental involvement and both the involvement of teachers in key school decisions, as perceived by the principal, and the principal's skill in dealing with the community, as perceived by the teachers. If the educational administrator has skill in handling interpersonal relations generally, he may be able to handle a high level of activity by multiple subgroups, even when they are in conflict with each other.

Strategies for Change

If we accept the evidence that equality of educational opportunity does not exist in our society and that the important decisions concerning schools are made by a small proportion of those who are affected by them, what can be done to correct these imbalances in the schools' external environment? There are three general strategies for change at this level of the learning system:

(1) to redistribute the educational resources and burdens more equitably. This can involve moving children as well as manipulating the budget or the school boundaries;

(2) to redistribute power, by raising the level of participation in school affairs to include a greater cross-section of the community and to apply constant pressure on the schools to provide this kind of environment in which children can learn;

(3) to raise the level of participation but to do it outside the public school system, by setting up new schools or programs which will be more congruent with the experiences and needs of the students and will involve their parents and other members of the immediate community.

Redistribution—of Resources and Burdens

School desegregation is the most ambitious strategy of the first type. Desegregation attempts to overcome the combined disadvantages of race and place by reassigning children so that the racial-ethnic distribution in each school mirrors that of the larger society. Proponents of desegregation claim that this will bring about a fairer distribution of resources, since "advantaged" citizens who heretofore have isolated themselves in privileged schools cannot escape the problems of the schools by simply moving away from them. For the racially and economically disadvantaged, the alternative of compensatory educational programs is discounted because it does not provide an adequate substitute for the most important resource in any school—the other students. Thus disadvantaged children in segregated schools have a double educational disadvantage—lacking the background that contributes to success in school themselves, they interact with schoolmates who have the same limitations.

Counter-arguments are not limited to racial supremacists and those who fear adverse economic effects (say, white working-class home owners.) Doubts also have been raised by more sophisticated analysts, including some who formerly were advocates of desegregation. For example, in an article which has stirred up considerable debate among government officials as well as behavioral scientists, Bickel (1970) argues that even if it were desirable, true desegregation is unlikely in the near future, because too many people do not want it. This includes minority group spokesmen who advocate racial separatism, as well as whites who respond to attempts to desegregate local schools by moving away in large numbers. Furthermore, integration "creates as many problems as it purports to solve,[6] and no one can be sure that, even if accomplished, it would yield an educational return." Instead of forcing through a policy that no one wants, the educational system should "proceed with education," that is, should take major commitments to improving schools as they now exist.

The Bickel argument raises two separate questions about school desegregation: (1) its *feasibility* or extensiveness—how far has desegregation progressed and what are the chances of future progress?; and (2) its *effectiveness*—to what extent does desegregation have positive effects upon students' attitudes and performance and how strong are these effects relative to alternative modes of educational reform? Most of the available materials on either of these questions consist of policy statements or abstract, ideological arguments, with little reference to research data. In the case of the feasibility question, precise answers are difficult because the figures on present and projected desegregation are shifting as well as incomplete. Future developments also will depend upon the outcome of several present unknowns—the extent to which present and future federal administrations will press for full desegregation, in schools and housing, and the outcome of legal maneuvers such as the appeals to the decision in the case of the Los Angeles schools handed down by Judge Gitelson in February 1970.

According to Pettigrew (1967) and Dentler (1965, 1966b), school segregation was not substantially reduced, in the North or South, in the cities or suburbs, during the decade following the 1954 Supreme Court decision. In fact, says Dentler, segregation is so pronounced in large northern cities that if schools were placed on a continuum ranging from all white to all nonwhite, the great majority would cluster at the two extremes. Of the six largest northern cities, three (New York, Chicago, and Philadelphia) were *more* segregated in 1964 than in 1954, and only one (Detroit) had made substantial gains.[7] There is a certain irony in the situation, in that *de jure* segregation has been decreasing in all parts of the country but it cannot offset the rate of increasing *de facto* segregation caused by rapidly increasing segregation in *housing* in virtually every metropolitan area of the United States. "Consequently, the ever-growing Negro ghettoes combine with the neighborhood school principle to establish an increasingly entrenched pattern of racially-separate education throughout the urban North and South" (Pettigrew, 1967: 299). Pettigrew also points out that the students who stand to gain the most from racially "balanced" education are the hardest to desegregate—in particular lower-SES blacks, who generally live deepest in the ghetto, and elementary school children, whose schools are tied most closely to the neighborhood principle.

Pettigrew and Dentler do concede that the problems of big cities may be unique. (An issue raised by the Los Angeles case is whether, with the best intentions in the world, true school desegregation can be achieved in a city that covers 714 square miles and in which residential segregation is virtually total.) The barriers to desegregation are less formidable in smaller cities and suburbs.[8]

Ironically, the area which was politically and emotionally most resistant to racial desegregation—the South—is the area in which it has been most extensive. As one analyst has pointed out, this is because, "from a technical standpoint Southern school districts can generally be desegregated fairly efficiently through the use of affirmative neighborhood zoning, pairing of schools, consolidation of schools, or some combination of these" (Rilling, 1970: 17–18). In the eleven southern states, the proportion of black children in desegregated schools increased from 2% in 1965 to 18.4% in 1969. (The rate was higher in some states than others—it was as low as 10.5 in the most resistant states of Alabama, Georgia, Louisiana, Mississippi, and South Carolina.) Thus one can conclude that desegregation in the South has increased but still is far from covering most minority group children.

Another irony in the desegregation situation is that resistance may be less strong than the mass media—and even the scholarly—accounts suggest. A recent summary of public opinion poll data showed that not only do the vast majority of black parents want their children to go to school with whites,[9] but that by the end of the 1960's, close to a majority of whites were, if not enthusiastic, at least resigned to desegregation. A 1970 Harris poll found that 50% of the whites interviewed were willing to have black children in the schools in their neighborhood and over 40% were willing to consider programs involving the bussing of white children (Orfield, 1970).

What then are the results of the desegregation that has occurred so far?

Part of the resistance stems from lack of factual information, and a common fear is that desegregation will automatically lower academic standards. Prior to the Coleman report, some studies of selected American cities had shown that Negro students had greater academic growth in racially integrated than in segregated schools (Katz, 1964; and Lesser *et al.,* 1964). The report was, however, the first large-scale study to show that not only do black children benefit from being in integrated schools, but, perhaps more important from the point of view of educational policy makers with white constituents, the performance of white middle-class children will not be adversely affected by attendance at racially balanced schools.

There is a dearth of good case studies on school districts that have tried to desegregate. For example, although one might like to conclude that the Berkeley plan is a success, there is still too little hard data on which to base a reasonable judgment. Not all of the administrative and operational details have been worked out fully, and the evaluation that exists is largely impressionistic. Desegregation has been accompanied by other educational innovations. Tracking has been reduced, and there are plans to eliminate it altogether—except for English and some mathematics classes. The use of team teaching and of teaching aides has been increased. Some schools now have learning laboratories where students can work on special projects, and centers where special teachers work individually with children who have learning and behavior problems. A study of tenth graders indicated that black students who had been in integrated schools for three years had higher grade point averages than those who had attended for only one year. Finally, most Berkeley residents feel that the wounds caused by the desegregation battle are healing, though some still feel that educational "quality" was sacrificed in the name of social progress.

Probably the most systematic analysis of the effects of desegregation is being carried out by McPartland, whose study of the effects of classroom and school racial composition was discussed in Chapters 7 and 11. His further analysis has shown that:

> . . . the difference in achievement between the average Negro in a segregated classroom and his counterpart in a mostly white classroom is on the order of one-half standard deviation. In other words, desegregation serves to cut the racial achievement gap in half. The longer the Negro student spends in a desegregated situation, the more dramatic the improvement in achievement. These results cannot be explained away because the students who wind up in desegregated schools might have been different to begin with, for the same impact of desegregation shows up when initial differences of students are statistically controlled (McPartland, 1970: 22).

McPartland's work underscores the point made by Coleman that the achievement of advantaged students is not threatened by having minority group classmates, though McPartland notes that this conclusion is *condi-*

tional—desegregation does not have adverse effects on the performance of white children in schools *with at least 50% white students*. Academic opportunities *are* likely to be affected when schools are "swamped" by sudden influxes of low-income minority group children, as has happened in the central city schools of many large metropolitan areas. This is because the gains in achievement of disadvantaged students are best explained as "due to the exposure to fellow students who come from families that place high value on academic achievement and have the resources to give strong support to their children's efforts in school" (McPartland, 1970: 22). As long as such children remain in the majority in a school, no one's academic progress appears to suffer, and the chances of success for children from deprived backgrounds is enhanced substantially.

McPartland also underscores the point that it is the social class, not the racial, composition of the school that matters. Deprived children in an all-black school which contained a high proportion of students from high-income, well-educated families probably would show the same kind of gains they display in desegregated schools. Unfortunately, "there simply are not presently enough advantaged black families to accomplish social class desegregation without racial desegregation" (McPartland, 1970: 22).

Finally, the fear that the strains of being in schools with whites will have detrimental effects upon the morale and performance of black children seems to be ungrounded. Clinical case studies of the first black children to enter previously all-white southern schools (Coles, 1968) indicated that the children felt strains no greater than those they had experienced in their previous relations with whites and that the new strains were more than offset by the knowledge that the education they were receiving in the new setting was superior to what they could obtain in all black schools. Similarly, McPartland found no evidence that severe psychological problems were any more frequent in desegregated than in segregated schools. Another kind of morale problem, that of resegregation within the desegregated school, was found to exist but not to have negative effects upon learning unless it manifested itself organizationally, through systematic division of black and white students into different classes or tracks. As we have noted at several previous points in this book, what produces satisfying group relations is not the same thing as what produces academic success, and "studies show that as long as the black student is attending desegregated classes, he will benefit from the student environment in these classes even though he may not have any close friends who are white" (McPartland, 1970: 24).

Redistribution—of Power

The second kind of strategy focuses upon activating a greater portion of the citizenry to involvement in their schools. Community control is in some respects a response by frustrated minority group members to the

slow pace of racial desegregation. The hope of community control advocates is to give local residents (particularly the residents of ghetto neighborhoods) a sense of dignity and pride in themselves as well as concrete
influence over the way their schools are run.

As applied to large city school systems, community control would divide
the total system into a number of smaller districts, compatible as far as
possible with traditional neighborhood and other local identities. The New
York City plan, for example, called for 30 to 33 such districts. Each district would have its own school board elected by the local residents, the
purpose being to make school administration more accessible and responsible to the community.

Community control advocates have been among the most vocal in demanding the publication of standard test scores and other statistical information measuring the performance of children in different schools.
While the immediate purpose of civil rights activists is to make schools
accountable for lack of results among their own children, it is interesting
to note that it may be the activists rather than the scholars who will provide the impetus for making generally available quantitative data on learning in schools.

It is impossible to make any judgment of this strategy yet, since the few
experiments in community control that have been attempted (the Ocean
Hill-Brownsville and P.S. 201 demonstration projects in New York) have
become so bogged down in political battles that no fair test of their educational potential can be carried out.[10] It should also be noted that community control as currently articulated is an almost purely political strategy.
It does not include any systematic plans for changes in teaching procedures
or for any other alterations in the schools. Nor does it necessarily have any
direct effect upon parental involvement. Whether gains in political power
will lead to changes in the learning environment, or whether they will
lead to the kind of upgraded self-image which in turn can lead to the
communication of academic motivation and skills to children, cannot be
assessed until we have more empirical evidence.

Accountability is also the theme of *contract* teaching, a strategy whereby
a school system makes an agreement for a private educational firm to
teach specified academic skills, and the firm is paid according to how
well students perform on tests at the end of the contract period. Unlike
community control, the mechanisms for determining accountability are
built into the terms of the contract. The contract technique is essentially
an application of behavior modification theory, in this case to the teaching
component of the learning system. The "teacher" (that is, the firm) is
rewarded in proportion to success in getting children to read, compute, or
demonstrate whatever learning behavior is stated in the contract. (The
students also may be included in the contract arrangement, receiving
prizes, such as sports equipment or transistor radios, in return for passing
tests at a given level.) A few school systems, San Diego among them,

already have made contracts with educational firms, and an estimated 150 others have entered the negotiating phase. There are, however, as yet no empirical data on which to judge the ultimate value of contract teaching.

New Schools

Not everyone has maintained faith in American public education. The strategy for those who want to involve local residents in their schools but who have given up hope that the public school system will ever provide adequate educational opportunities for their children is to set up new schools which will not only equip children with the traditional intellectual skills but will also inculcate them with a sense of racial identity and self-respect. Students sometimes are trained to be agents of change in their own communities. For example, students in Mississippi freedom schools participated with their teachers in voter registration drives or efforts to persuade black parents to enroll their children in formerly all-white schools.

Application of this strategy is still on a very small scale. Community schools, freedom schools, and other experimental schools, typically set up on an independent basis by ghetto parents with the help of a few professional teachers and educational activists, are often exciting, but they still reach too few children to have had any real impact upon urban education. (Most of the handful of such schools have enrollments of fewer than fifty students.) Without solid financial backing, most are run on a day-to-day basis with a high component of volunteer help. In the opinion of a sympathetic journalist who has visited several of the most significant ones, we can conclude only that they are "showing a tenacious ability to endure in the face of very steep odds" (Featherstone, 1967).[11]

The few usable studies of innovations based upon this approach are inconclusive. For example, a study of 22 children enrolled in a New York City freedom school, in which personality and attitude questionnaires and interviews were administered at two different points in the course, showed slight changes toward more positive attitudes toward self, Negroes, whites, and civil rights among boys but virtually no changes for girls (Johnson, 1967). One weakness of this study was that most of the students came from middle-class homes with one or both parents involved in the civil rights movement, and few of them had negative self-images and racial attitudes to begin with.

Finally mention should be made of the proposed education *voucher* system, which combines aspects of all three general strategies. Under the scheme proposed by the Office of Economic Opportunity, an "Educational Voucher Agency," financed by federal, state, and local funds, but locally controlled, will issue vouchers to parents to cover the cost of educating their children at a school of their own choice. Equalization of resources (strategy 1) will be brought about by having all vouchers equal the full payment of the child's education, and by the stipulation that all participating schools must offer every applicant a roughly equal chance of admission and accept every child's voucher as full payment for his education. (In fact, vouchers for children from low-income families will have a somewhat higher redemption value, reflecting the fact that schools with high proportions of such children tend to have a disproportionate share of expensive educational problems.)

Under a voucher system, parents will have greater power as educational "consumers," since they rather than the school board will decide where their children go to school (strategy 2). Furthermore, vouchers can be used for either public or private schools (strategy 3). Supporters of the voucher model (see Jencks, 1966 and 1970) claim that it will stimulate the development of new schools in both sectors—with new private schools catering especially to children with vouchers; and new public schools being opened by school boards to attract families who otherwise would withdraw their children from the public system. Public or private, schools which cannot attract and hold enough applicants will go out of business.

Since there are no voucher systems in operation,[12] there is no way to evaluate their feasibility or effectiveness in practice. Opponents of the system, including many civil rights groups, fear that the system will increase rather than prevent racial and economic segregation, since schools will try to cream off the most easily educated middle- and upper-SES children; and fear that parents who can afford to supplement their vouchers will be able to gain an even larger share of communities' educational resources than they do already. At the other extreme, is the fear that regulation of all participating schools by a single public agency will cause the legal and administrative entanglements which now threaten to strangle large city school systems to spread even further. The outcome depends, of course, upon how the voucher agencies are organized and how actively they enforce the nondiscriminatory regulations built into the scheme. The relevant point here is that the voucher system is one of the first which represents a direct attack upon the structural defects of schools in relation to their external environments and that it encompasses aspects of all the general strategies for change at this level of the learning system.

Conclusions

The frustration of trying to deal with the subject of this chapter is a double one. On the one hand, the kinds of data needed to construct an adequate model relating success in school to the various components in the environment simply are not available in the form of quantity required. On the other hand, the clues we can piece together are as disheartening as they are incomplete. One is left with the feeling that the patterns of interaction within and between the groups comprising the social environment are not only complex but contrived to impede the adaptation of school systems to the needs of students.

Two general conclusions seem irrefutable, both of which have clear implications with regard to educational reform. One is the almost overwhelming effect of the socioeconomic level of the community surrounding the school. From the point of view of the ambitious parent with school-age children, clearly the best strategy is to locate his family in a metropolitan suburb in the North or West. There his children will be likely to attend schools with high proportions of other students who succeed academically, which will in turn enhance his own children's probability of academic success. For those concerned with "doing something" about the schools as a whole, any serious reform must include mechanisms for distributing the burdens and resources more evenly among the schools in a given area. As Burkhead points out, the policy implications of the present, grossly inequitable distribution—

> . . . are not particularly pleasant to face up to. Taken at face value this means that in large cities for a very great number of low-income children—perhaps for an increasing number—there is no reasonable expectation for an important improvement in the quality of education unless something dramatic is done to ameliorate the socioeconomic conditions of existence. This may require programs, public and private, on a scale which now looks nothing short of utopian (Burkhead, 1967: 88–89).

The second conclusion is that, contrary to our educational ideology, schools as systems are very much enmeshed in politics. As Gittell and Hollander put it, city schools "reflect the city in microcosm. The general character of community interest and level of organization of various segments of the public in local affairs is likely to be replicated in school affairs" (Gittell and Hollander, 1968: 197). In contrast to the usual reformist maxim that education should be outside of politics and should be left to the professionals, Gittell and Hollander argue that in the large cities where this has been done, the results have been disastrous. When such systems need, they conclude, is not less politics but the active political participation of a broader cross-section of community groups and interests.

Finally, regrettable though it may be, the model which describes the dynamics of the schools' external environment is a *conflict* model—groups with conflicting interests are in competition for the limited resources available to the educational system; and the educational arrangements which provide the maximum environment for learning are not necessarily those which are most feasible politically.

Some strategies for change at this level of the learning system were described, although little reliable evaluative evidence is available. Desegregation focuses upon redistributing educational resources and burdens more equitably. By making school populations mirror the class and racial distributions of the total society, it aims to place the disadvantaged in environments where the climate is conducive to learning and to prevent the advantaged from escaping the problems of the schools by simply moving away from them. What data are available indicate: that desegregation has been increasing since 1954, although unevenly and at a pace that no longer satisfies those who are most punished by educational inequality; and that while desegregation is not the panacea for all our educational problems, it has had greater impact upon the academic lives of educationally disadvantaged students than any other large-scale educational reform attempted so far. Both Coleman and McPartland have offered convincing if not conclusive evidence that under appropriate conditions, desegregation has positive effects upon low-income and minority group children without deterring the progress of their more advantaged classmates. This evidence is the more impressive in that the alternative most often proposed by opponents of large-scale desegregation, compensatory programs for ghetto schools, has to date shown virtually no evidence of positive effects.[13]

The second kind of strategy focuses upon distributing educational power more equitably, either by activating a greater proportion of the citizenry to provide a counter-force to the excessive influence of entrenched educational bureaucracies or by having those who provide teaching services held accountable for the learning results, or lack of them. A third strategy provides alternatives to the public school system in the form of new schools or programs which raise the student's confidence in himself and his learning ability. None of these schemes has moved beyond the stage of preliminary trials, so neither their feasibility nor their effectiveness can be stated.

Thus the weight of evidence now favors the strategy of desegregation, but alternative strategies have not yet been given a fair test. What does seem clear is: (1) that the linkages of schools with their external environments have such a powerful effect upon schools and students that they must be a part of any comprehensive educational planning; and (2) that the solutions at this level that have any chance of raising the overall level of educational productivity will change radically school and school systems as we now know them.

Notes

1. See Griffiths, 1966; and Gross, 1958. The latter study, like Coleman's, testifies to the value of doing educational research within a framework of broad sociological conceptualization. Gross was more interested in general problems of role analysis than in particular problems of educational systems per se. The role of the superintendent was chosen because, in Gross's opinion, it represented one of the most cross-pressured roles in our society.

2. Baltimore, Chicago, Detroit, Philadelphia, and St. Louis.

3. The study sample consisted of eight northern and seven southern school systems, selected by a modified random process from cities having a population over 250,000, of which at least 10% was Negro. Data were gathered by

teams of graduate students who spent ten man-days in each city interviewing school administrators, board members, civil rights leaders, political leaders, and members of the civic elite.

4. Crain's term, "civic," seems preferable to Gross's "professional," since it avoids confusion with the professional educational staff.

5. This is analogous to the small amount of research on teachers as an organized peer group relative to research on the individual teacher in the classroom.

6. For example, negative effects upon black children bussed into racist white schools.

7. Whether a given school is segregrated or desegregated depends partly upon one's definition. Dentler uses the U.S. Department of Health, Education and Welfare definition which classifies Negro students in terms of whether or not they attend schools which are 50% or more white.

8. The experience of Berkeley, California, is a case in point. In 1968, Berkeley put into effect what is probably the most comprehensive integration plan outside the South. The heart of the plan is a two-way bussing program, of about 40% of the elementary school students, which limits all elementary schools in the white and middle-to-upper class neighborhoods to kindergarten through grade three and sends all fourth, fifth and sixth graders to formerly black schools. Although Berkeley has a clear pattern of racial and economic segregation in housing, the city maintains a slight majority of whites, and it is small enough (population 120,000) so that there is only one high school and so that the bussing involves an average ride of only twenty minutes.

9. 82% in a 1966 Harris poll; over 90% in a 1968 Survey Research Center Study of black attitudes in 15 cities; and 88% in a 1969 national survey commissioned by *Newsweek* (Orfield, 1970). For data on *changes* in white attitudes toward blacks' intelligence and school desegregation, see Pettigrew, 1967: 297 and 301.

10. For a series of journalistic accounts of the New York crisis, see Featherstone, 1967; 1968; 1969.

11. For supporting arguments underlying this strategy, and possible new kinds of school-community relationships, see Katz, 1964; Newman and Oliver, 1967; Green, 1969. Note that the conclusion that public schools are not good learning environments is not limited to the poor. The free schools described in Chapter 9 serve mainly middle- and upper-SES children, although there have been some attempts to initiate free schools which will enroll a broad social cross-section of children. The difference between the "new" schools for the well-to-do and those for the disadvantaged are that the latter are generally trying to provide for ghetto children the very qualities of white suburban schools which the free school founders have rejected. To put it another way, the former stress creativity and joy in learning; the latter stress academic achievement as conventionally defined, and also stress racial identity.

12. The OEO hopes to fund an experimental voucher system in some community by 1971.

13. See especially the thorough review of evaluative research on Head Start, Title I programs, the More Effective Schools project, and other compensatory programs, by McDill *et al.*, 1969.

Educational practices are not phenomena that are isolated from one another; rather, for a given society, they are bound up in the same system all the parts of which contribute toward the same end: it is the system of education suitable to this country and this time. Each people has its own, as it has its own moral, religious, economic systems, etc. . . . . Consequently, through comparison, by abstracting the similarities and eliminating the differences from them, one can certainly establish the generic types of education which correspond to the different types of societies.   Emile Durkheim

In a society like ours, academic patterns change more slowly than others. In my lifetime, in England, they have crystallized rather than loosened. I used to think that it would be about as hard to change, say, the Oxford and Cambridge scholarship examination as to conduct a major revolution. I now believe I was over-optimistic.   C. P. Snow

There is nothing wrong with the school as a social environment, except what is wrong with America.   Edgar Z. Friedenberg

Although the schools are under constant pressures from the external environment, there are also at periodic intervals crises and criticisms of a special sort. These have to do with whether "our" (American) schools are good enough or as good as some other nation's. Such crises on the national level usually are precipitated by some outside event which is viewed as a test or a threat to our national superiority—technological, moral, or otherwise—or our competitive position with respect to some other country. Such was the launching of Sputnik. One consequence of the flow of words set off by Sputnik was the emergence of Admiral Rickover as the major proponent for a particular view of the school's function and their current efficiency. The Rickover view is expressed in the following excerpt:

Sputnik dramatized the fact that today a nation's position in the world is closely related to the number and competence of its scientists and technologists, as well as to the educational level of the general population . . . We fail to recognize that life in all modern industrial countries now calls for much the same kind of intellectual competence, and that this competence can be acquired in no other way than by formal schooling. Many Americans have almost as fervent an attachment to our present school system as to the Constitution . . .

I have tried for years to combat these illusions by collecting and publishing concrete facts about European education. We must be realistic. It is European education we should equal—better still excel: there is no doubt we do splendidly in comparison with education in the Congo or Outer Mongolia. . . . What has to be kept in mind is that the educational value of a school year in Europe is at least a third higher than in America (Rickover, 1965).

Although the substantive validity of Rickover's argument can be substantiated, or disproved, only with the kind of empirical data which we shall consider later in this chapter, the excerpt itself constitutes a form of sociological data, insofar as it is an influential view of what American schools should be like. To Rickover, the function of a national education system is a competitive one—we want to win in a kind of international achievement contest. Participation in the contest, moreover, is limited to industrially developed societies and to the kinds of learning which can contribute directly to science and technology. Presumably what is good enough for the Congo and Outer Mongolia is not good enough for Americans; so they are not in the same game.

A recent explosion of national concern over our schools followed publication of some of the results of the International Project for the Evaluation of Educational Achievement, which will be discussed at length in this chapter. It is interesting to note here that what was reported in the mass media was the poor showing of American students. An especially humiliating comparison was with Japan, which ranked at or near the top on all achievement measures, because the Japanese education system breaks some of the cardinal rules of American pedagogy (for instance, Japanese classes average over 40 at the secondary level, disproving the innate value of the small class).

In this final chapter dealing with substantive research findings, we reach the outer limits of the learning system as it was mapped in Chapter 1. We shall consider here the relationship of the total society to its education system and the ultimate effect upon learning and achievement of that society's schools. The types of variables with which we shall be concerned are diagrammed in Exhibit 13–1. Following a consideration of some of the special problems of comparative educational research, we shall turn to empirical studies which link up the three components of this model.

Exhibit 13-1

The Relationship of the Total Society and Its Learning System

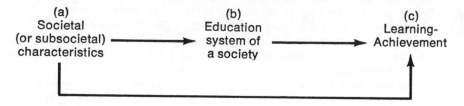

The Field of Comparative Education

The basic questions to which comparative education addresses itself coincide with the basic policy alternatives of a national education system. These are: *how many* persons are to be educated in a formal school setting; *what* they are to be taught; and *how* they are to be taught. Comparative education is an old and active subdivision of educational research, with an extensive literature and its own textbooks and journals. From a sociological point of view, however, it is a conceptually and methodologically underdeveloped field. As one sociologist puts it: "Although comparative education is rapidly growing in popularity, the field remains characterized by a 'buzzing confusion' regarding optimal strategies for its advancement as a scientific discipline." To date, its output consists "mainly of a large collection of concrete descriptions of the educational institutions of many nations, a growing but disjointed literature on the determinants of various educational activities, and a continuous flow of methodological discussions of the difficulties inherent in comparative research" (Livingstone, 1968: 11, 1).

What are the problems peculiar to crosscultural research? First, simply the logistics and the expense. Think, for example, of replicating the *Educational Opportunity* survey in other countries. To obtain an equivalent set of data in each country would multiply the cost—assuming that one could translate the concept of educational equality, as well as specific questions, into the terms of other societies. To economize by cutting down on the size of the sample or the scope of the measuring instruments would lower the likelihood of obtaining unbiased and truly comparable data.

The major difficulty is in ensuring comparability of data from one country to another. Categories of classification are often different. For example, not all countries have "comprehensive" high schools, and what constitutes a comprehensive school may differ from one country to another. (Husen, 1967: Vol. II, 287). National school systems also differ not only in the structure or classification of schools and the content of the curriculum but in starting age and minimum school-leaving age, and the proportion of the total population in school at various levels.

To assure the comparability of test materials, administrative instruction, and data processing procedures, when there are language differences, is problematic. A final headache is that:

> nearly all the sources of error are country-specific, and thus there is no possibility for randomization of errors. . . . In one study, it was said that the key-punching errors reflected differences in national character; Germany showed a total absence of random errors in key-punching; whenever an error occurred, it was a systematic error that appeared in all cards; in Italy the errors were scattered with apparent Latin abandon. Apocryphal though these stories may be, they point to the sobering fact that errors are highly correlated with country, and the cross-country comparisons on which such studies depend must be made warily. In the . . . [International Project for the Evaluation of Educational Achievement], it was discovered too late for changing proofs that all the results reported for Finland were incorrect, due to poor communication—so the book carries a note at the front that is a solemn reminder of the special methodological problems of cross-national studies (Coleman, 1969: 98).

Given the difficulties in executing and interpreting crosscultural studies, why bother with them? Apart from the pure interest of crosscultural comparisons, and the larger perspective they give on our own educational systems and problems, crosscultural comparisons are the only way we can answer certain questions, in particular the question of whether a relationship between a set of components in our own learning system is unique to that system and is explained by some characteristics of the larger society, or whether the relationship is characteristic of learning systems in general.

We shall begin our survey of crosscultural research findings by examining data on internation differences in academic achievement (component c of Exhibit 13–1), and then move back to see to what degree we can explain these differences.

Crosscultural Differences in Achievement

The International Project for the Evaluation of Educational Achievement (hereafter called the IEA) has completed a comparison of mathematics achievement in twelve countries,[1] based upon a sample of 132,775 students (between 2500 and 38,000 in each country) and almost 19,000 teachers in over 5000 schools. The overall goal of the IEA was to assess the productivity of participating countries' education systems and to see what school characteristics, teaching approaches, and student characteristics are related to achievement. The results to date are published in two volumes, the first describing the design and administration of the survey; the second being a compilation of results. Although the editor emphasizes that the study was not conceived as an "international contest," clearly this has been the stance of the mass media reporting of the findings.

Mathematics was chosen as the first subject area to be investigated,[2] because it presents fewer measurement problems than say history or literature, and because, "Most countries represented are at present concerned with improving their scientific and technical education, at the basis of which lies the learning of mathematics" (Husen, 1967: Vol. I, 33. This justification somewhat belies the editor's plea for a noncontest approach).

The UNESCO Institute for Education, in Hamburg, Germany, supplied administrative and technical coordination service for the project, with some of the costs met by a U.S. Office of Education grant. A council of representatives from each participating nation met annually from 1960 through 1965, to oversee the conceptualization and carrying out of the project, and additional committees dealt with special problems (for instance, sampling, test construction).

The original goal was to test at two major turning points in the school career: (1) the last point at which all of an age group was still in full-time schooling (age 13); and (2) the preuniversity year. One problem was that although virtually all thirteen-year-olds were in school, they were not necessarily at the same level of the education ladder:

> . . . the per cent of 13-year-olds who are not in the normal grade for 13-year-olds ranges from 1 per cent in one country to 29 per cent in another. As a result it was decided to test both populations, that is, all 13-year-olds (designated as Population 1a) and all pupils in the grade where the majority of 13-year-olds are (designated 1b). . . . To avoid disparity, it was agreed for this project that it would be the grade where the majority of the 13-year-old pupils were within 3 months of the end of the current school year.
>
> [Students in the pre-university year] . . . were divided into two target populations, that is, those students taking mathematics (designated population 3a) and those not (designated 3b).
>
> Between the 13-year-old level . . . and the pre-university year there are various major terminal points in the school systems. For example, the end of compulsory schooling is 14 years in Germany and 16 in Sweden; there are also major examination points such as 1er partie du baccalaureat in France or GCE "O" level in England. It was decided that countries could choose the population(s) they wished to test at these intermediate points in terms of their own plans for national investigations (Husen, 1967: Vol. I, 45–46).

Having defined the target populations, the goal was to sample as many different schools, with as few students per school, as possible (to decrease the likelihood of bias due to the unique characteristics of individual schools).[3]

The problem of test construction was exacerbated by the linguistic and cultural differences among the participating countries. Nine different languages were used in the twelve countries sampled. After each national center prepared a report on the content and objectives of mathematical learning for students within the age range of the study, with suggested examples of appropriate test items, an international committee drew up an overall "blueprint" and a series of pre-tests which were tried out on small samples in three countries. The final test contained 174 items, mainly multiple choice, in ten separately prepared test booklets, graded in difficulty, with a time limit of one hour per booklet. In addition to the achievement tests, questionnaires were designed to measure students' perception of their school and their attitudes toward mathematics, school, learning in general, and the world around them.[4]

After administration, the test booklets were first collected in national centers, where responses were transferred on to punch cards or special sheets designed for the IBM 1230. These data were sent to the University of Chicago Computer Center for editing, sorting, filing, and most of the analysis. Despite the great care to ensure that materials arrived on time and in correct form, there were a number of small mistakes, as well as the boner, mentioned earlier, concerning the Finnish data.

The data analysis includes comparisons at both macro and micro levels. That is, as well as the comparisons between total or mean achievement scores among countries as a whole, there are *within*-country comparisons (for example, of achievement differences between students in comprehensive and specialized schools). An additional analysis compares subgroups of the total sample (for instance, the top 4% in each country).

The basic macro-level comparison, which shows the rough standing of each country in each of the four target populations, is summarized in Exhibit 13–2. The placement of each nation in the figure represents the deviation of that country's national mean from the grand mean of all countries. Especially noticeable are the overall good showings of Japan and Israel (although the latter had a very small sample and in only two of the four target populations) and the poor showing of the United States. Some countries displayed different performance patterns at the two different age levels. For example, France's deviation is below the overall mean at the 13-year-old level, when all the children in the age-group are still in school, but rises toward the top after the school-leaving age apparently produces a more selective population in the schools.

The study found much variation in school entry and leaving ages, with no clear relations with math achievement. The median entry age was 6, and the countries in this category produced, *on the average,* higher test scores at age 13 than at an entry age of 5. Apparently the extra year of schooling in England and Scotland does not have a direct positive effect upon later mathematical competence. Of the two countries with an entry age of 7, one (Sweden) had as high a score as the median of the 6-year-old entry group, while the other (Finland) had the lowest score of all (Husen, 1967: Vol. II, 77–78).

The findings on size are also ambiguous. Within the wide range of school sizes in the sample, the best test performance by most 13-year-olds was

Exhibit 13-2
National Means Expressed as Deviations from the Grand Mean

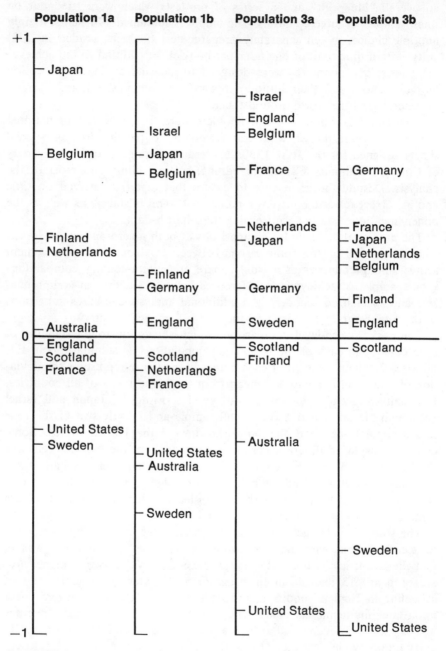

Husen, 1967: Vol. ii, 27.

in schools with enrollments greater than 800, although in a few types of schools small enrollments went with higher scores. For older students the evidence was contradictory, and at this age level, national differences accounted for more of the variation than size of school. Classroom size ranged from means of 24 and 25 in Belgium and the Netherlands to 41 in Japan. (The United States mean in this sample was 29.) On the national level, students in the countries with larger mean class size scored higher at the age 13 level (the rank order correlations by country between average math scores and average class size are $+.29$ and $+.43$ for samples 1a and 1b), but this relationship was reversed at the preuniversity level (rank order correlations for samples 3a and 3b were $-.41$ and $-.23$). Within most countries there were no statistically significant differences in math scores among students in small, medium, and large classes. One interpretation suggested by the authors is that at the earlier age, when enrollments still include almost all children at that age, the best teachers often are assigned to the larger classes because they are thought better able to cope with them, but by the preuniversity year, there is a tendency toward smaller classes for the more able and advanced students. At the later level, the class size variable is further complicated by "varying selection mechanisms affecting both the ability distribution and the social class composition of the classes" (Husen, 1967: Vol. II, 297). The general conclusion is the same one reached in Chapter 8: it is difficult to separate out the effects of class size from the effects of other variables, but merely reducing class size is not likely to increase achievement markedly.

A third system characteristic correlated with achievement was retentivity, or the proportion of the age group still in school at the terminal level. The general question here is whether "more means worse" in academic terms, whether an educational system which tries to keep high proportions of young people in school up to relatively high levels will sacrifice overall quality of education. Exhibit 13–3 synthesizes the IEA answers to this question. The countries are ranked according to the proportion of the total age group still in school at the preuniversity year, beginning with the most selective (or least retentive) system. As Column 2 of Exhibit 13–3 shows, the average level of math performance was inversely related to the proportion of the age group still in school (the correlation between Columns 1 and 2 is $-.62$). Thus more does seem to mean worse, in the sense that countries which retain a high percentage to this stage produce on the average lower standards of achievement than do the more elitist countries. However, when equal proportions of the total age group are compared, the results are quite different. These results are shown in Column 3. With one exception (Belgium, which has a 4% retentivity rate), the means go up when only the highest performance students are included, with the greatest increases in the countries with the highest retentivity rates. There are also changes in the relative standing of the countries:

Exhibit 13–3

Mathematics Test Scores by Retentivity Ranks

	(1)	(2)	(3)
		Mean Math Score	
	% Retentivity	**Total Sample**	**Upper 4%**
Belgium	4	34.6	34.6
Germany	4.7	28.8	31.5
England	5	35.2	39.4
France	5	33.4	37.0
Netherlands	5	31.9	34.7
Scotland	5.4	25.5	29.4
Israel	7	36.4	41.7
Finland	7	25.3	32.1
Japan	8	31.4	43.9
Australia	14	21.6	33.7
Sweden	16	27.3	43.7
United States	18	13.8	33.0

Adapted from Husen, 1967: Vol. II, 118 and 122.

The rank correlation between the two sets of means is +.45. This indicates that one can predict only moderately well the mathematics performance of the upper 4 per cent of the *age group in each country* from the mathematics performance of the students in full-time schooling. . . . Downward shifts occur in Belgium, which moves from third to seventh place; Germany, which moves from seventh to eleventh place; and Scotland, which moves from ninth to last place. Upward shifts occur in Japan, which moves from sixth to first place, Sweden, which moves from eighth to second place; and the United States, which moves from twelfth to ninth place. In general, those countries with the least restrictive policies as to who will continue in school show the greatest upward shifts, while those countries with stricter selection policies and practices show the greatest downward shifts . . .

The *range* of difference between high and low performance countries also decreases when only the most able students are compared: the range in Colunm 2 is from 13.8 for the United States to 36.4 for Israel, a difference of 22.6 score points; in Column 3 the mean score ranges from 29.4 for Scotland to 43.9 for Japan, a difference of only 14.5:

This would support the proposition that countries do *not* differ considerably in the proportions of students talented in math, but that the differences in selection policies and practices cloud the picture. It is at least a feasible suggestion that the "cream" of mathematical talent is distributed equally over the various countries and that it is only the procedures for diluting the cream that vary from country to country.

These findings can have important implications for educational policy and practice. The view that the lowering of selection barriers would lead to decline in achievement and, especially, a reduction in achievement among the cream of a nation's talent is questioned by these data. The results indicate that the most talented students continue to achieve at a high level, even when as much as 70 per cent of the age group is enrolled in full-time schooling (Husen, 1967: Vol. II, 122–123).

Another way to consider the retentivity issue is to select some level of test performance as an international "standard" and then to see what proportions of students in various countries achieve these scores or higher. The IEA data showed that the proportion of a total age group achieving a predetermined test score was positively related to the proportion still in school, suggesting that a country can increase its "total mathematical yield" by increasing its "intake" of students (Husen, 1967: Vol. II, 134).

A school system characteristic also used as an independent variable was specialization—that is, whether a student attends a school which provides a single course of study (academic, vocational, or general) or a comprehensive school which provides a variety of courses. The authors' prediction was that the level of math achievement would be higher in the former than the latter. The data analysis was complicated and the findings disappointingly ambiguous. The problem of classifying schools in different countries in terms of a uniform measure of comprehensiveness has been pointed out already, and it appears that any conclusive interpretation of the data already collected waits upon a more adequate codification of this dimension. All that the authors could conclude from an extended comparison of different types of schools both within and between countries was that any initial advantage gained by students in specialized academic preparatory schools over their peers in more comprehensive schools is largely overcome by the preuniversity level. The presence of students with lower ability or students following general or vocational courses of study does not in itself have a negative effect upon those headed for universities. Moreover, nonacademic students in comprehensive schools seemed to do rather better than students following similar courses in separate schools (Husen, 1967: Vol. II, 101–102).

The effects upon achievement of two of the individual student characteristics we have studied already are much clearer than the effects of school structural attributes. One individual characteristic is socioeconomic background. A regression analysis aimed at assessing the relative contribution of a number of different independent variables to the differences in test scores indicated that family background accounted for the greatest share of the variation (Husen, Vol. II, Chapter 6). For the 13-year-olds, the relationship between father's education and mathematics performance is significant in all cases (with the single exception of Finland in Population 1a). A similar relationship occurs between father's occupation and math scores. For the older students, on the other hand, the correlations are smaller and occasionally in the opposite direction (in Finland, Sweden, and Germany, the lower-SES students had higher test scores than the upper-SES students). This apparently reflects the fact that, except in the United States, the selection process is such that only the most able students in the lower-SES groups are still in school by the preuniversity year (Husen, 1967: Vol. II, 208–209).

The study provides replications of the sex differences which were the subject of Chapter 5. At every level and in most countries, boys were more interested in mathematics than girls and outperformed them. The exceptions were France and England, where the girls who were specializing in math (Population 3a) had higher interest scores than their male counterparts. "This may be understood in terms of these girls being so highly selected (almost six boys for every girl) that those girls admitted to mathematics specialization must be among the most highly motivated students" (Husen, 1967: Vol. II, 258).

Some clues to understanding the social forces influencing these sex differences are provided by comparing the attitudes and achievements of boys and girls in coeducational and single-sex schools. With regard to achievement, within a given country the differences between boys and girls are less in coed than in single-sex schools, and at the level of total societies, sex differences are smallest in countries where the majority of students are in coeducational schools (for example, in the United States and Sweden). The implication is that girls' capability for learning mathematics is not markedly lower than boys' and that when the learning conditions are similar, the achievement differences will be reduced. Ironically though, sex differences in mathematics *interest* are slightly greater in coed schools. Apparently in the very settings where the opportunities for learning math are more nearly equal for boys and girls, the heightened awareness of sex role differences may have negative effects upon girls' attitudes and self-expectations!

Although the effects of both family background and sex appear to be universal, it is important to remember that neither variable explains away the large differences *between* countries that is the core finding of the IEA survey. Children from families at the highest occupational and educational levels in some countries (Sweden, Australia, the United States) score at or below the level of children from the lowest-SES levels in other countries (Japan and Israel). Similarly, the girls in some countries outperform the boys in others, even though they are nearly always inferior to the boys in their own country. On the whole, educational differences among the countries in this sample far outweigh any of the social differences within them.

Finally, achievement in mathematics on the national level was correlated with attitudes toward learning. In general, the countries with the highest average math scores were those in which the highest proportions of respondents:

felt that mathematics was important to the future of human society;

expressed liking for school and school learning (the least favorable attitudes were expressed by students from the U.S., followed by the other English-speaking countries. Japanese students were most likely to express positive attitudes);

felt that man has effective control of and mastery over his environment (Husen, 1967: Vol. II, 44–48).

The Internal Dynamics of National Education Systems

Although the IEA study is a major contribution to the educational research literature, it is limited to one component of the crosscultural model diagrammed in Exhibit 13–1. That is, it dealt with the creation of adequate measures of one kind of academic achievement and documented the differences between a sample of nations (component c). Although the authors attributed the differences they found to differences in the organization of the total system (component b), "which, in turn, mirror differences in cultural values" (component a), they were not very successful in identifying the important system characteristics which were related to mathematics performance (with the exception of the findings with respect to retentivity rates).

The IEA researchers can scarcely be blamed for failing to fill in the entire crosscultural learning model. With the resources available to them, they were wise to limit their focus to an area which could be handled in a systematic fashion, giving a great deal of attention to the problems of test construction and data gathering and analysis. One of the few systematic analyses of component b of Exhibit 13–1 is Livingstone's model of the internal structure of national education systems (1968). Like the IEA study, it focuses upon defining the principal variables and intrarelationships of a single area of the model, but unlike the IEA, Livingstone's is a theoretical paper, based upon an extensive review of available studies but not itself contributing any empirical findings.

Livingstone postulates the following as the basic "activities" which comprise any national learning system: (1) legal provisions; (2) financing; (3) staff development and maintenance; (4) educational research; (5) program control (or degree of centralization); (6) provision of educational facilities; (7) provision of auxiliary services; (8) instruction; and (9) administration of students.[5] By using these as the components or "focal subsystems" of his model, Livingstone formulates almost three hundred hypotheses about their interdependencies. Some of the major variables, which act as unifying themes organizing sets of hypotheses, are: enrollment (how many or what proportions of young people are in school); the number and types of different educational programs offered and at what point in his school career a student must make a firm choice of specialty; the extent of centralization of the system (is there a national education ministry, and if so how great is its control over curriculum and the allocation of students?); and the range and extensiveness of services offered beyond classroom teaching (say, guidance or financial aid). Here are some of the major hypotheses formulated around these themes, as paraphrased by this writer:

Enrollments at different levels of the education system are related; the greater the attendance rates at one level, the greater the rates at other levels.

The greater the enrollment rates at a given level,
the more predominant are ability groupings of students and specialized subject teaching;
the greater the basic education and formal training required of teachers and the higher the proportion of teachers who are formally qualified;
the greater the number of teachers per school, but also the higher the ratio of administrators to teachers;
the less the centralization, especially of program policy.

The greater the proportion of urban students at a given level,
the greater the enrollment rates;
the higher the educational expenditure (per capita and the proportion of the national income devoted to education) and the greater the proportion of public education expenditure allocated to special education;
the greater the proportion of female students.

The greater the religious homogeneity of enrollment at a given level,
the lower the educational expenditure;
the lower the proportion of female students;
the greater the proportion of students in private schools.

The greater the centralization in one area or activity of the system (say, program policy), the greater the centralization in another (say, guidance services or financial support). The greater the centralization, especially in program control,
the greater the likelihood of external examinations to determine entrance to and graduation from schools or programs;
the sooner the differentiation into specialized curriculum and the greater the proportion of students enrolled in vocational and other non-academic programs;
the lower the acceleration rate and the greater the degree of retardation at respective levels;
the greater the proportions of secondary and higher level students receiving financial aid;
the greater the proportion of rural students.

The longer the basic education program, or the later the differentiation into specialized curriculum,
the smaller the proportion of the total school enrollment at the primary level and the higher the proportion pursuing advanced degrees;

the greater the range and the more balanced the enrollments in
  level programs.
The greater the number of alternative curricula offered at elementary
  secondary levels,
  the lower the enrollment rates within the compulsory age limits;
  the lower the proportion of students enrolled in strictly academic
    programs;
  the greater the likelihood of external examinations for admittance to or
    graduation from these programs.

Although most of Livingstone's hypotheses, like the majority of crosscultural studies, make comparisons only at the level of the education system
as a whole, he emphasizes that this is more a consequence of the availability of data than of optimum research design. One of the most valuable
—and unusual—features of the IEA study was that comparisons within as
well as among societies could be made with respect to such variables as
class or school size, comprehensiveness and specialization, and so on. The
results made us constantly aware that "the educational systems of different
nations are not internally homogeneous nor do they exhibit identical degrees of variation," a point that is often lost in the superficiality and the
"penchant for slick, sterile generalization" that plague so much crosscultural work (Livingstone, 1968: 7–8).

Relations Between Societies and Schools

One of the first sociologists to recognize and describe the relationship
between a society and its schools was Durkheim. As the quotation at the
beginning of this chapter indicates, Durkheim saw education as a social
creation, as the means by which a society assured its own continuity by
socializing the young in its own image. The components of the education
system—which themselves "constitute perfectly defined facts and which
have the same reality as other social facts" (Durkheim, 1956: 94)—are
interrelated. They are interrelated internally, so that a given education system has unity and consistency, and also externally, so that the education
system reflects a society's moral and intellectual values.

While Durkheim postulated a close relationship between the external
and internal characteristics of a society's learning system, he did not spell
out what he considered the crucial variables. Much of the literature on
comparative education has been an attempt to specify these variables.
Havighurst (1968) believes that the way to understand a society's educational system is to understand how it is related to the other basic institutions of that society, in particular the family, the church, the state, and the
economy. Certain historical periods have been characterized by the dominance of one of these basic institutions. In the Middle Ages in Europe,
the church was dominant, but later the national state assumed major importance, with corresponding changes in the nature and structure of the

schools, from the composition of the curriculum to the composition of the student body. Similarly, modern societies can be distinguished by the relative strength of their basic institutions. In most modern industrialized societies the alliance between the state and the economy is close. In communist-socialist societies, such as those of Russia and China, not only are the economic and education systems under the aegis of state planning, but the schools are designed to be an intrument for economic development. Thus 70% of the students in Russian universities major in engineering and science; and in Communist China many schools are set up in factories, workshops, and farms, and emphasis is placed upon the skills necessary for increasing national production (Havighurst, 1968: Chapters III and VI). There are few modern societies in which the family or the church is the dominant institution, although Holland illustrates a kind of exception. Here religious influences remain relatively strong, and both Protestant and Roman Catholic "voluntary" schools, as well as the schools established by public authorities, receive financial assistance from public funds (Havighurst, 1968: Chapter XII).

Two decisions which must be made by any society are what subjects and skills are required for that society's maintenance and further development, and how many students are needed by—and can be supported by—the economy. Societies at a low level of industrial development can utilize only a small number of highly educated persons. "Under such conditions much of the effort of the schools and the external examining system is to find ways of rejecting the majority of students at various points in the educational system and to discover the talented few who are to be given advanced educational opportunity" (Bloom, 1968: 12). Highly developed nations, on the other hand, must find ways to increase the proportion of persons with secondary and higher education. In an economy that requires the range and complexity of skills required in the United States, investment in education may pay off at a greater rate than capital investment. In fact, it may be cheaper to educate nearly everyone at a given age level than to invest a great deal in the prediction and selection of talent. "The problem is no longer one of finding the few who can succeed. The basic problem is to determine how the largest proportion of the age group can learn effectively those skills and subject matter regarded as essential" (Bloom, 1968: 12).

Societies undergoing rapid social change or modernization have special problems in adapting the educational system to the manpower needs in the other segments of the society. Developing nations often suffer shortages of persons with special kinds of learning (in engineering and other technical fields), and may have difficulty keeping persons with valuable skills once they have completed their education (as a result of "brain drains"). On the other hand, the institutional imbalances caused by rapid change may produce a temporary surplus of persons with higher levels of education. For example, although India suffers a shortage of persons trained in agriculture, technical fields, and the health professions, it has an excess of students in the classical academic courses of study, who cannot find work commensurate with their education. In India, the intense competition for the limited supply of degrees and diplomas of the sort required for desirable government and other white-collar positions explains the great amount of cheating on examinations endemic to some colleges. Those who fail constitute a pool of the discontented susceptible to the appeals of extremist political and social movements. Although our sources of information on Communist China are limited and not entirely dependable, the information available suggests that China may be experiencing some discrepancy between educational output and the ability of the labor market to absorb it:

> It may be that by 1970 China will find herself burdened with a surplus of secondary-school graduates for whom there will be no semi-skilled labor market, as was true in the USSR in the 1950's. There are already complaints that "second rate sons" are multiplying too fast. Those who are neither outstanding students nor outstanding Communists complete their secondary education only to find there are no better jobs for them than the manual labor to which they would have been assigned as illiterates (Havighurst, 1968: 125–126).

A sharp increase in the numbers or proportions of students at the higher levels may produce problems of adaptation for the students as well as for the society. In a paper on educational policy presented before a congressional committee on science and astronautics, Green (1970) cautioned:

> . . . an increase in the social demand for formal education experienced as a sequential requirement in the lives of people, may be dysfunctional because in practice, it constitutes an extraordinary extension of adolescence at precisely the time when people are maturing earlier. It means, among other things, the extended deferment of entrance upon meaningful work. . . . The result cannot help but be frustrating and indeed alienating in a society that has promised much to be gained from extended education and then has progressively deferred the reward (Green, 1970: 6).

Stinchcombe's study of rebellious California students (discussed in Chapter 11) suggested that lack of perceived articulation between in-school learning and the requirements of future roles is a cause of poor academic performance and social alienation. Similar results were obtained in a study of Israeli high school students (Adler, 1967), which found that the major difference between dropouts and nondropouts was that the former were vague about their future plans and saw little likelihood of fulfilling their aspirations via their current course of study.

In addition to deciding how many students will be educated and in what kinds of programs, societies must decide how entry into the more prestigious schools and programs is to be determined. Studies of highly elite systems, such as those of England and France, have emphasized that the degree of elitism in the school reflects the status system of that society as a whole, including its patterns of social stratification and its opportunities for social mobility. As Turner puts it, in a comparison of American and English schools, the "accepted mode of upward mobility shapes the school system, directly and indirectly through its effects on the values which implement social control" (Turner, 1968: 219). Turner distinguishes between "sponsored" and "contest" modes of mobility. Under the former, illustrated by English society and education, "elite recruits are chosen by the established elite or their agents, and elite status is *given* on the basis of some criteria of supposed merit and cannot be *taken* by any amount of effort or strategy. Upward mobility is like entry into a private club where each candidate must be 'sponsored' by one or more of the members" (Turner, 1968: 220). In contest mobility, characteristic of the American style, status is achieved through the individual's talents and efforts. Ideally, all members of the society have an opportunity to try for its prizes, and more than one strategy is available for obtaining them. Thus the American ideal (however much deviation there may be in actual practice) is to have within most schools a variety of courses of study as well as a cross-section of social class and ability.

Egalitarian societies also differ from elitist ones in the *source* of their valuation of education:

> Education has a *functional* value when it is used *directly* to accomplish a purpose. For example, when a person takes an engineering course and becomes an engineer, his education has had a functional value for him. Education has a *symbolic* value when it is used as a *symbol* of status. For example, when a person takes a doctor's degree in medicine and uses the degree as a symbol of status, but does not practice medicine, his education has a symbolic value. Or when an uneducated man earns a good deal of money in business and then sends his son to a selective private school before the son enters the family business, the son's education has a symbolic value (Havighurst, 1968a: 137–138).

Havighurst feels that Russia and China, with their ideology of a "classless" society, have gone further than any other societies toward evaluating education in functional terms, though the United States is not far behind.

While nations and their schools can be placed in some kind of order along an equalitarianism-elitism continuum, the present arrangement should not be thought of as static or permanent. The most egalitarian of modern societies and systems typically emerged from systems that were oriented toward training a small, often aristocratic, elite for positions of importance in the larger society. Similarly, in the countries which are currently at the elitist end of the continuum, there are forces toward extending educational opportunities toward a greater portion of the young and toward revising the curriculum and methods of instruction to be more congruent with the present-day world.[6]

It should be noted that greater educational equalization generally requires an increase in educational and training opportunities (in particular, more openings in selective schools and programs), but that such an increase does not by itself bring about reductions in differential social class attendance rates. For example, data presented at a recent international conference on educational planning indicated that in those countries in which the proportion of an age group educated in selective schools had increased markedly (for example, England and the Netherlands), there had not been a comparable increase in attendance by lower-SES children. Even in the United States, where the aspiration for higher education has diffused relatively rapidly among all social strata, attendance at selective schools and universities has tended to be, disproportionately, a higher-status phenomenon. What seems to happen is that as educational opportunities increase, attendance follows a process of "class succession," with the upper-strata reaching near-satiation of their demands before the strata below them begin to increase their rates of attendance.

Exceptions to this general pattern can be found in some of the newly developing countries (for instance, Puerto Rico—see Sussman, 1962) and in countries which have made conspicuous efforts to overhaul their educational systems. The two nations in the IES sample in which major reform has occurred during the past two decades are Sweden and Israel. The focus of the "new" education in both cases is upon equalizing opportunities for previously disadvantaged groups and at the same time upon lessening the invidious distinctions between academic education and technical or vocational education. In Israel, children of "Oriental" Jewish families comprised over half of the primary school population in 1966, but accounted for only 25% of the high school and 12% of the higher education population. Moreover, although Israel has a crying need for agricultural and technical experts, about three-fourths of the secondary students pursued the academic curricula (Braham, 1966). In Sweden, where the old dual system is being replaced by new comprehensive *grindskola,* there is already evidence that the near monopoly of the upper middle class on university education is being broken and that the relative attendance of students from rural areas has increased; also, that students of all social classes are more likely to plan for more education if they attend a comprehensive school than if they are enrolled in the traditional dual system (for a discussion of equalitarian trends in Swedish education, see Tomasson, 1965).

The strong shift toward equalitarianism that has occurred in Sweden and Israel seems to require, among other things, a strong centralized education ministry with real power over educational policy. Degree of centralization, or "program control," was one of the variables in Livingstone's model. Lack of central decision-making and control has been suggested as a source of weakness in the American education system, and the IEA findings suggest that it may have some bearing upon the quality of academic performance and that it is not simply a function of such other system characteristics as elitism-egalitarianism—for example, both France and Sweden have a national education ministry. However, until further empirical analysis of the effects of centralization is carried out, our conclusions must remain speculative.

Socialization

The preceding section has suggested some of the ways in which the structure of a society's education system may be related to and explained by its other institutions. We have not yet given much attention to the family, which, even if it is not the dominant institution in a given period or place, is the one responsible for the initial socialization of children and their preparation for the student role. It was noted in Part Two that the relationship between family background and academic performance is a universal phenomenon, documented in an extensive crosscultural literature. In all the countries for which data are available, it has been found that children from some families begin their educational career with an advantage over children from others and that this initial gap widens as the school career progresses. The most extensive recent findings are contained in the English study, *Children and Their Primary Schools,*[7] which serves as a crosscultural replication of many of the Coleman report findings. The Plowden report incorporates findings from: a national survey, based upon a random sample of children within a random sample of English primary schools; data from interviews with the parents of the children in the national survey sample; a longitudinal study of child development in one city; and a study of resource allocation to the schools in that same city. The last two sets of findings showed that children's achievement in the first years of school was strongly related to the status of their parents, and furthermore, that children from lower-status families were more likely to go to schools with relatively limited resources. The national survey showed that, even by age 14, more of the variance between and within schools was explained by the social and economic position of the students' parents than by any of the school factors included in the analysis. "Teacher quality" was the strongest predictor among the school variables, but even though the children in this sample were matched with their present teachers (a matching which the *Equality of Educational Opportunity* study did not make), the greater precision of the teacher measure did not markedly improve the survey's predictive power relative to the students' family characteristics.

A wide range of background, attitudinal, and behavioral information was collected in the parents' interviews. The family variable which explained the greatest amount of student achievement variance was a multi-item dimension termed "literacy of home." This included such things as the content and amount of reading done by parents and children, and whether the family belonged to a library. In fact, literacy of home was more strongly related to achievement than either parental interest (for instance, how much parents talked to their children about school work, and how much they played with them) or social position (including father's occupation and education—although parents' literacy was obviously related to their social position).

Also of interest with respect to family socialization is whether there are crosscultural differences in child-rearing patterns which explain differences in intellectual attitudes and performance. As we saw in Chapter 4, the linkages between specific modes of socialization and academic success in our own society are not understood fully. On the crosscultural level, the data are even spottier, but they do provide some clues about the kinds of family experiences that facilitate or impede learning.

Independence

In Chapter 4 we saw that independence of the sort that motivates the child to handle learning tasks without constant adult supervision and support was a characteristic of high-achieving children. We shall examine here (1) whether there are crosscultural differences in parental encouragement of their children's self-sufficiency and (2) whether the apparent relationship between independence and achievement is a general phenomenon or one which differs from one society to another.

One of the few sociological analyses of a sizable sample of families is Kandel and Lesser's comparison of American and Danish parent-adolescent interaction. Data collected from all students in three U.S. high schools (N = 2327) and twelve Danish secondary schools (N = 1552) showed differences in the distribution of patterns of parental authority. Joint decision-making by the child and his parents was more prevalent in Danish families than in American ones, where the predominant pattern was for the parents to make most of the decisions relevant to the adolescent ("joint authoritarianism" in the authors' terminology). The Danish adolescent "is not only treated more like an adult by his parents[8] but also feels subjectively more independent from his parents than does the American. . . . An inescapable conclusion from these results is that in the United States, parents treat their adolescents as children longer than in Denmark. Danish adolescents are expected to be self-governing; American adolescents are not" (Kandel and Lesser, 1969: 353, 358).

While there are contrasts between the two countries in the distribution of family patterns and of youthful initiative, the interrelationships between family authority and the adolescent's attitudes toward his family and himself are similar in both countries. In both countries, "students who feel they get enough freedom from their parents are more likely to feel extremely close to them, to enjoy doing many things with them, to talk most problems over with them, to depend upon their parents for advice, to want to be like their parents in many ways" (Kandel and Lesser, 1969: 357).

Another study which demonstrates crosscultural differences in the dominant family authority patterns but crosscultural similarities in their effects is Kohn's comparison of his Washington, D.C., sample (described in Chapter 3) with a parallel sample of 861 Italian parents of fifth-grade children. The American parents were more likely than the Italian parents to value happiness, popularity, and consideration; the Italian parents more likely to value obedience, seriousness, and good manners. In both countries, however, middle-class parents placed less emphasis upon the child's obedience and conformity to adult standards, more upon his becoming self-directed. The behavioral conservatism of the working-class parents in both countries is interpreted as reflecting the universal lack of autonomy of the working man in his own occupational role. "It seems the lot of the worker that he must accord respect to authority and teach his children to do so" (Pearlin and Kohn, 1966: 471).

Neither the Kandel-Lesser nor the Pearlin-Kohn study tests the hypothesis that socialization to independence produces academic achievement, since neither study links up the socialization patterns studied with either the structure of the schools or the performance of students in school.[9] The best evidence relating family structure with educational attainment is Elder's secondary analysis of data from approximately a thousand interviews in the United States, England, West Germany, Italy, and Mexico. Parental dominance[10] was negatively associated with the probability of reaching secondary school in all the above countries. Size of birthplace, religion, and social class were also associated with the dependent variable; those who had secondary education were more likely to be from urban than rural areas, to be Protestant rather than Catholic, and to be from middle-class families. Where these other independent variables reflect the availability of educational opportunity, they may affect the strength of the parental authoritarianism effect, but they never completely erase it. For example, in very isolated rural areas of Mexico, there are few opportunities for acquiring a secondary education and few residents of such areas, no matter what their other individual characteristics, have reached the secondary level:

> Yet even under these conditions parent-youth relations have some effect on educational attainment. The fact that the effect of parent-youth relations is markedly stronger among urban-born Mexicans indicates that in a favorable social and educational context a motivating family environment substantially encourages social advancement (Elder, 1965: 86).

Where educational opportunities are most available and valued (both within and between countries), development of the motivation and skills to reach higher education levels is apparently most impaired by parental dominance. Thus the strongest relationship between family structure and educational attainment, as well as the highest levels of attainment, is found in urban America, the lowest relationship and level of attainment among rural-born Mexicans and Italians.

The hypothesis that academic success is fostered by a nonauthoritarian family environment in which the autonomy of the children is encouraged is a satisfying one. However, the evidence of either clear crosscultural differences in independence training or of linkages between such differences and academic performance is far from substantial. For example, a study somewhat similar to Kandel and Lesser's, one which compared a sample of American and Swiss children, showed that the American children achieved independence earlier, but as in the Danish case, there are no comparable data on learning differences.

A second piece of evidence which casts doubt on the hypothesis comes from the Elder study itself. Although the parental dominance effect was replicated in each of the societies studied, there is also evidence that the effect may be a diminishing one. Comparison of the oldest and youngest persons in the sample indicated that in each of the five countries the relationship between family structure and educational attainment was less for the younger interviewees. Moreover, the "declines" are greatest in the United States, England, and Germany, though in the less modern Italy there is greater change in the industrialized North than in the more slowly developing South. In other words, the effect of what goes on in the family is strongest in societies or parts of societies in which the family retains its traditional strength as an institutional force. Social change and modernization, which open up new educational and occupational opportunities, as well as increase the impertance of persons and institutions outside of the family, may diminish the effect that family status and socialization patterns have upon the child's chances in school and the larger society.[11]

Finally the hypothesis that socialization for independence within the family leads to academic achievement in the school fails to explain the extraordinary performance of the Japanese children in the IEA study. Much of the evidence we have on Japanese child-rearing patterns is anthropological, but it presents a fairly uniform picture of the Japanese family as having a highly authoritarian structure—which still remains after the great changes following World War II and the Allied occupation.[12] While the Caudill study cited in Chapter 3 was about Japanese *Americans,* Caudill's explanation for the success of individuals of Japanese background in American schools and jobs was the strength which the traditional Japanese family, with its emphasis upon strong parental authority, retained even when transplanted to American soil. (Caudill's clinical data also indicated that the coexistence of a strong striving for success with an almost total submission to family authority produced dissonance and ambivalence with respect to authority among the second- and third-generation young, the result of which seems to be displayed in the current unrest and rebellion among oriental youth in American Chinatowns). The general point is, though, that the hypothesis which says that academic achievement is caused by early socialization to independence, is not supported by enough data and is not even supported by all of the available data. If it is a useful hypothesis, it appears to be true only in some societies and/or only under certain conditions, which remain to be specified.

Achievement Motivation

We also saw in Chapter 4 that the motive to achieve, at least as presently measured, was not a good predictor of actual academic behavior. We shall reexamine this motive here to see if it clarifies any of the cross-cultural differences we have discovered. McClelland's ambitious study, *The Achieving Society,* compares a large number of societies, both contemporary and historical, on three motives (need-for-affiliation and need for power, as well as *n* Achievement), several value categories (for example, other-directedness, or the sensitivity to the expectations of others and the strength of the desire to meet them), and indices of economic development ranging from national income to per capita kilowatt hours of electricity produced. McClelland's thesis is that nations which get ahead economically are those which value success and which socialize their members to believe in hard work as the means of achieving it. He is concerned primarily with how inter-nation differences in achievement motivation are related to economic development in general and the production of business entrepreneurs in particular,[13] but he perceives the impetus for development in stories and other modes of the communication of values to children in the home and school.

To measure *n* Achievement at the level of the total society, McClelland applied his theme-analysis techniques to a sampling of children's stories, from as many of the world's nations as he could obtain them, and at two different points in time. After assembling second-, third-, and fourth-grade readers from twenty-three countries for the period around 1925 and from forty countries for the period around 1950, twenty-one stories were selected at random for each country, were translated when necessary, and were typed up in a standard form using code names for all of the characters in order to mask the identity of the source country. The final total of over 1300 stories were then coded on *n* Achievement and the other motive and value dimensions.

McClelland did find empirical support for his hypothesis that countries with the fastest rates of economic development would combine high *n* Achievement with high other-directedness:

> It may come as something of a shock to realize that more could have been learned about the rate of future economic growth of a number of these countries in 1925 or 1950 by reading elementary school books than by studying such presumably more relevant matters as power politics, wars and depressions, economic statistics, or governmental policies governing international trade, taxation, or public finance. The reason apparently lies in the fact that the readers reflect sufficiently accurately the motives and values of key groups of men in a country which *in the long run* determine the general drift of economic and political decisions and their effects on productivity. Economic and political policies are of course the means by which economic change is brought about, but whether policies will be implemented, or even decided on in the first place, appears to depend ulti-

mately on the motives and values of men as we have succeeded in detecting them in the stories they think it is right for their children to read (McClelland, 1961: 202).

What is relevant to this chapter, however, are the relationships between the societal orientations measured by McClelland and the kinds of internation achievement differences reported in the IEA study. The following list gives the 1950 mean *n* Achievement scores, in rank order, for the countries in the IEA sample:

Australia	2.38
France	2.38
Israel	2.33
United States	2.24
Germany	2.14
England	1.67
Sweden	1.62
Finland	1.52
Netherlands	1.48
Japan	1.29
Belgium	.43
Russia	2.10

(Scotland is the one country in the IEA sample which was not in McClelland's sample. Russia was added to the list, although it was not in the IEA sample, because it is typically seen as our major rival in all areas of international competition and because data on Russia from other studies are presented in this chapter.)

Since the IEA and McClelland studies differ in so many aspects of research objective and design, no statistical comparisons have been attempted, but looking at the above list along with Exhibits 13–2 and 13–3 does not reveal any meaningful relationships between the two sets of findings. Australia, which shares with France the highest mean *n* Achievement score, was among the lowest ranking nations in all of the IEA target populations. Close behind are Israel and the United States, again a high and low performing nation on the math achievement tests. Conversely, Japan and Belgium, which rank high on the IEA indices, are the lowest in *n* Achievement. Nor does the introduction of McClelland's other indices clarify the picture. England, which retains one of the most elitist educational systems, had the highest ranking of the IEA nations on other-directedness.

In sum, the McClelland findings do not explain or clarify the IEA findings, nor do they at this point offer an alternative model to explain crosscultural differences in education systems and academic achievement. All one can conclude at present is: (1) that there is no evidence, either within or between societies, that academic success is explained to any great extent by present measures of achievement motivation or need; and (2) that what produces scholastic learning and success and what produces economic development and success are not the same.

Group Orientation

Another aspect of socialization which has large implications for the design of school systems and scholastic behavior is the extent to which and the manner in which the child identifies with important groups and ideas outside of his home. By contrast with societies and schools which place major emphasis upon the development of the individual character and intellect,[14] some societies foster a commitment to a larger group or groups by the approved method of child-rearing and the structure of the schools. Two of the most interesting examples are Russia and Israel.

Although systematic study of Russian child-rearing and educational techniques is generally forbidden to Westerners, we are fortunate in the work of Urie Bronfenbrenner, who was given permission to travel in Russia in the late 1950's and whose knowledge of the Russian language enabled him to supplement the "official" information given to him with informal conversations in restaurants and stores. (For example, although in Bronfenbrenner's early trips, he was not allowed to visit Soviet elementary schools, he was able to compare the official teacher's manual given him with a conversation with three elementary teachers he met by chance in a restaurant.) According to his report, the process of "collective socialization" begins when the child enters school; the focus of evaluation is not upon the individual child but upon subgroups of students within the class. Competition is not eliminated—on the contrary, the use of competition as a motivating device is a crucial part of the design of Soviet schools— but it is at the level of the group rather than the individual. Even in the earliest grades,

> records are kept for each row from day to day for different types of tasks so that the young children can develop a concept of group excellence over time and over a variety of activities, including personal cleanliness, condition of notebooks, conduct in passing from one room to the other, quality of recitations in each subject matter, and so on. In these activities, considerable emphasis is placed on the externals of behavior in dress, manner, and speech. There must be no spots on shirt or collar, shoes must be shined, pupils must never pass by a teacher without stopping to give greeting, there must be no talking without permission, and the like. Great charts are kept in all the schools showing the performance of each row unit in every type of activity together with their total overall standing. "Who is best?" the charts ask, but the entries are not individuals but social units—rows, and later the "cells" of the communist youth organization which reaches down to the primary grades (Bronfenbrenner, 1968: 61).

As the children grow older, competition is initiated among classes, and then among schools, regions, and so on. At the same time, the source of evaluation is shifted from the teacher to the students themselves. Even in the first grade, children act as monitors for some activities. Within the next few years, they learn to evaluate themselves and their peers, and to state their criticisms publicly.

These patterns of classroom socialization reflect the thinking of Makarenko, a thinker and writer whose influence parallels that of Dr. Spock in our country and whose work Bronfenbrenner had studied before his visits to Russia. Like Spock, Makarenko developed his ideas about children out of a lifetime of practical experience. He was, however, a teacher rather than a physician, and his earliest experiences were in setting up rehabilitation programs in the 1920's for children orphaned and made homeless by the civil wars. The focus of his philosophy is the need to develop in children a sense of group responsibility and commitment to group work goals, using the group itself as the major disciplining agent. In such a scheme, full personal development comes only through productive activity in a social collectivity. The first "collective" most children experience is the family (one of Makarenko's most widely read books is a manual for parents akin to Spock's *Baby and Child Care*). But this collective must be supplemented, and ultimately supplanted, by other collectives, in schools and community groups, later in factories and other occupational settings. All collectives share a common goal of developing socialist "morality," and at the same time producing concrete goods and services for the state. "This aim is accomplished through an explicit regimen of activity mediated by group criticism, self-criticism, and group oriented punishments and rewards" (Bronfenbrenner, 1968: 60).

Since Russia has loosened some of its restrictions on travel in the past decade, Bronfenbrenner has made nine return trips. His most recent publication, *Two Worlds of Childhood* (1970), is a comparison between family, school, and community environments of Russian and American children. In this book, Bronfenbrenner's develops more extensively his theme that, in each setting, the Soviet child is a member of a collective group which emphasizes self-discipline and effort for the sake of the group, and that there is a congruency and unity of purpose from one setting to another. By contrast, the American child has greater independence from the group, which produces a spontaneity and expressiveness absent in Russian schools but which also may reflect an abdication of responsibility by the family, school, and community for the development of the young. Bronfenbrenner worries that in the absence of a clear ideology of child rearing and a clear commitment by adult institutions to guiding the child, socialization occurs more and more in the peer group (which, as we saw in Chapter 11, provides in addition a kind of protection from the stresses of the individualistic competition characteristic of American schools). If the current trends toward "affluent neglect" continue, says Bronfenbrenner, "we can anticipate increased alienation, indifference, antagonism and violence on the part of the younger generation in all segments of our society," in sum, the "unmaking of the American child."

The preceding discussion also should make clear that the dimension of group orientation is not a simple one. While in Bronfenbrenner's terms, children in our society have a high degree of individualism and a low degree of "collectivity commitment," they are by other definitions very sensitive to the opinions and expectations of others. McClelland, for instance, found that high proportions of the American children he studied engage in group activities outside of school, by comparison to, say, German children, who were more likely to engage in such individualistic activities as hiking, collecting stamps, or playing musical instruments (McClelland, 1961; 197ff.), and that through such activities they build up what seems to some observers an excessive sensitivity to the opinions of others. Bronfenbrenner's point is not that American children are lacking in group orientation but rather that in the absence of attention and systematic guidance from adult institutions, the child's "other-directedness" is virtually all toward his age peers, and that he never develops a true commitment to the community or society as a whole.

Another experiment in collective living, which combines a theory of child rearing and education with a theory of economic organization, can be found in the kibbutzim and other cooperative settlements in Israel. We have seen the IEA evidence that the overall output of the Israeli educational system is high, even given the egalitarian ideology of the nation as a whole and the practical difficulties of assimilating a large influx of relatively unschooled Oriental Jews. Of course, the kibbutz is not representative of Israel as a whole—kibbutz schools enroll only about five per cent of the nation's children—but its influence (both ideologically and as a source of national leaders) has been disproportionate to its quantitative strength. Thus consideration of the kibbutz techniques of child rearing and schooling are relevant to a discussion of socialization with respect to group or collectivity orientation.

Among the distinctive features of the kibbutz educational system noted by Bruno Bettelheim, in a seven-week visit in 1964, were the following:

Children are reared apart from their natural parents, with a group of their age-peers. Most see their parents during daily visits, but the general responsibility for day-to-day care is assigned to trained "metapelets" or nurses.

All children receive the same education and the same preparation for school. Although the wide differences in individual ability are recognized, no child starts school at a disadvantage because of his social position. Similarly, students neither skip grades nor are held back because of their intellectual skills—the age-group stays together both in school and in the residence house throughout childhood and adolescence.

Academic learning is combined with "real" work in the kibbutz from the earliest years. Even young children help with the care of animals and in the maintenance of their residence house. "As the child grows older, he works more after-school hours at the farm or in the shop and is given ever more absorbing and responsible tasks" (Bettelheim, 1969: 49).

Children regularly see their parents and other adults, as well as older children, engaged in work that is understandable in itself and visibly meaningful to the life of the community.

Virtually all students stay in school to the end, because the usual reasons for dropping out are absent. Since the kibbutz is a communal society, there is no chance to earn money by leaving school. In the absence of TV and other forms of entertainment, and with all of his age-mates in school, there would be nothing for a dropout to do but sit in the children's house. Finally, the lack of individualistic competition in the classroom means that the classroom does not have to be a punishing experience for those less endowed intellectually.

In sum, "kibbutz education is so much a part of a common way of life, so embodies the youngsters' future aspirations that, however much they sometimes tire of learning, what they never feel is a split between them and the educational system" (Bettelheim, 1969: 50).

Most of the accounts of kibbutz life are rich in descriptive detail[15] but short on systematic data collection and analysis, and much of the interpretation of the effects of the educational system upon definite areas of academic achievement is biased by the author's prior views on child rearing and/or the kibbutz (in other words, by Rosenthal effects), and by lack of facility in the Hebrew language. One of the few behavioral scientists who has investigated the kibbutz modes of socialization with a tightly structured research design is Eifermann, whose large-scale study of children's games has indicated that the spontaneous behavior of school children reflects the collective orientation of the surrounding community. By comparison with children from other rural settlements, kibbutz children favored games which "demand cooperation toward the achievement of a common aim, but within an overall competitive framework," as opposed to games which are exclusively cooperative or which emphasize individualistic competition (Eifermann, 1969: 13). Although Eifermann's work to date has not related play behavior to academic behavior, it suggests a promising line of research.

In understanding the kind of education a child receives in a kibbutz, two important but often overlooked general characteristics should be noted. One is that, although the kibbutz modes of communal child rearing and educating have now taken on the aura of an ideology, their origins, as Bettelheim points out, were purely pragmatic. They were arrived at in a hasty and piecemeal fashion to allow a band of young pioneers to throw off the traces of their own childhood in European Jewish ghettoes and at the same time to survive in an underdeveloped land surrounded by enemies. In other words, the specific techniques of this very humane— and by many standards very effective—way of raising children did not evolve out of a general theory of child development, but rather the theory evolved gradually out of a series of improvisations implemented to meet the most pressing needs of the moment. A second general point is that a system that provides such a high level of integration among and cooperation between all its major institutions "can only exist where a consensus society is the universal ideal. This includes a far-reaching acceptance by the individual of the community's right to shape his own life and that of his children" (Bettelheim, 1969: 45–46).

Conclusions

The evidence in this chapter has indicated that there are great differences between societies in what and how children learn, and that these differences hold up when other social factors related to achievement are controlled. Indeed, the between-nation differences are often considerably greater than within-nation differences based upon such important independent variables as socioeconomic status and sex.

The general theme of this chapter is that schools reflect the larger society of which they are a part, an idea introduced by Durkheim and continuing through much of the literature on comparative education. This means that in order to understand the schools of any society, one must understand the society itself, including the structure and interrelations of its most important institutions and the values and techniques which underly the rearing of children. For example, if the economy of the society is characterized by overproduction and underconsumption, with high rates of unemployment, there are likely to be pressures toward keeping the young in school longer, regardless of whether this meets the needs and desires of the young and regardless of whether they are learning efficiently. A correlary of this is that if one wants to "do something" about the schools one must "do something" about the other societal systems that interact with the educational system.

Crosscultural studies have replicated the well-documented finding from our own society that the kinds of experiences a child has in his home have more impact upon his success in school than anything the school does on its own. Especially important are the family's intellectual habits, including what and how much they read, though a family's literacy is largely a function of its socioeconomic position. In general, those countries, or subgroups within countries, where the educational achievement is highest are those in which the adults feel autonomous with respect to their own lives and where they communicate this sense of control and independence to the young.

Although there is a worldwide trend toward increasing the amount of education and the equalization of educational opportunity, neither in the United States nor in most European countries has the expansion of opportunities per se removed social class differences in educational attainment. Instead there has been a "filtering down" process whereby educational "demand" is satiated in the upper social strata before there is a great increase in noncompulsory school attendance by working-class or lower-SES children. Some countries are making conspicuous efforts to change this pattern (for instance, Sweden and Puerto Rico), but nowhere do the schools overcome the inequalities with which children begin school.

An obvious conclusion of this chapter is that the available data do not allow us to be very precise about the effects of crosscultural variables upon academic achievement and their interaction with other independent variables. There is a wealth of case study materials describing national education systems, past and present, and there are some crosscultural studies on the experiences of children outside of school that may affect their attitudes toward learning and their performance in formal educational settings. However, with the exception of the IEA, there are virtually no systematically conceived and conducted comparisons between sizable samples of students in a number of different societies. Livingstone's paper, which does not itself get past the hypothesis-building phase, illustrates the magnitude of the task of moving educational system classification to a higher level of sophistication. The present state of the matter is well summarized by Husen: "It seems that we still have a long way to go before we will have cross-nationally codified independent variables to describe the most important dimensions of school systems" (Husen, 1967: Vol. II, 287).

This brings us to the end of our examination of empirical data and to the point where we want to see what it all "adds up to." In Part Five, we shall draw some conclusions and implications from the preceding parts. In addition, we shall look into the future, examining a few educational innovations that incorporate sociological principles and speculating upon how sociological knowledge and educational reform can be improved. In sum, we shall end the book by considering where we are and where we are going—and by considering also possible means and measures for our progress.

Notes

1. Australia, Belgium, England, Federal Republic of Germany, Finland, France, Israel, Japan, Netherlands, Scotland, Sweden, and the United States.

2. In the original conception of the study, mathematics was to be its first phase; succeeding phases were to be devoted to other subject areas and to cognitive style in general. However, due to the formidable technical and administrative requirements, not to mention the expense, at present there are no concrete plans to continue.

3. For a full report on the sampling problems and procedures, see Volume I, Chapter 9.

4. A full discussion of test construction can be found in Volume I, Chapter 5.

5. For detailed definitions and discussions of these activities, see Livingstone, 1968: 25–48.

6. The Plowden report and Hilde Himmelweit's work in England, and the Brunold Circulars in France, have documented the bias against working-class children and have called for reform of the national educational system to obtain "maximum social unity." There is still some feeling, however, that equality of educational opportunity goes against the French and English national character! See, for example, Havighurst, 1968: Chapter II.

7. Central Advisory Council, 1967. This study is more commonly known as the Plowden report.

8. Measured by the number of rules parents had for the teenagers in the family.

9. Also, since neither Denmark nor Italy was in the IEA sample, the findings cannot be compared directly. To suggest a very tenuous connection, if one thinks of Denmark as to some degree representative of Scandinavian societies and educational systems, one might speculate that the superior performance of Scandinavian compared with American students may be explained partially by socialization differences of the sort described by Kandel and Lesser. It must be emphasized, however, that this is purely speculation.

10. Measured by interviewees' responses to the following two questions: As you were growing up, let's say when you were around 16, how much influence do you remember having in family decisions affecting yourself? (much influence; some, none); At around the same time, if a decision was made that you didn't like, did you feel free to complain? (felt free; felt a little uneasy; it was better not to complain).

11. Note that this finding also illustrates the kinds of insights which can only be obtained by crosscultural studies. To evaluate our educational problems using only data from our own society not only impresses one with the overwhelming influence of the student's family upon his school career, but also limits one's ideas for improving academic performance. What the Elder data suggest is that to widen the range of alternatives available in the larger society, or to manipulate the expectations of significant others outside of the family, may be as effective in upgrading academic performance as trying to upgrade or change the structure of the family itself.

12. The best known study of Japanese national character is Ruth Benedict's *The Chrysanthemum and the Sword,* 1946. See also Haring, 1946.

13. Recently McClelland and his associates have been developing training procedures for increasing the supply of entrepreneurs in underdeveloped nations, via exercises designed to raise individuals' n Achievement levels as well as their confidence that they have the power to change themselves and their environment.

14. An example of the individualistic orientation: "We must recognize that the Frenchman is, generally speaking, not given to cooperation. . . . This distaste is due, in part, to the fact that we have insufficiently developed the community spirit in a youth whose activity is sometimes marked by excessive individualism" (Fraser, 1968: 25).

15. In addition to Bettelheim's book, the best known and most interesting are Spiro, 1965; and Neubauer, 1965.

PART FIVE

Conclusion

Where We Are   Chapter 14
and Where We Are Going

I am entirely certain that 20 years from now we will look back at education as it is practiced in most schools today and wonder that we could have tolerated anything so primitive.   John Gardner

[Many] people depend heavily on the continuing irrelevance of most school curricula. . . . Operating in these matters is a kind of variation of Parkinson's Law of Triviality: The enthusiasm that community leaders display for an educational innovation is in inverse proportion to its significance to the learning process.   Neil Postman and Charles Weingartner

Any teacher who can be replaced by a machine should be.
                                             attributed to B. F. Skinner

The inescapable conclusion to be drawn from Chapters 3 through 13 is that the major determinants of school performance are factors external to the school. That is, things outside the school matter more than the things inside in explaining what and how well children learn. In several large and well-designed surveys, variables describing the background characteristics and home experiences of individual students and the composition of the school's student body explained considerably more of the variance in achievement than did school facilities, characteristics of the teachers and the curriculum, and other features of the internal educational system. In large metropolitan areas, the average income of the communities in which schools are located explains between 45% and 85% of the variance in mean academic performance. Although there are large differences between different cities, types of communities, and geographical regions, there is no area of the United States where the economic level of the surrounding neighborhood or community is not a powerful predictor of academic success. Similarly, although the relative dominance of the family as an institution may be declining, the influence of family position and experiences accounts for many more of the differences in school success than any of the measurable characteristics of schools themselves. Finally, the achievement differences between nations are great, often greater than the internal differences explained by such factors as social status and sex. In most international comparisons, the performance of American students does not compare favorably with that of numerous other industrialized nations, including Japan as well as Western European countries.

The learning potential of many children is hampered by multiple disadvantages. In our society, Negro and other minority group children encounter direct discrimination because of their race, and they are also discriminated against indirectly because (1) their families are less likely to train them to play the student role skillfully and (2) they are more likely to live in racially segregated neighborhoods which raises the probability that they attend inferior schools. Thus the initial disadvantages of many children are reinforced at every step of their educational career, and the schools do not close the gap.

The immediate implication of these findings is that the way in which to have a dramatic impact on educational performance is to do something dramatic about the socioeconomic conditions of the environments surrounding weak schools. The question is whether a society's members are willing to make the effort required, since what seems to be involved is not just a more equitable distribution of present educational resources (in itself no mean political feat) but a substantially greater *total* investment in education. The pattern of teacher strikes and voting down of school bond issues during the late 1960's is not indicative of the motivation to make this kind of investment.[1]

On the other hand, dollars alone do not have a significant impact upon learning in schools. While there are disagreements among researchers over the interpretation of available data, academic achievement has not been shown to be strongly related to any simple measures of expenditures on school facilities and programs, nor is a society's affluence an accurate predictor of its ranking on standardized intellectual achievement indicators. The kinds of values and attitudes toward learning that children bring to school, their feelings about their own capacities for understanding and controlling their world, the structure of the student "society," and the degree to which school learning is clearly linked to roles and activities outside of school seem to have more impact upon the learning differences within and between schools than the size of financial expenditures.

Why is it that our schools have so little measurable effect? One reason undoubtedly is that in a fast-changing, information-rich society like ours, the school's influence relative to other "educators"—in particular, television and the student peer group—is declining. Since this book has focused upon the school only, we have no way of deciding here the relative weight of the potential educators in children's lives (though the relative weights of adults and peers was discussed in Chapter 11). What our analysis has indicated, however, is that apart from its competition with other institutions, the school has the following characteristics as a social system which prevent it from being as effective as it might be.

1. The reward system, based upon individualistic competition in which good grades are treated as scarce resources, has a number of unfortunate consequences. Among them: there are few winners and many losers; there are pressures to keep down the whole level of performance; and there is no motivation for students to help each other to learn—in fact, they are usually punished for doing so, since this is defined as cheating.

2. The teacher is in control of most of the action and does most of the talking. The student role is essentially passive—with students having little to say about what they learn and how they learn it.

3. There is some reason to believe that students learn better when their teachers know about them as individuals and expect them to perform well. Unfortunately, in many societies, including ours, there are subgroups or categories of children who are not expected to do well in school, and, to date, such children (especially the poor and those from racial minority groups) have been fulfilling our low expectations for them.

4. The student role as conventionally defined is incongruent with other roles which may be more attractive to the young. The disappointing performance of boys in the earliest years of school, of girls in the late high school and college years, and of boys of all ages from neighborhoods where "being a man" is greatly valued, may be explained, partially at least, by conflicting role expectations and rewards.

5. Students who do not see meaningful connections between what they do in school and what they expect or would like to do in their own future lives are not likely to perform well academically. The result may be passive withdrawal from classroom involvement and dropping out of school at the earliest opportunity, or active rebellion. To keep adolescents in school for more and more years to meet some other societal needs (caused, say, by an overcrowded labor market) may be dysfunctional both for learning and for the stability of the larger society. We do not know to what extent the current campus unrest is due to an increase in the numbers of young people who stay in school because of lack of reasonable alternatives rather than because of real commitment to their formal course work.

6. The conventional classroom situation allows academic success through a very limited range of intellectual approaches or styles. Most curricula, and teachers, reward skill in rote learning and a cognitive style characterized by analytical, abstract modes of thinking. Children who have other modes of thinking are out of luck. In particular, more rational

cognitive styles, and the "playful contemplation" that is an important ingredient of creativity, are discouraged in most classrooms.

It should be kept in mind, however, that to make schools more potent environments for learning is more than a matter of raising students' "motivation" or making school life more "enjoyable." The appeal of the education-and-ecstacy and the free school arguments[2] notwithstanding, our evidence has indicated that while education and ecstacy are not mutually exclusive, they are not synonymous either. Sanford's gloomy prognosis that:

> It may turn out that in the culture of today it is impossible to be both mentally healthy—or mature or highly developed—and highly educated, and that it is necessary at some point to choose between the two (Sanford, 1962: 37),

probably overstates the other side of the argument, but we have seen that at no level of the learning system does academic achievement necessarily follow from individual motivation or from good group dynamics. Achievement motivation and actual achievement have not been found to be strongly related in much of the empirical research to date, and disadvantaged children do not differ greatly from their age-peers in their desire to succeed. Similarly, students often perform as well or better in authoritarian classes as in the supposedly more satisfying democratic ones, and minority group students in newly desegregated schools often show gains in achievement despite the interpersonal strains involved. In sum, students, like factory workers and members of work groups generally, "produce" when it is to their self-interest to do so and when group norms call for achievement.

Where We Are Going

To point to the defects in the learning system is not, however, to abandon hope—hope that it will become more effective. In fact, some educational experiments already in existence go far toward overcoming some of the defects of formal education and allow us to end this book on a more optimistic note.

In their review of the open classroom, Gross and Gross note that one of the most valuable features of the Plowden report (see Chapter 13) is that it "does not just discuss the theory and marshal the evidence from various fields and disciplines. It goes the further step of showing that it can be done, that in fact it already is being done" (Gross and Gross, 1970: 73). In this section we shall describe some innovations in learning that are "being done." This will not be a comprehensive outline of educational innovations but a selection of examples which illustrate the application of sociological principles to practical educational problems. Nor are the innovations described finished products; in some cases, their ultimate success— even their survival—is still in question. But for the moment they are living evidence that meaningful change in the learning system is possible.

At the Classroom Level

At the Chadwick School in Palos Verdes, California, Ken Bullin's seventh- and eighth-grade history classes are undergoing a transfomation that, at present, makes them resemble a combination of art studio and chemistry lab. Rather than reading textbooks or listening to lectures, the students are:

> using chemicals to process negatives or color slides; talking into a tape recorder; taking pictures from books and magazines with a 35 mm camera on a copying stand; listening to music; viewing slides; or in a heated debate with a peer over the Barbaric Invasions of Europe in relation to today's happenings.
>
> , . . except for the age difference, a visitor might think that he has gotten into a faculty workshop, since the students are doing things that teachers usually do. Also, it is difficult for a visitor to locate the teacher in this classroom scene. This is because the teacher is working in the same manner as the students in preparation for the next episode of this classroom drama.

Each new unit begins with a very condensed taped lecture on a particular historical period, which the students listen to while viewing colored slides relating to the main point in the tape. After the teacher presents his interpretation of the unit, students discuss it in small groups. They are free to replay the tape to clarify points they missed the first time. After that:

> each student is on his own to develop, through research, his personal interpretation of an aspect of the unit covered. After the student completes his research, he tapes his lecture, makes his slides, chooses a musical recording, and presents his visual and taped interpretation of history to the class—he becomes the teacher!
>
> The student's presentation must be his own interpretation of a parallelism of history—not just facts copied from a book (California Association of Independent Schools, 1969: 5).

Bullin is constantly tinkering with his course. Currently he is preparing a new meeting place for the class, in which desks and the other paraphernalia of the formal classroom will be replaced by overstuffed chairs, pillows and rugs, bookcases filled with resource materials, and a soft drink machine. An adjoining laboratory contains the equipment for producing tapes, slides, and cultural artifacts. The general objective remains to create a setting like that of a professional social scientist, where each student, working at his own pace, considers the total range of historical materials and at the end comes to his own conclusions about the meaning of his findings. Bullin also claims that any student who does not get along with the teacher can proceed though the entire course without having to deal with him personally.

Bullin's class illustrates how an imaginative individual, relying heavily upon his experience with children, his flair for the dramatic, and his own intuition, can bring about radical change in a single school. A more far-reaching reform at the classroom level, which uses developmental psychology in general and the work of Piaget in particular to justify its methods, is the open classroom. The most extensive reports on the open classroom movement and methods are contained in the Plowden report and in a series of articles written for *The New Republic* by Joseph Featherstone. The following excerpt, describing an "infant school" (for children aged 5 to 7) in a working-class housing development, gives some of the flavor of what is going on in many English classrooms, although it cannot do justice to the breadth and depth of these reforms:

> If you arrive early, you find a number of children already inside, reading, writing, painting, playing music, tending to pets. Teachers sift in slowly and begin working with students. Apart from a religious assembly (required by English law) it's hard to say just when school actually begins, because there is very little organized activity for a whole class to do together. The puzzled visitor sees some small group work in mathematics ("maths") or reading, but mostly children are on their own, moving about and talking quite freely. The teacher sometimes sits at her desk, and the children flock to her for consultations, but more often she moves about the room, advising on projects, listening to children read, asking questions, giving words, talking, sometimes prodding . . .
>
> Classrooms open out onto the playground, which is also much in use. A contingent of children is kneeling on the grass, clocking the speed of a tortoise, which they want to graph against the speeds of other pets and people. Nearby are five-year-olds, finishing an intricate, tall tower of bricks, triumphantly counting as they add the last one, "23, 24." A solitary boy is mixing powders for paint; on a large piece of paper attached to an easel, with very big strokes, he makes an ominous, stylized building that seems largely to consist of black shutters framing deep red windows. "It's the hospital where my brother is," he explains, and pulls the visitor over to the class-library corner, where a picture book discusses hospitals. He can't read yet (he's five), but says he is trying. And he is; he can make out a number of words, some pretty hard, on different pages, and it is clear that he has been studying the book, because he wants badly to know about hospitals. At another end of the hall there is a quieter library nook for the whole school. Here two small boys are reading aloud; the better reader is, with indifferent grace, correcting the grateful slower boy as he stumbles over words.
>
> The rooms are fairly noisy—more noisy than many American teachers or principals would allow—because children can talk freely. Sometimes the teacher has to ask for quiet. With as many as 40 in some classes, rooms are crowded and accidents happen . . .
>
> In these classes there are no individual desks, and no assigned places. Around the room (which is about the size of one of ours) there are different tables for different kinds of activities: art, water and sand play, number work. (The number tables have all kinds of number lines—strips of paper with numbers marked on them in sequence on which children learn to count and reason mathematically—beads, buttons and odd things to count; weights and balances; dry and liquid measures . . .
>
> In a school that operates with a free day, the teacher usually starts in the morning by listing the different activities available. A lot of rich ma-

terial is needed, according to the teachers, but the best stuff is often home-made; and, in any case, it isn't necessary to have 30 or 40 sets of every-thing, because most activities are for a limited number of people. "Six children can play in the Wendy House," says a sign in one classroom. The ground rules are that they must clean up when they finish, and they mustn't bother others (Featherstone, 1967a: 17–18).

Both Bullin's class and the English one described by Featherstone illus-trate an approach to teaching that "discards the familiar elementary class-room setup and the traditional, stylized roles of teacher and pupil, for a far freer, highly individualized, child-centered learning experience" (Gross and Gross, 1970: 71). Both classes are characterized by a high level of activity and autonomy for the students, with the teacher acting as a con-sultant and co-learner. Both illustrate Piaget's tenets that children are capable of learning through their own discoveries, and that this mode of learning requires an environment in which they are encouraged to pose questions and then to seek the answers through first-hand experience. "Open" should not be confused with "empty." The open classroom is a very full room, and its success depends upon a rich supply of materials, including things to manipulate and equipment to make things.

A third example of learning innovation at this level is the simulation game, which was introduced at the end of Chapter 10 as a potential tech-nique for analyzing the effectiveness of schools. In the typical instructional simulation, certain features of the socioeconomic environment—for ex-ample, the labor market, a national election, legislative sessions, or family interaction—are reproduced, and players make decisions and take action as if they were in the real-life roles (employers and employees, politicians, parents, and so forth) simulated by the game. At various points partici-pants receive "feedback" on the consequences of their action, which is cal-culated by the teacher, the students themselves, or a computer. Social simulations for use in elementary and secondary school classes have been developed by R. Garry Shirts, at the Western Behavioral Sciences Institute, by Jerome Bruner's group at the Educational Development Center; and by the group at Johns Hopkins University.

To date, empirical evidence on the effects of games from adequately designed field tests is very limited (for a review of findings up to 1968, see Boocock and Schild, 1968). Designers of instructional games are still working largely from theoretical "hunches" about what well-designed social simulations could do. Among these hunches are, first, that games can break down the barrier between the school world and the community or larger social world, allowing the child to *play at* those roles that he must assume in earnest when he enters adult society. His academic task is not to carry out assignments, but to "survive" in the simulated environment.

Second, simulation games appear to restructure classroom role relation-ships in ways that are productive of learning. Because games are self-disciplining, in that players must all obey the rules if the game is to con-tinue, and self-judging, in that the outcome decides the winner and a player knows he has won or lost by his own actions, the teacher is freed from the role of judge and disciplinarian.

Third, games may affect attitudes, in particular the individual's attitude toward his sense of control of environment. While the antecedents of this attitude are still imperfectly understood, one possibility is that absence of sense of control is derived from insufficient experience with situations where the actor clearly *has* control—which is, upon examination, a realistic definition of the actual real-life situation of the culturally deprived child and his family. Extended experience in simulated environments could be a remedy for this cultural deficiency. Perhaps most important, instructional gaming treats play as a respectable form of learning, bringing into the classroom the strategic planning and the informal atmosphere which characterize the way many professional scholars work.

At the School Level

In Chapter 8, we examined the findings of some studies which showed how the techniques of behavior modification could, by changing the reward system of the classroom, produce quite remarkable increases in learning behavior. The organization of a whole school around a system of positive pay-offs is illustrated in a project at the National Training School for Boys in Washington, D.C. The students consisted of a group of convicted juveniles, whose offenses ranged from auto theft to armed robbery and homicide. The only thing all shared in common was school failure—85% were school dropouts; the few who were still in school when sentenced were retarded for from three to six academic years.

The initial screening of the boys was for the sole purpose of determining their present academic level. That is, a boy's past history, and what he thought about himself and his behavior was not built into his diagnosis or treatment:

> His actual educational program is based upon his measured performance on a large series of tests, specific tests in such areas as multiplication, divison, subtraction and complex reading tasks, and more general tests such as the Stanford Achievement Test and the Gates Reading Survey.
>
> After the individual has gone through his entry tests and we have been able to identify his deficiencies in specific areas (e.g., long division) and in general areas (e.g., reading), he is given a set of programmed instruction material based upon his present repertoire . . .
>
> If an individual can read numbers (2 + 2), we start there. By pretesting the students and assigning them programmed instruction at a level where they can successfully perform, we guarantee success for each individual no matter on what level he begins. Thus, each individual is on his own track and becomes programmed for success in contrast to his past educational environment in which he was basically programmed for failure. Little by little, each student inmate finds out that he is able to perform 90 per cent or better in his test work.

. . . We all learn because there is something in it for us. We read our books in school and took our tests because there was somehing in it for us. The "something in it" might have been a job or $5.00 for each "A." Today, for some college students, a grade of "C" or better is the ticket for staying out of Vietnam. . . . If we can take as a basic premise that every individual needs to have some payoff, some system of reinforcement, then the question we need to ask is "When, and on what schedule?" Unlike the Jesuit who will wait until his final hour for his reinforcement, God and Heaven, our delinquent student inmates are not willing to wait for good report cards, diplomas, and the rest of the delayed reinforcements. They want to know, "Man, what's the payoff now?" For these non-Jesuit types we use an extrinsic immediate reinforcer, money, to get the academic behaviors started . . .

We converted an old facility (an existing cottage on the prison grounds) into a 24-hour learning environment. We created a point economy using money as the generalized reinforcer. We established schedules of reinforcement and hired the students to work for us on some 140 programmed educational courses and 18 programmed classes. Each student becomes, and is addressed as, a Student Educational Researcher, working for the corporation. His product is intellectual wealth in general and academic work in particular. When the students perform on tests at 90% or better, they get paid off in points, and each point is equal to one penny (in money). With what he earns, the student pays for his room, his food, his clothing, his gifts, and he pays an entrance fee and tuition for special classes. He can also rent a private office. A student who does not have sufficient funds goes on relief—sleeps on an open bunk and eats food on a metal tray—no student has ever been on relief more than two weeks. We thus created a society full of choices and prerequisites normally not available in a prison, but available to the average wage-earning American. A system of time clocks located throughout the building established our basic measurement tool. We set up new evaluation methods for parole upon objective academic measurements and recordable social behaviors . . .

Group reinforcement is extremely powerful. We attempted to program some of this into the system. For example, not only was the student paid off in points, but when he did well on an exam (earned 100%), the staff was instructed to bring the accomplishment to the attention of all the students and say all kinds of good things like "Gosh, that was great," or "Man, that's cool." This is recognition for a task performed. However, one must not approve just any task, but only those that require some competent behavior or a large effort—for the student knows the difference between a task requiring lots of competent behavior to get a job "well done" and a "mickey mouse" task.

The importance of producing a contingency oriented environment which increases academic skills and maintains these newly acquired behaviors is not just to demonstrate and prove a learning theory and develop an educational technology. These newly acquired educational skills act as a program which reinstates in the young deviant the promise that he can be "normal." "Normal" in this case means that he can be successful in an area where he formerly was unsuccessful and, furthermore, that this success will provide him with the ticket to re-enter the mainstream of the American adolescent world—the public school system and the choices of opportunities that follow (Cohen, 1967: 1–3).

Another school committed to redoing the total system of the high school is John Adams High School, a public high school in Portland, Oregon, which opened in the fall of 1969 in a brand new building. The student body covered all socioeconomic status levels and was about 25% black. The model for Adams High was the medical teaching hospital, a service institution seen by the school's creators as "much more successful than schools in developing structural arrangements which allow them continuously to generate, nurture, evaluate and disseminate ideas" (Fletcher, 1970: 24). Thus the Adams plan includes the components of:

training. This includes not only in-service training and practice teaching but also the development of programs for special groups. One is a group of candidates for regular teaching credentials who would not normally have been accepted for teacher training—nearly all are ghetto blacks, most have spotty educational records, and some have police records.

research and evaluation. The school staff includes two research coordinators who also hold appointments at a university or educational research laboratory. Research activities range from systematic interviewing of a 10% random sample of school members to measure school climate to a computerized analysis of the costs and outputs of alternative programs within the school.

development and dissemination of new curricula. One curricular innovation is a series of "mini-courses," lasting only a few weeks each and ranging in subject from a course of high student interest but minimal intellectual context, such as "how to buy a used car," to short but erudite courses in a particular period of history, such as "Cotton Mather's Massachusetts," Mini-courses may be taught by students or by members of the outside community as well as by the regular faculty. Another curricular innovation is the Mobile School program, for about 60 students who entered Adams High defining school as totally irrelevant. Home base for the Mobile School program is a bus, and most of the school hours are spent away from school—for these students, education is quite literally a "community" affair.

reflection and regeneration. Something that is absent from virtually all organizations, but especially from new and innovative ones where many new things are being tried out simultaneously, are built-in mechanisms for periodic review of the total program. The blueprint for Adams High School includes a planning committee assigned to "set up procedures for periodically reviewing the status of each of the aspects of the school to determine progress toward general and program objectives" (Fletcher *et al.,* 1970: 32).

At the Level of the School and Its Environment

One of the core problems at this level of the learning system is the feeling of many students that life in school is somehow not "real," and one of the most aggressive attempts to break down the barriers between the classroom and the outside world is the "school without walls." At the time of this writing, two examples of schools without walls were in operation: the Parkway Program, begun in Philadelphia in January, 1969; and Metro, a Chicago public high school which opened a year later.

The curriculum in both schools is based upon a series of two-way interchanges between the school and its urban environment. In addition to the regular faculty, a variety of individuals are brought in to teach about their particular field of expertise, and the students go out into the community to seek information or instruction.[3] For example, the initial curriculum at Metro included:

a course on the newspaper, run by the *Chicago Sun Times,* during which students accompanied reporters on assignments;

a course on "Dissent" taught by the American Civil Liberties Union;

a course on the ethnic and economic structure of the city, based upon student interviews with people on the streets of Chicago;

a Spanish course in which students spent time conversing with residents of the city's Spanish-speaking communities.

The thrust of curriculum development can be summarized by the comment of one student interviewed by a newspaper reporter: "We are learning from people who actually know things instead of people who know only by reading out of books" (*Los Angeles Times,* July 24, 1970).

Both students and faculty have a say in the choice of curriculum and teachers, and open criticism of both is allowed. Although the student body is chosen by lottery,[4] there is no ability tracking. Students attend most classes together, and they receive credit for courses passed satisfactorily rather than conventional grades.

The most ardent supporters of the school-without-walls principle admit that the costs probably would be prohibitive for a whole metropolitan school system (including the energy drain on the faculty as well as the tax on community resources)—and that probably it would not work with many students and teachers, even if it was economically feasible. It also should be recognized that while the linkage between the school and the larger society is greatly enhanced in a program of this sort, it is still far from the total integration found in the Israeli kibbutz. (Other examples of total integration between the educational system and the other societal institutions probably can be found in Chinese and Soviet experiments in raising children in communes, but we still lack the first-hand accounts needed to describe and evaluate them accurately.) Some reformers, Bettelheim among them, feel that none of the child-rearing and educational innovations tried in our society go far enough to meet the needs of severely deprived children, and they urge us to overcome our political and emotional scruples enough to consider dispassionately some more extreme reforms, including reforms which would remove children from clearly destructive homes and schools.

Another extreme view of educational reform would eliminate the barriers between schools and their environments by eliminating compulsory education altogether. Such critics argue that not only can no nation afford a truly effective national education system, but that excessive faith in formal education perpetuates rather than eliminates social caste systems, both within and between nations. Rather than continuing to pour ever more resources into formal educational systems, we should put our efforts into matching up individuals who want to learn a particular subject or skill with someone who will teach it to them, or organizing groups of individuals who wish to pursue some topic of common interest.[5]

In our consideration of educational innovation, there has been so far almost no mention of the much touted technological revolution in education. Although the National Training School program is built around the use of programmed instruction, and Adams High School researchers plan to use a computer for analyzing alternative modes of instruction, there has been little emphasis upon technology or technological innovation as such.

Our purpose is not to downgrade technology. On the contrary, it seems that a relevant education for any American child must include an introduction to the nature and implications of technology. However, it also seems that the importance of any given educational device lies less in the details of its mechanical operation than in its effect upon the structure of the learning environment. For example, one of the most intriguing findings in connection with Omar Moore's "responsive environment" is that the major appeal of the "Talking Typewriter" is the *increased social interaction* facilitated—a voice always responds to the child's behavior. In fact, Moore has found that many of the impressive learning results occur just as regularly when the child works at a regular typewriter with a teacher beside him as when he uses the computer-based equipment (Moore, 1966).[6]

In other words, it is *how* a given technological device is used that is important. In fact, most devices can be used in very different ways. For example, to date, educational television has been used mainly for mass instruction—large groups of students gather in one place to hear a televised lecture or demonstration.[7] However, the response to the "Sesame Street" television programs for preschool children suggests that the same media can provide a very individualized form of instruction. In most of the cities where "Sesame Street" can be seen, it is run two or more times a day, with an additional rerun of the entire week's series during the weekend. The program thus can be viewed at the convenience of the "student" and his mother, and it can be seen more than once (or in segments). What is perhaps more significant is that the usual viewing pattern is for a child to watch it alone in his own home, at most with a brother or sister, a few friends, or occasionally with his parents. The moral to be learned from the success of "Sesame Street" is not only that learning can be made attractive to very young children, but that we have the technology to eliminate not only the teacher but the school system itself as we now know it. What we do with television, or computers, or any other technological innovation, is a social rather than a technical question and "in thinking about the future of schools, it is not nearly as important to consider the attainable technology as it is to consider the social and institutional changes that will be necessary if that technology is to be widely adopted" (Green, 1969: 251. See also Green, 1970, for some predictions about the employment of technology in public education).

All of the innovations selected for this chapter have in common a commitment to redoing the learning environment, using technological devices where they are congruent with the total learning model. All innovations involve a substantial increase in student activity and autonomy. Equally important, however, are the ways in which they vary, an indication that there is a rather high degree of consensus on the need for change but much less agreement on how it should be brought about.

One of the dimensions on which these examples vary is the degree to which the students themselves set the goals of the learning system and the degree to which the success of the innovation depends upon an unusually large amount of trust between different roles. The open classroom, the Adams High School, and the school-without-walls models are at one end of this continuum. Proponents of the former admit that it is:

> precariously based on a kind of trust little evident in education today. Teachers must trust children's imagination, feelings, curiosity, and natural desire to explore and understand their world. They also must learn to trust themselves—to be willing to gamble that they can retain the children's interest and respect once they relinguish the external means of control: testing, threats, demerits, petty rules, and rituals. School administrators, in turn, must trust teachers enough to permit them to run a classroom that is not rigidly organized and controlled but, rather, is bustling, messy, flexible, and impulsive. Parents must trust school people to do well by their children, without the assurance provided by a classroom atmosphere recognizable from their own childhoods and validated, however emptily, by standardized tests (Gross and Gross, 1970: 85).

At the other end of the continuum, the reform school built on the behavior modification model makes no attempt to involve students either in setting the goals for the school or in specifying the means of reaching them. In fact, there is not even any attempt to justify the system to the students. They are simply told as clearly and honestly as possible how the system works. The only choice left to the student is whether or not to try for the rewards offered by the system. A parallel example for younger children is the Bereiter-Engelmann compensatory education program, the core of which is a series of brief (1 or 2 minute) but sharply focused drills in basic language and arithmetic skills. Teachers adhere to a rigid, repetitive presentation pattern (usually memorized), and the children reply, in unison, in answers that are brief, unambiguous, and designed to be shouted out in a rhythmic pattern. Indeed visitors to the Bereiter-Engelmann classes at the University of Illinois often compare the mode of teaching to a military drill.[8]

Simulation gaming falls in the middle of this dimension. All but the most open-ended role playing exercises have a set of rules for play—and a game cannot proceed unless everyone follows the basic rules—but a simulation game usually presents a rather complicated problem and there is, in contrast to a textbook problem, usually more than one winning strategy. Moreover, given that games typically require players to move about the room or to gather in small groups to argue over points of strategy, the teacher has to trust that most of the conversation is over matters related to the task at hand and that the action will not get "out of hand."

A second dimension on which educational innovations differ is in the extent to which they help children to adapt to and succeed in the existing society versus developing their unique potentialities regardless of how these mesh with the "real" world. The reform school program is clearly at the former end of the continuum, as are most of the compensatory programs for the disadvantaged. So is the kibbutz school. (Although the kibbutz society is very different from the American middle-class one, child-rearing and educational techniques all focus upon fitting the child into his community.) At the opposite extreme is the free school model, and, to a lesser degree, the open classroom (the assumption of the latter is that the best way for a person to become a productive adult is to live fully as a child).

Some educational reforms aim not only to change the student but to turn him into an agent of change in the larger society. The freedom school movement[9] shares with the kibbutz philosophy the view of children as full and active members of their communities, but while kibbutzniks feel that they have already made the kind of society that is best for children to be members of, the organizers of freedom schools define society as so defective that it must be reconstructed by the next generation.

Another way in which these innovations vary is in the extent to which they are consciously constructed upon theoretical principles. The National Training School program is a direct translation of behavior modification principles, and the open classroom is built upon ideas from Piaget's developmental theory. Bullin's history laboratory, on the other hand, seems to have evolved more from his intuition and from practical experiment than from a conscious application of educational, sociological, or psychological theory. It is, of course, impossible to classify any innovation finally on this dimension. It is clear from Featherstone's reports, for example, that many of the most successful teachers and administrators do a great deal of improvising in the open classroom and are unable to articulate what they are doing or trying to do. On the other hand, many of Bullin's innovations may well be the result of his reading and other theoretical influences of which he is no longer consciously aware. The distinction being made here is one of a general approach to or strategy with respect to innovation—whether one works from the abstract and builds new schools and methods upon general theoretical principles or whether educational reforms evolve from day-to-day experiences in school life.

The Means

It would be naïve to assume that because a handful of researchers have had some gratifying successes with a new learning technique and can produce some evidence of its educational worth, it will be adopted automatically by school systems and used correctly by classroom teachers. Educational history is full of good ideas that never got beyond the superintendent's office. And Featherstone has observed that a large metropolitan school system such as New York City's has tried every educational innovation—once.

Furthermore, the more innovative a new technique is, the greater the difficulties of dissemination—and all of the approaches discussed in this chapter fall toward the "more" end of the innovation continuum. To provide a classroom with a new kind of slide projector is not going to change things much, and is not likely to meet much resistance, but techniques that produce more noise and less visible order than the lecture-recitation situation, and that require the teacher not only to master new materials but also to learn a whole new way of thinking about children, present greater problems of acceptance and correct usage. At the level of the school and its environment, where the major determinants of school success are now found, the repercussions of change are even greater. For example:

> A basic attack on segregation would force to the forefront a host of difficult political problems. We would have to confront questions about the validity of school district boundary lines, the propriety of massive pupil transportation systems, the usefulness of fixed racial quotas, the need for a basically new type of multi-neighborhood school building, efforts to alter housing patterns, massive new federal aid programs, and a variety of other difficult issues (Orfield, 1970: 35).

In recent years an extensive literature has been accumulating on the diffusion of educational innovation.[10] The most important conclusion that can be drawn from this work is that no change in the learning system can be viewed as an isolated phenomenon. Rather, the introduction of change in one part of the system will change other parts.[11]

Teacher support and performance are enhanced by bringing teachers into the planning process early enough so they have a feeling of participating in the change rather than having it imposed upon them, and by adequate training in the concrete skills demanded by the innovation. (Bruner, for example, will not allow his new social studies units to be sold to any school system which does not agree to send its teachers for a lengthy, and expensive, training program at the center where the material was developed.) It is also a good strategy to make special efforts to develop positive attitudes among those teachers who are looked to for information and advice by other teachers.

The principal and the outside administrator of a new program, unlike those who evaluate it, should be biased in its favor. Although currently there is strong feeling in this country in favor of reducing the power of the "central office," the English experience indicates that the educational bureaucracy can itself be a vehicle for reform. One of Featherstone's explanations for the speed with which the open classroom concepts have spread in English elementary schools is the change in the role of the governmental inspector, from educational policeman to agent for disseminating new ideas. The moral of the story for Featherstone is that, while external rules enforced from without tend to "rigidify through fear," the use of outside professionals who have no administrative responsibilities except to spread ideas and train teachers in new methods can have positive effects upon schools. Given the predictions of some educational analysts that the current "demands by both community and teachers for greater participation in the control and management of the schools will peak in the next few years and thereafter taper off. . . . After establishing their claim to a role in decision and policy-making, they will weary of the chore and want to turn the responsibility over to the professional expert" (Melbo, 1970), innovations in the structure and operation of the professional bureaucracy are worthy of our serious consideration.

In fact, public enthusiasm for a specific innovation does not seem to be necessary for its adoption, although strong public opinion can prevent its continuation. (The intense community conflicts over sex education courses are a case in point—many school administrators misread the strength of feelings against having this subject taught in the schools.) The best strategy for the administrator with respect to the public, as with respect to the teachers, is to have good and frequently used lines of communication, even if the information communicated is of a very vague sort. What seems to be conducive to an innovative school or school system generally is positive public attitudes toward the overall school program—attitudes improved by the public's feeling that they are being kept informed.

Observers of the educational scene disagree about the depth of the change that is occurring in the learning system. Some feel that we are undergoing a true revolution in education (see, for example, Bruner, 1964: 1), and would agree with John Gardner's prognosis for the future quoted at the beginning of this chapter. These observers also point to evidence that the educational innovation cycle of development, testing, diffusion, and adoption has speeded up along with the general acceleration of technological development (Miles, 1968: Chapter 1). Other observers feel equally strongly that the so-called revolution in education reflects developments in gadgetry and packaging, tacked onto the present school structure at points of least resistance, rather than changes in basic attitudes toward learning and children. "To date, no group—in or out of the educational establishment—has been willing to face the complexity of an attack on the total problem of institutional change and comprehensive curriculum development" (Wilson, 1967; 160. See also Goodlad, 1967).

There is also disagreement over strategy. The general issue is whether the educational reformer should push for the kinds of innovations which would truly close the opportunity and achievement gaps in the learning system—which would in effect end the public educational system as we now know it—or should settle for measures which are less than ideal but which would be palatable to a greater cross-section of the citizenry. Should one accept no change in the distribution of students to schools short of total racial and class desegregation (by massive bussing and/or educational parks), or should one experiment with solutions which would give students some interracial experience but not outlaw the neighborhood school principle (for example, "part-time" schools in a central location, where students from several different "home" schools would come together for special events and programs)? Should one build a new curriculum from scratch or try to introduce new subjects and techniques in such a way as to minimize the strains of adaptaion (and the likely resistance of schools and teachers)?

Certainly there should be no disagreement about the need for change. Indeed, it does not seem unduly alarmist to say that our national survival depends upon reducing the monumental inequalities in our schools and making them environments in which the young can truly prepare for the "surprises" of the future.

The Measures

One of the difficulties of living in a nation and age of change is in maintaining some sense of how well our institutions are serving their major functions. In order to decide whether our schools are effective, we need both good sources of information and intelligent analyses and interpretation of the information. The preceding chapters have left the distinct impression that the quality of research in the sociology of learning is uneven. Some studies are sophisticated and elegant; others are almost absurd in content and design.

The classroom, the heart of the learning system, presents the most confusing picture. Although it is true in a sense that we cannot teach students anything but can only remove the obstacles to their learning, it is also true that the teacher and the techniques he or she uses are important to the learning process. We still cannot say with certainty who or what the effective teacher is or does. The only general conclusion possible at this point is that no characteristic or technique is indispensable, that none produces the best results with all students in all areas of learning. We need more carefully designed studies matching student characteristics with specific teacher characteristics and instructional procedures.

We also need to follow Jackson's example and, quite literally, take another look at "life in classrooms." Neither the black-box model, relating input and output measures without examining their actual interaction in the classroom situation,[12] nor the reports of teachers and students, who for a variety of reasons seldom are able to report fully and accurately on their experiences, are adequate. It is also time to go beyond the detail-rich but structure-poor "exposes" of classroom life (e.g., Holt, 1964; Kohl, 1967; and Herndon, 1968) to more structured kinds of observation which link up specific classroom events with specific learning outcomes.

Another major research direction would be to study more concretely what happens to children outside of school to affect their chances of school success. This calls for controlled studies of the specific aspects of socialization that are linked, directly or indirectly, to formal learning. For example, we have strong clues that independence, of the sort that nurtures self-direction with respect to learning tasks, and a feeling of potency with regard to one's environment and one's ability to have an impact on it, are both conducive to success in school. What we need to know more about are (1) how such attitudes are induced in the family and other socialization groups and (2) how or under what conditions they lead to high levels of achievement. We also have clues that the resources of well-to-do homes and neighborhoods—from the availability of books and magazines to the level of the conversation at the dinner table—have a stronger impact upon ultimate school success than the resources of the schools themselves, but we still know very little about what it is in such homes and neighborhoods that is most important and how the use of resources gets translated into academic skills. Research on outside-of-school effects should include in-depth studies of individual children and families and also intergroup, including crosscultural, studies designed to answer such questions as: Is there a "culture of poverty" that makes it difficult for the poor to succeed in school under any circumstances?; Are the relatively permissive child-rearing practices approved by mental health experts congruent with academic excellence?; What kinds of home and community experiences are characteristic of nations or national subgroups with unusually high, or low, achievement patterns? Of course, our understanding of the relationship of outside-school experiences and in-school success does not guarantee that we can put it to use. It is difficult to change basic modes of socialization. But understanding at least would let us know what we are up against in treating our educational ills.

Research on student peer groups, an agent of socialization operating both inside and outside the school system, already has indicated quite clearly that many young people will not apply their best efforts to learning tasks unless such application is consistent with the norms of their informal cliques and friendship groups. The need here is for imaginative research which will point to ways of channeling these potentially powerful group influences toward intellectual goals.

In addition to basic research on the social factors related to learning, a sociology of learning should help in the evaluation of alternative modes of teaching and in the development of new learning environments. The innovations described in this chapter were selected because they seemed to be among the most interesting attacks upon structural defects in the learning system and to be ones which also have demonstrated some capacity for survival; yet none of them has really proven its worth in terms of the standards of evaluation set in Chapter 2. This is not to take the stance of anxious parents and educators whose response to any new method of teaching is to ask how children educated in the new way will fare in conventional settings and on standard tests. The evidence from the new approaches that have received fairly extensive testing (among them, simulation gaming and the open classroom) has consistently shown that children taught in the new way do not over the long-run perform any worse on standard tests than children who spend the same amount of time in conventional learning environments—*even though the new method was not intended to teach the things measured by most standard tests.* Even allowing for novelty effects, almost any new way of teaching does about as well as the traditional ways —at teaching the traditional, as well as new, things! However, as we noted in the first chapter, schools may teach many things in addition to the standard academic skills of reading, writing, and mathematics (which can be measured readily by standardized achievement tests), and new teaching methods may be oriented toward the production of good citizenship, success in the world of work, interpersonal skills, such behavioral norms or characteristics as independence and achievement motivation, and even individual self-development and happiness. (For a recent sociological analysis of what is learned in school in addition to book learning and technical skills—or what is *learned* in school as opposed to what is *taught* there— see Dreeben, 1968.) Thus, the question of whether children really learn better or learn different things in any of the new learning environments is unanswerable until one specifies *what* it is they are supposed to be learning. Few educational innovators have developed good indicators of the effects their innovations are supposed to have and then shown experimentally that they do in fact produce these effects.

The kinds of innovations we have been considering present special problems of evaluation. For one thing, they affect the learning system so broadly that it is hard to decide what effects are the most important ones to measure. What, for instance, of all the activities and changes in relationships in Adams High School should be selected for evaluation—or, to put it another way, what measurable results or output of the school would justify its existence or show that it was doing a "good job"? Similarly, what aspects of the kibbutz educational system should be taken as representing the effectiveness of the whole system? With what other educational systems, or parts of systems, should the output of a kibbutz school or Adams High School be compared? (Although it is quite true that to compare a new teaching approach with a traditional approach on standardized test results is unfair to the new approach, this leaves unanswered the question of what *is* a fair comparison.)

A second problem is that the students most affected by one of these innovative learning environments are often the very ones who do not "test" well. For example, one of the rewarding aspects of using instructional games is that games often bring to the fore students who have not done well in the conventional classroom—in particular, nonverbal students and those in rebellion against teachers or school in general. Such students were often observed making very shrewd moves in games—and making them repeatedly enough to indicate that they were not simply random or lucky moves. They were, however, seldom able to explain in words what they had done. The point is that it will be impossible to test the hypothesis that simulation games are especially valuable for poor school performers without designing some new measures of learning.

The experience of Head Start and other compensatory programs for disadvantaged children suggests that the development of new evaluation techniques is a high priority item. As McDill's appraisal of these program evaluations has pointed out, it is impossible to say to what degree their apparent lack of positive results is due to weaknesses in the programs themselves as opposed to weaknesses in the evaluation instruments. Apart from knowledge about learning we would gain from evaluation of such programs, their survival or future direction depends upon showing fairly soon some concrete evidence that they are worth the investment of taxpayers' money.

The innovations described in this chapter have hardly begun to exploit the implications of the findings reported in earlier chapters. Among the studies that not only raised potentially powerful ideas about learning but also indicated strategies for implementing them are Rosenthal's experiment on teacher expectations (Chapter 7) and Jensen's study of ability development (Chapter 6). Faults of research design and interpretation of data have been attacked in both studies, and neither can be said to have made its point conclusively. However, at the risk of sounding pompous, we would suggest that it would be more profitable (though more difficult) to divert energy and ingenuity from writing clever critiques of Rosenthal's and Jensen's work to devising intelligent replications of some of their ideas. In the case of Rosenthal's work, all kinds of manipulations of the classroom situation and roles could be tested to see which produces the most positive forms of the self-fulfilling prophecy. In the case of Jensen's, we already have the example of the Bereiter and Engelmann program (see page 322) to support Jensen's idea that the concrete skills required for school success are more susceptible to intervention and manipulation than IQ scores. But other kinds of programs testing this general principle would add greatly to our knowledge of how children learn.

Finally, to the pessimists who claim that the learning system is beyond help, we can answer that neither integration nor compensatory education nor any of the other major educational reforms proposed in the last few years has been given a fair test—which means that we must introduce such reforms in new ways and on scales that reflect accurately their underlying principles and then evaluate the results accurately and in depth. We have not demonstrated that the most intelligent ideas for change in the learning system cannot succeed. Perhaps they can. Now would be a good time to find out.

Notes

1. Some analysts feel that the cost of a truly effective educational system is beyond the means of *any* nation. "Everywhere in the world school costs have risen faster than enrollments and faster than GNP; everywhere expenditures on schools fall even further behind the expectations of parents, teachers, and pupils. . . . The U.S. is proving to the world that no nation can be rich enough to afford a school system that meets the demands this same system creates simply by existing. Rather than calling equal schooling temporarily unfeasible, we must recognize that it is, in principle, economically absurd" (Illich, 1970: 11).

2. See George Leonard's *Education and Ecstasy* (1968); on free schools, see the description and references in Chapter 7.

3. Note the parallels to the mini-courses and the Mobile School program at Adams High School.

4. This is to give all applicants an equal chance of admission, although in practice applications are weighted by race, to obtain a student body comparable to the total Chicago public school population.

5. Ivan Illich is one of the most articulate exponents of this view. His article on "Why We Must Abolish Schooling" (1970), describes some interesting experiments in "matching partners for educational purposes." Serious alternatives to a national educational system are still largely in the proposal stage.

6. This author's experience with simulation games has been similar. Although our original belief was that computer games would raise both motivation and learning, early field tests showed that what appealed to the participants was the social restructuring of the classroom (in particular the freedom to talk with peers). Indeed, the complexity of most early computer games confused students, making it more difficult for them to analyze the causal relationships in a given sequence of play and thus to learn the general principles built into the game model.

7. One pessimistic observer of current trends in mass instruction has noted that: "The scope of our technological effort makes possible errors of great magnitude. For example, one teacher lecturing to 30 or 300 students with minimal feedback is inefficient enough. But it took the ingenuity and grandeur of American technology to enable (on "educational" TV) one teacher to lecture simultaneously to hundreds of thousands of students with no feedback whatever" (Leonard, 1968: 188).

8. For a fuller discussion of the underlying principles and the specific sequences of activities, see Bereiter and Engelmann, 1966. This is one of the *very* few compensatory education programs which has shown some consistent and long-term effects upon children's academic success (McDill *et al.,* 1969).

9. Not to be confused with the free schools. See Chapter 12.

10. Among the most comprehensive treatments are Miles, 1964: and Lin, 1965.

11. The positive implication of this conclusion is that although total system reform is the most rational, an intelligent change at any level can lead to positive changes at other levels.

12. "The truth is that learning is a kind of black box; teaching goes in, and student performance comes out, and no one really knows what goes on inside the box" (Dubin and Taveggia, 1968: 10).

Bibliography

Adler, Chaim
1967 "Some social mechanisms affecting high school drop-out in Israel." Sociology of Education 40: 363–366.

Alexander, C. N., and E. Q. Campbell
1964 "Peer influences on adolescent educational aspirations and attainments." American Sociological Review 29: 568–575.

Alkin, M. C.
1967 Toward an Evaluation Model: A Systems Approach. Center for the Study of Evaluation of Instructional Programs, University of California, Los Angeles.

Anderson, K. E.
1950 "A frontal attack on the basic problem in evaluation: the achievement of the objectives of instruction in specific areas." Journal of Experimental Education 18: 163–174.

Aries, Philippe
1962 Centuries of Childhood. New York: Knopf.

Armor, David J.
1969 The American School Counselor. New York: Russell Sage Foundation.

Astin, A. W.
1961 "A re-examination of college productivity." Journal of Educational Psychology 52: 173–178.

Atkinson, John W.
1965 "The mainsprings of achievement-oriented activity." Pp. 25–66 in J. D. Krumboltz (ed.), Learning and the Educational Process. Chicago: Rand McNally.

Atkinson, John W.
1966 An Introduction to Motivation. Princeton, New Jersey: Van Nostrand.

Bales, R. F.
1952 "Some uniformities of behavior in small social systems." Pp. 146–159 in G. E. Swanson et al. (eds.), Readings in Social Psychology, revised edition. New York: Holt.

Bales, R. F., and E. F. Borgatta
1955 "Size of group as a factor in the interaction profile." Pp. 396–413 in P. Hare et al. (eds.), Small Groups. New York: Knopf.

Barker, R. G., et al.
1962 Big School—Small School. A report to the Office of Education, U.S. Department of Health, Education and Welfare, from the Midwest Psychological Field Station, University of Kansas.

Bavelas, A.
1962 "Communication patterns in task-oriented groups." Pp. 669–682 in D. Cartwright and A. Zander (eds.), Group Dynamics. Evanston, Ill.: Row, Peterson and Company.

Becker, Howard
1968 "The teacher in the authority system of the public schools." Pp. 298–309 in R. R. Bell and H. R. Stub (eds.), The Sociology of Education, revised edition. Homewood, Ill.: Dorsey Press.

Benedict, Ruth
1946 The Chrysanthemum and the Sword. Boston: Houghton Mifflin.

Bereiter, Carl, and Siegfried Engelmann
1966 Teaching Disadvantaged Children in the Preschool. Englewood Cliffs, New Jersey: Prentice-Hall.

Bernstein, Abraham
1967 The Education of Urban Populations. New York: Random House.

Bernstein, Basil
1961 "Social class and linguistic development." Pp. 288–314 in A. H. Halsey *et al.* (eds.), Education, Economy and Society. New York: Free Press.

Bettelheim, Bruno
1969 The Children of the Dream. New York: Macmillan.

Bickel, Alexander
1970 "Desegregation: where do we go from here?" New Republic 162: 20–22.

Bidwell, Charles E.
1965 "The school as a formal organization." Pp. 972–1022 in J. G. March (ed.), Handbook of Organizations. Chicago: Rand McNally.

Bidwell, Charles E.
1969 "The sociology of education." Pp. 1241–1254 in R. Ebel (ed.), Encyclopedia of Educational Research, fourth edition. New York: Macmillan.

Blalock, Hubert M.
1960 Social Statistics. New York: McGraw-Hill.

Blau, Peter
1955 The Dynamics of Bureaucracy. Chicago: University of Chicago Press.

Bloom, Benjamin S.
1968 "Learning for mastery." UCLA Evaluation Comment 1: 1–12.

Boocock, Sarane S., and E. O. Schild
1968 Simulation Games in Learning. Beverly Hills, Calif.: Sage Publications.

Borgotta, Edgar
1969 Sociological Methodology: 1969. San Francisco. Jossey-Bass.

Boulding, Kenneth
1966 "Expecting the unexpected: the uncertain future of knowledge and technology." Report prepared for the first area conference, Designing Education for the Future, Denver, Colorado.

Bowles, Samuel
1968 "Toward equality of educational opportunity?" Harvard Educational Review 38: 89–99.

Boyle, R. P.
  1966 "The effect of the high school on students' aspirations." American Journal of Sociology 71: 628–639.

Braham, R. L.
  1966 Israel: A Modern Education System. U.S. Department of Health, Education and Welfare, Office of Education. Washington, D.C.: U.S. Government Printing Office.

Brim, O. G.
  1960 "Family structure and sex-role learning by children." Pp. 482–496 in N. W. Bell and E. F. Vogel (eds.), A Modern Introduction to the Family. Glencoe, Ill.: Free Press.

Brittain, C. V.
  1963 "Adolescent choices and parent-peer cross-pressures." American Sociological Review 28: 385–390.

Bronfenbrenner, Urie
  1958 "Socialization and social class through time and space." Pp. 400–425 in E. E. Maccoby *et al.* (eds.), Readings in Social Psychology, third edition. New York: Henry Holt.

Bronfenbrenner, Urie
  1968 "Soviet methods of character education." Pp. 57–65 in R. J. Havighurst (ed.), Comparative Perspectives on Education. Boston: Little, Brown.

Bronfenbrenner, Urie
  1970 Two Worlds of Childhood: U.S. and U.S.S.R. New York: Basic Books-Russell Sage Foundation.

Bruner, Jerome
  1964 "The new educational technology." Pp. 1–7 in A. de Grazia and D. A. Sohn (eds.), Revolution in Teaching. New York: Bantam Books.

Bruner, Jerome
  1966 "Theorems for a theory of instruction." Pp. 196–211 in J. Bruner (ed.), Learning about Learning. U.S. Department of Health, Education and Welfare, Office of Education. Washington, D.C.: U.S. Government Printing Office.

Burkhead, Jesse
  1967 Input and Output in Large-City High Schools. Syracuse, New York: Syracuse University Press.

Bushnell, J. H.
  1962 "Student culture at Vassar." Pp. 489–514 in N. Sanford (ed.), The American College. New York: Wiley.

Buswell, M. M.
  1954 "The relationship between the social structure of the classroom and the academic success of the pupils." Journal of Experimental Education 22: 37–52.

Cahman, W. J.
  1949 "Attitudes of minority youth: a methodological introduction." American Sociological Review 14: 543–548.

California Association of Independent Schools
  1969 "Teaching history at Chadwick School." C. A. I. S. Review 2: 5.

Campbell, D. T., and J. C. Stanley
1963 "Experimental and quasi-experimental designs for research on teaching." Pp. 171–246 in N. L. Gage (ed.), Handbook of Research on Teaching. Chicago: Rand McNally.

Campbell, E. Q., and C. N. Alexander
1965 "Structural effects and interpersonal relations." American Journal of Sociology 71: 284–289.

Campbell, E. Q.
1969 "Adolescent socialization." Pp. 821–859 in D. A. Goslin (ed.), Handbook of Socialization Theory and Research. Chicago: Rand McNally.

Carroll, J. B.
1965 "Learning over the long haul." Pp. 249–269 in J. D. Krumboltz (ed.), Learning and the Educational Process. Chicago: Rand McNally.

Cartwright, Dorwin, and Alvin Zander
1962 Group Dynamics, second edition. Evanston, Ill.: Row, Peterson.

Caudill, William, and George De Vos
1966 "Achievement, culture, and personality: the case of the Japanese Americans." Pp. 208–228 in S. W. Webster (ed.), The Disadvantaged Learner. San Francisco: Chandler.

Center for Research and Development in Higher Education
1969 SCOPE: Grade Eleven Profile. New York: College Entrance Examination Board.

Central Advisory Council on Education
1967 Children and Their Primary Schools. London: Her Majesty's Stationery Office.

Cervantes, L. F.
1965 "The isolated nuclear family and the drop-out." Sociological Quarterly 6: 103–118.

Charters, W. W.
1963 "The social background of teaching." Pp. 715–813 in N. L. Gage (ed.), Handbook of Research on Teaching. Chicago: Rand McNally.

Cicourel, A. V., and J. I. Kitsuse
1963 The Educational Decision-makers. Indianapolis: Bobbs-Merrill.

Clark, Burton
1962 Educating the Expert Society. San Francisco: Chandler.

Clark, Kenneth
1965 Dark Ghetto. New York: Harper and Row.

Cogan, M. L.
1958 "The behavior of teachers and the productive behavior of their pupils." Journal of Experimental Education 27: 89–124.

Cohen, H. L.
1967 "The educational model." IRCD Bulletin 3: 1–3.

Cohen, Rosalie
1968 "Cognitive styles, culture conflict and non-verbal tests of intelligence." Paper presented at the 38th annual meeting of the Eastern Sociological Society.

Coleman, James S.
1961   The Adolescent Society. New York: Free Press.
Coleman, James S.
1962   "Reward structure and allocation of effort." Pp. 119–132 in J. H. Criswell *et al.* (eds.), Mathematical Methods in Small Group Processes. Stanford, Calif.: Stanford University Press.
Coleman, James S.
1964   "Research chronicle: The Adolescent Society." Pp. 184–211 in P. E. Hammond (ed.), Sociologist at Work. New York: Basic Books.
Coleman, James S., Ernest Q. Campbell, *et al.*
1966   Equality of Educational Opportunity. U.S. Department of Health, Education and Welfare, Office of Education. Washington, D.C.: U.S. Government Printing Office.
Coleman, James S.
1969   "The methods of sociology." Pp. 86–114 in R. Bierstedt (ed.), A Design for Sociology: Scope, Objective and Methods. Philadelphia: American Academy of Political and Social Science.
Coles, Robert
1968   Children of Crisis. New York: Delta.
Conant, James B.
1959   The American High School Today. New York: McGraw-Hill.
Corwin, Ronald G.
1965   A Sociology of Education. New York: Appleton-Century-Crofts.
Crain, Robert L.
1968   The Politics of School Desegregation. Chicago: Aldine.
Crandall, Virginia, *et al.*
1960   "Maternal reactions and the development of independence and achievement behavior in young children." Child Development 31: 243–251.
Crandall, Virginia
1964   "Achievement behavior in young children." Young Children 20: 77–90.
Dave, R. H.
1963   The Identification and Measurement of Environmental Process Variables that are Related to Educational Achievement. Unpublished doctoral dissertation, University of Chicago.
Davis, James
1963   "Intellectual climates in 135 American colleges and universities." Sociology of Education 37: 110–128.
Dentler, Robert A.
1965   "Community behavior and Northern school desegregation." Journal of Negro Education 34: 258–267.
Dentler, Robert A.
1966a   "Equality of Educational Opportunity: a special review." The Urban Review 1: 27–29.
Dentler, Robert A.
1966b   "Barriers to Northern school desegregation." Daedalus 95: 45–63.

Deutsch, Martin
1963 "The disadvantaged child and the learning process." Pp. 163–179 in A. H. Passow (ed.), Education in Depressed Areas. New York: Columbia University-Teachers College Press.

Deutsch, Morton
1949 "The effects of cooperation and competition upon group process." Human Relations 2: 129–152 and 199–231.

Dewey, John
1928 Democracy and Education. New York: Macmillan.

Dodd, P. C.
1965 Role Conflicts of School Principals. Final Report No. 4, Cooperative Research Project No. 853. Graduate School of Education, Harvard University.

Douvan, Elizabeth
1962 "Motivational factors in college entrance." Pp. 199–224 in N. Sanford (ed.), The American College. New York: Wiley.

Dreeben, Robert, and Neal Gross
1965 The Role Behavior of School Principals. Final Report No. 3, Cooperative Research Project No. 853. Graduate School of Education, Harvard University.

Dreeben, Robert
1968 On What is Learned in School. Reading, Mass.: Addison-Wesley.

Dubin, R., and T. C. Taveggia
1968 The Teaching-learning Paradox: A Comparative Analysis of College Teaching Methods. Eugene, Oregon: Center for the Advanced Study of Educational Administration.

Durkheim, Emile
1956 Education and Sociology. Glencoe, Ill.: Free Press.

Durkheim, Emile
1961 Moral Education. Glencoe, Ill.: Free Press.

Dyer, H. S.
1968 "School factors and equal educational opportunity." Harvard Educational Review 38: 38–56.

Eckland, B. K.
1967 "Genetics and Sociology: a reconsideration." American Sociological Review 32: 173–194.

Edgar, D. E., and R. Warren
1969 "Power and autonomy in teacher socialization." Sociology of Education 42: 386–399.

Eifermann, R. R.
1969 "Cooperativeness and egalitarianism in kibbutz children's games." Department of Psychology, Hebrew University, unpublished paper.

Eisenstadt, S. N.
1956 From Generation to Generation. New York: Free Press.

Elder, Glen H.
1965 "Family structure and educational attainment." American Sociological Review 30: 81–96.

Elkin, F., and W. A. Westley
1955   "The myth of adolescent culture." American Sociological Review 15: 680–684.

Entwisle, Doris R.
1966   "Developmental sociolinguistics: a comparative study in four sub-cultural settings." Sociometry 29: 67–84.

Entwisle, Doris R.
1968   "Developmental linguistics: inner city children." American Journal of Sociology 74: 37–48.

Entwisle, Doris R., and Ellen Greenberger
1969   "Racial differences in the language of grade school children." Sociology of Education 42: 238–250.

Entwisle, Doris R.
1970a   "Semantic systems of children; some assessments of social class and ethnic differences." In F. Williams (ed.), Language and Poverty: Perspectives on a Theme. Chicago: Markham.

Entwisle, Doris R.
1970b   "To dispel fantasies about fantasy-based measures." Baltimore: Johns Hopkins University, mimeographed paper.

Epperson, D. C.
1964   "A re-assessment of indices of parental influence in The Adolescent Society." American Sociological Review 29: 93–96.

Faltermayer, E. K.
1968   "More dollars and more diplomas." Fortune 77: 140–145.

Farber, Jerry
1969   The Student as Nigger. North Hollywood, Calif.: Contact Books.

Featherstone, Joseph
1967a   "Schools for children: what's happening in British classrooms." The New Republic 157: 17–21.

Featherstone, Joseph
1967   "Notes on community schools." The New Republic 160: 16–17.

Featherstone, Joseph
1968   "Community control of our schools." The New Republic 160: 16–19.

Featherstone, Joseph
1969   "Off to a bad start." The New Republic 161: 19–22.

Field, W. F.
1951   The Effects of Thematic Apperception upon Certain Experimentally Aroused Needs. Unpublished doctoral dissertation, University of Maryland.

Flanagan, J. C., et al.
1962   Studies of the American High School. Project Talent Office, University of Pittsburgh.

Flanders, Ned A.
1960   Teacher Influence, Pupil Attitudes and Achievements. U.S. Department of Health, Education and Welfare, Office of Education, Cooperative Research Monograph No. 12.

Fletcher, Jerry, *et al.*
1970 The School as a Center for Educational Change: A Prospectus. Portland, Oregon: John Adams High School, mimeographed report.

Fox, D. J.
1968 "Conclusions of the Center's MES evaluation." The Urban Review 2: 17.

Fraser, W. R.
1968 "Education and society in modern France." Pp. 13–37 in R. J. Havighurst (ed.), Comparative Perspectives on Education. Boston: Little, Brown.

Freedman, D. G.
1969 "The survival value of the beard." Psychology Today 3: 36–39.

Freedman, M.
1956 "The passage through college." Journal of Social Issues 12: 12–28.

Friedenberg, Edgar Z.
1968 "The school as a social environment." Pp. 186–198 in R. R. Bell and H. R. Stub (eds.), The Sociology of Education. Homewood, Ill.: Dorsey Press.

Fruchter, Benjamin
1954 Introduction to Factor Analysis. New York: Van Nostrand.

Furstenberg, F. F.
1970 "Premarital pregnancy among black teen-agers." Transaction 7: 52–55.

Gagne, Robert M.
1965 "Educational objectives and human performance." Pp. 1–24 in J. D. Krumboltz (ed.), Learning and the Educational Process. Chicago: Rand McNally.

Gerard, R. W.
1952 "The biological basis of imagination." Pp. 226–251 in B. Ghiselin (ed.), The Creative Process. Berkeley: University of California Press.

Getzels, Jacob W., and Philip W. Jackson
1962 Creativity and Intelligence. New York: Wiley.

Gittell, Marilyn, and T. Edward Hollander
1968 Six Urban School Districts: A Comparative Study of Institutional Response. New York: Praeger.

Glaser, Robert
1968 Reply to A. Oettinger and S. Marks, "Educational Technology: New Myths and Old Realities." Harvard Educational Review 38: 739–746.

Goffman, Erving
1959 The Presentation of Self in Everyday Life. New York: Doubleday Anchor.

Goldberg, Marian L., *et al.*
1966 The Effects of Ability Grouping. New York: Columbia University-Teachers College Press.

Goldhammer, K., and F. Farner
1964 The Jackson County Story. Eugene, Oregon: Center for the Advanced Study of Educational Administration.

Goldhammer, K., and F. Farner
 1968   Jackson County Revisited. Eugene, Oregon: Center for the Advanced Study of Educational Administration.

Goodlad, John I.
 1966   School, Curriculum, and the Individual. Waltham, Mass.: Blaisdell Publishing Company.

Goodlad, John I.
 1967   "The educational program to 1980 and beyond." Pp. 46–60 in E. L. Morphet and C. O. Ryan (eds.), Implications for Education of Prospective Changes in Society. Report of the Second Area Conference, Designing Education for the Future, an Eight-State Project.

Goodman, Paul
 1960   Growing up Absurd. New York: Random House.

Goodman, S. M.
 1959   The Assessment of School Quality. Albany, N.Y.: New York State Education Department.

Gordon, Chad
 1969   Self-conceptions, Race and Family Factors as Determinants of Adolescent Achievement Orientations. Cambridge: Harvard University, Department of Social Relations. Unpublished manuscript.

Gordon, C. Wayne
 1957   The Social System of the High School. Glencoe, Ill.: Free Press.

Gordon, C. Wayne, and Leta M. Adler
 1963   Dimensions of Teacher Leadership in Classroom Social Systems. Los Angeles: University of California, Department of Education. Mimeographed report.

Gottlieb, David, and Jon Reeves
 1963   Adolescent Behavior in Urban Areas. New York: Free Press.

Greeley, Andrew M., and Peter H. Rossi
 1966   The Education of Catholic Americans. Chicago: Aldine.

Green, Arnold W.
 1946   "The middle class male child and neurosis." American Sociological Review 11: 31–41.

Green, R. L., and L. J. Hofmann
 1965   "A case study of the effects of educational deprivation on southern rural negro children." Journal of Negro Education 34: 327–341.

Green, R. L., and W. W. Farguar
 1965   "Negro academic motivation and scholastic achievement," Journal of Educational Psychology 56: 241–243.

Green, Thomas F.
 1969   "Schools and communities: a look forward," Harvard Educational Review 39: 221–252.

Green, Thomas F.
 1970   "Education and schooling in post-industrial America: some directions for policy." Paper presented to the Committee on Science and Astronautics, U.S. House of Representatives, Ninety-first Congress.

Griffiths, Daniel E.
1966 The School Superintendent. New York: Center for Applied Research in Education.

Gronlund, Norman E.
1959 Sociometry in the Classroom. New York: Harper.

Gross, Beatrice, and Ronald Gross
1970 "A little bit of chaos." Saturday Review May 16: 71–73, 84–85.

Gross, Neal, *et al.*
1958 Explorations in Role Analysis. New York: Wiley.

Gross, Neal
1965 Who Runs our Schools? New York: Wiley.

Gross, Neal, and Robert E. Herriott
1965 Staff Leadership in Public Schools. New York: Wiley.

Gross, Ronald, and Judith Murphy (eds.)
1964 The Revolution in the Schools. New York: Harcourt, Brace and World.

Haggard, E. A.
1957 "Socialization, personality, and achievement in gifted children." School Review winter: 318–414.

Halpern, A. W.
1962 "Problems in the use of communication media in the dissemination and implementation of educational research." Educational Research, Third Annual Phi Delta Kappan Symposium: 176.

Hamblin, R. L., *et al.*
1969 "Changing the game from 'get the teacher' to 'learn.' " Transaction 6: 20–31.

Haring, D. G.
1946 "Aspects of personal character in Japan." Far Eastern Quarterly 6: 12–22.

Harman, H. H.
1967 Modern Factor Analysis. Chicago: University of Chicago Press.

Hartley, Ruth E.
1959 "Sex-role pressures and the socialization of the male child." Psychological Reports 5: 457–468.

Hartley, Ruth E.
1960 "Children's concepts of male and female roles." Merrill-Palmer Quarterly 6: 84–91.

Hartley, Ruth E., and F. P. Hardesty
1964 "Children's perceptions of sex roles in childhood." Journal of Genetic Psychology 105: 43–51.

Hansen, D. A.
1967 "The uncomfortable relation of sociology and education." Pp. 3–35 in D. A. Hansen and J. E. Gerstl (eds.), On Education: Sociological Perspectives. New York: Wiley.

Havighurst, Robert J.
1966 "Who are the socially disadvantaged?" Pp. 20–29 in S. W. Webster (ed.), The Disadvantaged Learner. San Francisco: Chandler.

Havighurst, Robert J. (ed.)
1968 Comparative Perspectives on Education. Boston: Little, Brown.

Havighurst, Robert J.
1968a "Education, social mobility, and social change in four societies." Pp. 129–144 in R. R. Bell and H. R. Stub (eds.), The Sociology of Education. Homewood, Ill.: Dorsey Press.

Heil, L. M., *et al.*
1960 Characteristics of Teacher Behavior and Competency Related to the Achievement of Different Kinds of Children in Several Elementary Grades. New York: Office of Testing and Research, Brooklyn College. Mimeographed report.

Henrysson, Sten
1957 Applicability of Factor Analysis in the Behavioral Sciences. Stockholm: Almquist and Wiksell.

Herndon, James
1968 The Way It Spozed to Be. New York: Bantam Books.

Herriott, Robert E., and Nancy Hoyt St. John
1966 Social Class and the Urban School. New York: Wiley.

Herzog, Elizabeth
1970 Boys in Fatherless Homes. Children's Bureau, Office of Child Development, Department of Health, Education and Welfare.

Hess, R. D., V. Shipman, and D. Jackson
1965 "Some new dimensions in providing equal educational opportunity." Journal of Negro Education 34: 220–231.

Hieronymus, A. N.
1951 "A study of social class motivation: relationships between anxiety for education and certain socio-economic and intellectual variables." Journal of Educational Psychology 42: 193–205.

Hollingshead, A. B.
1949 Elmtown's Youth. New York: Wiley.

Holt, John
1964 How Children Fail. New York: Delta.

Holt, John
1967 How Children Learn. New York: Pitman.

Holt, John
1969 The Underachieving School. New York: Pitman.

Homans, George C.
1941 Fatigue of Workers: Its Relation to Industrial Production. New York: Reinhold.

Homans, George C.
1950 The Human Group. New York: Harcourt, Brace.

Hughes, E. C., *et al.*
1962 "Student culture and academic effort." Pp. 515–530 in N. Sanford (ed.), The American College, New York: Wiley.

Hunt, J. McV.
1961 Intelligence and Experience. New York: Ronald Press.

Husen, Torsten (ed.)
1967 International Study of Achievement in Mathematics. Vols. I and II. New York: Wiley.

Hyman, H. H.
1953 "The value systems of different classes: a social psychological contribution to the analysis of stratification." Pp. 426–442 in R. Bendix and S. M. Lipset (eds.), Class, Status and Power. Glencoe, Ill.: Free Press.

Illich, Ivan
1970 "Why we must abolish schooling." The New York Review 15: 9–15.

Jackson, Philip
1968 Life in Classrooms. New York: Holt, Rinehart and Winston.

Jahoda, Marie, and Neil Warren
1965 "The myths of youth." Sociology of Education 38: 138–149.

Jencks, Christopher
1966 "Is the public school obsolete?" The Public Interest 2: 18–27.

Jencks, Christopher
1969 "What color is IQ?" New Republic 162: 25–29.

Jencks, Christopher
1970 "Education vouchers." New Republic 163: 19–21.

Jensen, A. R.
1969 "How much can we boost IQ and scholastic achievement." Harvard Educational Review 39: 1–123.

Johnson, D. W.
1967 "The effects of a freedom school on its students." Pp. 226–244 in Robert Dentler *et al.* (eds.), The Urban R's: Race Relations as the Problem in Urban Education. New York: Praeger.

Kagan, J., *et al.*
1960 "Conceptual style and the use of affect labels." Merrill-Palmer Quarterly 6: 261–278.

Kagan, J., *et al.*
1963 "Psychological significance of styles of conceptualization." Pp. 73–112 in J. C. Wright and J. Kagan (eds.), Basic Cognitive Processes in Children, Monograph in Social Research on Child Development 28, No. 2.

Kagan, J.
1964 "The child's sex role classification of school objects." Child Development 35: 1051–1056.

Kagan, J.
1969 "Check one: male, female." Psychology Today 3: 39–41.

Kahl, J. A.
1953 "Educational and occupational aspirations of 'common man' boys." Harvard Educational Review 23: 186–203.

Kahn, R. L.
1956   "The prediction of productivity." Journal of Social Issues 12: 41–49.

Kandel, Denise, and Gerald S. Lesser
1969   "Parent-adolescent relationships and adolescent independence in the United States and Denmark." Journal of Marriage and the Family 31: 348–358.

Kandel, Denise, and Gerald S. Lesser
1969a   "Parental and peer influences on educational plans of adolescents." American Sociological Review 34: 212–223.

Katz, Fred E.
1964   "The school as a complex social organization." Harvard Educational Review 34: 428–455.

Katz, Irwin
1964   "Review of evidence relating to effects of desegregation on the intellectual performance of negroes." American Psychologist 19: 381–399.

Keppel, Francis
1966   The Necessary Revolution in American Education. New York: Harper and Row.

Kerr, N. D.
1964   "The school board as an agency of legitimation." Sociology of Education 38: 34–59.

Kohl, Herbert
1967   36 Children. New York: Signet Books.

Kohn, M. L.
1959a   "Social class and parental values." American Journal of Sociology 64: 337–351.

Kohn, M. L.
1959b   "Social class and the exercise of parental authority." American Sociological Review 24: 352–366.

Kohn, M. L.
1963   "Social class and parent-child relationships: an interpretation." American Journal of Sociology 68: 471–480.

Kohn, M. L., and C. Schooler
1968   "Class, Occupation, and Orientation." Unpublished paper.

Komarovsky, Mirra
1953   Women in the Modern World: Their Education and Their Dilemmas. Boston: Little, Brown.

Krasner, L., and L. P. Ullman (eds.)
1965   Case Studies in Behavior Modification. New York: Holt, Rinehart and Winston.

Krasner, L., and L. P. Ullman
1966   Research in Behavior Modification: New Developments and Implications. New York: Holt, Rinehart and Winston.

Krauss, Irving
1964   "Educational aspirations among working class youth." American Sociological Review 29: 867–879.

Leavitt, H. J.
1958   "Some effects of certain communication patterns on group perform-ance." Pp. 546–563 in E. E. Maccoby *et al.* (eds.), Readings in Social Psychology, third edition. New York: Holt.

Leonard, George B.
1968   Education and Ecstacy. New York: Dell.

Lesser, G. S., *et al.*
1964   "Some effects of segregation and desegregation in the schools." Inte-grated Education 2: 20–26.

Lewin, K., R. Lippitt, and R. K. White
1939   "Patterns of aggressive behavior in experimentally created 'social climates.' " Journal of Social Psychology 10: 271–299.

Lin, Nan, *et al.*
1965   The Diffusion of an Innovation in Three Michigan High Schools. Michigan State University, Institute for International Studies in Education and Department of Communication

Livingstone, David W.
1968   A General Model of the Internal Structure of National Education Systems. Baltimore: Johns Hopkins University, Department of Social Rela-tions.

Lyford, Joseph P.
1966   The Air-tight Cage. New York: Harper and Row.

McAbee, H. V.
1958   "Time for the job." NASSP Bulletin 42: 41.

McClelland, David *et al.*
1953   The Achievement Motive. New York: Appleton-Century-Crofts.

McClelland, David *et al.*
1955   "Religious and other sources of parental attitudes toward independ-ence training." Pp. 389–397 in D. McClelland (ed.), Studies in Motivation. New York: Appleton-Century-Crofts.

McClelland, David
1961   The Achieving Society. New York: Free Press.

Maccoby, Eleanor (ed.)
1966   The Development of Sex Differences. Stanford: Stanford University Press.

McDill, Edward L., *et al.*
1967   "Institutional effects on the academic behavior of high school stu-dents." Sociology of Education 40: 181–199.

McDill, Edward L., *et al.*
1969   Strategies for Success in Compensatory Education: An Appraisal of Evaluation Research. Baltimore: Johns Hopkins Press.

McKeachie, W. L.
1962   "Procedures and techniques of teaching: a survey of experimental studies." Pp. 312–364 in N. Sanford (ed.), The American College. New York: Wiley.

McNeely, A., and J. Buck
   1967   "A study of guidance counselors at three high schools." Johns Hopkins University, Department of Social Relations. Unpublished paper.

McPartland, James
   1967   The Relative Influence of School Desegregation and of Classroom Desegregation on the Academic Achievement of Ninth Grade Negro Students. Baltimore: Johns Hopkins University, Center for the Study of Social Organization of Schools.

McPartland, James
   1970   "Should we give up on school desegregation?" Johns Hopkins Magazine 21: 20–25.

Mauch, James
   1962   "A systems analysis approach to education." Phi Delta Kappan 43: 158–161.

Mayr, Ernst
   1967   "Biological man and the year 2000." Daedalus 96: 832–836.

Medley, D. M., and H. E. Mitzel
   1963   "Measuring classroom behavior by systematic observation." Pp. 247–328 in N. L. Gage (ed.), Handbook of Research on Teaching. Chicago: Rand McNally.

Melbo, I. R.
   1970   "Educational trends in the 1970's." Los Angeles Times, Jan. 18, Section G: 7.

Meranto, Philip
   1967   The Politics of Federal Aid to Education in 1965. Syracuse, N.Y.: Syracuse University Press.

Miles, Matthew B.
   1964   Innovation in Education. New York: Teachers College, Columbia University Press.

Miller, Harry L.
   1967   Education for the Disadvantaged. New York: Free Press.

Miller, Leonard M.
   1963   "The dropout: schools' search for clues to his problems." School Life May: 3.

Minuchin, P.
   1964   "Sex role concepts and sex typing in childhood as a function of school and home environments." Paper presented at American Orthopsychiatric Association annual meetings.

Moeller, Gerald
   1968   "Bureaucracy and teachers' sense of power." Pp. 236–250 in R. R. Bell and H. R. Stub (eds.), The Sociology of Education. Homewood, Ill.: Dorsey Press.

Moise, Edwin
   1964   "The new mathematics program." Pp. 171–187 in A. de Grazia and D. A. Sohn (eds.), Revolution in Teaching. New York: Bantam Books.

Mollenkopf, W. G., and S. D. Melville
1956 A Study of Secondary School Characteristics as Related to Test Scores. Research Bulletin 56–6. Princeton, N.J.: Educational Testing Service.

Moore, G. A.
1967 Realities of the Urban Classroom. Garden City, N.Y.: Doubleday Anchor Books.

Moore, O. K.
1966 "Education for the future." Paper presented at American Sociological Association annual meetings.

Moynihan, Daniel P.
1965 The Negro Family: The Case for National Action. Washington, D.C., Office of Policy Planning and Research, United States Department of Labor.

Musgrove, F.
1964 Youth and the Social Order. Bloomington: Indiana University Press.

NEA
1968 Ability Groupings: Research Survey 53. Washington, D.C.: National Education Association.

National Manpower Council
1957 Womanpower. New York: Columbia University Press.

Neill, A. S.
1961 Summerhill. New York: Hart.

Neubauer, P. B. (ed.)
1965 Children in Collectives: Child-rearing Aims and Practices in the Kibbutz. Springfield, Ill.: Thomas.

Newcomb, Theodore M.
1952 "Attitude development as a function of reference groups: the Bennington study." Pp. 420–430 in G. E. Swanson *et al.* (eds.), Readings in Social Psychology. New York: Holt.

Newcomb, Theodore M.
1962 "Student peer-group influence." Pp. 469–488 in N. Sanford (ed.), The American College. New York: Wiley.

Newman, F. M., and D. W. Oliver
1967 "Education and community." Harvard Educational Review 37: 61–106.

Nisbet, John
1961 "Family environment and intelligence." Pp. 273–287 in A. H. Halsey *et al.* (eds.), Education, Economy and Society. New York: Free Press.

Oettinger, A. G.
1968 "The myths of educational technology." Saturday Review May 18: 76–77, 91.

Ojemann, R. H., and F. R. Wilkinson
1939 "The effect on pupil growth of an increase in teachers' understanding of pupil behavior." Journal of Experimental Education 8: 143–147.

Orfield, Gary
1970 "The debate over school desegregation." New Republic 162: 32–35.

Pace, R., and G. G. Stern
1958 "An Approach to the measurement of psychological characteristics of college environments." Journal of Educational Psychology 49: 269–277.

Parsons, Talcott, and Robert F. Bales
1955 Family Socialization and Interaction Process. Glencoe, Ill.: Free Press.

Parsons, Talcott
1959 "The school class as a social system: some of its functions in American society." Harvard Educational Review 29: 297–318.

Parsons, Talcott
1962 "Youth in the context of American society." Daedalus 91: 97–123.

Pearlin, L. I., and M. L. Kohn
1966 "Social class, occupation, and parental values: a cross-national study." American Sociological Review 31: 466–479.

Perlmutter, H. V., and G. DeMontmollin
1952 "Group learning of nonsense syllables." Journal of Abnormal and Social Psychology 47: 762–769.

Pettigrew, T. F.
1964 A Profile of the American Negro. Princeton, N.J.: Van Nostrand.

Pettigrew, T. F.
1966 "Negro American intelligence: a new look at an old controversy." Pp. 96–116 in J. L. Frost and G. R. Hawkes (eds.), The Disadvantaged Child: Issues and Innovations. Boston: Houghton Mifflin.

Pettigrew, T. F.
1967 "Extending educational opportunities: school desegregation." Pp. 293–307 in M. Gittell (ed.), Educating an Urban Population. Beverly Hills, Calif.: Sage Publications.

Piaget, Jean
1948 The Moral Judgement of the Child. New York: Free Press.

Piaget, Jean
1951 The Child's Conception of the World. New York: Humanities Press.

Piaget, Jean
1952 The Origins of Intelligence in Children. New York: International University Press.

Pines, Maya
1965 "What the talking typewriter says." New York Times Magazine May 9: 23, 74–80.

Pitcher, E. G.
1963 "Male and female." Atlantic 211: 87–91.

Portola Institute
1970 The Big Rock Candy Mountain. Menlo Park, Cal.: Portola Institute.

Postman, Neil, and Charles Weingartner
1969 Teaching as a Subversive Activity. New York: Delacorte

Radin, N., and C. K. Kamii
1965 "The child-rearing attitudes of disadvantaged negro mothers and some educational implications." Journal of Negro Education 34: 138–145.

Rhodes, A. L., and C. B. Nam
1970 "The religious context of educational expectations." American Sociological Review 35: 253–267.

Richer, S.
1967 "Issues in reference group theory, with special reference to grouping practices in education." Johns Hopkins University, Department of Social Relations. Dittoed paper.

Rickover, H. G.
1965 "The illusions of American schools." Baltimore Sun, January 31, Section D: 3.

Riesman, David, and Christopher Jencks
1962 "The viability of the American college." Pp. 74–192 in N. Sanford (ed.), The American College. New York: Wiley.

Riessman, Frank
1962 The Culturally Deprived Child. New York: Harper.

Riley, M. W., et al.
1954 Sociological Studies in Scale Analysis. New Brunswick, N.J.: Rutgers University Press.

Riley, M. W., et al.
1955 "Adolescents talk to peers and parents." Rutgers University, Department of Sociology. Mimeographed working paper.

Riley, M. W., et al.
1961 "Adolescent values and the Riesman typology: an empirical analysis." Pp. 370–386 in S. Lispet and L. Lowenthal (eds.), Culture and Social Character. New York: Free Press.

Riley, M. W.
1963 Sociological Research, Vol. I. New York: Harcourt, Brace and World.

Rilling, P. M.
1970 "Desegregation: the south *is* different." New Republic 162: 17–19.

Roethlisberger, F. J., and W. J. Dickson
1939 Management and the Worker. Cambridge, Mass.: Harvard University Press.

Rogers, David
1968 110 Livingston Street: Politics and Bureaucracy in the New York City School System. New York: Random House.

Rogoff, N.
1961 "Local social structure and educational selection." Pp. 241–251 in A. H. Halsey et al. (eds.), Education, Economy and Society. New York: Free Press.

Rosen, B. C.
1956 "The achievement syndrome: a psychocultural dimension of social stratification." American Sociological Review 21: 203–211.

Rosen, B. S., and R. D'Andrade
1959 "The psycho-social origin of achievement motivation." Sociometry 22: 185–217.

Rosen, B. C.
1961 "Family structure and achievement motivation." American Sociological Review 26: 574–585.

Rosenberg, L. A., *et al.*
1966 "The Johns Hopkins perceptual test." Paper presented at Eastern Psychological Association annual meetings.

Rosenthal, Robert, and Lenore Jacobson
1966 "Teachers' expectancies: determinants of pupils' IQ gains." Psychological Reports 19: 115–118.

Rosenthal, Robert
1966a Experimenter Effects in Behavioral Research. New York: Appleton-Century-Crofts.

Rosenthal, Robert, and Lenore Jacobson
1968 Pygmalion in the Classroom. New York: Holt, Rinehart and Winston.

Rossi, Peter H.
1961 "Social factors in academic achievement." Pp. 269–273 in A. H. Halsey *et al.* (eds.), Education, Economy and Society. New York: Free Press.

Ryan, F. J., and J. S. Davie
1958 "Social acceptance, academic achievement and academic aptitude among high school students." Journal of Educational Research 52: 101–106.

Sadler, M. E.
1900 How Far Can We Learn Anything of Practical Value from the Study of Foreign Systems of Education? London: Guilford.

Sanford, N.
1956 "Personality development during the college years." Journal of Social Issues 12: 1–71.

Sanford, N.
1959 "Motivation of high achievers." Pp. 34–38 in O. D. David (ed.), The Education of Women. Washington, D.C.: American Council on Education.

Sanford N. (ed.)
1962 The American College. New York: Wiley.

Schrag, Peter
1965 Voices in the Classroom. Boston: Beacon Press.

Schrag, Peter
1967 Village School Downtown. Boston: Beacon Press.

Schramm, Wilbur, *et al.*
1961 Television in the Lives of our Children. Stanford, Calif.: Stanford University Press.

Secord, P. F., and C. W. Backman
1964 Social Psychology. New York: McGraw-Hill

Segel, D., and O. J. Schwarm
1957 Retention in High Schools in Large Cities. U.S. Department of Health, Education and Welfare, Office of Education. Washington, D.C.: U.S. Government Printing Office.

Selltiz, Clair, *et al.*
1959 Research Methods in Social Relations. New York: Holt.

Sewell, W. H., *et al.*
1957 "Social status and educational and occupational aspiration." American Sociological Review 22: 67–73.

Sewell, W. H., and V. P. Shah
1968 "Social class, parental encouragement and educational aspirations." American Journal of Sociology 73: 559–572.

Shaw, M. E.
1932 "A comparison of individuals and small groups in the rational solution of complex problems." American Journal of Psychology 44: 491–504.

Shaycoft, M., *et al.*
1965 The Identification, Development and Utilization of Human Talents: Studies of a Complete Age Group—Age 15. University of Pittsburgh, Project Talent Office.

Shaycoft, M.
1967 The High School Years: Growth in Cognitive Skills. Pittsburgh: American Institutes for Research and School of Education, University of Pittsburgh.

Shriner, T. H.
1968 "Social dialect and language." Paper presented at Eastern Illinois Conference on Dialectology.

Shuey, A. M.
1966 The Testing of Negro Intelligence. New York: Social Science Press.

Simon, William, and John Gagnon
1969 "Psychosexual development," Transaction 6: 9–17.

Simpson, R. L.
1962 "Parental influence, anticipatory socialization and social mobility." American Sociological Review 27: 517–522.

Snow, C. P.
1961 "Miasma, darkness and turpidity." New Statesman, 42: 1587.

South, E. B.
1927 "Some psychological aspects of committee work." Journal of Applied Psychology 11: 437–464.

Spiro, Melford E.
1965 Children of the Kibbutz. New York: Schocken.

Stake, R.
1968 Comments on Professor Glaser's paper entitled, "Evaluation of instruction and changing educational models." Center for the Study of Evaluation of Instructional Programs, University of California, Los Angeles.

Stern, G. C.
1962 "Environments for learning." Pp. 690–730 in N. Sanford (ed.), The American College. New York: Wiley.

Stinchcombe, Arthur L.
1964 Rebellion in a High School. Chicago: Quadrangle Books.

Stodolsky, S. S., and G. S. Lesser
1967 "Learning patterns in the disadvantaged." Harvard Educational Review 37: 546–593.

Stretch, B. B.
1970 "The rise of the 'free school.'" Saturday Review June 20: 76–79, 90–93.

Strodtbeck, Fred L.
1958 "Family interaction, values, and achievement." Pp. 135–194 in D. C. McClelland *et al.* (eds.), Talent and Society. Princeton, N.J.: Van Nostrand.

Sussman, Leila
1962 High School to University in Puerto Rico. Report to U.S. Office of Education on Cooperative Research Project no. 1018. Tufts University.

Terman, L. M., and M. H. Oden
1947 The Gifted Child Grows Up. Stanford, Calif.: Stanford University Press.

Thelan, Herbert A.
1967 Education and the Human Quest. New York: Harper.

Tomasson, R. F.
1965 "From elitism to egalitarianism in Swedish education." Sociology of Education 38: 203–223.

Turner, Ralph H.
1964 The Social Context of Ambition. San Francisco: Chandler.

Turner, Ralph H.
1968 "Sponsored and contest mobility and the school system." Pp. 219–235 in R. R. Bell and H. R. Stub (eds.), The Sociology of Education. Homewood, Ill.: Dorsey Press.

U.S. Commission on Civil Rights
1967 Racial Isolation in the Public Schools. Washington, D.C.: U.S. Government Printing Office.

Veroff, J., *et al.*
1962 "Achievement motivation and religious background." American Sociological Review 27: 205–217.

Wallach, M. A., and N. Kogan
1965a Modes of Thinking in Young Children: A Study of the Creativity-Intelligence Distinction. New York: Holt, Rinehart and Winston.

Wallach, M. A., and N. Kogan
1965b Cognitive Originality, Physiognomic Sensitivity and Defensiveness in Children. Final report to U.S. Office of Education on Cooperative Research Project No. 1316B. Duke University.

Wallach, M. A., and N. Kogan
1967 "Creativity and intelligence in children's thinking." Transaction 4: 38–43.

Wallace, W. L.
1965 "Peer influences and undergraduates' aspirations for graduate study." Sociology of Education 38: 377–392.

Waller, Willard
1932 The Sociology of Teaching. New York: Wiley.

Watson, F. G.
1963 "Research on teaching science." Pp. 1031–1059 in N. L. Gage (ed.), Handbook of Research on Teaching. Chicago: Rand McNally.

Webster, H., *et al.*
1962 "Personality changes in college students." Pp. 811–846 in N. Sanford (ed.), The American College. New York: Wiley.

Wechsler, David
1958 The Measurement and Appraisal of Adult Intelligence. Fourth edition. New York: Williams and Wilkins.

Weick, K. E.
1969 The Social Psychology of Organizing. Reading, Mass.: Addison-Wesley.

Weinberg, C., and R. Skager
1966 "Social status and guidance involvement." Personnel and Guidance Journal 44: 586–590.

Weisstein, Naomi
1969 "Woman as nigger." Psychology Today 3: 20–22, 58.

Werts, Charles E.
1966 Sex Differences in College Attendance. Evanston, Ill.: National Merit Scholarship Corporation Reports, Vol. 2, No. 6.

White, R., and R. Lippitt
1962 "Leader behavior and member reaction in three 'social climates.' " Pp. 527–553 in D. Cartwright and A. Zander (eds.), Group Dynamics. Evanston, Ill.: Row, Peterson.

White, Robert W.
1959 "Motivation reconsidered: the concept of competence." Psychological Review 66: 317–318.

Whiting, B. B. (ed.)
1963 Six Cultures: Studies of Child Rearing. New York: Wiley.

Wilson, Alan B.
1959 "Residential segregation of social classes and aspirations of high school boys." American Sociological Review 24: 836–845.

Wilson, Alan B.
1967 "Educational consequences of segregation in a California community." Pp. 165–206 in U.S. Commission on Civil Rights, Racial Isolation in the Public Schools. Washington, D.C.: U.S. Government Printing Office.

Wilson, Alan B.
1968 "Social class and equal educational opportunity." Harvard Educational Review 38: 77–84.

Wilson, E. C.
1967 "A model for action." Pp. 155–193 in NEA, Rational Planning in Curriculum and Instruction. Washington, D.C.: NEA Center for the Study of Instruction.

Winterbottom, M. R.
1953 The Relation of Childhood Training in Independence to Achievement Motivation. Unpublished doctoral dissertation, University of Michigan.

Woronoff, I.
1966 "Negro male identification problems and the education process." Pp. 293–295 in S. W. Webster (ed.). The Disadvantaged Learner. San Francisco: Chandler.

Wright, Sewall
1934   "The method of path coefficients." Annals of Mathematical Statistics
5: 161–215.

Wright, Sewall
1960   "Path coefficients and regression coefficients: alternative or complementary concept?" Biometrics 16: 189–202

Zeigler, H., and W. Peck
1970   "The political functions of the educational system." Sociology of
Education 43: 115–142.

Index

abilities: differences by sex of, 81–83; individual, 97–120; mental, 98, 118

ability grouping, 158–162

academic achievement, 98; and applicability of curriculum to future life, 311; anxiety and, 82–83; and behavior standards, 73–75; crosscultural comparisons of, 276–306; and educational reform, 108; effect of adolescent subculture on, 240 *n*; effect of child's independence on his, 295; effect of desegregation on, 124–125; effect of peer group on, 212–218, 226–228; effect of racial integration on, 226; effect of sociometric structure on, 169; and parent-child interaction, 62–70; and school facilities, 198–199; school level of, students' influence on, 200; and SES, 36; and student attitudes, 150–151; summary of national differences in, 304

achievement, academic. *See* academic achievement.

achievement behavior, 62, 64

achievement motivation, 170, 298–300; factors, 36–37, 312; interrelationship of birth order and SES with, 36; measurement, 74–75;

and religion, 55; and SES, 60–61; and social environment, 55–56

achievement syndrome, 37, 74

Adams, Henry, 179

Adams High School (Oregon), 320, 321

Adler, Chaim, 291

Adler, Leta M. (Gordon and Adler), 129, 132, 134, 143–149, 153 *n*

administration, school, 257–260; community control of, 269–270

adolescence, historical attitude toward, 8

adolescent: comparative independence in Denmark and U.S. of, 295; transitional state of, 213–214. *See also entries for* pupil; student

adolescent attitudes, Coleman study of, 212–218

adolescent society, 209–241; high school as, 253

The Adolescent Society, review of, 209–210

adolescent values, Coleman study of, 212–218

adult-child interaction, 65–67; and family size, 36; and linguistic development, 69 *See also* communication; expectations.

age, school entry, national variations in, 281

aggression, relationship to learning, 75

aggressiveness, and achievement, 82

Alexander, C. N. (Campbell, E. Q., and Alexander), 223, 224, 225